The Magic Touch

Oyayubi kara Romance

Vol. 9

Story & Art by Izumi Tsubaki

CONTENTS

The Magic Touch: Part 47 3

The Magic Touch: Part 48 33

The Magic Touch: Part 49 63

The Magic Touch: Part 50 95

The Magic Touch: Part 51 125

The Magic Touch: Final Story 155

Postscript 187

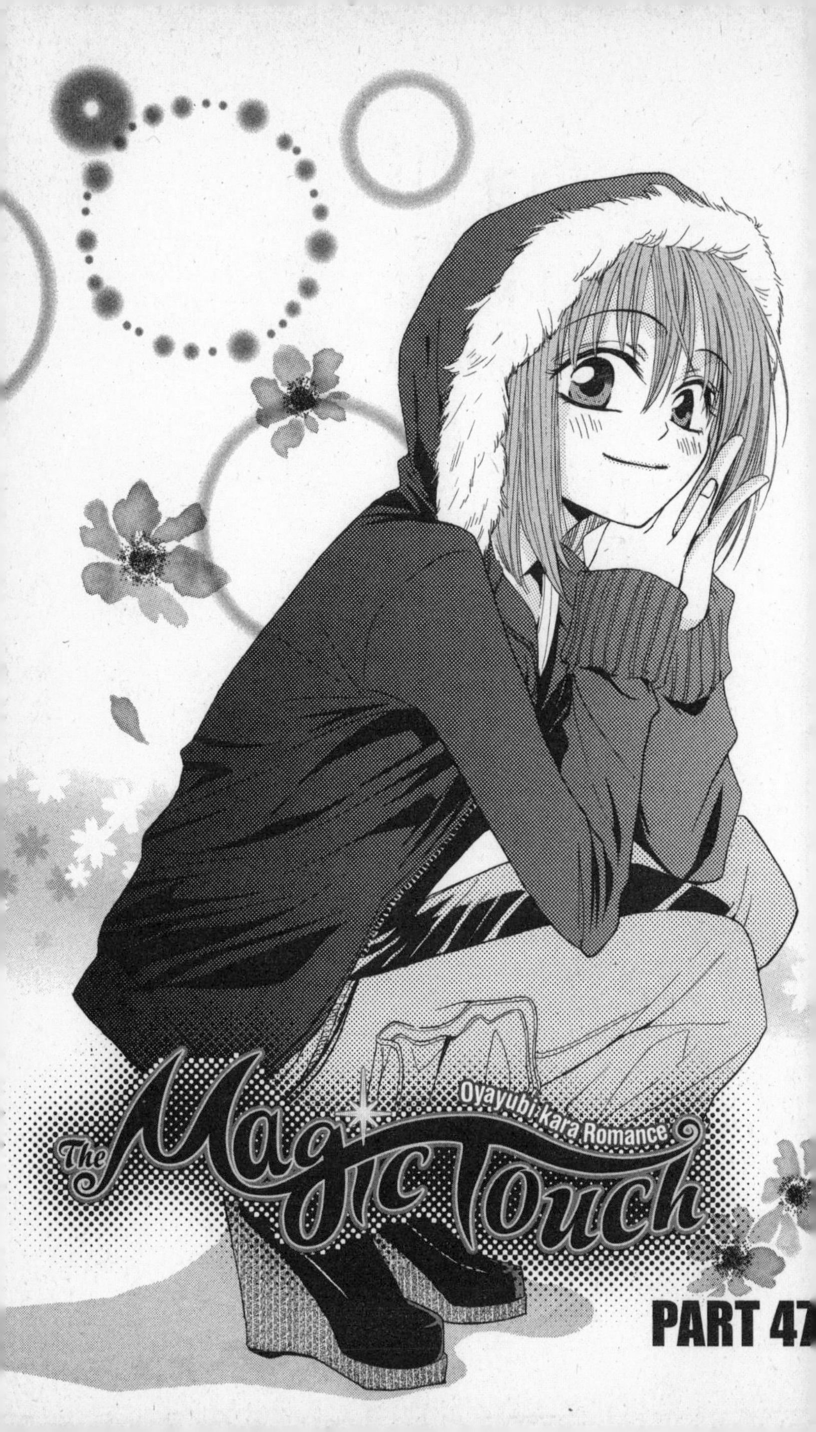
The Magic Touch
Oyayubi kara Romance
PART 47

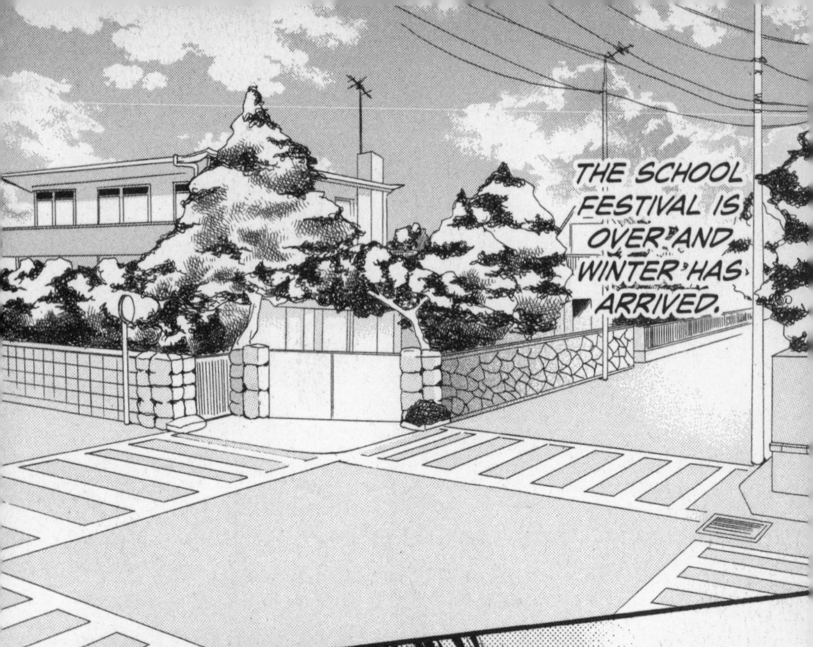
THE SCHOOL FESTIVAL IS OVER AND WINTER HAS ARRIVED.
IT FEELS LIKE WINTER IS IN MY SOUL AS WELL.
WHOOSH...

This Is the Final Volume

Because this is the final volume,
I had wonderful illustrations drawn by the assistant who helped me during the series! Now I'm finally realizing that it is over...
Since I put all of my youth into making this story, I feel very emotional about it. I really can't believe that I was able to finish school at the same time...
In any case, this is the final volume! Please enjoy it!

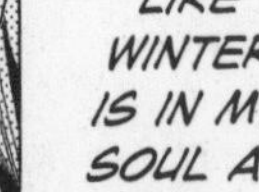
"Thanks for all of the support up to now."

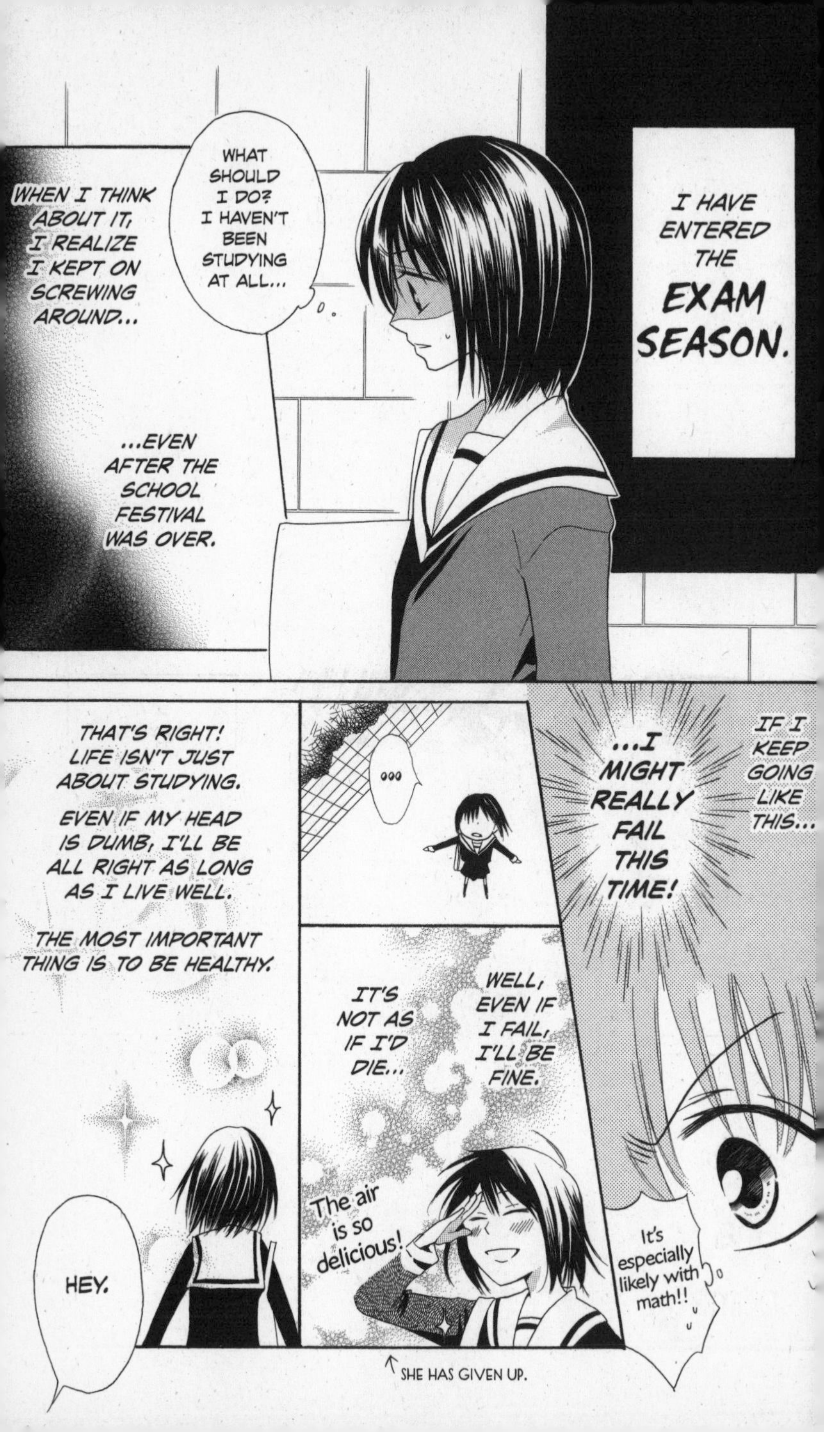
I HAVE ENTERED THE EXAM SEASON.
WHAT SHOULD I DO? I HAVEN'T BEEN STUDYING AT ALL...
WHEN I THINK ABOUT IT, I REALIZE I KEPT ON SCREWING AROUND...
...EVEN AFTER THE SCHOOL FESTIVAL WAS OVER.
IF I KEEP GOING LIKE THIS...
...I MIGHT REALLY FAIL THIS TIME!
It's especially likely with math!!
...
WELL, EVEN IF I FAIL, I'LL BE FINE.
IT'S NOT AS IF I'D DIE...
The air is so delicious!
SHE HAS GIVEN UP.
THAT'S RIGHT! LIFE ISN'T JUST ABOUT STUDYING.
EVEN IF MY HEAD IS DUMB, I'LL BE ALL RIGHT AS LONG AS I LIVE WELL.
THE MOST IMPORTANT THING IS TO BE HEALTHY.
HEY.

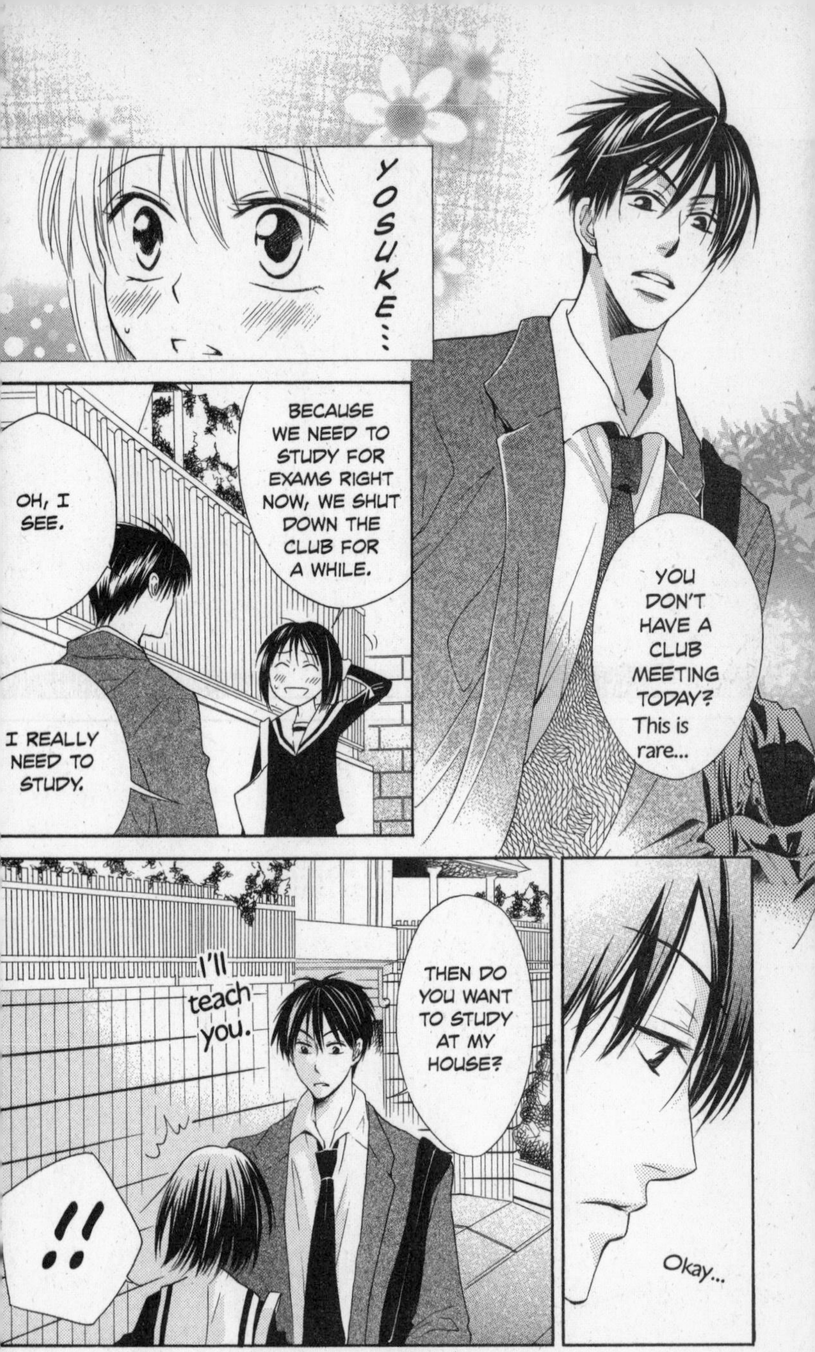
YOU DON'T HAVE A CLUB MEETING TODAY? This is rare...
YOSUKE...
BECAUSE WE NEED TO STUDY FOR EXAMS RIGHT NOW, WE SHUT DOWN THE CLUB FOR A WHILE.
OH, I SEE.
I REALLY NEED TO STUDY.
Okay...
THEN DO YOU WANT TO STUDY AT MY HOUSE?
I'll teach you.
!!

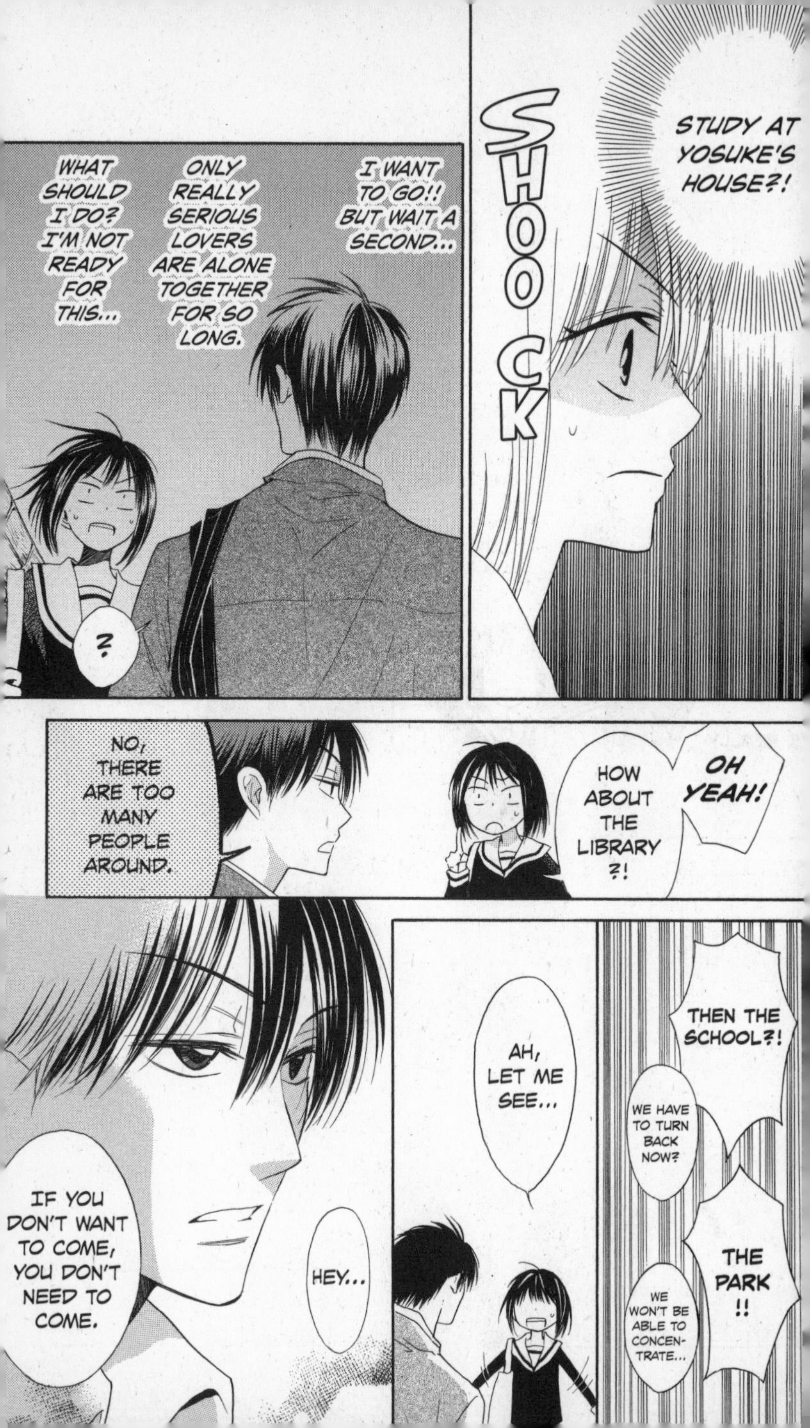
STUDY AT YOSUKE'S HOUSE?!
SHOCK
I WANT TO GO!! BUT WAIT A SECOND...
ONLY REALLY SERIOUS LOVERS ARE ALONE TOGETHER FOR SO LONG.
WHAT SHOULD I DO? I'M NOT READY FOR THIS...
?
OH YEAH!
HOW ABOUT THE LIBRARY?!
NO, THERE ARE TOO MANY PEOPLE AROUND.
THEN THE SCHOOL?!
WE HAVE TO TURN BACK NOW?
THE PARK!!
WE WON'T BE ABLE TO CONCENTRATE...
AH, LET ME SEE...
HEY...
IF YOU DON'T WANT TO COME, YOU DON'T NEED TO COME.

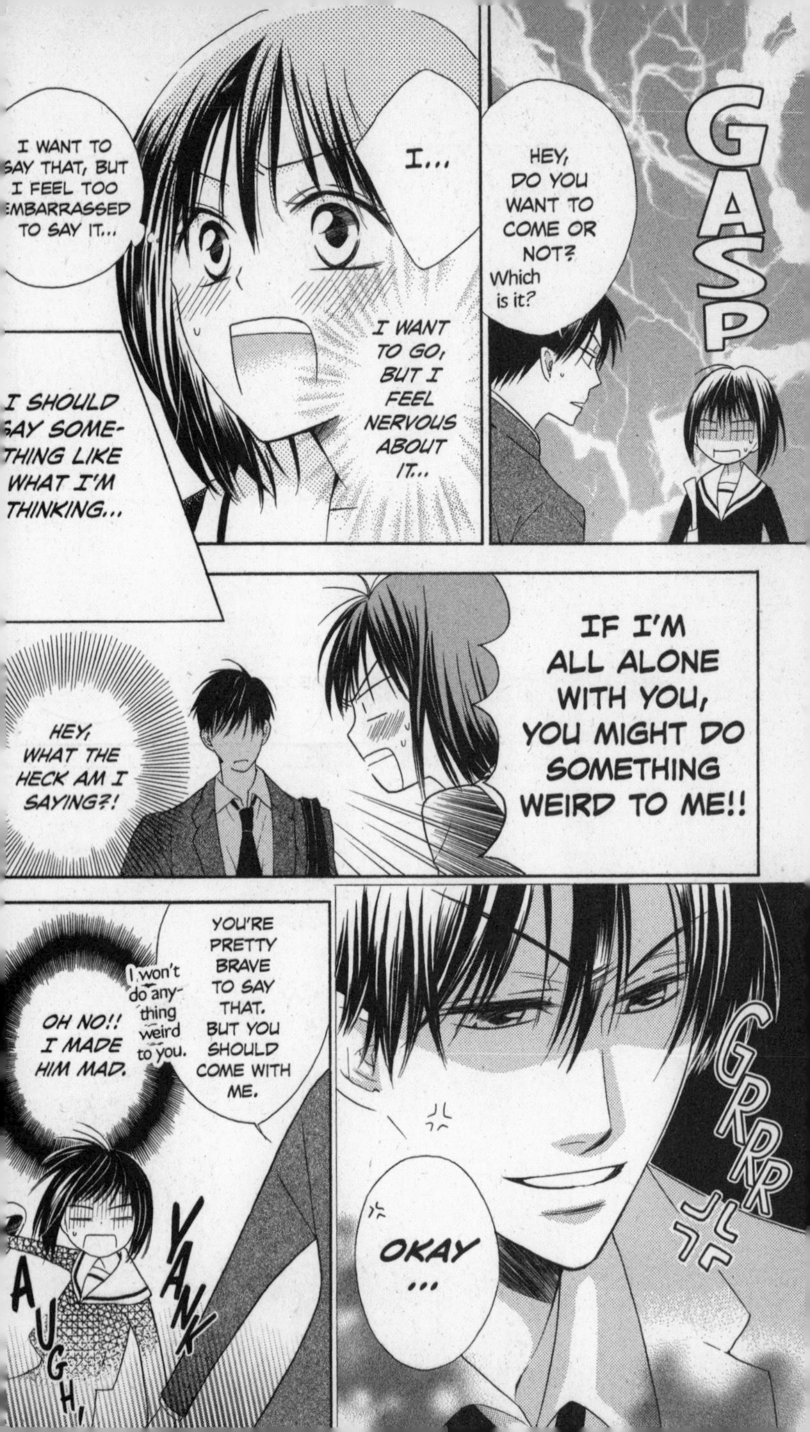
GASP
HEY, DO YOU WANT TO COME OR NOT? Which is it?
I...
I WANT TO GO, BUT I FEEL NERVOUS ABOUT IT...
I WANT TO SAY THAT, BUT I FEEL TOO EMBARRASSED TO SAY IT...
I SHOULD SAY SOME-THING LIKE WHAT I'M THINKING...
IF I'M ALL ALONE WITH YOU, YOU MIGHT DO SOMETHING WEIRD TO ME!!
HEY, WHAT THE HECK AM I SAYING?!
GRRR
OKAY...
YOU'RE PRETTY BRAVE TO SAY THAT. BUT YOU SHOULD COME WITH ME.
I won't do any-thing weird to you.
OH NO!! I MADE HIM MAD.
YANK
AUGH!

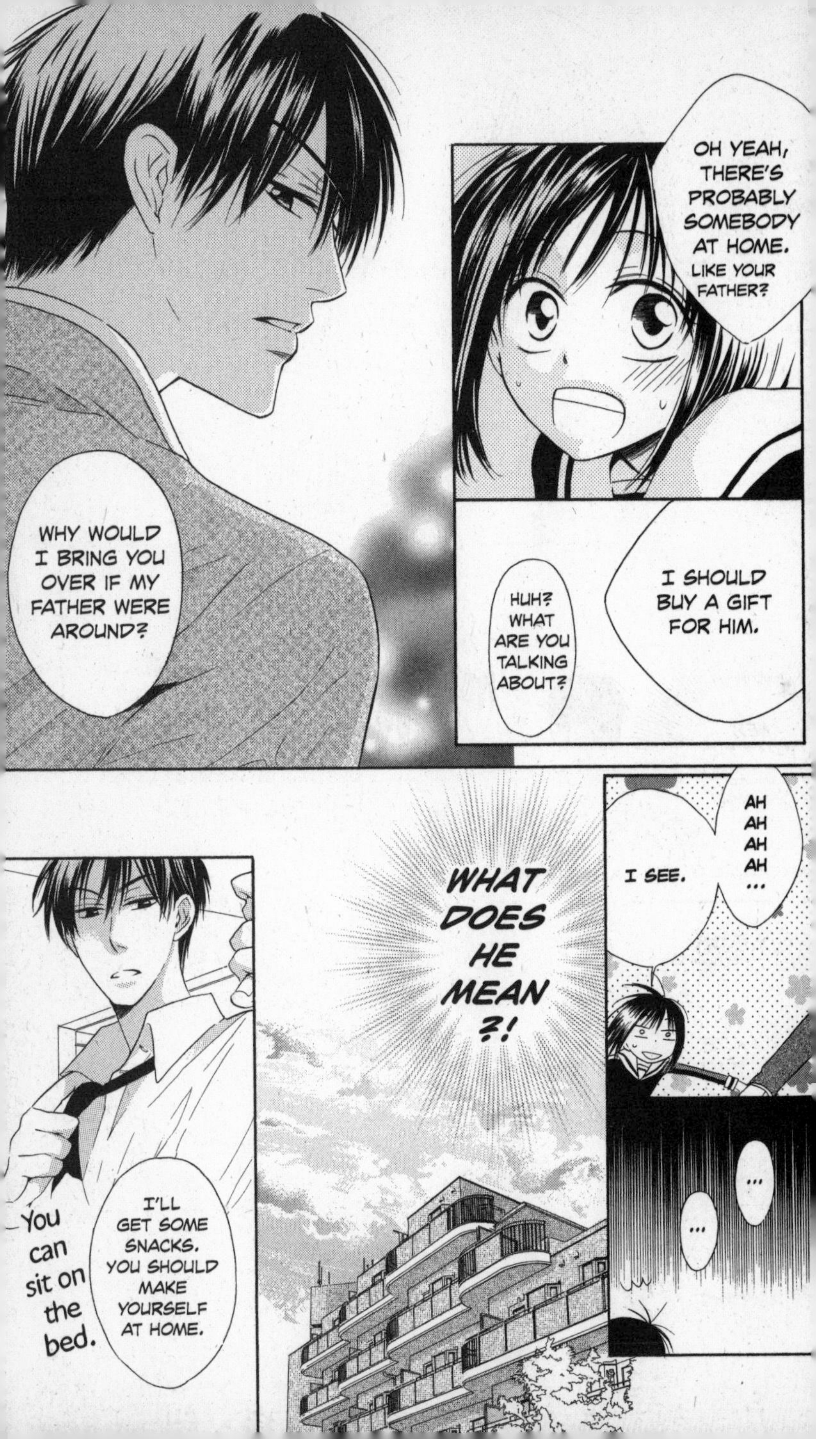
OH YEAH, THERE'S PROBABLY SOMEBODY AT HOME. LIKE YOUR FATHER?
I SHOULD BUY A GIFT FOR HIM.
HUH? WHAT ARE YOU TALKING ABOUT?
WHY WOULD I BRING YOU OVER IF MY FATHER WERE AROUND?
AH AH AH AH...
I SEE.
...
...
WHAT DOES HE MEAN?!
I'LL GET SOME SNACKS. YOU SHOULD MAKE YOURSELF AT HOME.
You can sit on the bed.

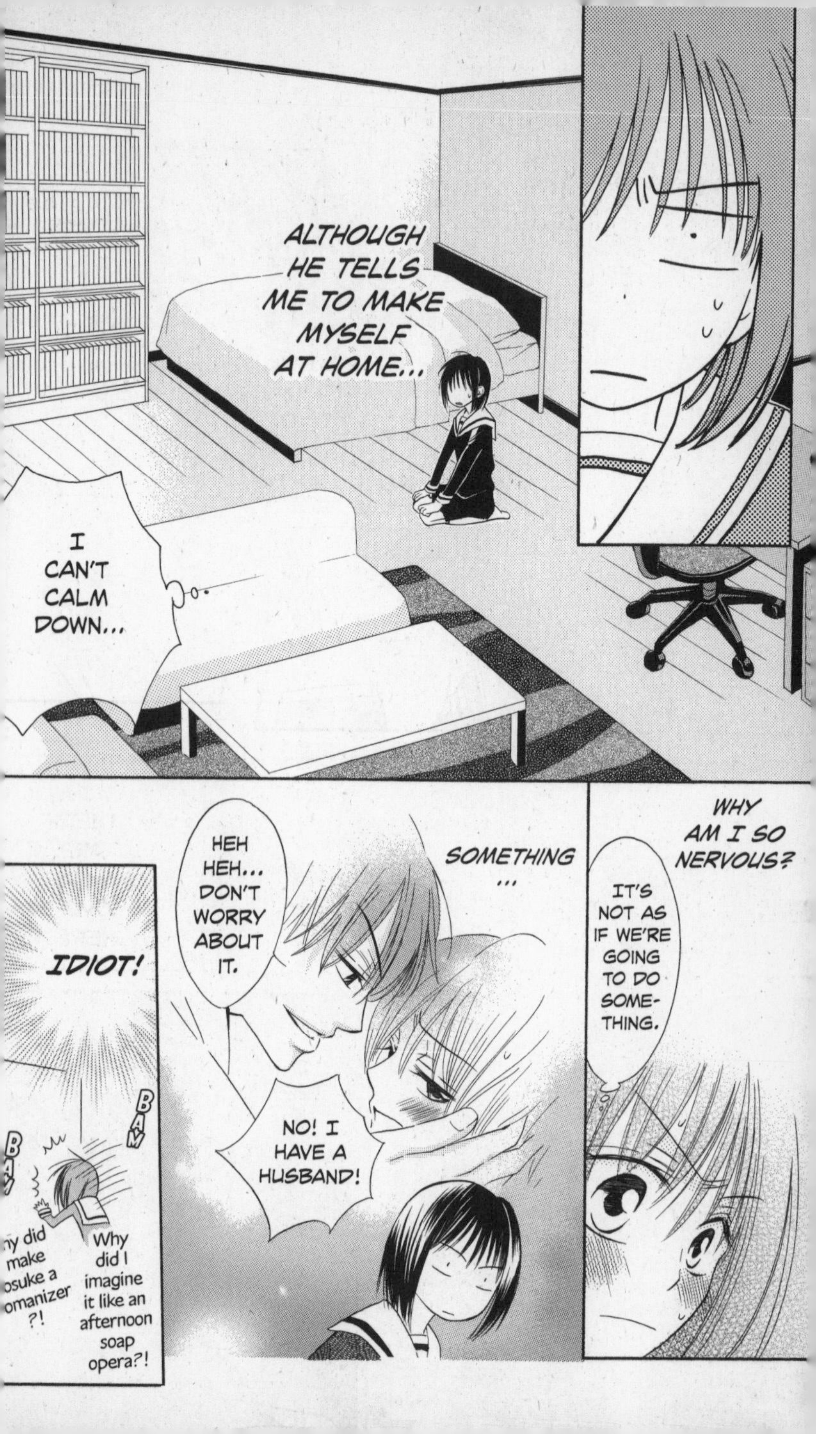
ALTHOUGH HE TELLS ME TO MAKE MYSELF AT HOME...
I CAN'T CALM DOWN...
WHY AM I SO NERVOUS?
IT'S NOT AS IF WE'RE GOING TO DO SOME-THING.
SOMETHING ...
HEH HEH... DON'T WORRY ABOUT IT.
NO! I HAVE A HUSBAND!
IDIOT!
BAM
BAM
Why did I imagine it like an afternoon soap opera?!
ny did make osuke a omanizer ?!

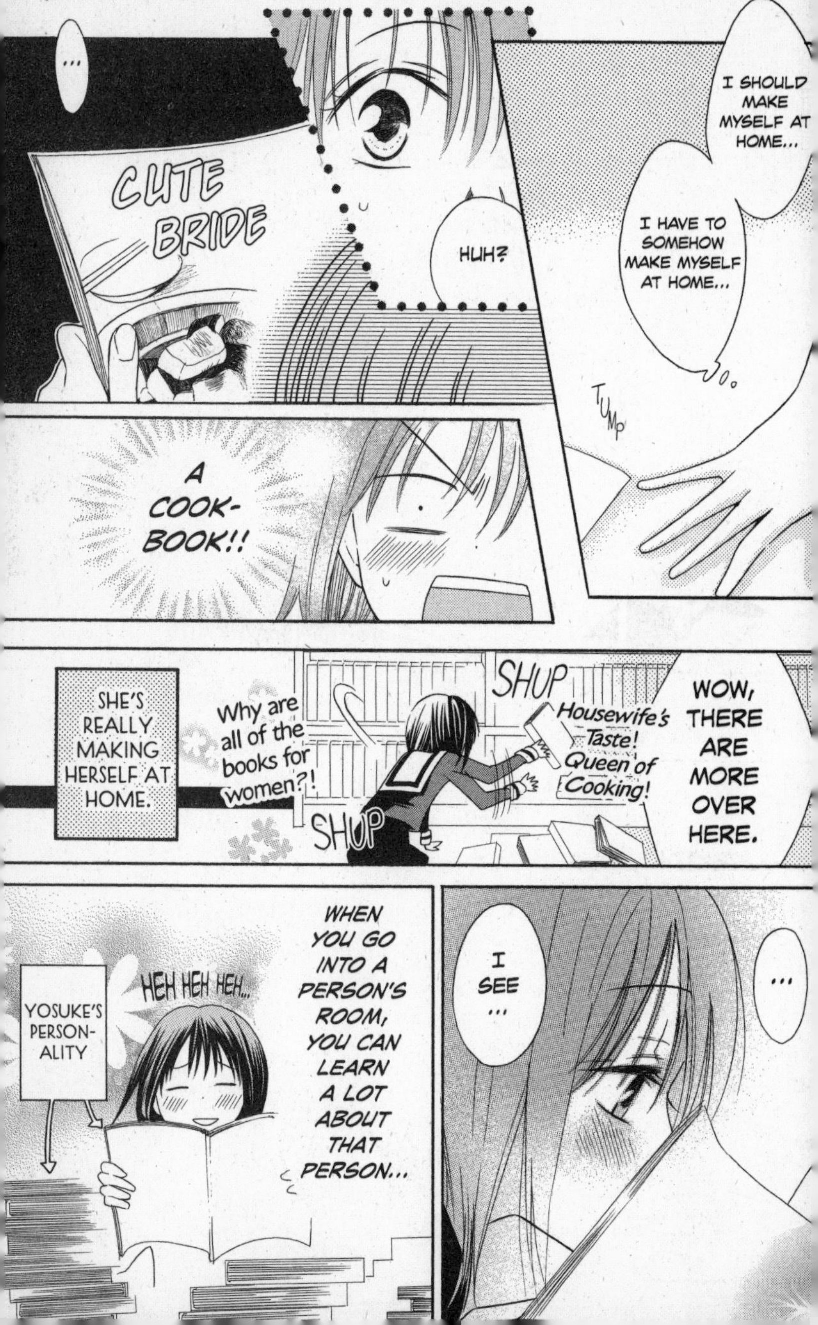
I SHOULD MAKE MYSELF AT HOME...
I HAVE TO SOMEHOW MAKE MYSELF AT HOME...
TUMP
...
HUH?
CUTE BRIDE
A COOKBOOK!!
WOW, THERE ARE MORE OVER HERE.
SHUP
Housewife's Taste! Queen of Cooking!
Why are all of the books for women?!
SHE'S REALLY MAKING HERSELF AT HOME.
SHUP
...
I SEE ...
WHEN YOU GO INTO A PERSON'S ROOM, YOU CAN LEARN A LOT ABOUT THAT PERSON...
HEH HEH HEH...
YOSUKE'S PERSONALITY

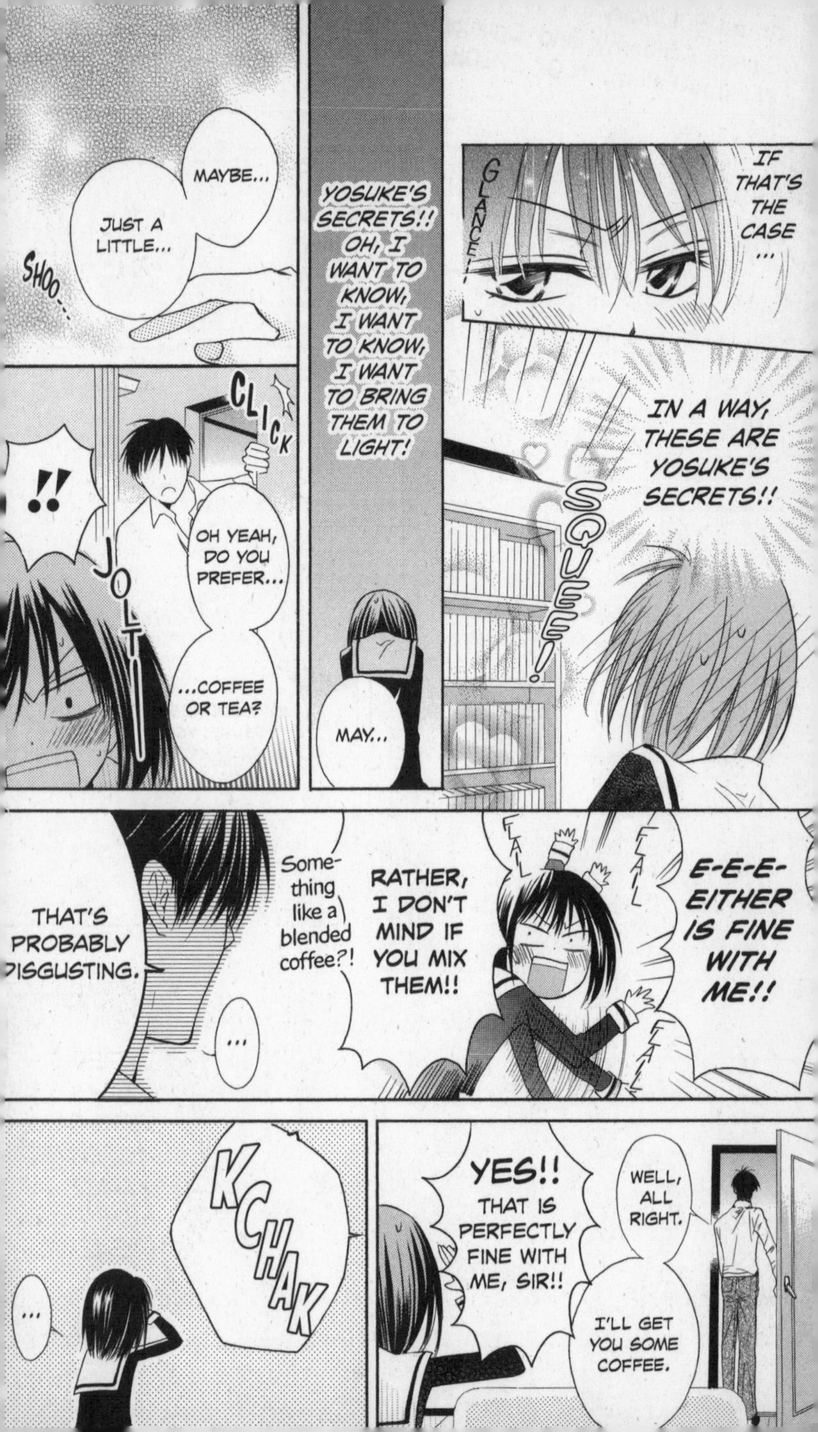

IF THAT'S THE CASE...
GLANCE!
IN A WAY, THESE ARE YOSUKE'S SECRETS!!
SQUEE!
YOSUKE'S SECRETS!! OH, I WANT TO KNOW, I WANT TO KNOW, I WANT TO BRING THEM TO LIGHT!
MAY...
MAYBE...
JUST A LITTLE...
SHOO...
CLICK
OH YEAH, DO YOU PREFER...
...COFFEE OR TEA?
!!
JOLT!
E-E-E-EITHER IS FINE WITH ME!!
FLAIL
FLAIL
FLAIL
RATHER, I DON'T MIND IF YOU MIX THEM!!
Something like a blended coffee?!
...
THAT'S PROBABLY DISGUSTING.
WELL, ALL RIGHT.
I'LL GET YOU SOME COFFEE.
YES!! THAT IS PERFECTLY FINE WITH ME, SIR!!
KCHAK
...

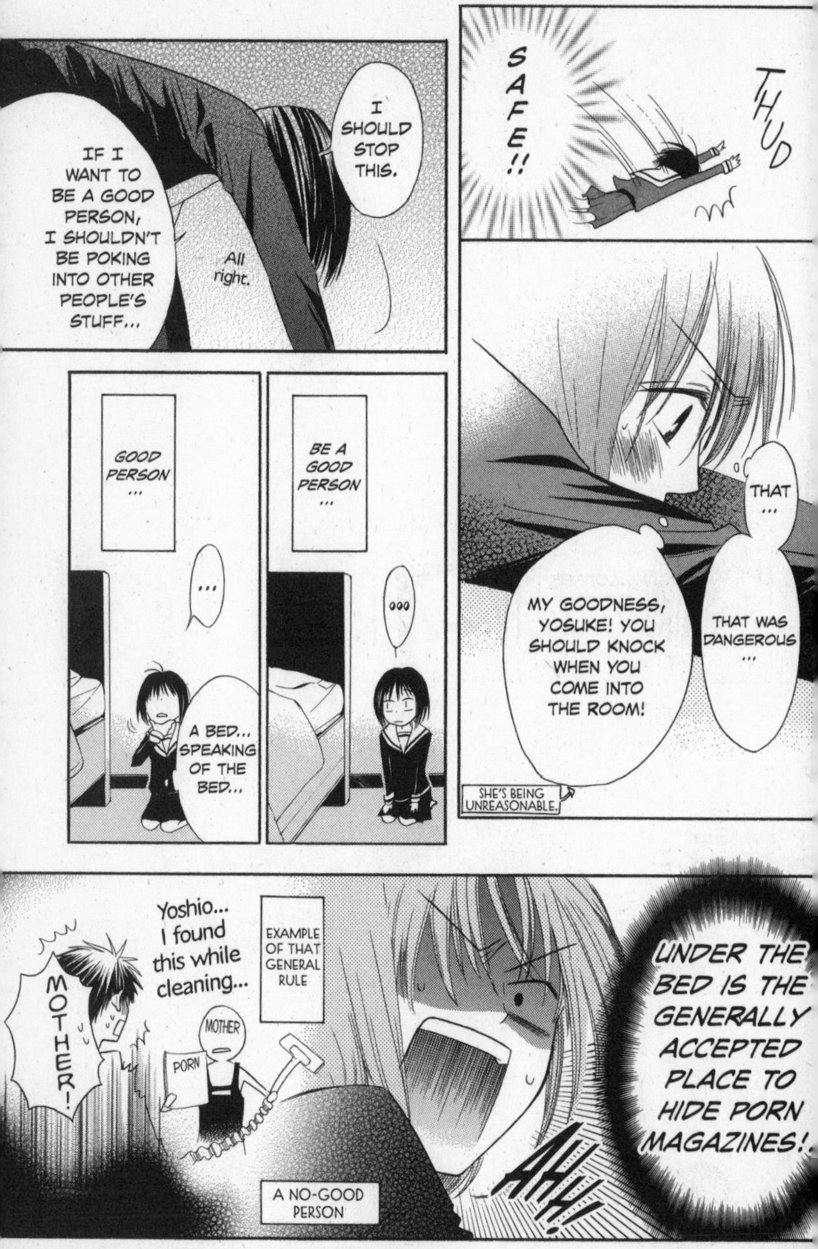
SAFE!!
THUD
THAT...
THAT WAS DANGEROUS...
MY GOODNESS, YOSUKE! YOU SHOULD KNOCK WHEN YOU COME INTO THE ROOM!
SHE'S BEING UNREASONABLE.
I SHOULD STOP THIS.
All right.
IF I WANT TO BE A GOOD PERSON, I SHOULDN'T BE POKING INTO OTHER PEOPLE'S STUFF...
BE A GOOD PERSON...
...
GOOD PERSON...
...
A BED... SPEAKING OF THE BED...
UNDER THE BED IS THE GENERALLY ACCEPTED PLACE TO HIDE PORN MAGAZINES!
AHH!
EXAMPLE OF THAT GENERAL RULE
Yoshio... I found this while cleaning...
MOTHER!
MOTHER
PORN
A NO-GOOD PERSON

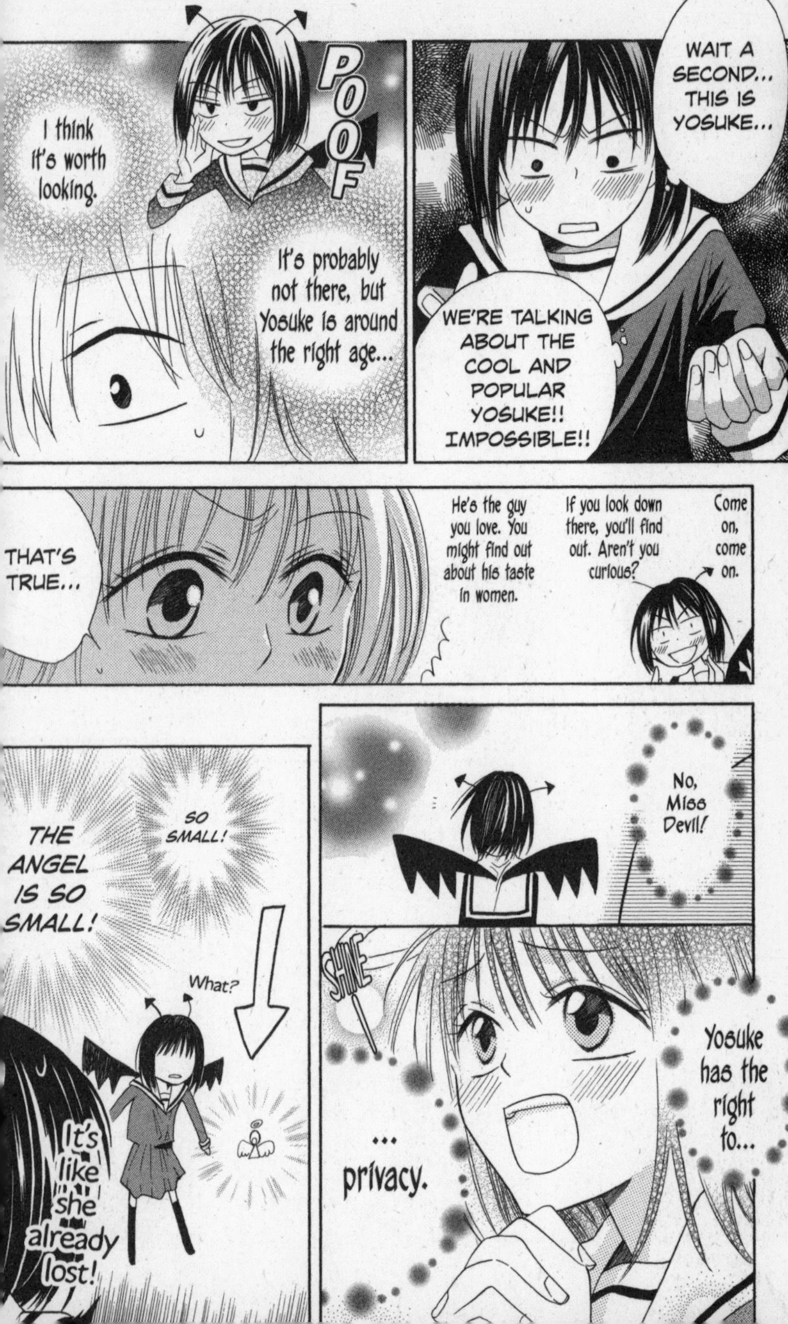
WAIT A SECOND... THIS IS YOSUKE...
WE'RE TALKING ABOUT THE COOL AND POPULAR YOSUKE!! IMPOSSIBLE!!
POOF
I think it's worth looking.
It's probably not there, but Yosuke is around the right age...
Come on, come on.
If you look down there, you'll find out. Aren't you curious?
He's the guy you love. You might find out about his taste in women.
THAT'S TRUE...
No, Miss Devil!
SHINE
Yosuke has the right to...
... privacy.
SO SMALL!
THE ANGEL IS SO SMALL!
What?
It's like she already lost!

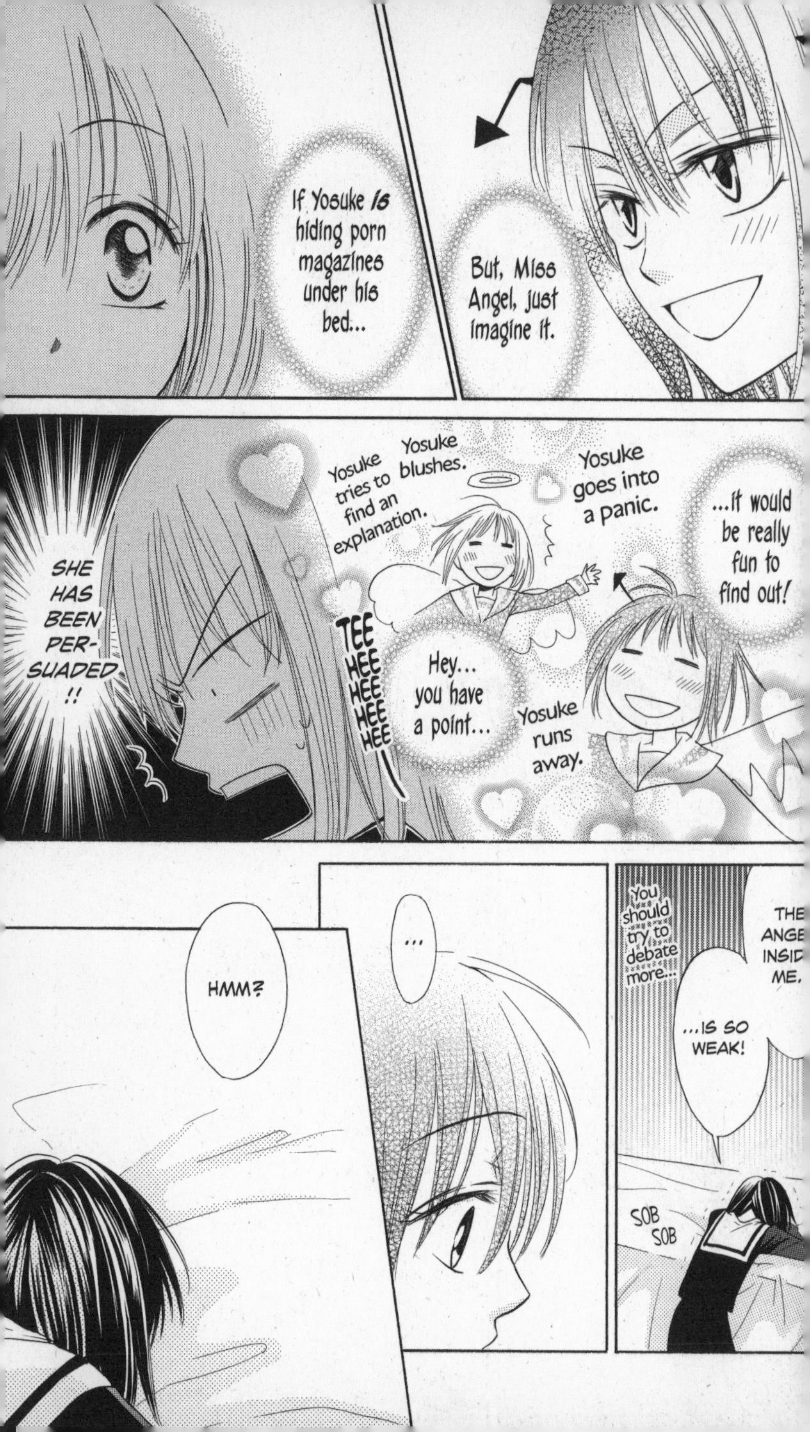
But, Miss Angel, just imagine it.
If Yosuke IS hiding porn magazines under his bed...
...It would be really fun to find out!
Yosuke goes into a panic.
Yosuke blushes.
Yosuke tries to find an explanation.
Yosuke runs away.
Hey... you have a point...
TEE HEE HEE HEE HEE
SHE HAS BEEN PER-SUADED!!
THE ANGE INSID ME.
...IS SO WEAK!
You should try to debate more...
SOB SOB
...
HMM?

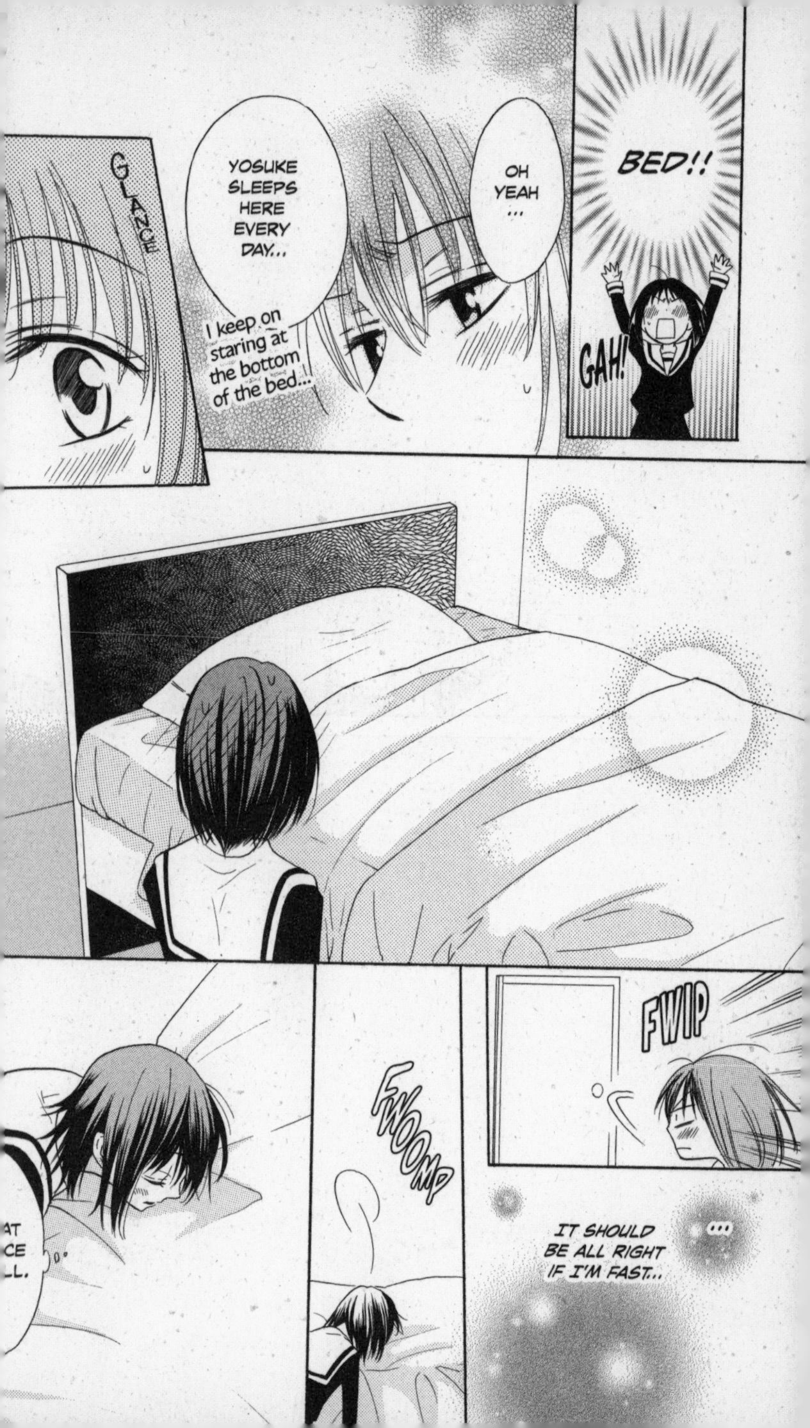
BED!!
GAH!
OH YEAH ...
YOSUKE SLEEPS HERE EVERY DAY...
I keep on staring at the bottom of the bed...
GLANCE
FWIP
...
IT SHOULD BE ALL RIGHT IF I'M FAST...
FWOOMP

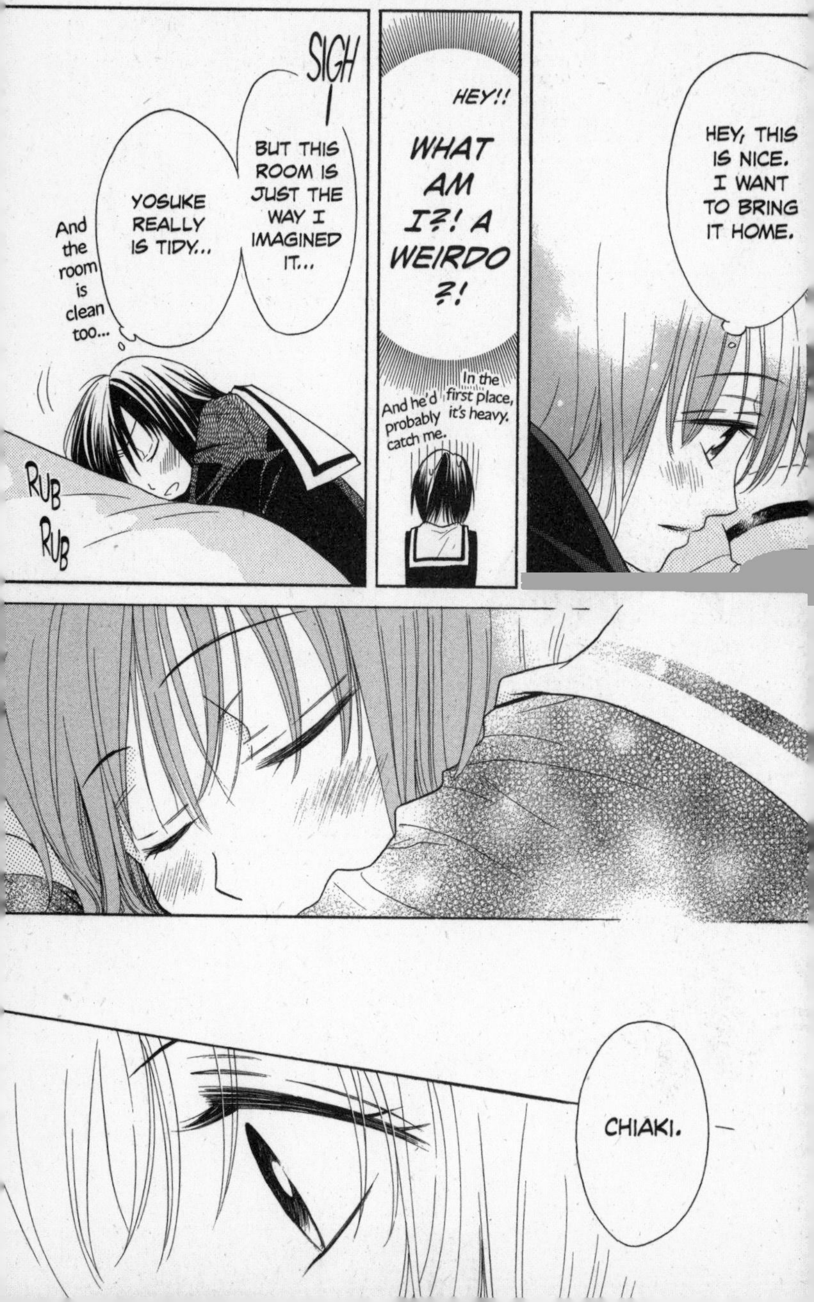
HEY, THIS IS NICE. I WANT TO BRING IT HOME.
HEY!!
WHAT AM I?! A WEIRDO?!
In the first place, it's heavy.
And he'd probably catch me.
SIGH
BUT THIS ROOM IS JUST THE WAY I IMAGINED IT...
YOSUKE REALLY IS TIDY...
And the room is clean too...
RUB RUB
CHIAKI.

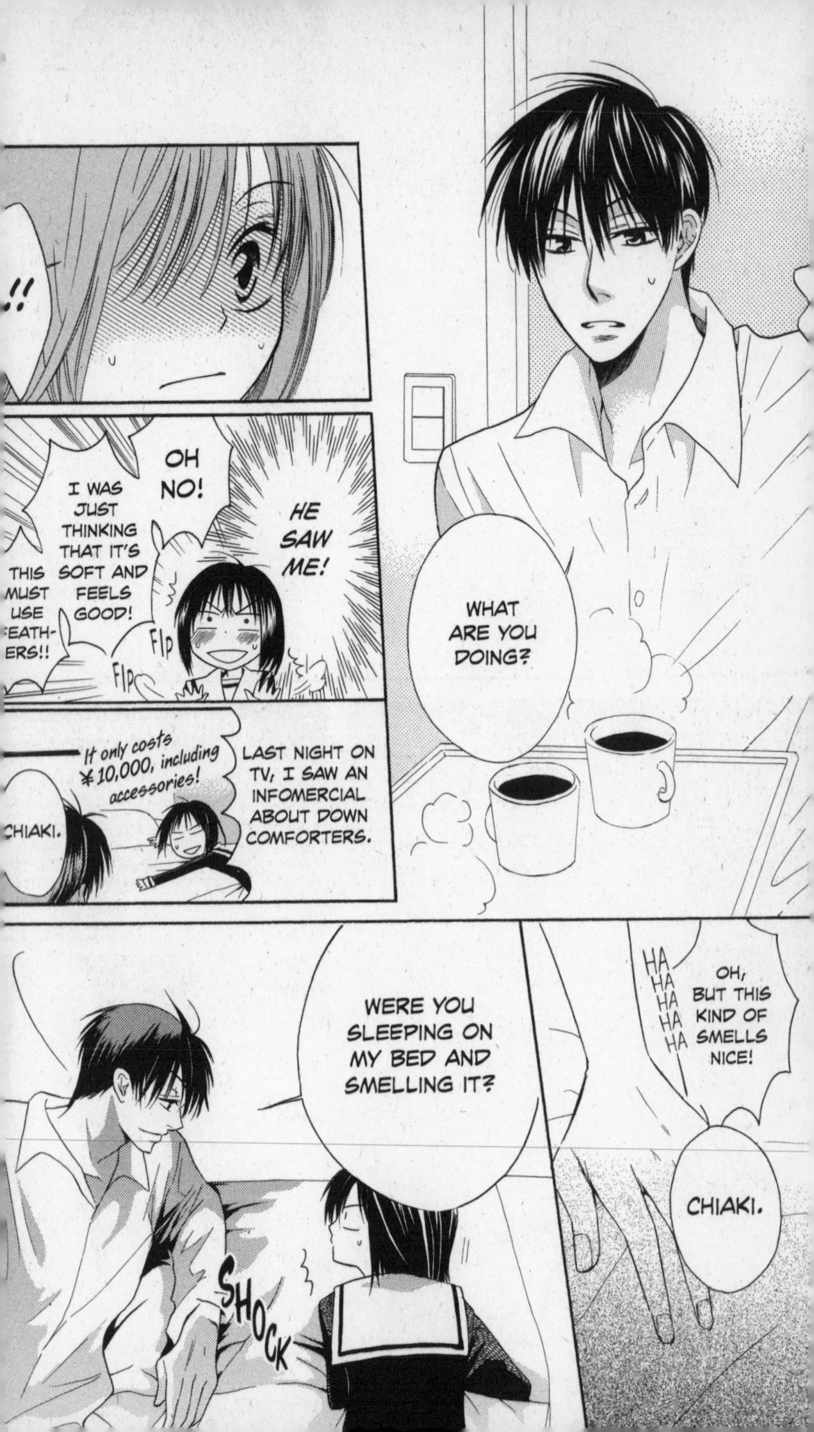
WHAT ARE YOU DOING?
!!
HE SAW ME!
OH NO!
I WAS JUST THINKING THAT IT'S SOFT AND FEELS GOOD!
THIS MUST USE FEATH-ERS!!
FLIP
FLIP
LAST NIGHT ON TV, I SAW AN INFOMERCIAL ABOUT DOWN COMFORTERS.
It only costs ¥10,000, including accessories!
CHIAKI.
OH, BUT THIS KIND OF SMELLS NICE!
HA HA HA HA HA HA
CHIAKI.
WERE YOU SLEEPING ON MY BED AND SMELLING IT?
SHOCK

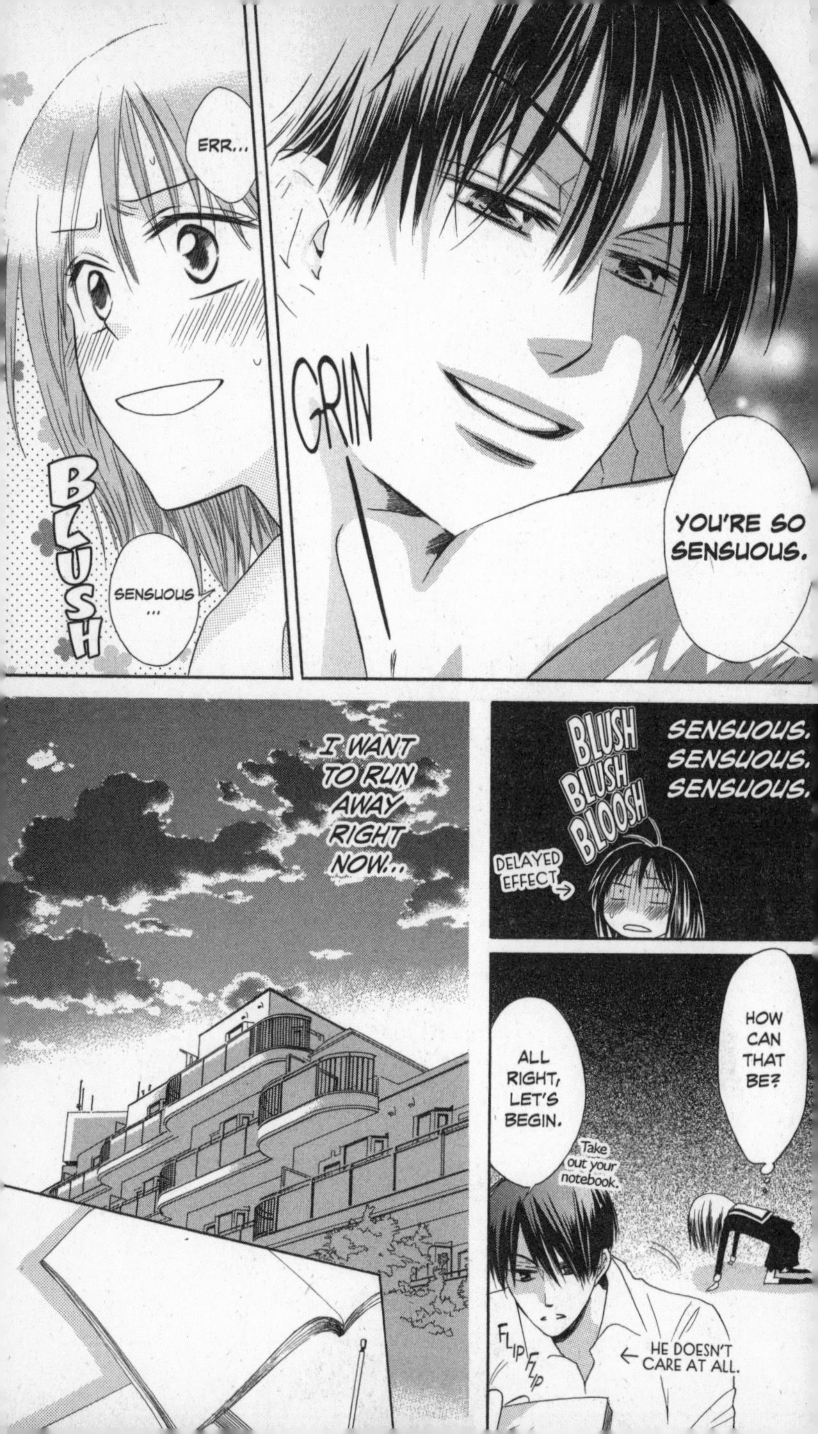
YOU'RE SO SENSUOUS.
GRIN
ERR...
SENSUOUS...
BLUSH
SENSUOUS. SENSUOUS. SENSUOUS.
BLUSH BLUSH BLOOSH
DELAYED EFFECT
HOW CAN THAT BE?
ALL RIGHT, LET'S BEGIN.
Take out your notebook.
FLIP FLIP
HE DOESN'T CARE AT ALL.
I WANT TO RUN AWAY RIGHT NOW...

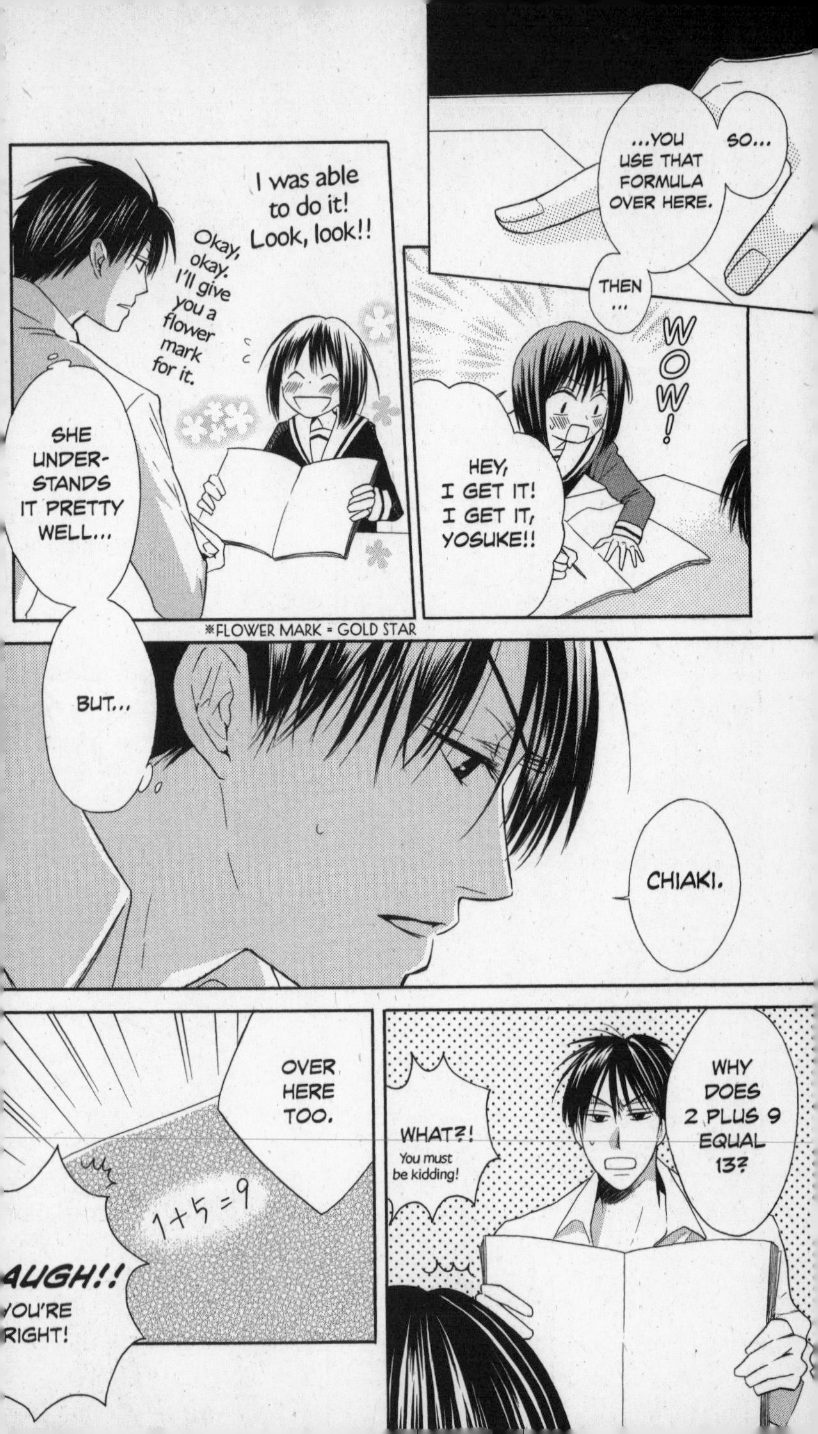
SO...
THEN ...
...YOU USE THAT FORMULA OVER HERE.
WOW!
HEY, I GET IT! I GET IT, YOSUKE!!
I was able to do it! Look, look!!
Okay, okay. I'll give you a flower mark for it.
SHE UNDERSTANDS IT PRETTY WELL...
※FLOWER MARK = GOLD STAR
BUT...
CHIAKI.
WHY DOES 2 PLUS 9 EQUAL 13?
WHAT?!
You must be kidding!
OVER HERE TOO.
1+5=9
AUGH!!
YOU'RE RIGHT!

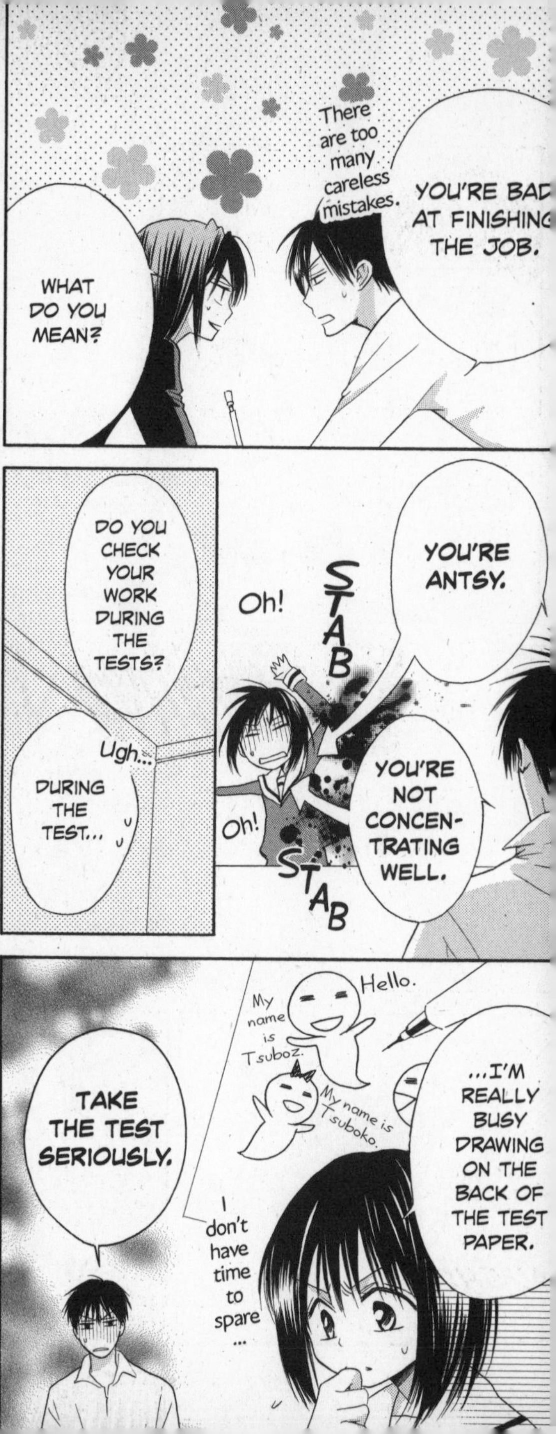
There are too many careless mistakes.
YOU'RE BAD AT FINISHING THE JOB.
WHAT DO YOU MEAN?
YOU'RE ANTSY.
STAB
Oh!
YOU'RE NOT CONCENTRATING WELL.
Oh!
STAB
DO YOU CHECK YOUR WORK DURING THE TESTS?
Ugh...
DURING THE TEST...
...I'M REALLY BUSY DRAWING ON THE BACK OF THE TEST PAPER.
I don't have time to spare...
Hello.
My name is Tsuboz.
My name is Tsuboko.
TAKE THE TEST SERIOUSLY.

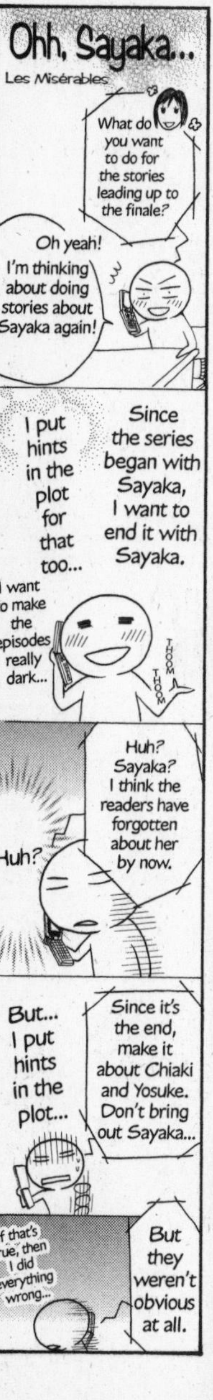
Ohh, Sayaka...
Les Misérables
What do you want to do for the stories leading up to the finale?
Oh yeah! I'm thinking about doing stories about Sayaka again!
Since the series began with Sayaka, I want to end it with Sayaka.
I put hints in the plot for that too...
I want to make the episodes really dark...
THOOM THOOM
Huh? Sayaka? I think the readers have forgotten about her by now.
Huh?
Since it's the end, make it about Chiaki and Yosuke. Don't bring out Sayaka...
But... I put hints in the plot...
But they weren't obvious at all.
If that's true, then I did everything wrong...

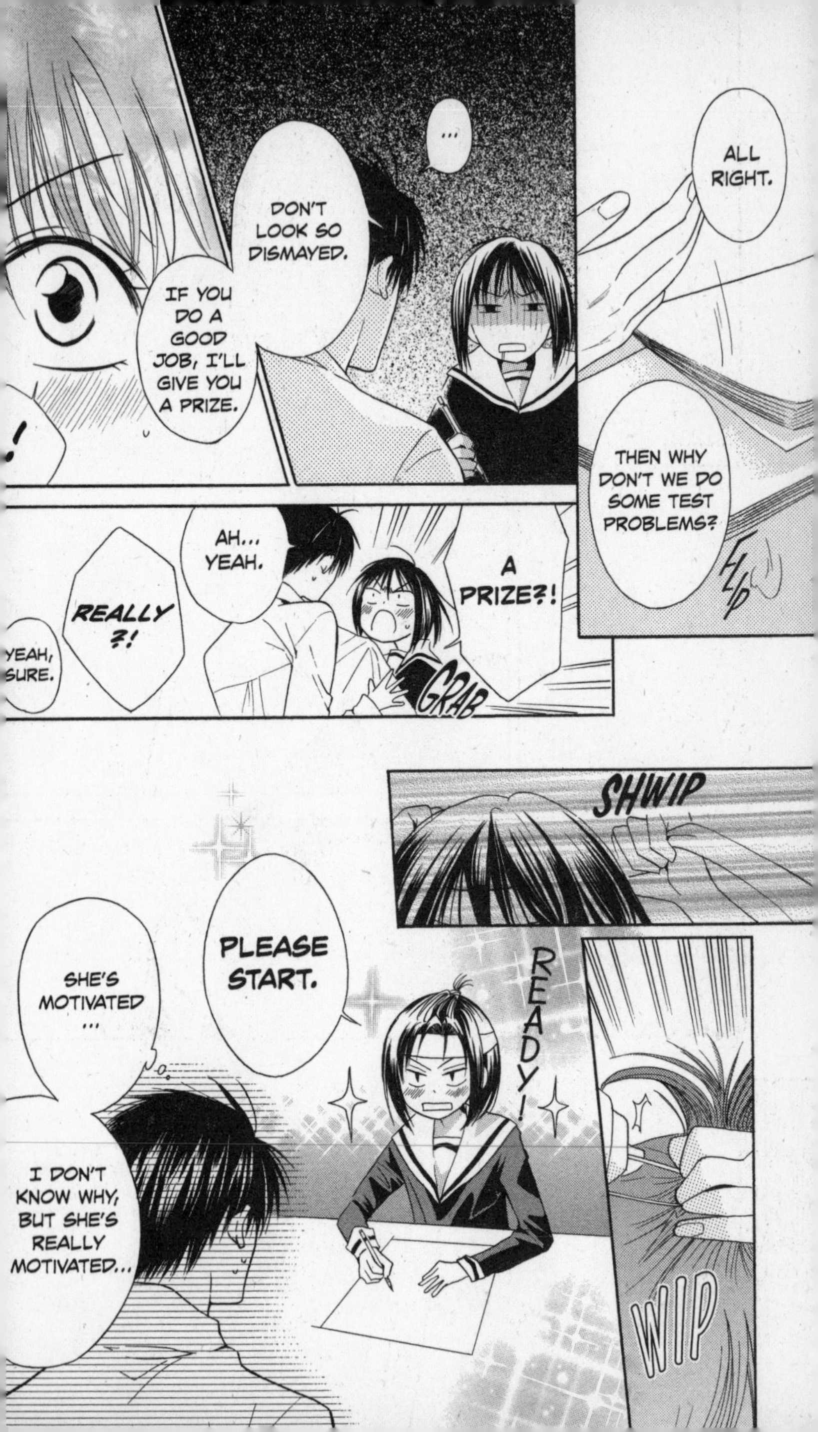
ALL RIGHT.
THEN WHY DON'T WE DO SOME TEST PROBLEMS?
FLIP
...
DON'T LOOK SO DISMAYED.
IF YOU DO A GOOD JOB, I'LL GIVE YOU A PRIZE.
A PRIZE?!
GRAB
AH... YEAH.
REALLY ?!
YEAH, SURE.
SHWIP
WIP
READY!
PLEASE START.
SHE'S MOTIVATED...
I DON'T KNOW WHY, BUT SHE'S REALLY MOTIVATED...

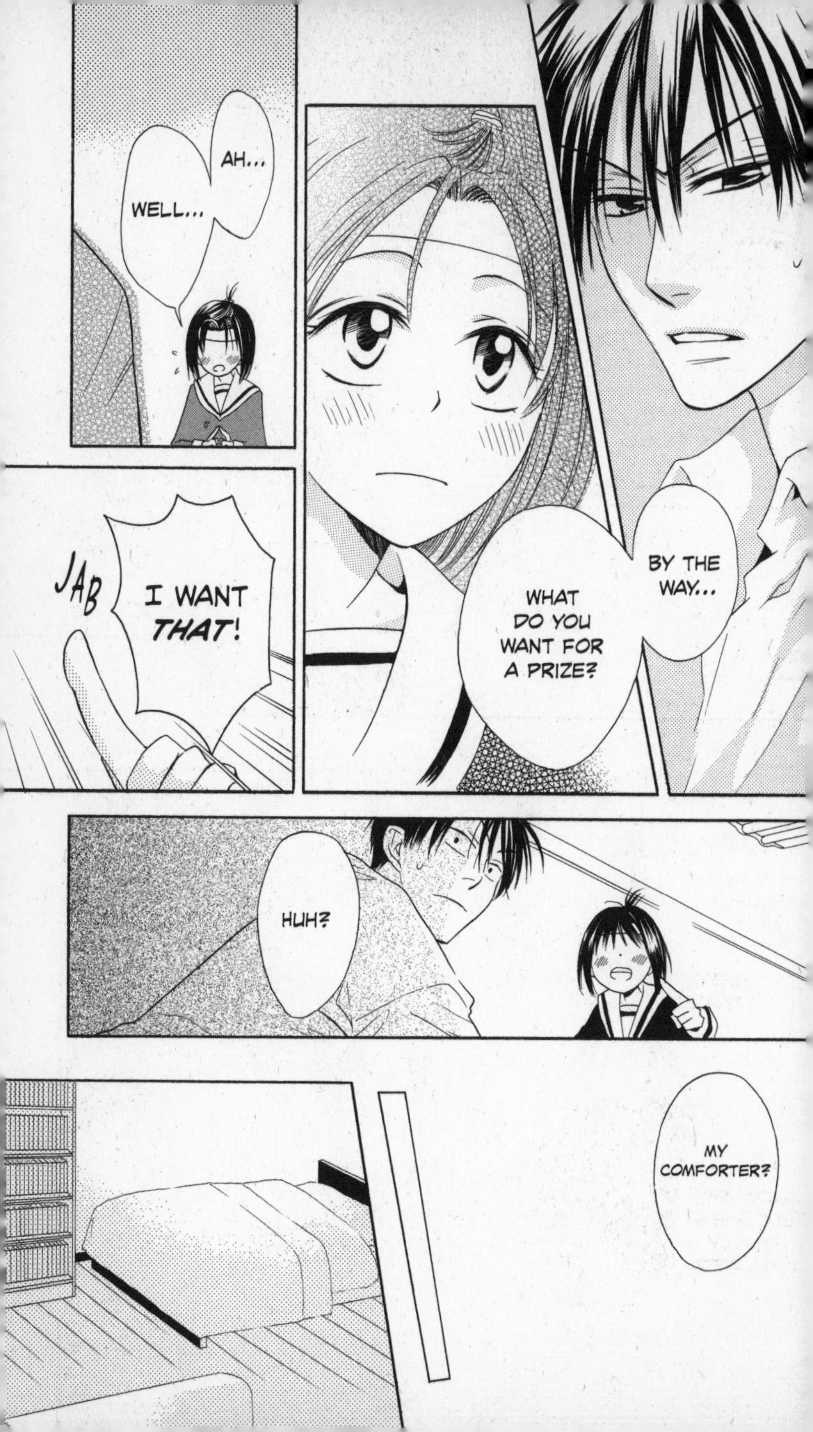
BY THE WAY...
WHAT DO YOU WANT FOR A PRIZE?
AH... WELL...
JAB
I WANT *THAT*!
HUH?
MY COMFORTER?

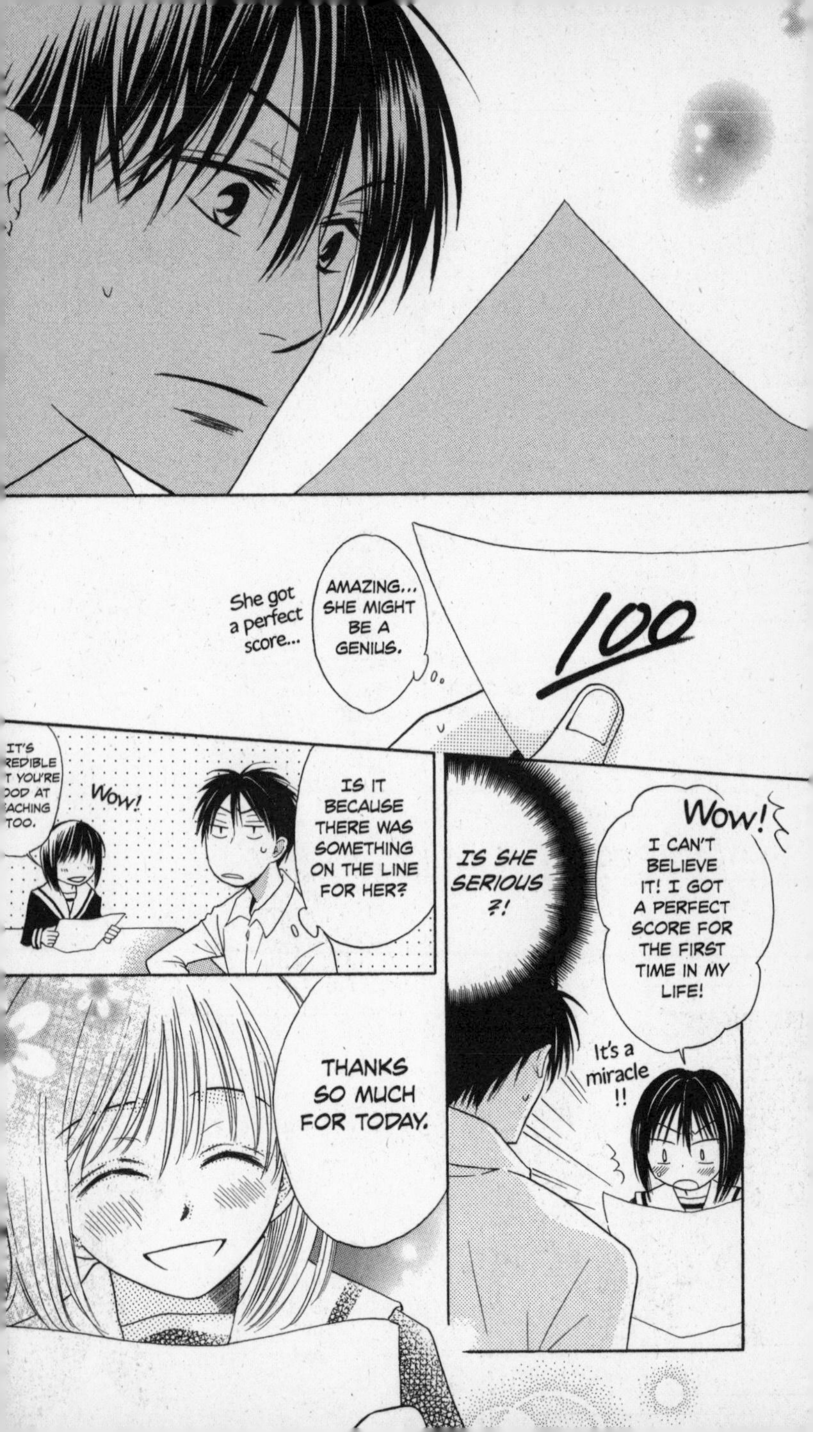
AMAZING... SHE MIGHT BE A GENIUS.
She got a perfect score...
100
Wow!
I CAN'T BELIEVE IT! I GOT A PERFECT SCORE FOR THE FIRST TIME IN MY LIFE!
IS SHE SERIOUS?!
It's a miracle!!
IS IT BECAUSE THERE WAS SOMETHING ON THE LINE FOR HER?
Wow!
IT'S REDIBLE T YOU'RE OOD AT ACHING TOO.
THANKS SO MUCH FOR TODAY.

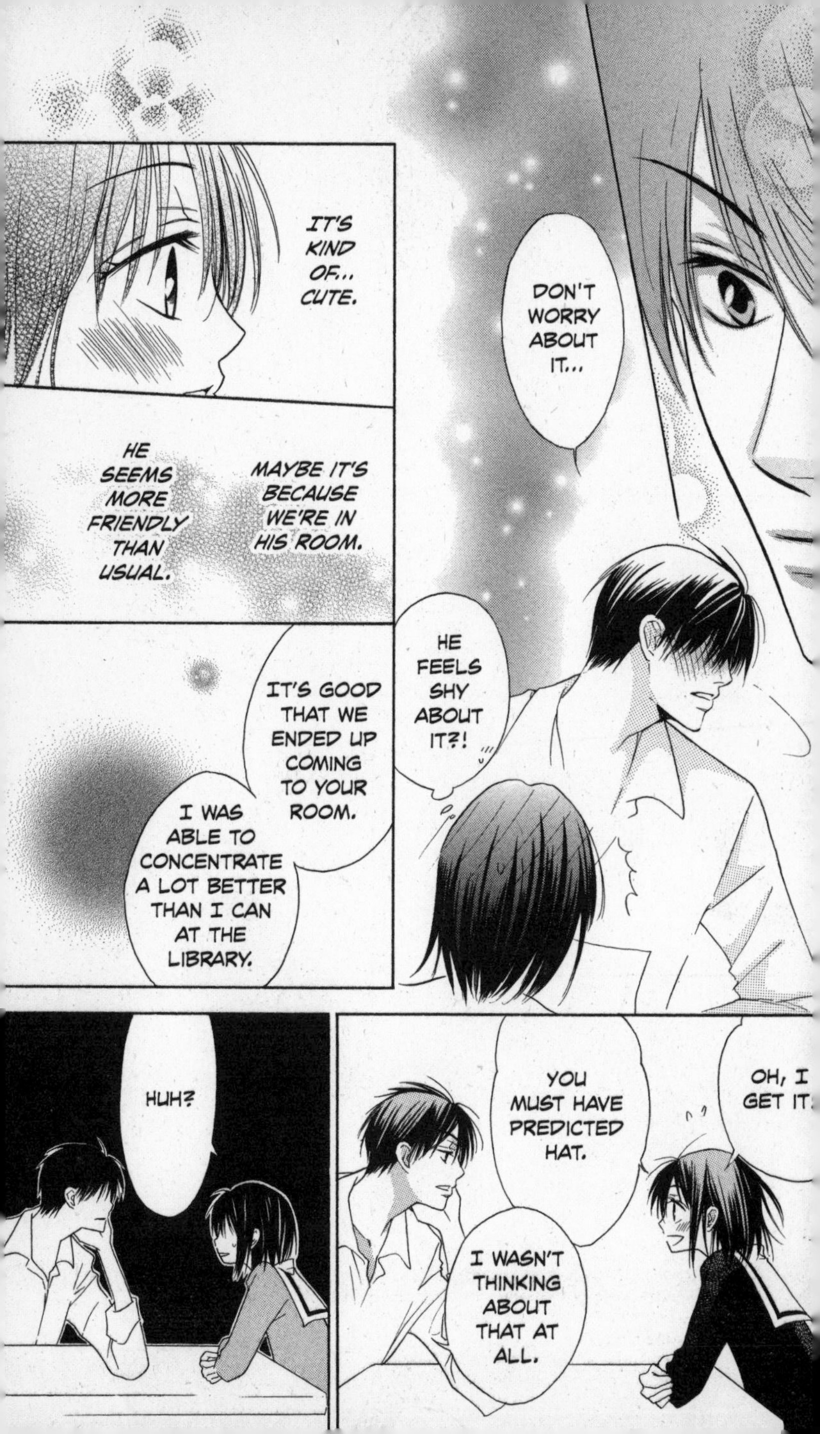
DON'T WORRY ABOUT IT...
HE FEELS SHY ABOUT IT?!
IT'S KIND OF... CUTE.
MAYBE IT'S BECAUSE WE'RE IN HIS ROOM.
HE SEEMS MORE FRIENDLY THAN USUAL.
IT'S GOOD THAT WE ENDED UP COMING TO YOUR ROOM.
I WAS ABLE TO CONCENTRATE A LOT BETTER THAN I CAN AT THE LIBRARY.
OH, I GET IT.
YOU MUST HAVE PREDICTED HAT.
I WASN'T THINKING ABOUT THAT AT ALL.
HUH?

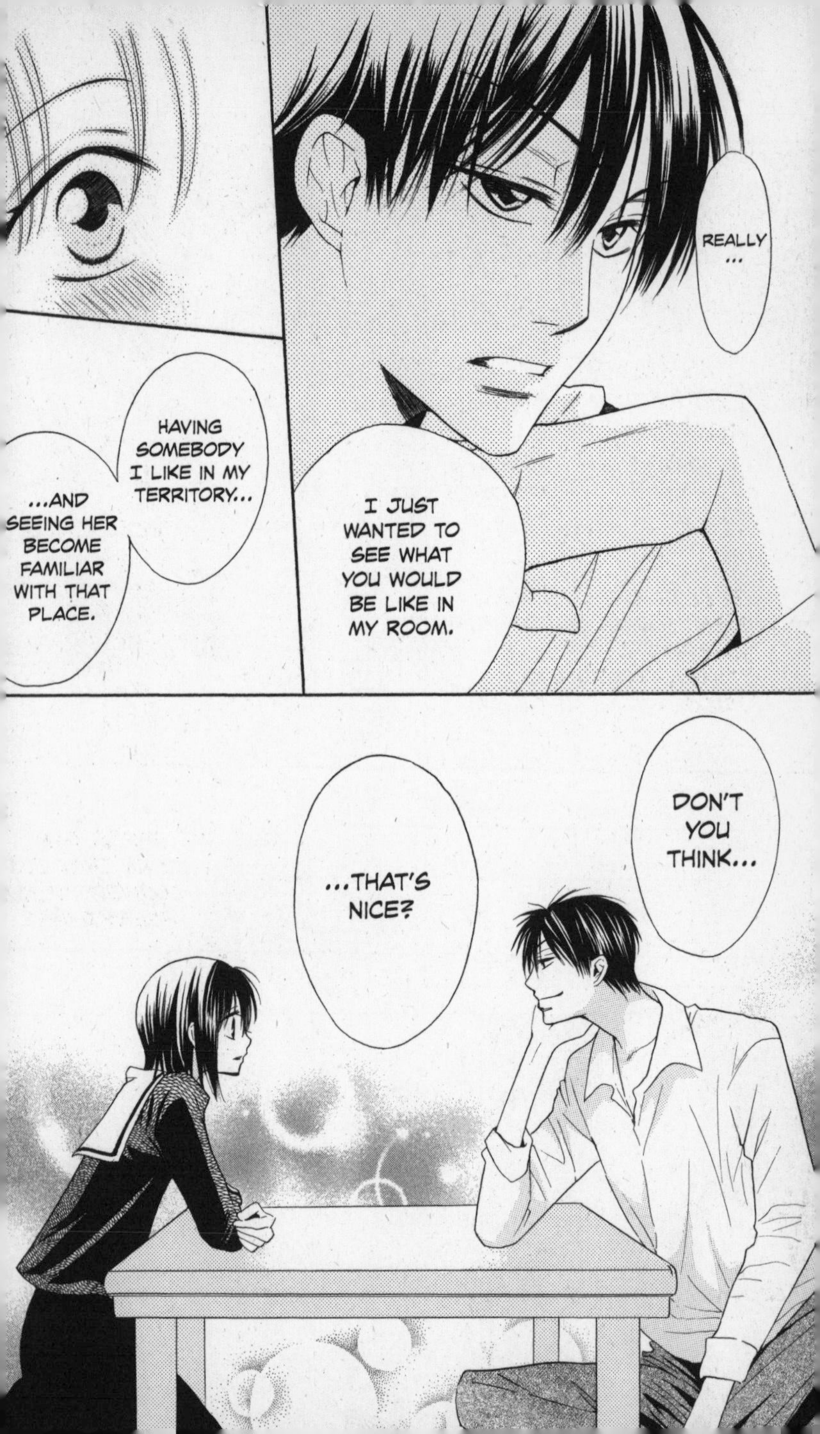
REALLY...
I JUST WANTED TO SEE WHAT YOU WOULD BE LIKE IN MY ROOM.
HAVING SOMEBODY I LIKE IN MY TERRITORY...
...AND SEEING HER BECOME FAMILIAR WITH THAT PLACE.
DON'T YOU THINK...
...THAT'S NICE?

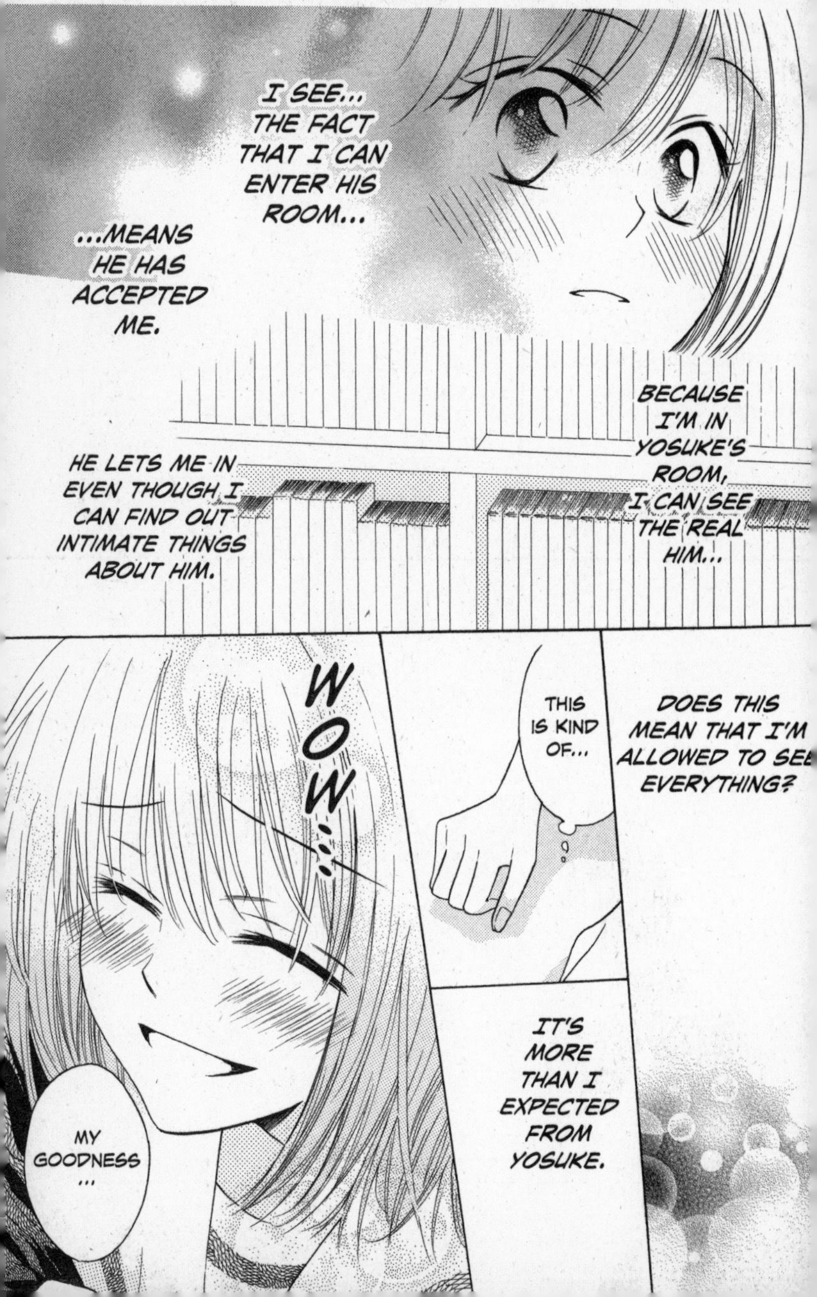
I SEE... THE FACT THAT I CAN ENTER HIS ROOM...
...MEANS HE HAS ACCEPTED ME.
BECAUSE I'M IN YOSUKE'S ROOM, I CAN SEE THE REAL HIM...
HE LETS ME IN EVEN THOUGH I CAN FIND OUT INTIMATE THINGS ABOUT HIM.
DOES THIS MEAN THAT I'M ALLOWED TO SEE EVERYTHING?
THIS IS KIND OF...
IT'S MORE THAN I EXPECTED FROM YOSUKE.
WOW...
MY GOODNESS...

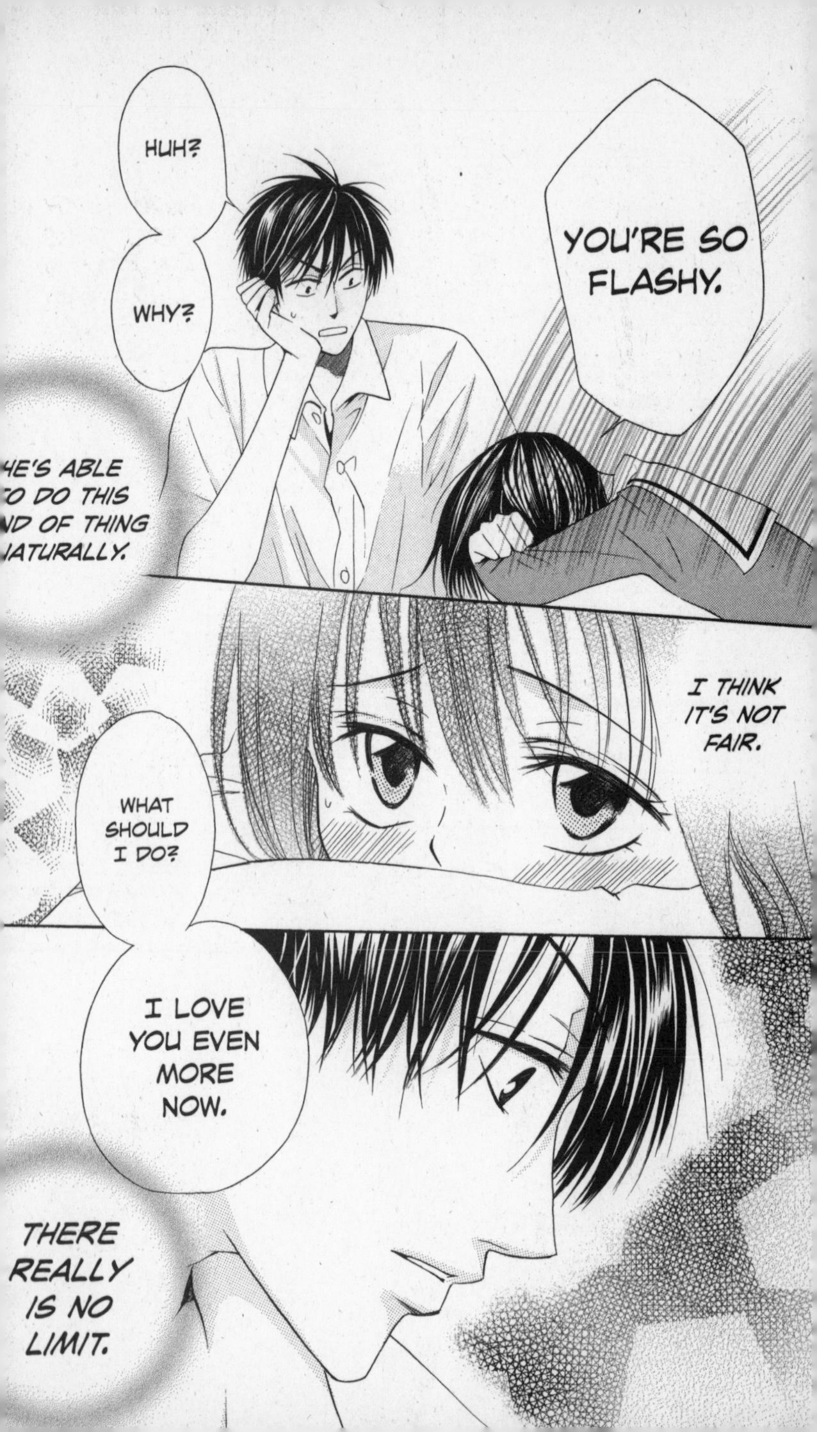
YOU'RE SO FLASHY.
HUH?
WHY?
HE'S ABLE TO DO THIS ND OF THING NATURALLY.
I THINK IT'S NOT FAIR.
WHAT SHOULD I DO?
I LOVE YOU EVEN MORE NOW.
THERE REALLY IS NO LIMIT.

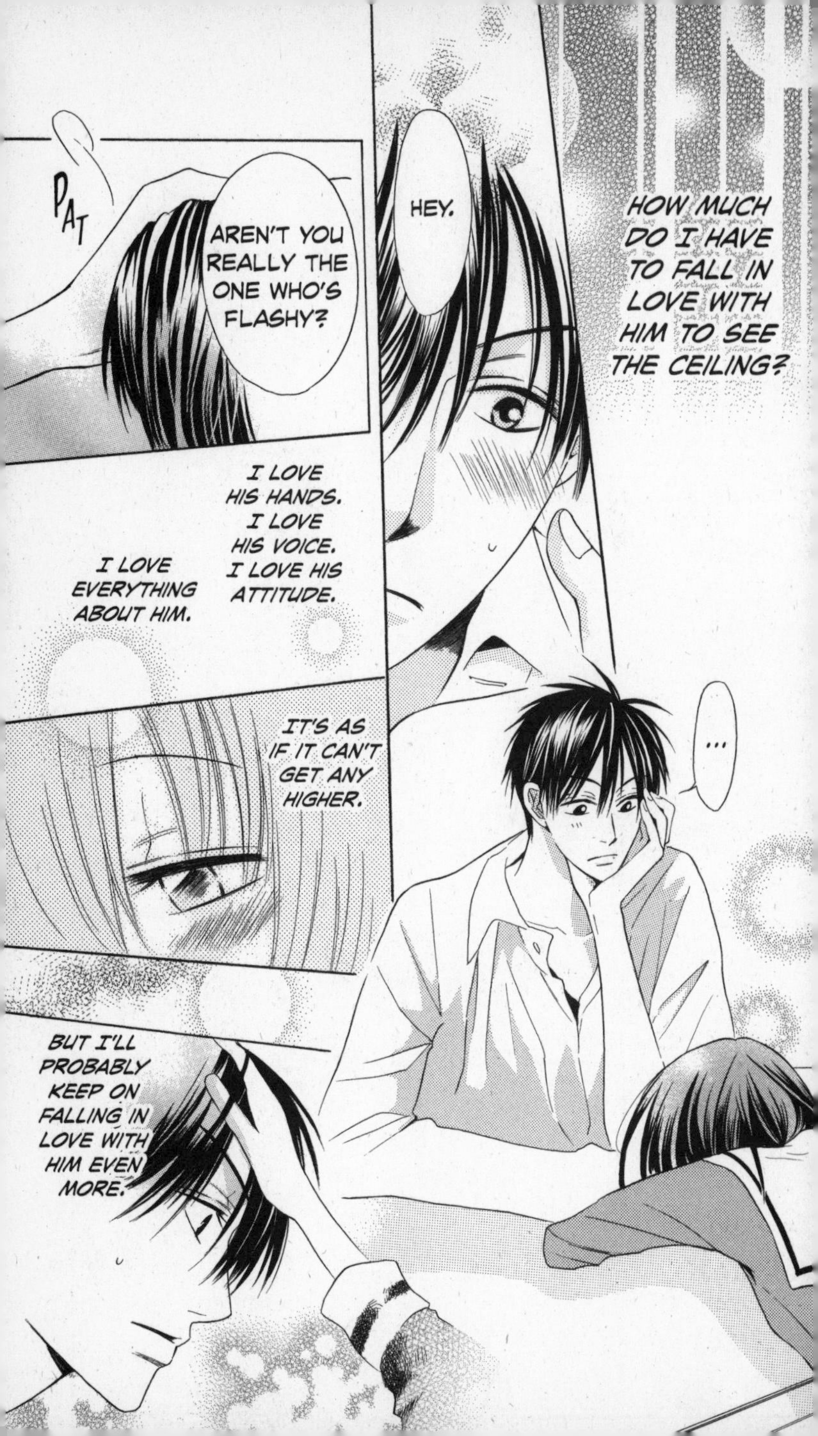

HOW MUCH DO I HAVE TO FALL IN LOVE WITH HIM TO SEE THE CEILING?
HEY.
ARE'NT YOU REALLY THE ONE WHO'S FLASHY?
PAT
I LOVE HIS HANDS. I LOVE HIS VOICE. I LOVE HIS ATTITUDE.
I LOVE EVERYTHING ABOUT HIM.
...
IT'S AS IF IT CAN'T GET ANY HIGHER.
BUT I'LL PROBABLY KEEP ON FALLING IN LOVE WITH HIM EVEN MORE.

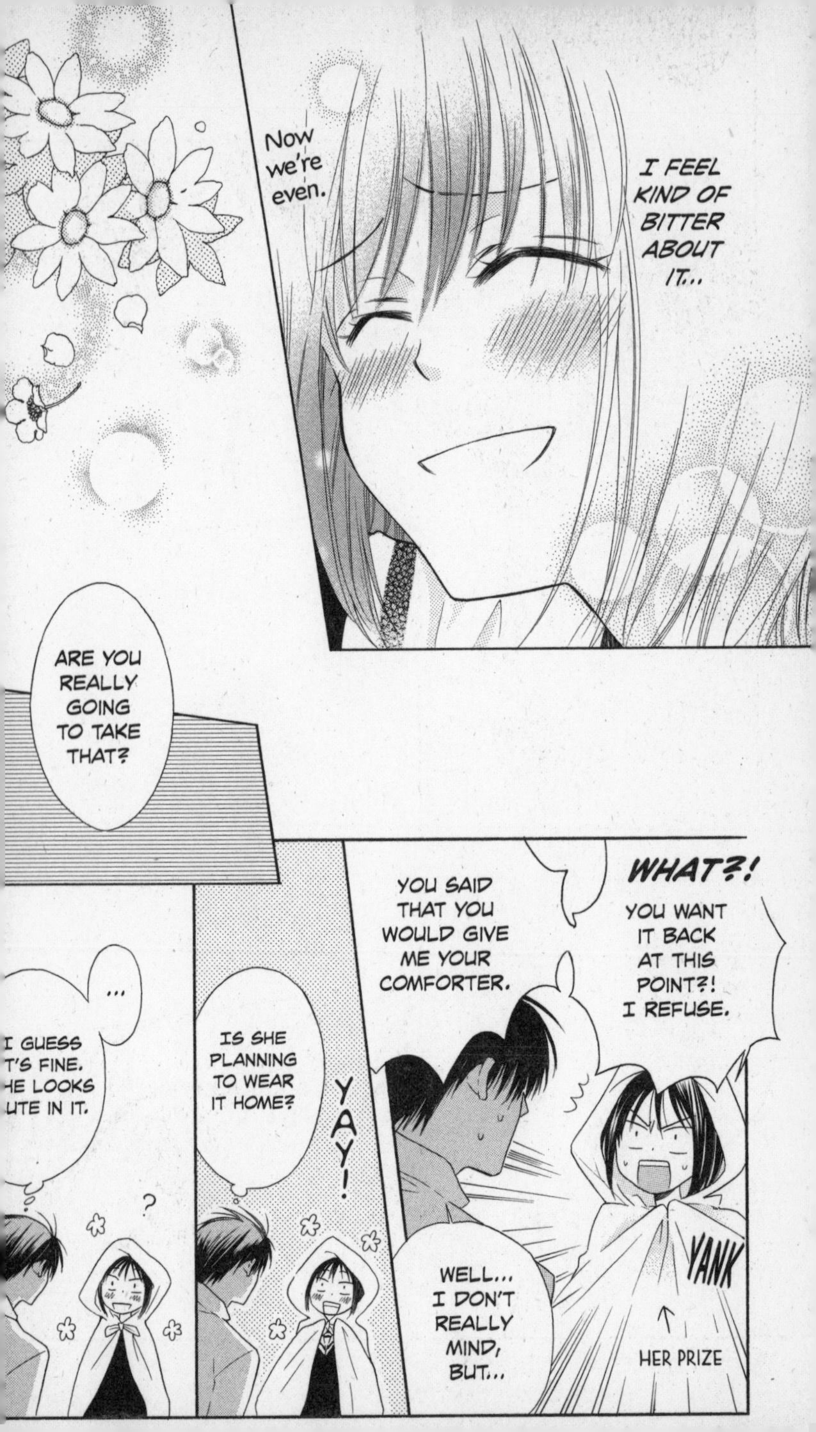
I FEEL KIND OF BITTER ABOUT IT...
Now we're even.
ARE YOU REALLY GOING TO TAKE THAT?
WHAT?!
YOU WANT IT BACK AT THIS POINT?! I REFUSE.
YOU SAID THAT YOU WOULD GIVE ME YOUR COMFORTER.
YANK
HER PRIZE
WELL... I DON'T REALLY MIND, BUT...
YAY!
IS SHE PLANNING TO WEAR IT HOME?
...
I GUESS
T'S FINE.
HE LOOKS
UTE IN IT.

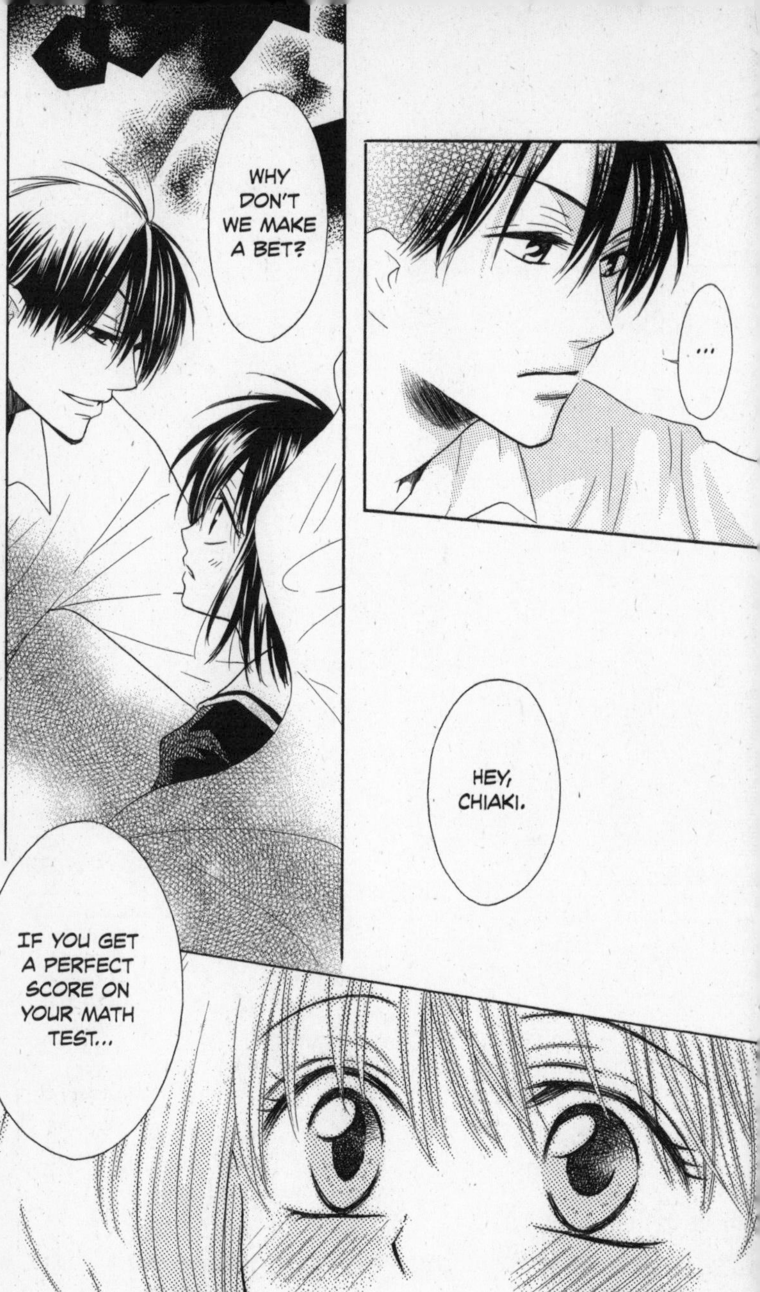
...
HEY, CHIAKI.
WHY DON'T WE MAKE A BET?
IF YOU GET A PERFECT SCORE ON YOUR MATH TEST...

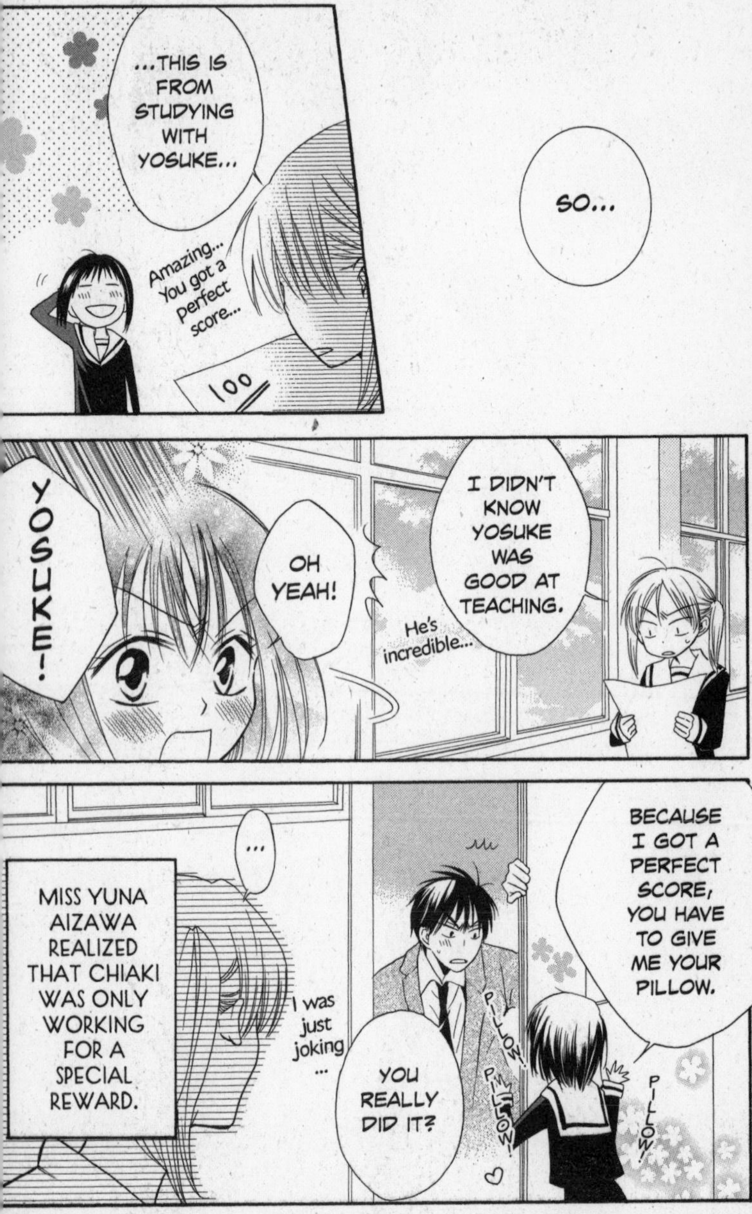
SO...
...THIS IS FROM STUDYING WITH YOSUKE...
Amazing... You got a perfect score...
100
I DIDN'T KNOW YOSUKE WAS GOOD AT TEACHING.
He's incredible...
OH YEAH!
YOSUKE!
BECAUSE I GOT A PERFECT SCORE, YOU HAVE TO GIVE ME YOUR PILLOW.
PILLOW!
PILLOW!
PILLOW!
YOU REALLY DID IT?
I was just joking ...
...
MISS YUNA AIZAWA REALIZED THAT CHIAKI WAS ONLY WORKING FOR A SPECIAL REWARD.

The Magic Touch, Part 47/The End

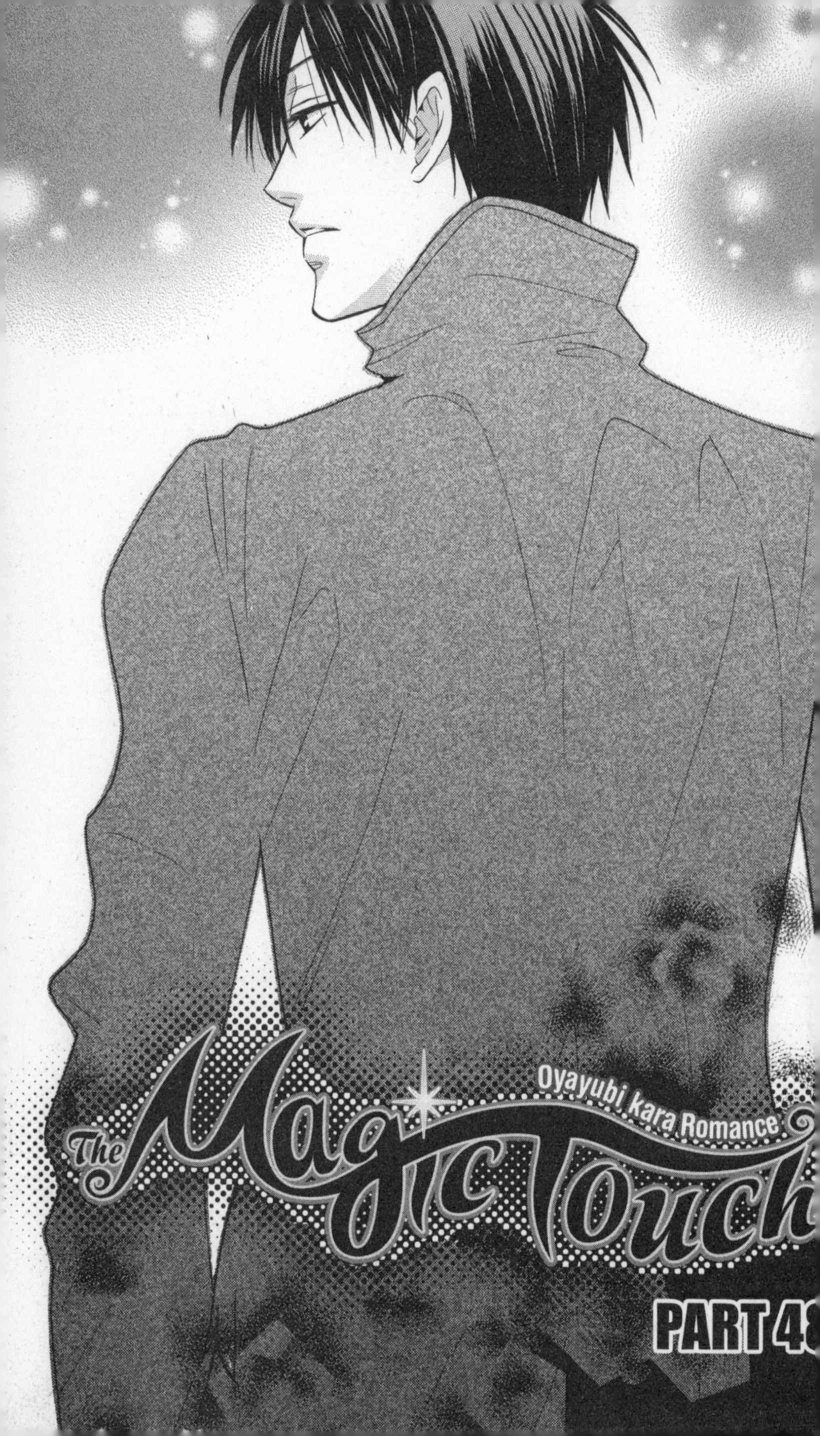
The Magic Touch
Oyayubi kara Romance
PART 48

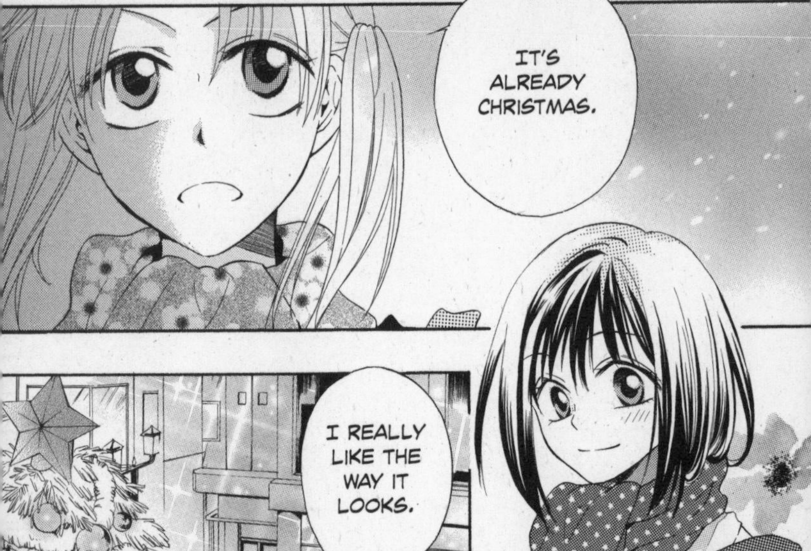
IT'S ALREADY CHRISTMAS.
YEAH.
I REALLY LIKE THE WAY IT LOOKS.
I REALLY LIKE THE WAY IT LOOKS.
IT FEELS LIKE A PARTY IS ABOUT TO START.
IT'S JUST THE MAGIC OF THE LIGHTS AND THE TREE.
OU SHOULDN'T BE FOOLED.

Favorite Characters

I didn't really notice it while writing the stories, but after the series ended, I realized that I liked certain characters because I still wanted to draw them. (It might also be because none of the characters but the main character got a resolution to their stories.)

So here are my top eight favorite characters!

1. Natsue
2. Mihime
3. Harumi
4. Tanaka
5. Sanae
6. Togu [Takeshi]
7. Sakuranomiya
8. Ohnuki

I feel like Chiaki and Yosuke are in a different category...
(It's not a question of liking or hating them.)

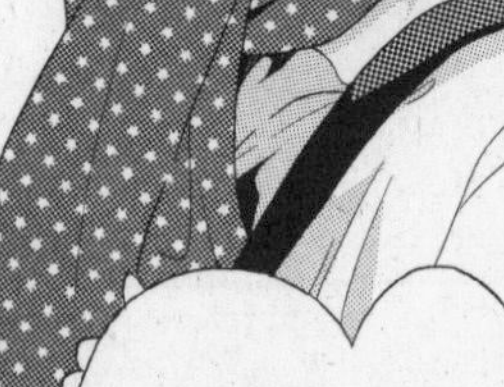

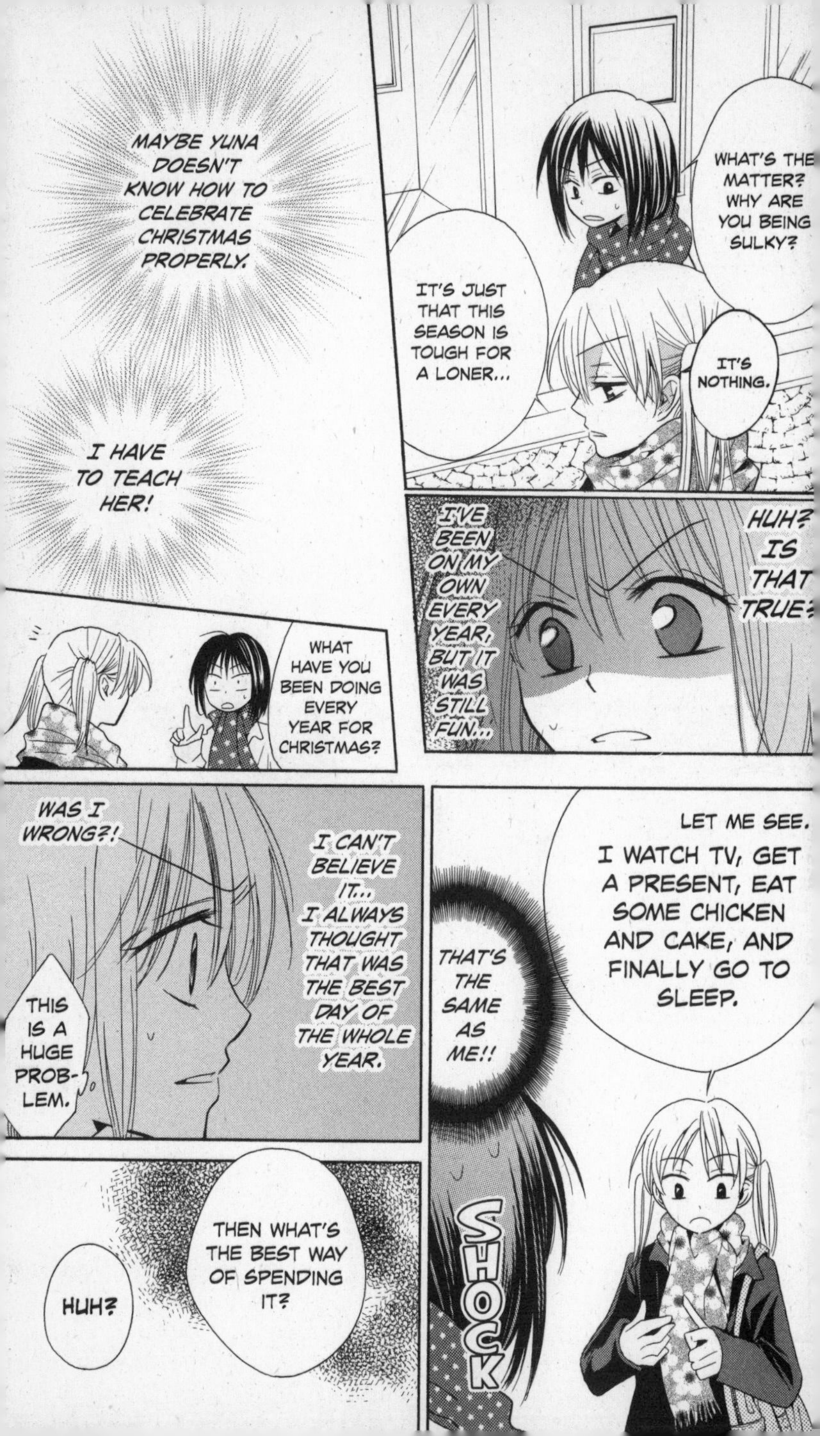
WHAT'S THE MATTER? WHY ARE YOU BEING SULKY?
IT'S NOTHING.
IT'S JUST THAT THIS SEASON IS TOUGH FOR A LONER...
HUH? IS THAT TRUE?
I'VE BEEN ON MY OWN EVERY YEAR, BUT IT WAS STILL FUN...
MAYBE YUNA DOESN'T KNOW HOW TO CELEBRATE CHRISTMAS PROPERLY.
I HAVE TO TEACH HER!
WHAT HAVE YOU BEEN DOING EVERY YEAR FOR CHRISTMAS?
LET ME SEE.
I WATCH TV, GET A PRESENT, EAT SOME CHICKEN AND CAKE, AND FINALLY GO TO SLEEP.
THAT'S THE SAME AS ME!!
SHOCK
I CAN'T BELIEVE IT... I ALWAYS THOUGHT THAT WAS THE BEST DAY OF THE WHOLE YEAR.
WAS I WRONG?!
THIS IS A HUGE PROB-LEM.
THEN WHAT'S THE BEST WAY OF SPENDING IT?
HUH?

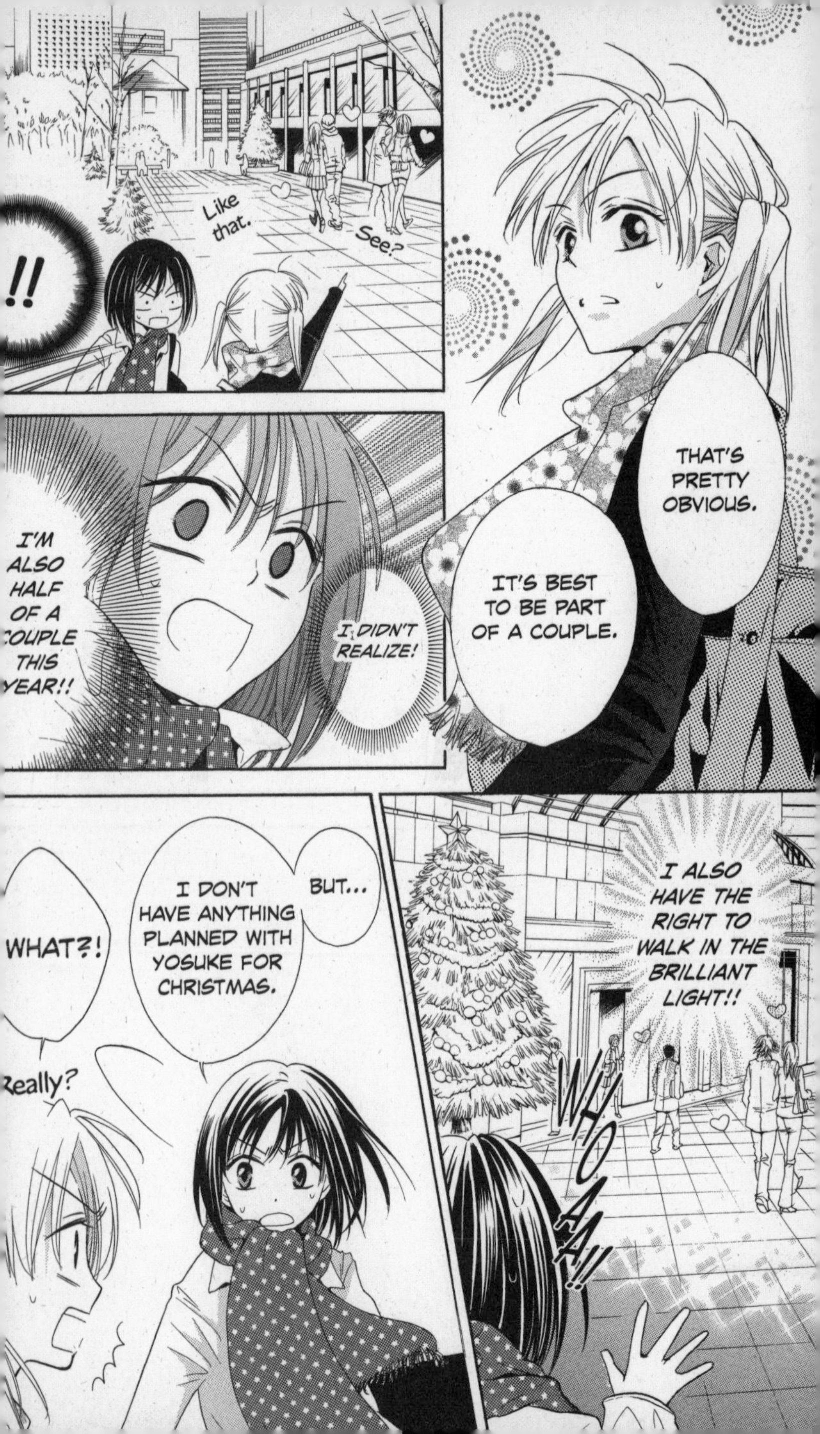
THAT'S PRETTY OBVIOUS.
IT'S BEST TO BE PART OF A COUPLE.
See?
Like that.
!!
I DIDN'T REALIZE!
I'M ALSO HALF OF A COUPLE THIS YEAR!!
I ALSO HAVE THE RIGHT TO WALK IN THE BRILLIANT LIGHT!!
WHOAA!!
BUT...
I DON'T HAVE ANYTHING PLANNED WITH YOSUKE FOR CHRISTMAS.
WHAT?!
Really?

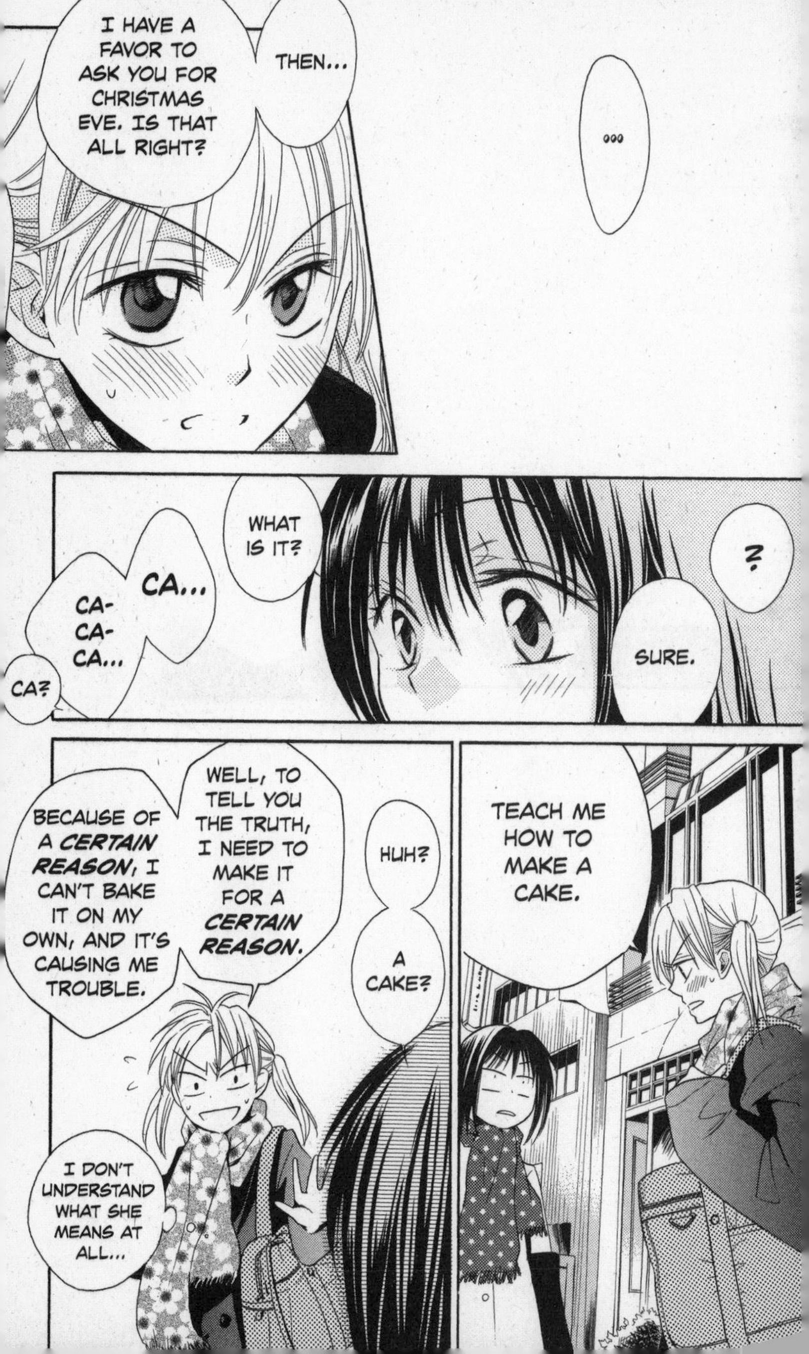
...
THEN...
I HAVE A FAVOR TO ASK YOU FOR CHRISTMAS EVE. IS THAT ALL RIGHT?
?
SURE.
WHAT IS IT?
CA...
CA-CA-CA...
CA?
TEACH ME HOW TO MAKE A CAKE.
HUH?
A CAKE?
WELL, TO TELL YOU THE TRUTH, I NEED TO MAKE IT FOR A *CERTAIN REASON*.
BECAUSE OF A *CERTAIN REASON*, I CAN'T BAKE IT ON MY OWN, AND IT'S CAUSING ME TROUBLE.
I DON'T UNDERSTAND WHAT SHE MEANS AT ALL...

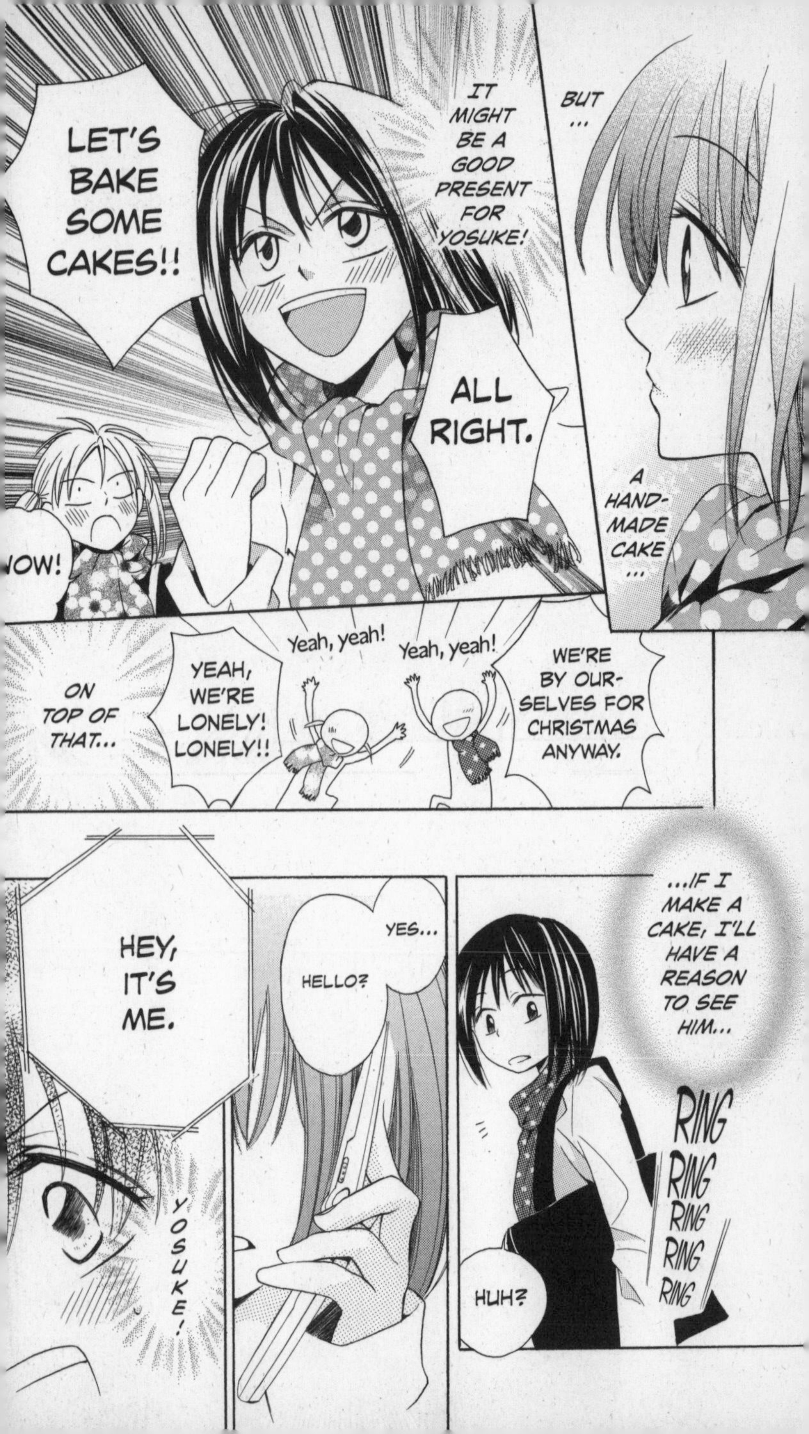

BUT ...
A HAND-MADE CAKE ...
IT MIGHT BE A GOOD PRESENT FOR YOSUKE!
ALL RIGHT.
LET'S BAKE SOME CAKES!!
NOW!
WE'RE BY OUR-SELVES FOR CHRISTMAS ANYWAY.
Yeah, yeah!
Yeah, yeah!
YEAH, WE'RE LONELY! LONELY!!
ON TOP OF THAT...
...IF I MAKE A CAKE, I'LL HAVE A REASON TO SEE HIM...
RING RING RING RING RING
HUH?
YES...
HELLO?
HEY, IT'S ME.
YOSUKE!

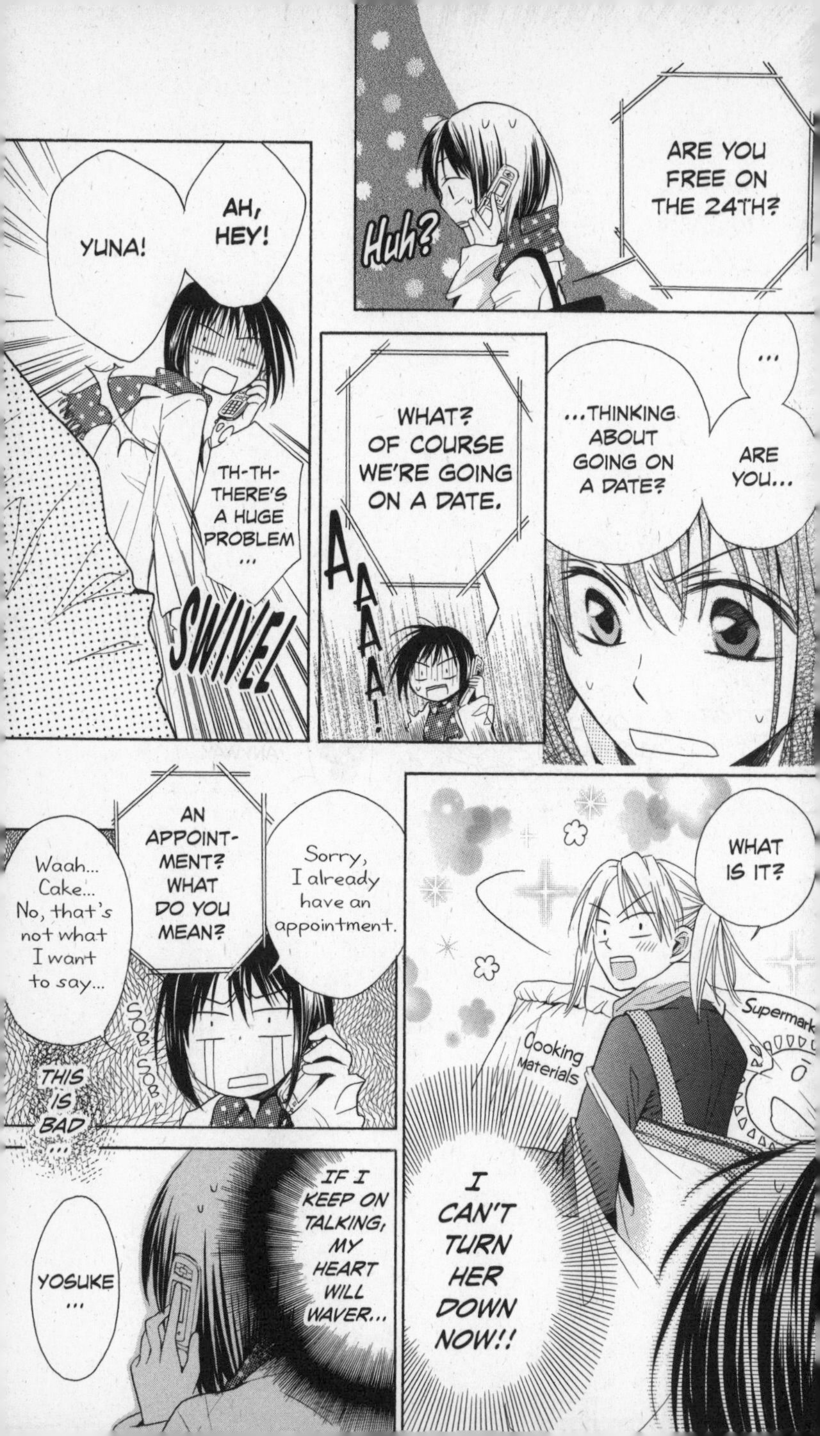
ARE YOU FREE ON THE 24TH?
Huh?
YUNA!
AH, HEY!
TH-TH-THERE'S A HUGE PROBLEM...
SWIVEL
...
ARE YOU...
...THINKING ABOUT GOING ON A DATE?
WHAT? OF COURSE WE'RE GOING ON A DATE.
AAAA!
WHAT IS IT?
Supermark
Cooking Materials
Sorry, I already have an appointment.
AN APPOINTMENT? WHAT DO YOU MEAN?
Waah... Cake... No, that's not what I want to say...
SOB SOB
THIS IS BAD...
I CAN'T TURN HER DOWN NOW!!
IF I KEEP ON TALKING, MY HEART WILL WAVER...
YOSUKE...

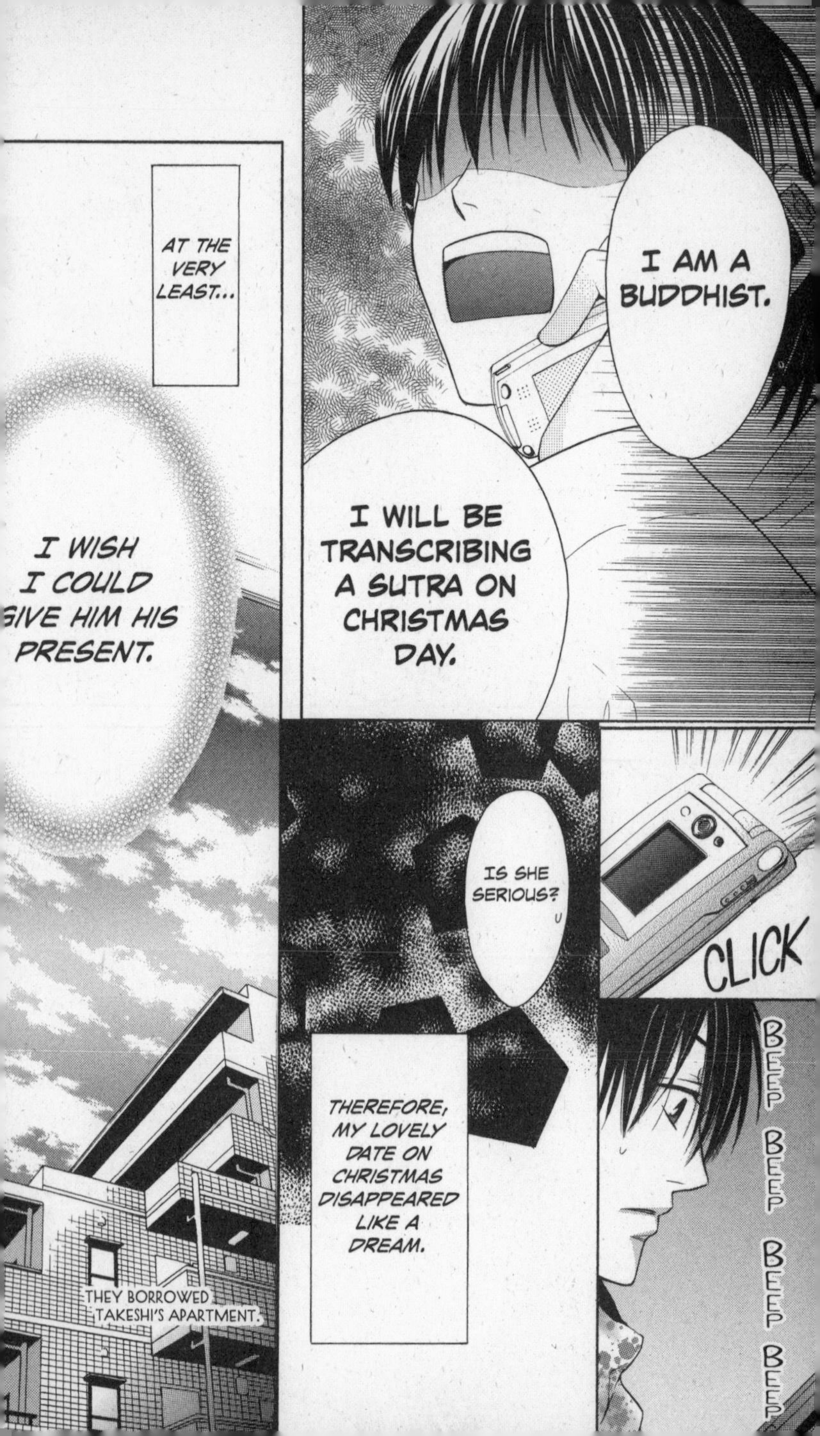

I AM A BUDDHIST.
I WILL BE TRANSCRIBING A SUTRA ON CHRISTMAS DAY.
CLICK
IS SHE SERIOUS?
BEEP BEEP BEEP BEEP
THEREFORE, MY LOVELY DATE ON CHRISTMAS DISAPPEARED LIKE A DREAM.
AT THE VERY LEAST...
I WISH I COULD GIVE HIM HIS PRESENT.
THEY BORROWED TAKESHI'S APARTMENT.

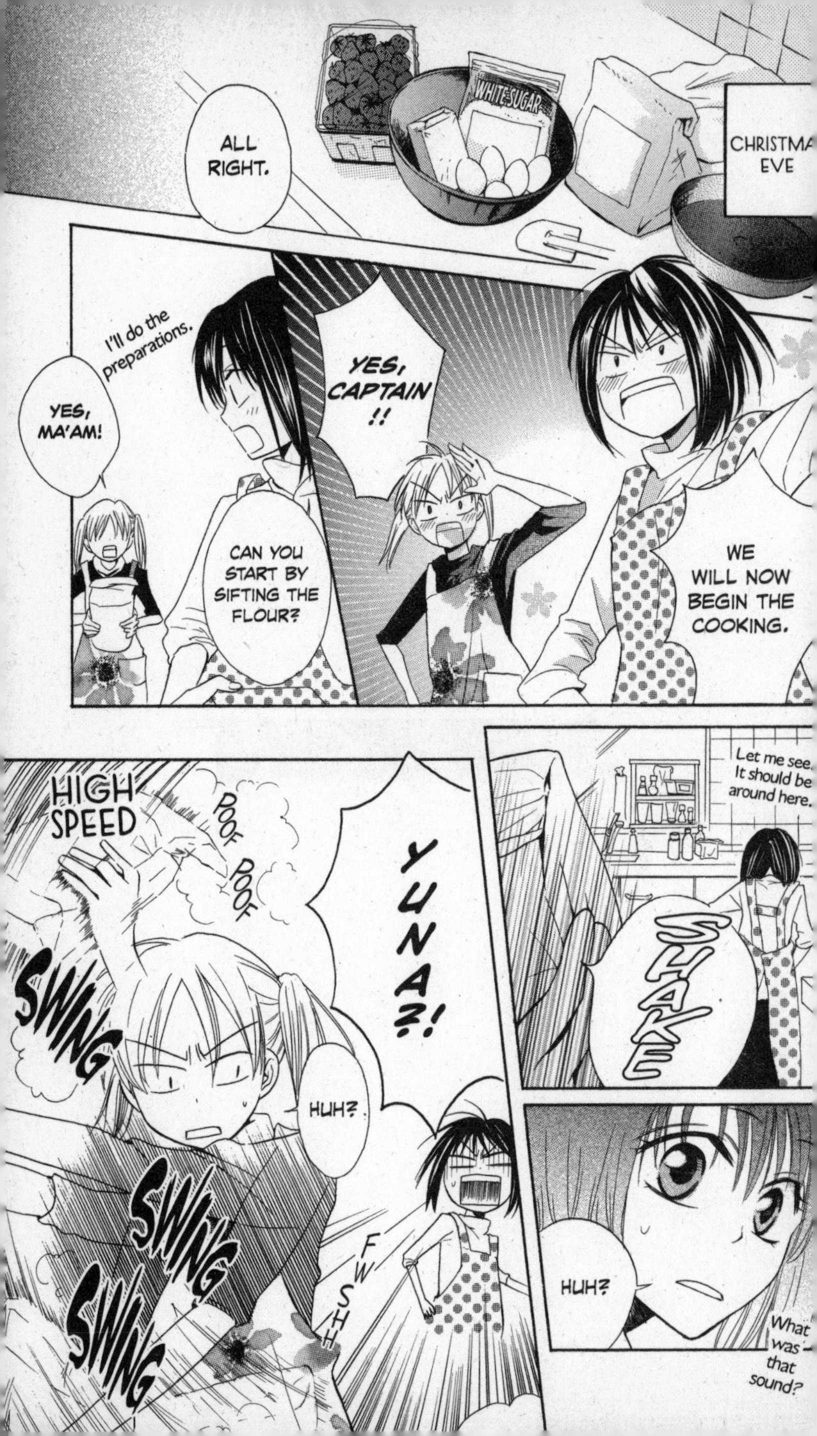
CHRISTMAS EVE
WHITE SUGAR
ALL RIGHT.
WE WILL NOW BEGIN THE COOKING.
YES, CAPTAIN !!
CAN YOU START BY SIFTING THE FLOUR?
I'll do the preparations.
YES, MA'AM!
Let me see. It should be around here.
SHAKE
HUH?
What was that sound?
YUNA?!
POOF POOF
HIGH SPEED
HUH?
SWING
FWSHH
SWING SWING

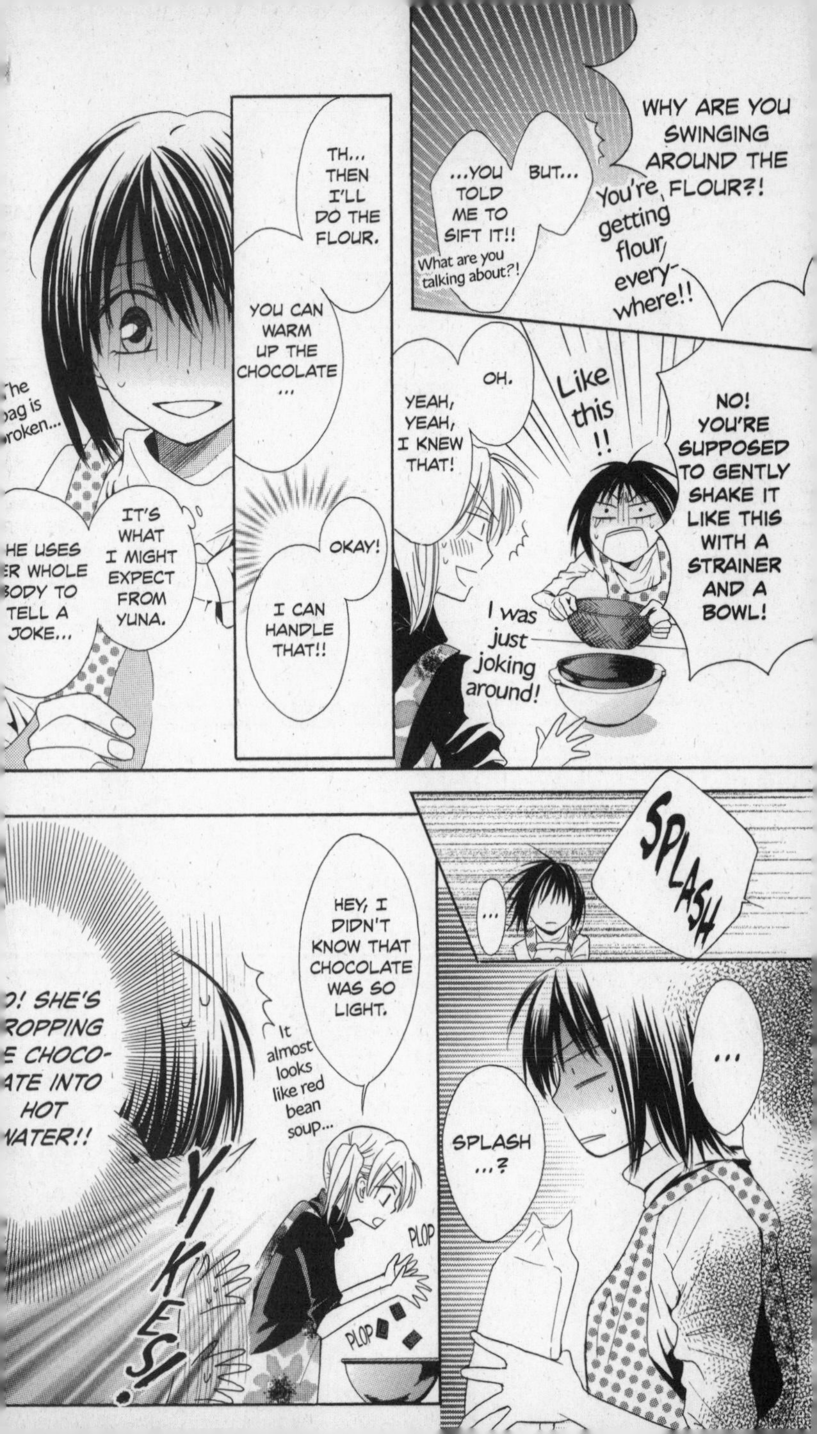
WHY ARE YOU SWINGING AROUND THE FLOUR?!
BUT...
...YOU TOLD ME TO SIFT IT!!
You're getting flour everywhere!!
What are you talking about?!
NO! YOU'RE SUPPOSED TO GENTLY SHAKE IT LIKE THIS WITH A STRAINER AND A BOWL!
Like this!!
OH.
YEAH, YEAH, I KNEW THAT!
I was just joking around!
TH... THEN I'LL DO THE FLOUR.
YOU CAN WARM UP THE CHOCOLATE...
OKAY!
I CAN HANDLE THAT!!
The bag is broken...
IT'S WHAT I MIGHT EXPECT FROM YUNA.
HE USES ER WHOLE BODY TO TELL A JOKE...
SPLASH
...
...
SPLASH...?
HEY, I DIDN'T KNOW THAT CHOCOLATE WAS SO LIGHT.
It almost looks like red bean soup...
PLOP
PLOP
YIKES!
O! SHE'S ROPPING E CHOCO- ATE INTO HOT VATER!!

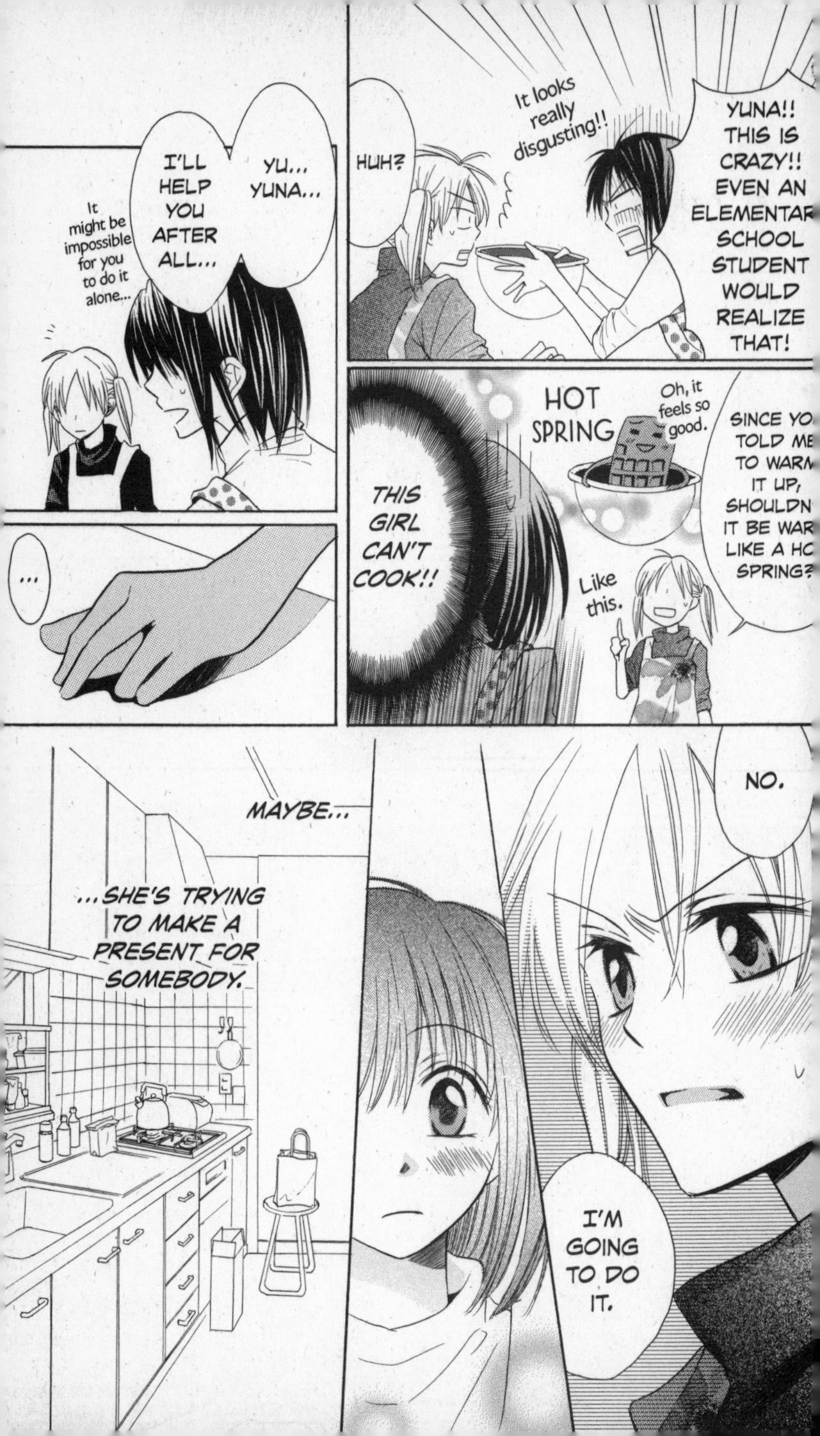
YUNA!! THIS IS CRAZY!! EVEN AN ELEMENTAR SCHOOL STUDENT WOULD REALIZE THAT!
It looks really disgusting!!
HUH?
SINCE YO TOLD ME TO WARM IT UP, SHOULDN IT BE WAR LIKE A HO SPRING?
Oh, it feels so good.
HOT SPRING
Like this.
THIS GIRL CAN'T COOK!!
YU... YUNA...
I'LL HELP YOU AFTER ALL...
It might be impossible for you to do it alone...
...
NO.
I'M GOING TO DO IT.
MAYBE...
...SHE'S TRYING TO MAKE A PRESENT FOR SOMEBODY.

THAT MIGHT BE THE REASON WHY SHE'S SO MOTIVATED...
Hey!! I used beef tallow instead of butter!!
...
Chiaki, is it all right to put in meat?!
BUT ...
I CAN'T HANDLE HER BY MYSELF!!

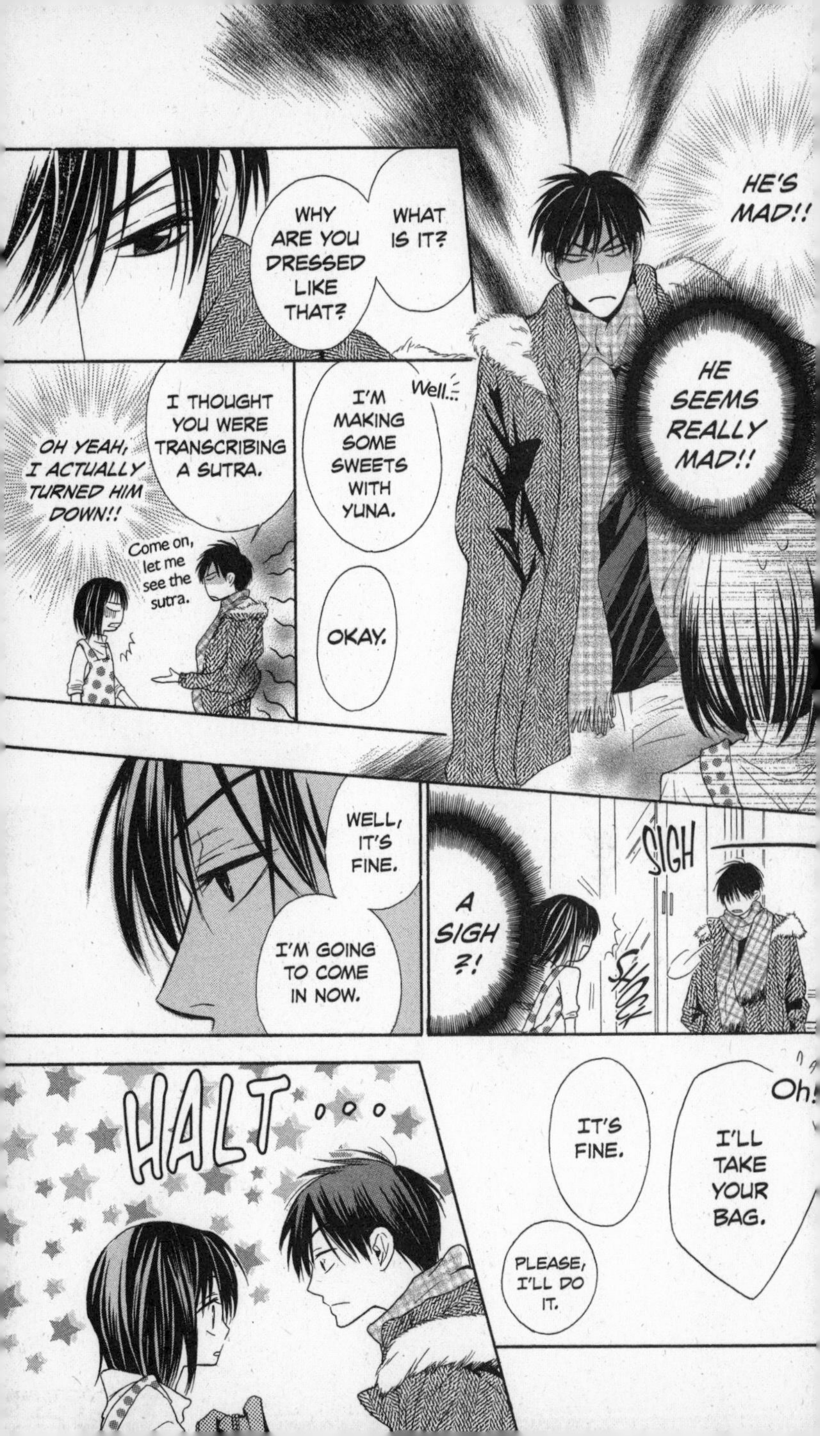
HE'S MAD!!
HE SEEMS REALLY MAD!!
WHAT IS IT?
WHY ARE YOU DRESSED LIKE THAT?
Well...
I'M MAKING SOME SWEETS WITH YUNA.
OKAY.
I THOUGHT YOU WERE TRANSCRIBING A SUTRA.
OH YEAH, I ACTUALLY TURNED HIM DOWN!!
Come on, let me see the sutra.
SIGH
SHOCK
A SIGH?!
WELL, IT'S FINE.
I'M GOING TO COME IN NOW.
Oh!
I'LL TAKE YOUR BAG.
IT'S FINE.
PLEASE, I'LL DO IT.
HALT...

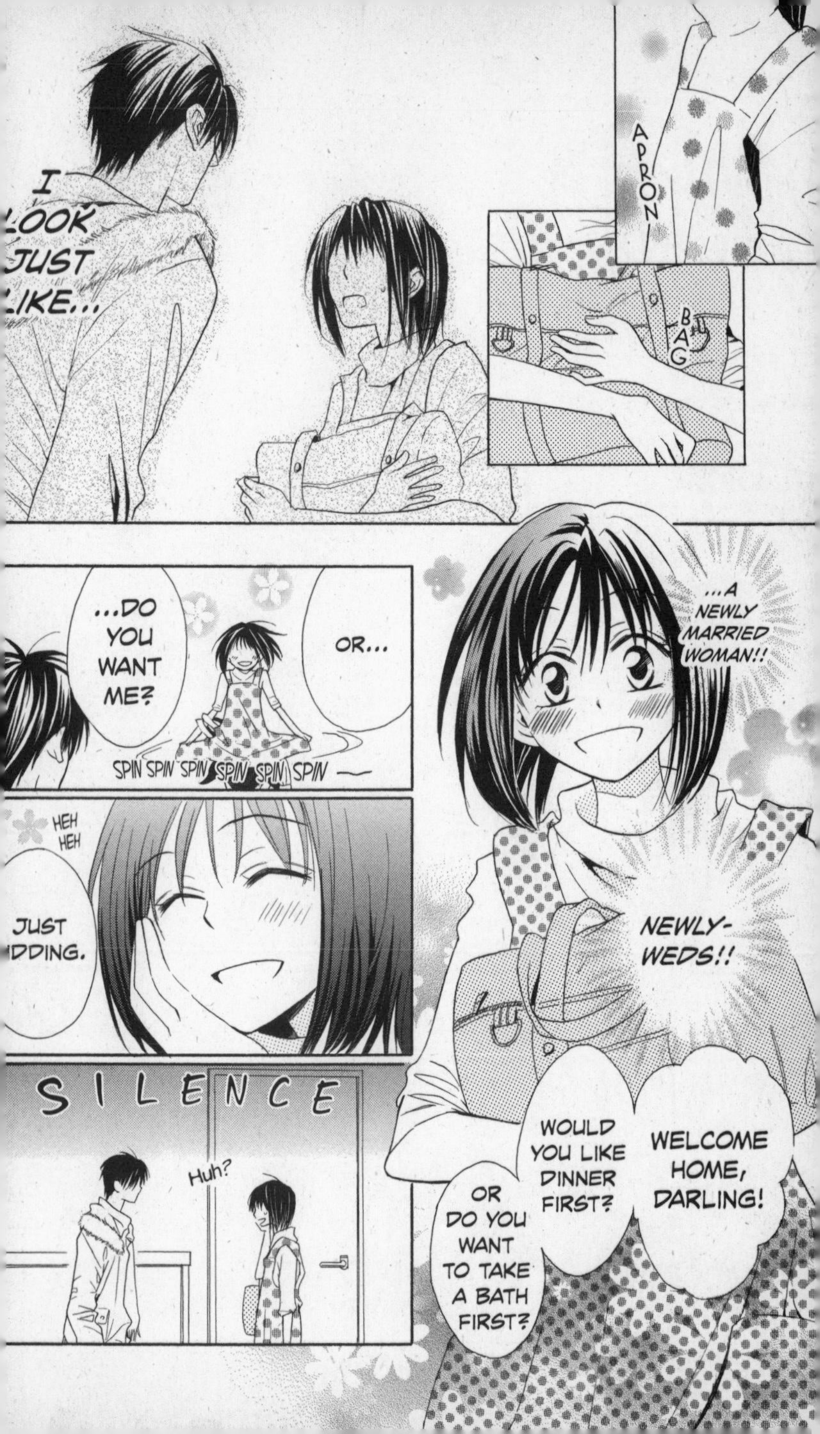
APRON
BAG
I LOOK JUST LIKE...
...A NEWLY MARRIED WOMAN!!
NEWLY-WEDS!!
WELCOME HOME, DARLING!
WOULD YOU LIKE DINNER FIRST?
OR DO YOU WANT TO TAKE A BATH FIRST?
OR...
...DO YOU WANT ME?
SPIN SPIN SPIN SPIN SPIN SPIN
HEH HEH
JUST KIDDING.
SILENCE
Huh?

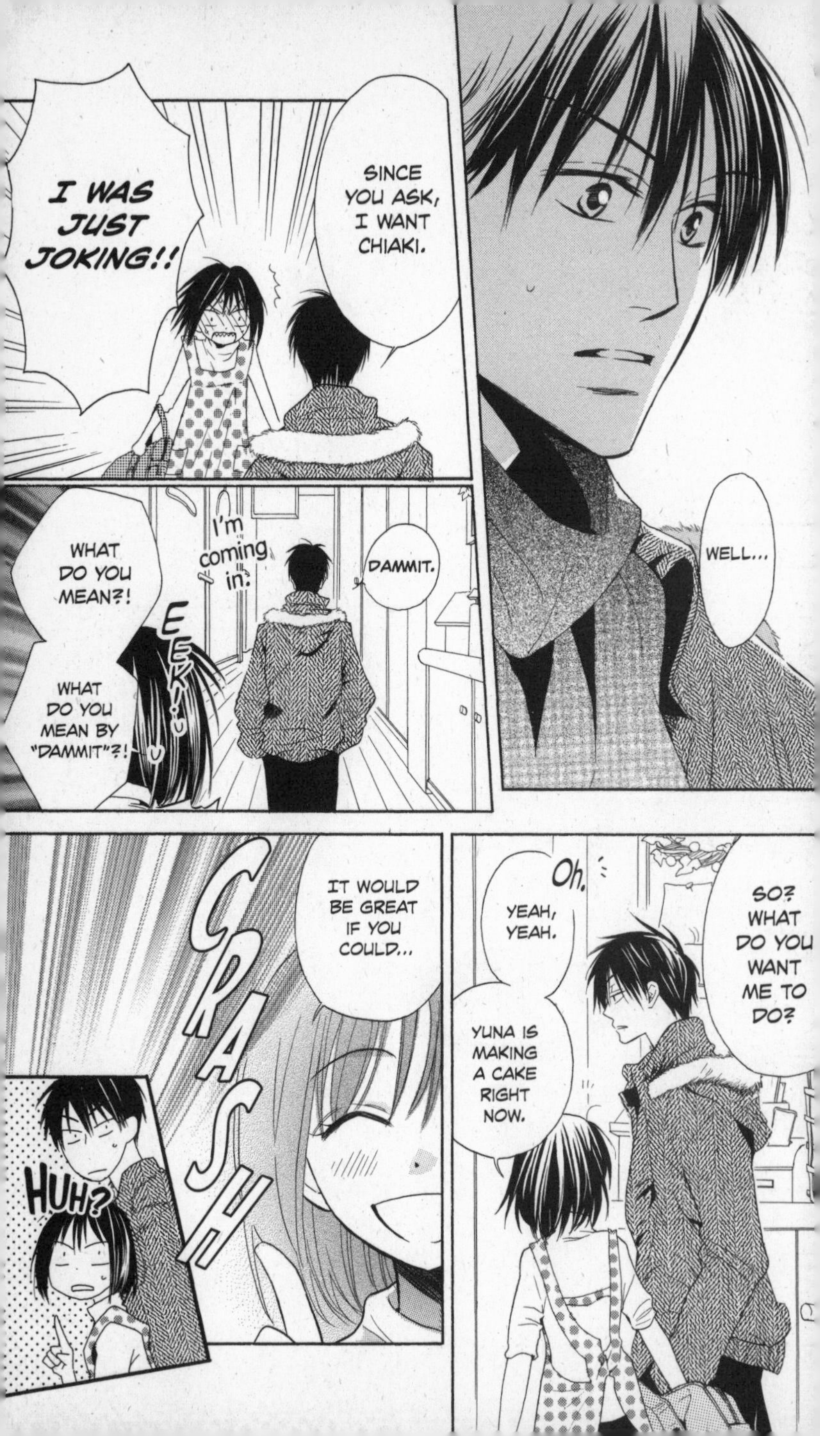
WELL...
SINCE YOU ASK, I WANT CHIAKI.
I WAS JUST JOKING!!
DAMMIT.
I'm coming in.
WHAT DO YOU MEAN?!
EEK!
WHAT DO YOU MEAN BY "DAMMIT"?!
SO? WHAT DO YOU WANT ME TO DO?
Oh.
YEAH, YEAH.
YUNA IS MAKING A CAKE RIGHT NOW.
IT WOULD BE GREAT IF YOU COULD...
CRASH
HUH?

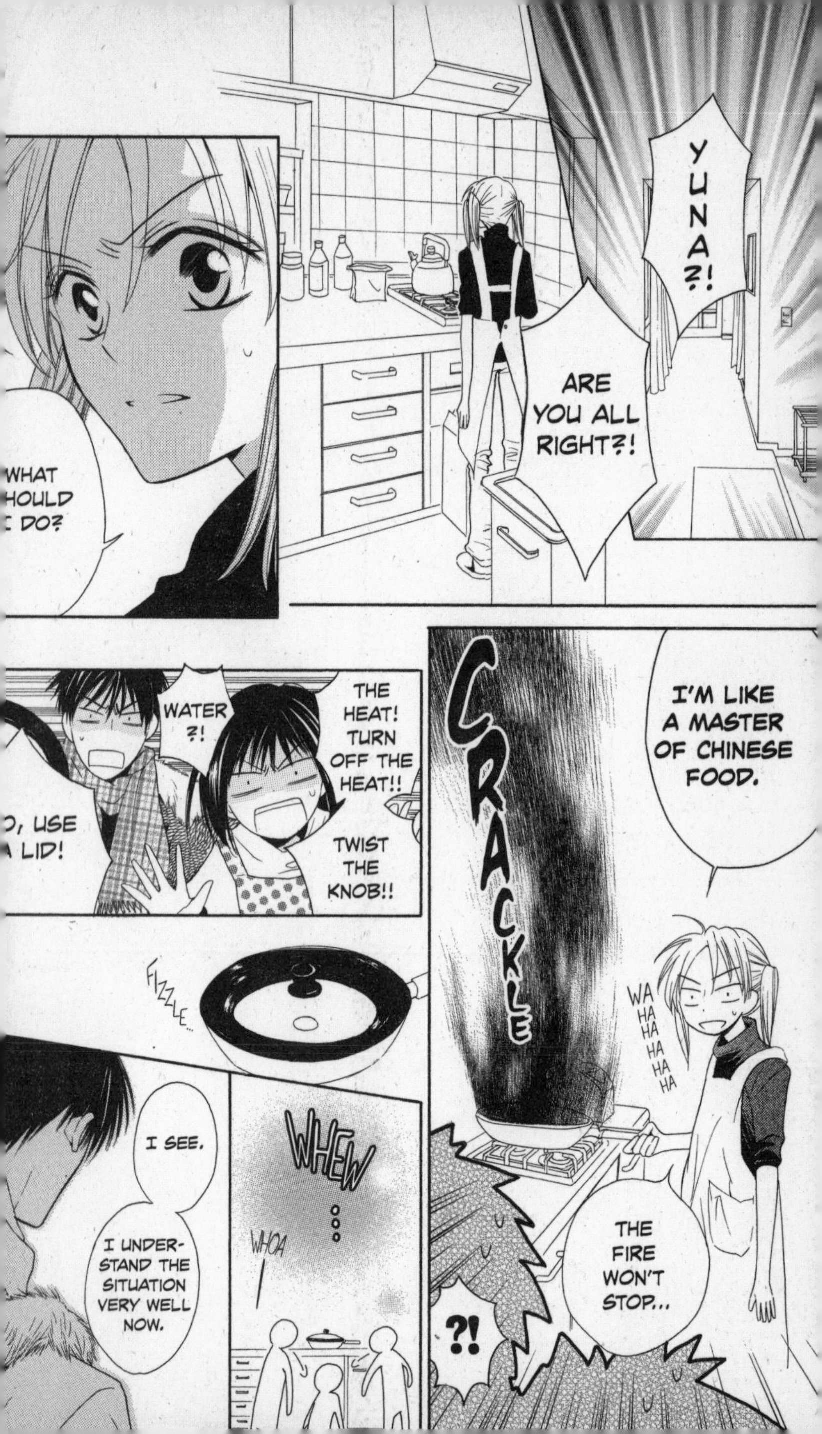
YUNA?!
ARE YOU ALL RIGHT?!
WHAT
HOULD
DO?
I'M LIKE A MASTER OF CHINESE FOOD.
CRACKLE
WA HA HA HA HA HA HA
THE FIRE WON'T STOP...
?!
THE HEAT! TURN OFF THE HEAT!!
TWIST THE KNOB!!
WATER?!
USE
LID!
FIZZLE...
WHEW...
WHOA
I SEE.
I UNDERSTAND THE SITUATION VERY WELL NOW.

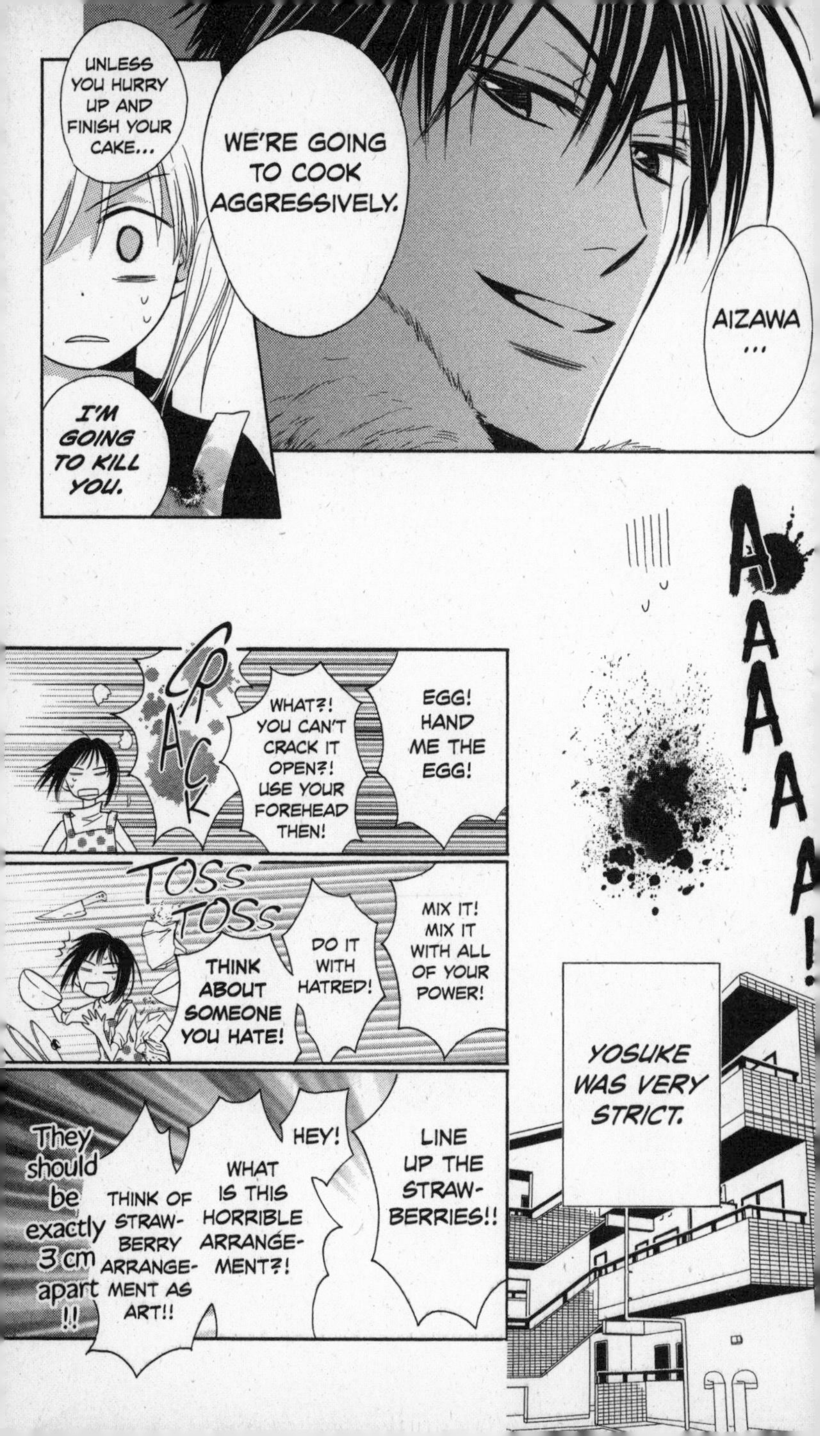
AIZAWA...
WE'RE GOING TO COOK AGGRESSIVELY.
UNLESS YOU HURRY UP AND FINISH YOUR CAKE...
I'M GOING TO KILL YOU.
AAAAA!
YOSUKE WAS VERY STRICT.
EGG! HAND ME THE EGG!
WHAT?! YOU CAN'T CRACK IT OPEN?! USE YOUR FOREHEAD THEN!
CRACK
MIX IT! MIX IT WITH ALL OF YOUR POWER!
DO IT WITH HATRED!
THINK ABOUT SOMEONE YOU HATE!
TOSS TOSS
LINE UP THE STRAW-BERRIES!!
HEY!
WHAT IS THIS HORRIBLE ARRANGE-MENT?!
THINK OF STRAW-BERRY ARRANGE-MENT AS ART!!
They should be exactly 3 cm apart!!

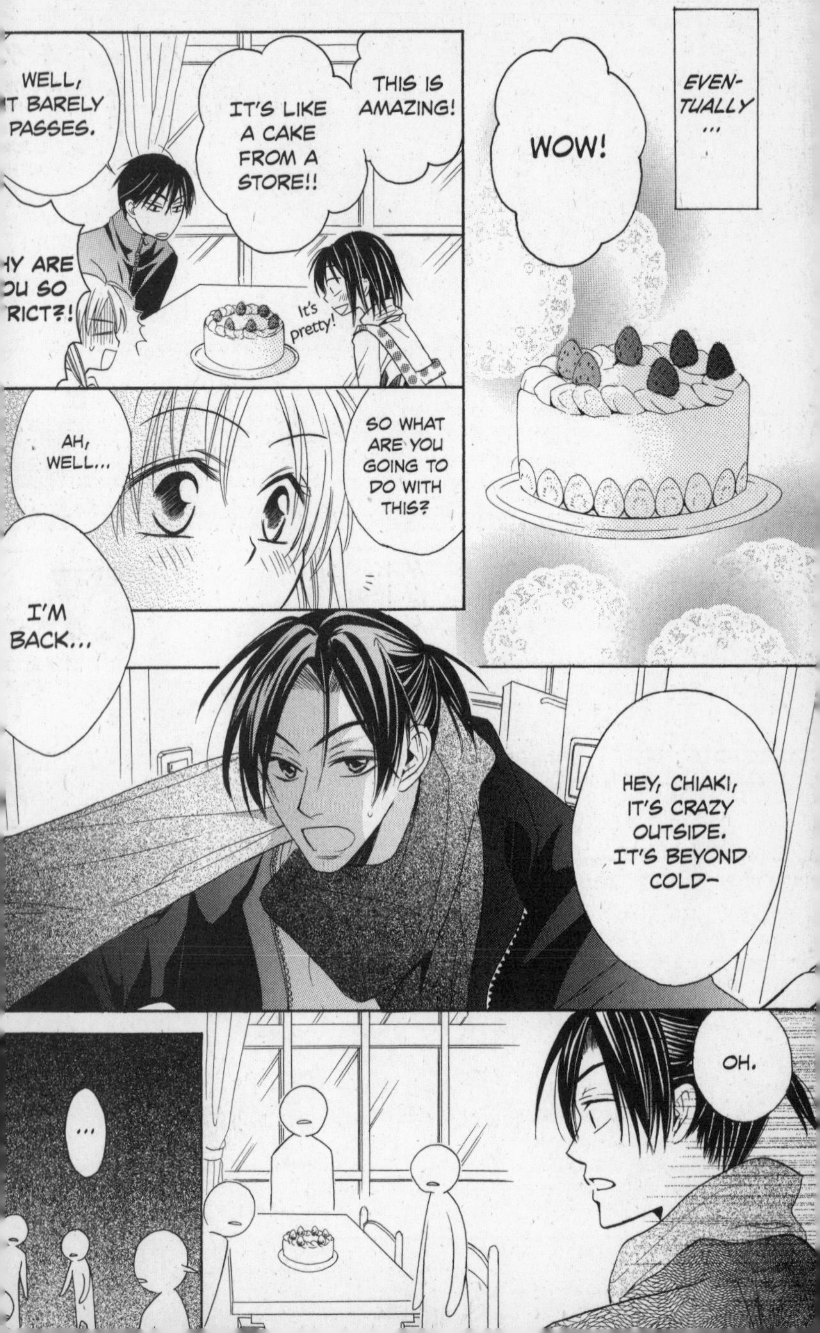
EVEN-TUALLY...
WOW!
THIS IS AMAZING!
IT'S LIKE A CAKE FROM A STORE!!
It's pretty!
WELL, T BARELY PASSES.
HY ARE OU SO RICT?!
SO WHAT ARE YOU GOING TO DO WITH THIS?
AH, WELL...
I'M BACK...
HEY, CHIAKI, IT'S CRAZY OUTSIDE. IT'S BEYOND COLD-
OH.
...

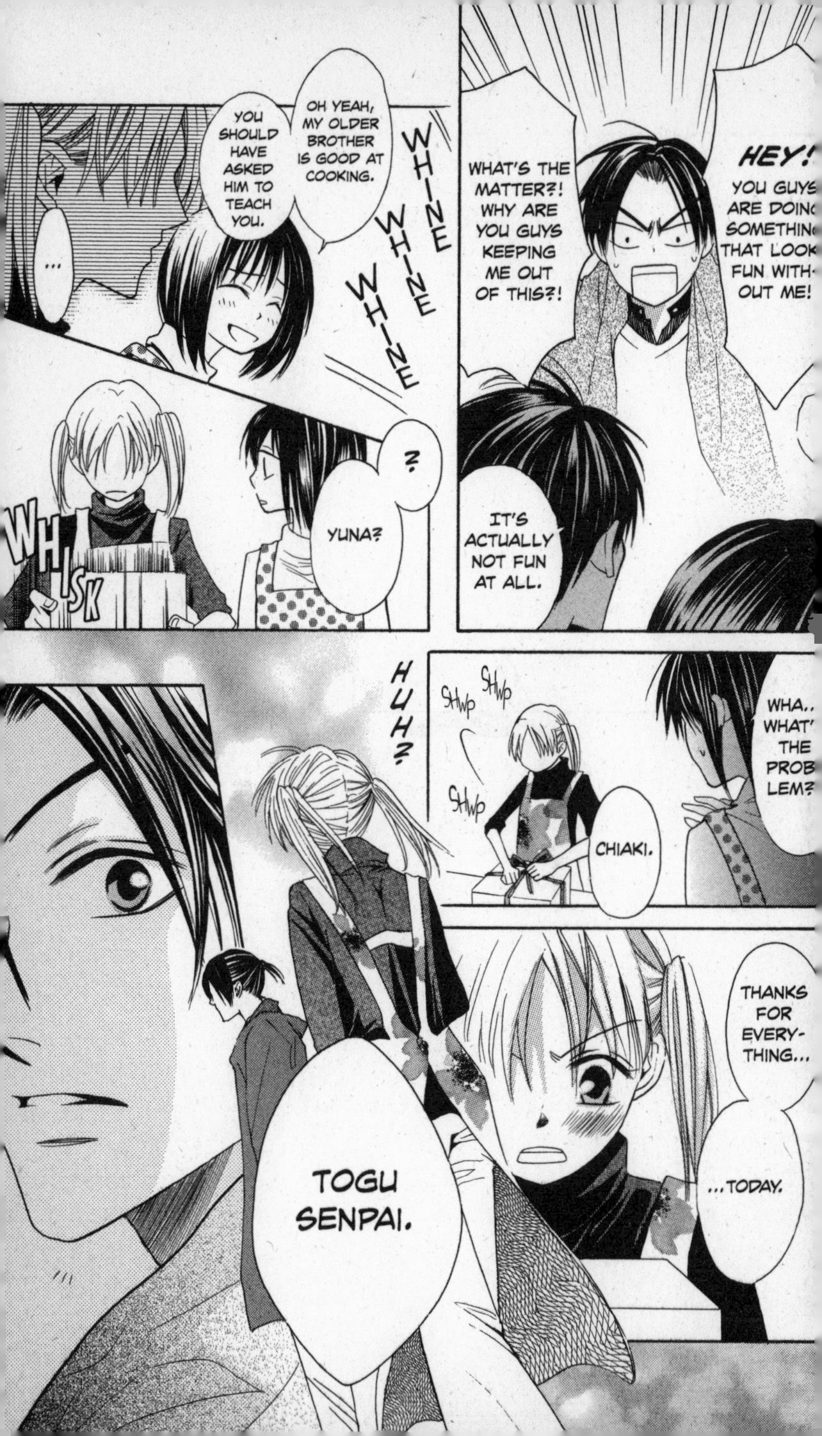
HEY!
YOU GUYS ARE DOIN SOMETHIN THAT LOOK FUN WITH-OUT ME!
WHAT'S THE MATTER?! WHY ARE YOU GUYS KEEPING ME OUT OF THIS?!
IT'S ACTUALLY NOT FUN AT ALL.
OH YEAH, MY OLDER BROTHER IS GOOD AT COOKING.
YOU SHOULD HAVE ASKED HIM TO TEACH YOU.
...
WHINE
WHINE
WHINE
?
YUNA?
WHISK
WHA.. WHAT' THE PROB LEM?
SHWP
SHWP
SHWP
CHIAKI.
THANKS FOR EVERY-THING...
...TODAY.
HUH?
TOGU SENPAI.

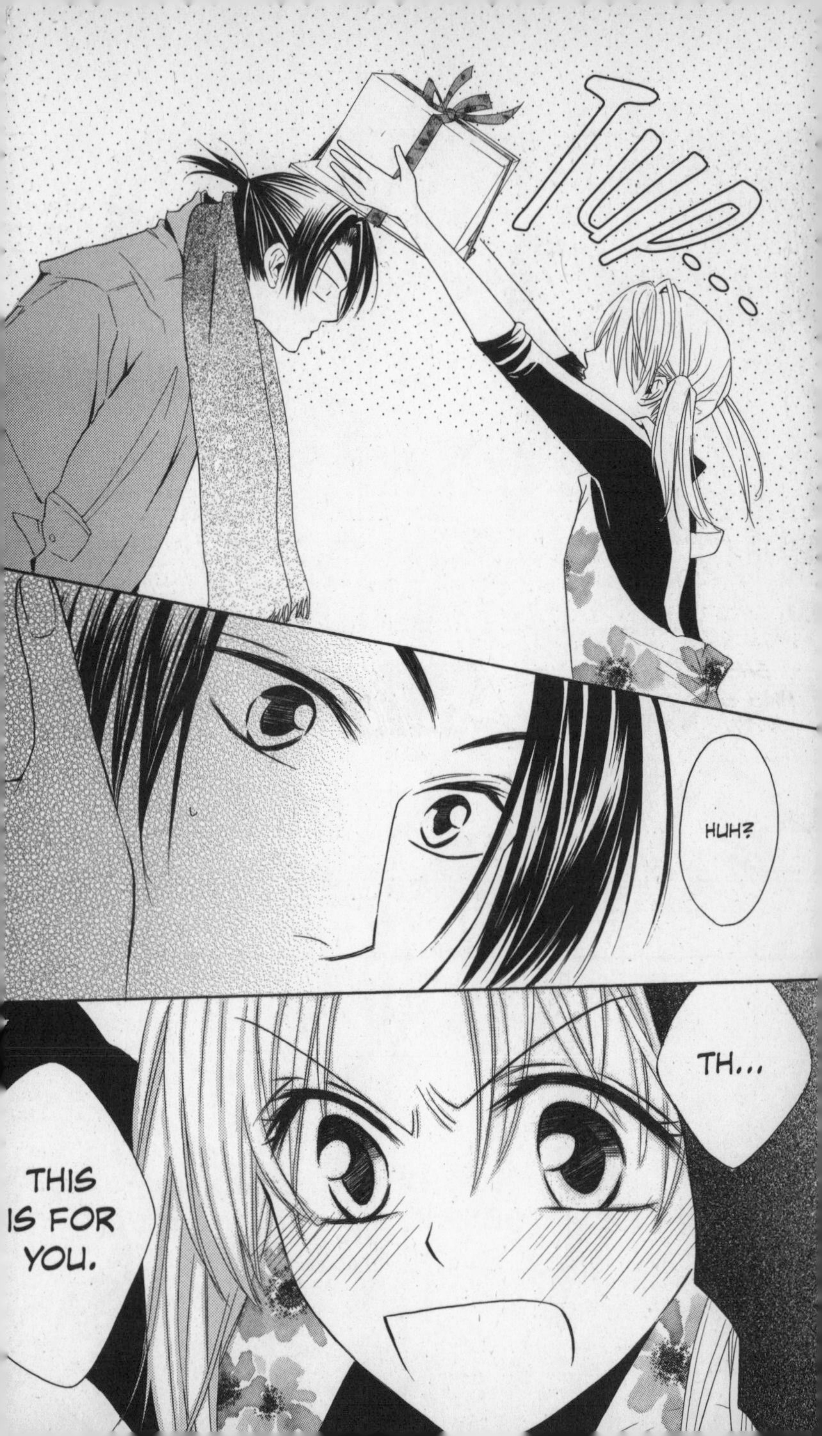
TUP...
HUH?
TH...
THIS IS FOR YOU.

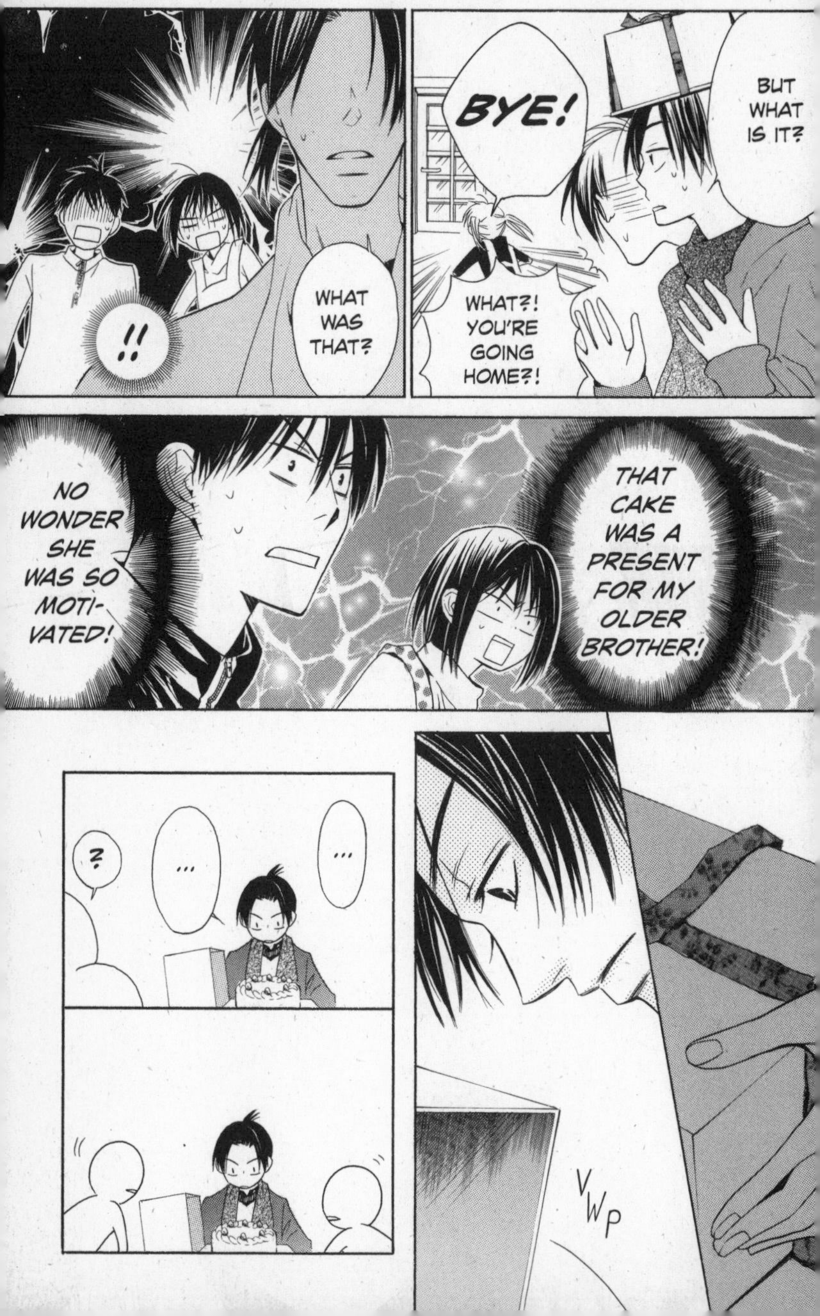
BUT WHAT IS IT?
BYE!
WHAT?! YOU'RE GOING HOME?!
WHAT WAS THAT?
!!
THAT CAKE WAS A PRESENT FOR MY OLDER BROTHER!
NO WONDER SHE WAS SO MOTI-VATED!
VWP
...
...
?

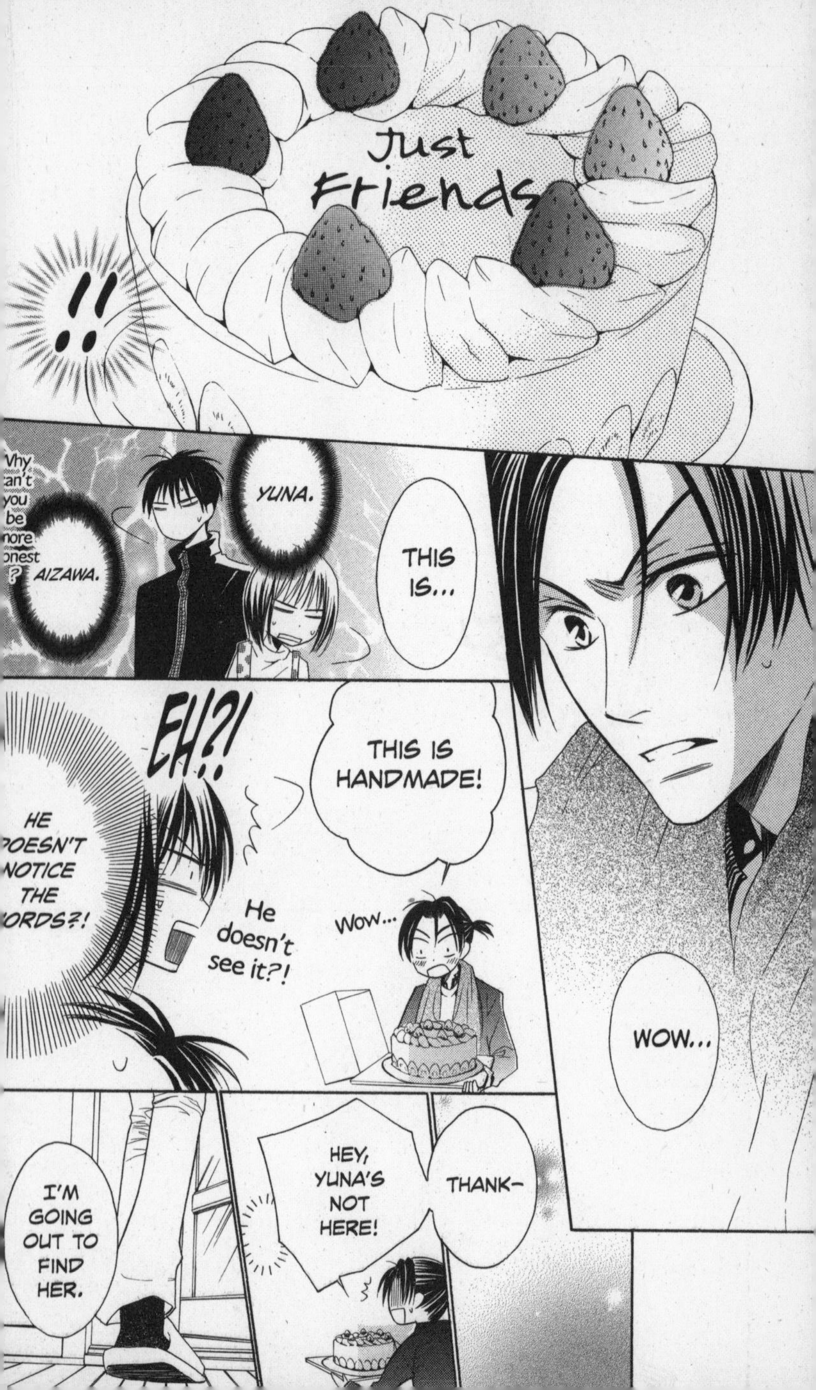
Just Friends
!!
WOW...
THIS IS...
YUNA.
Vhy an't you be nore onest ?
AIZAWA.
THIS IS HANDMADE!
EH?!
WOW...
He doesn't see it?!
HE OESN'T NOTICE THE ORDS?!
THANK-
HEY, YUNA'S NOT HERE!
I'M GOING OUT TO FIND HER.

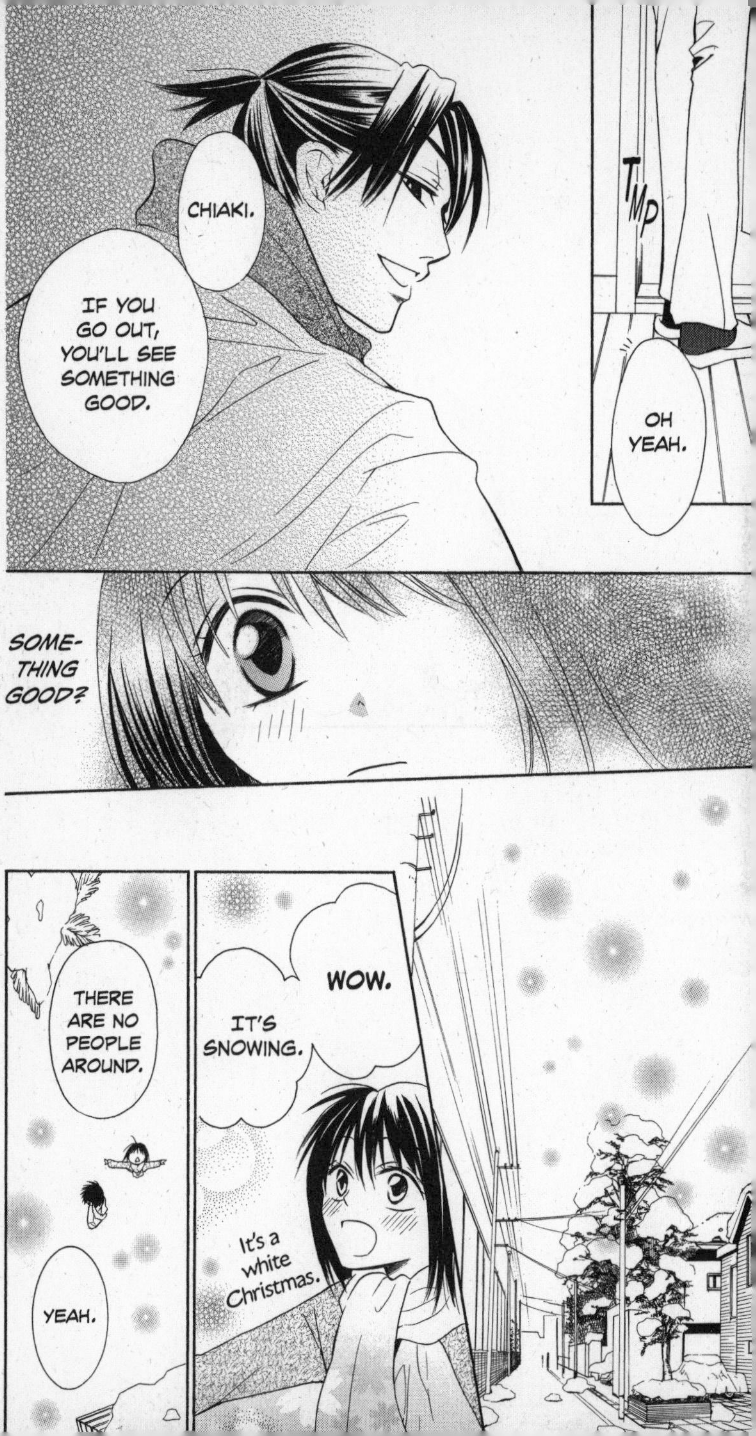
TMP
OH YEAH.
CHIAKI.
IF YOU GO OUT, YOU'LL SEE SOMETHING GOOD.
SOME-THING GOOD?
WOW.
IT'S SNOWING.
It's a white Christmas.
THERE ARE NO PEOPLE AROUND.
YEAH.

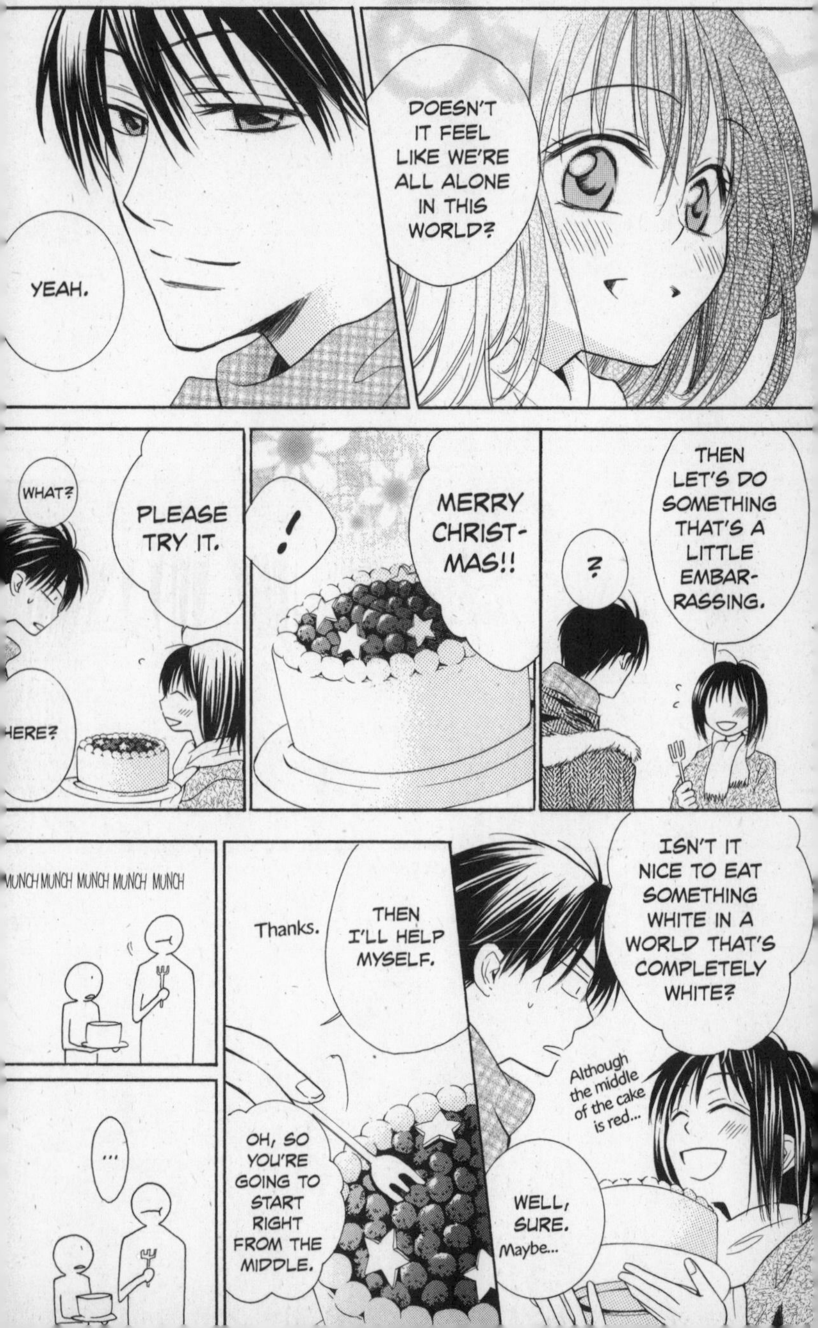
DOESN'T IT FEEL LIKE WE'RE ALL ALONE IN THIS WORLD?
YEAH.
THEN LET'S DO SOMETHING THAT'S A LITTLE EMBARRASSING.
?
MERRY CHRIST-MAS!!
!
PLEASE TRY IT.
WHAT?
HERE?
ISN'T IT NICE TO EAT SOMETHING WHITE IN A WORLD THAT'S COMPLETELY WHITE?
THEN I'LL HELP MYSELF.
Thanks.
Although the middle of the cake is red...
WELL, SURE.
Maybe...
OH, SO YOU'RE GOING TO START RIGHT FROM THE MIDDLE.
MUNCH MUNCH MUNCH MUNCH MUNCH
...

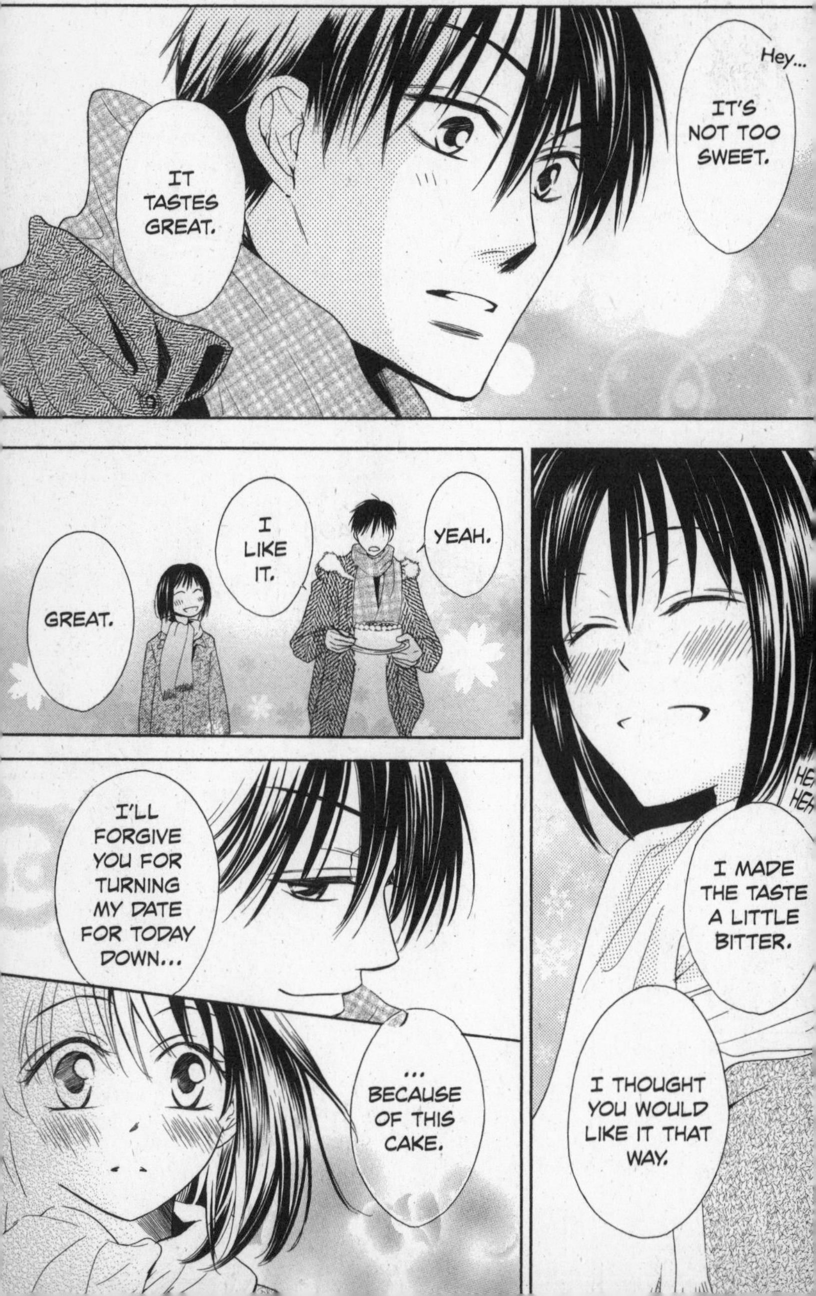
Hey...
IT'S NOT TOO SWEET.
IT TASTES GREAT.
I MADE THE TASTE A LITTLE BITTER.
I THOUGHT YOU WOULD LIKE IT THAT WAY.
YEAH.
I LIKE IT.
GREAT.
I'LL FORGIVE YOU FOR TURNING MY DATE FOR TODAY DOWN...
...BECAUSE OF THIS CAKE.

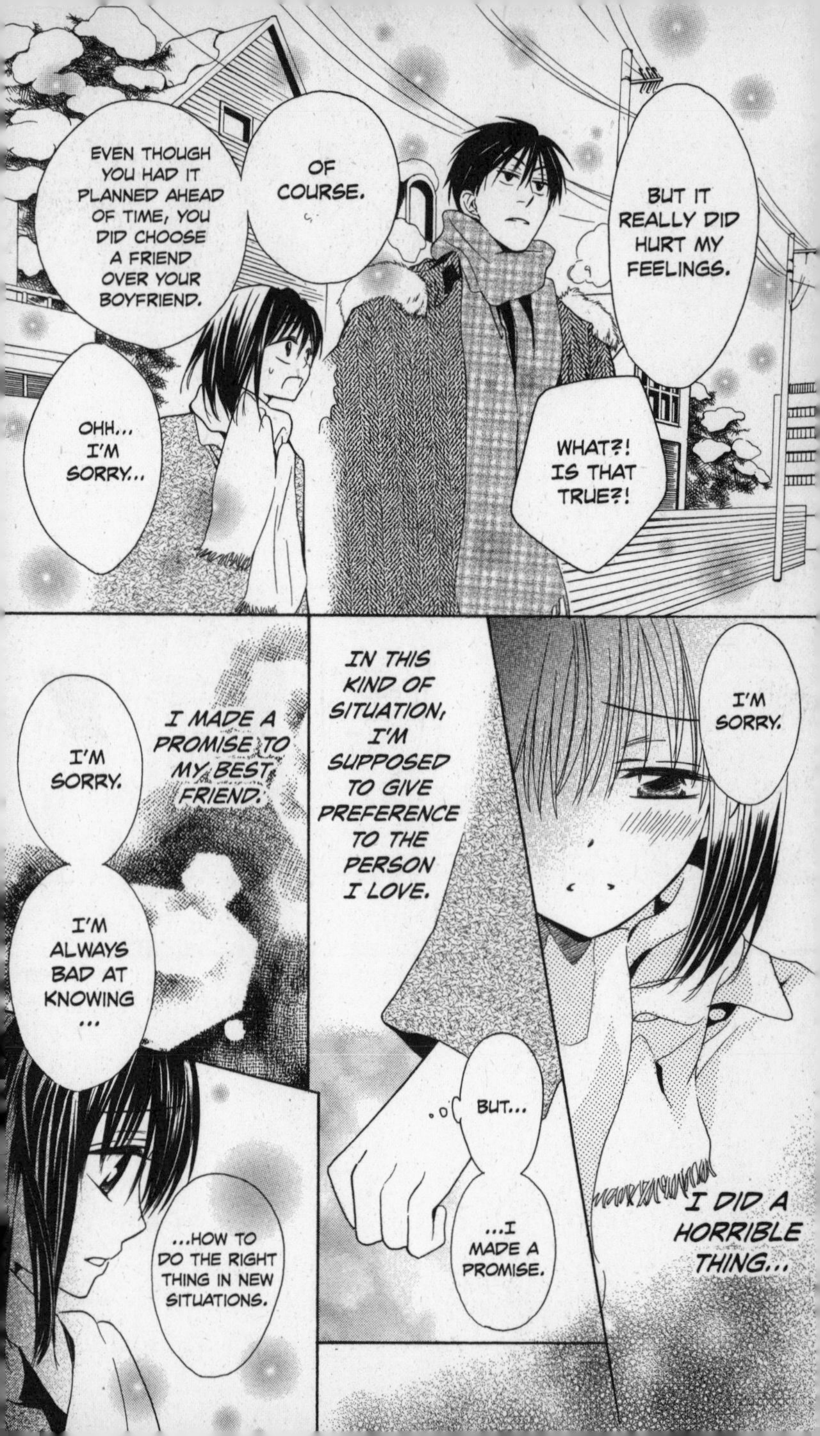
BUT IT REALLY DID HURT MY FEELINGS.
OF COURSE.
EVEN THOUGH YOU HAD IT PLANNED AHEAD OF TIME, YOU DID CHOOSE A FRIEND OVER YOUR BOYFRIEND.
WHAT?! IS THAT TRUE?!
OHH... I'M SORRY...
I'M SORRY.
I DID A HORRIBLE THING...
IN THIS KIND OF SITUATION, I'M SUPPOSED TO GIVE PREFERENCE TO THE PERSON I LOVE.
BUT...
...I MADE A PROMISE.
I MADE A PROMISE TO MY BEST FRIEND.
I'M SORRY.
I'M ALWAYS BAD AT KNOWING...
...HOW TO DO THE RIGHT THING IN NEW SITUATIONS.

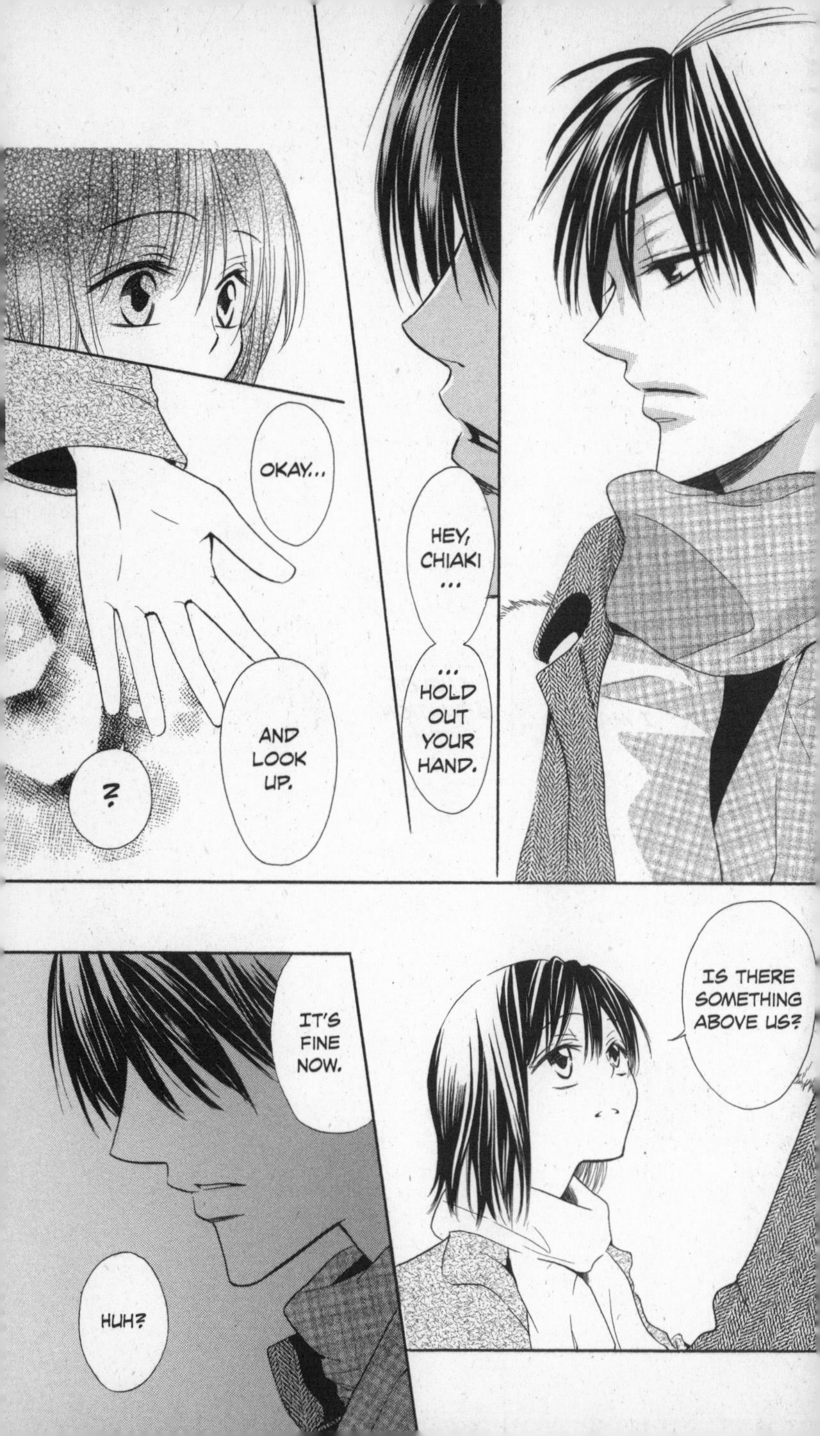
HEY, CHIAKI...
...HOLD OUT YOUR HAND.
OKAY...
AND LOOK UP.
?
IS THERE SOMETHING ABOVE US?
IT'S FINE NOW.
HUH?

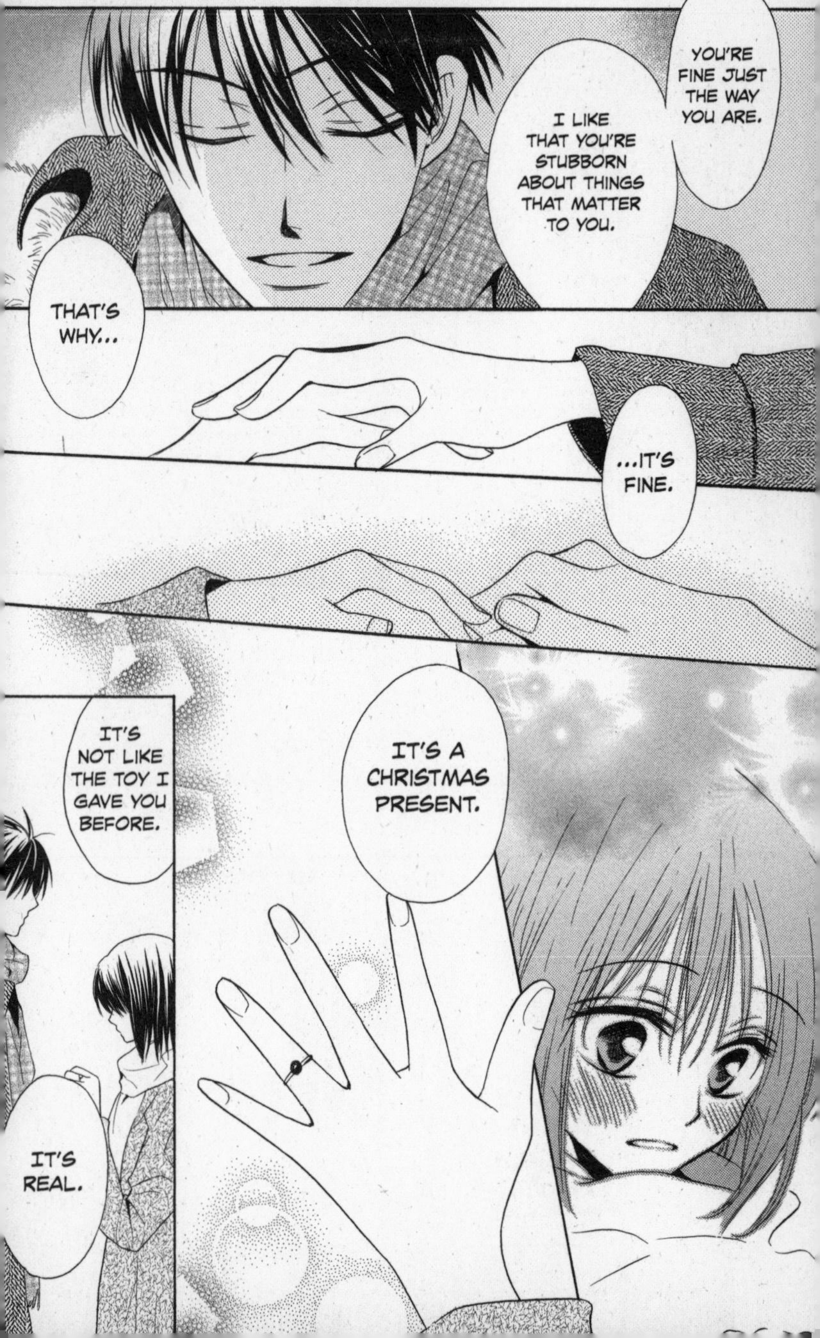
YOU'RE FINE JUST THE WAY YOU ARE.
I LIKE THAT YOU'RE STUBBORN ABOUT THINGS THAT MATTER TO YOU.
THAT'S WHY...
...IT'S FINE.
IT'S A CHRISTMAS PRESENT.
IT'S NOT LIKE THE TOY I GAVE YOU BEFORE.
IT'S REAL.

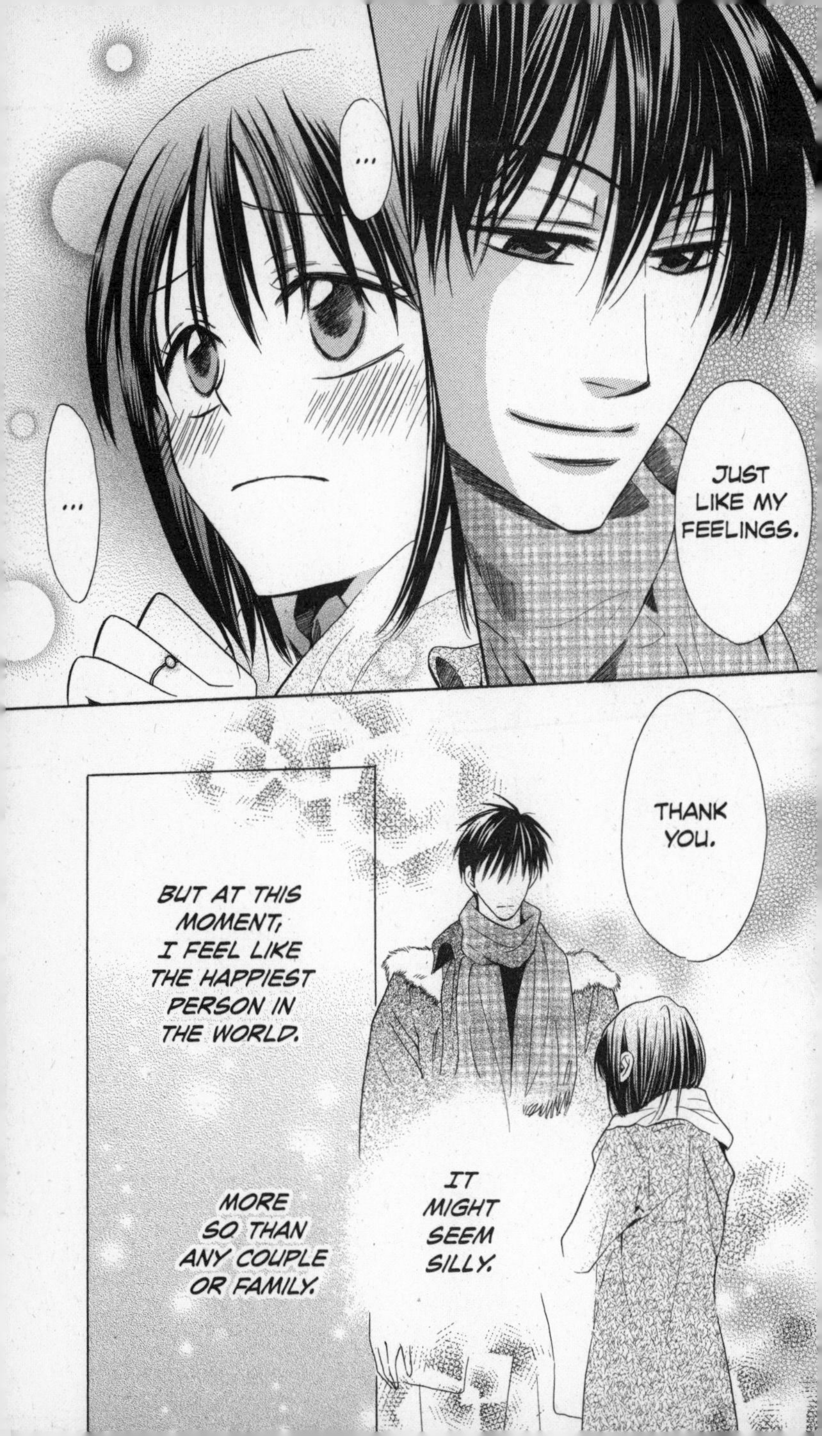
...
JUST LIKE MY FEELINGS.
...
THANK YOU.
IT MIGHT SEEM SILLY.
BUT AT THIS MOMENT, I FEEL LIKE THE HAPPIEST PERSON IN THE WORLD.
MORE SO THAN ANY COUPLE OR FAMILY.

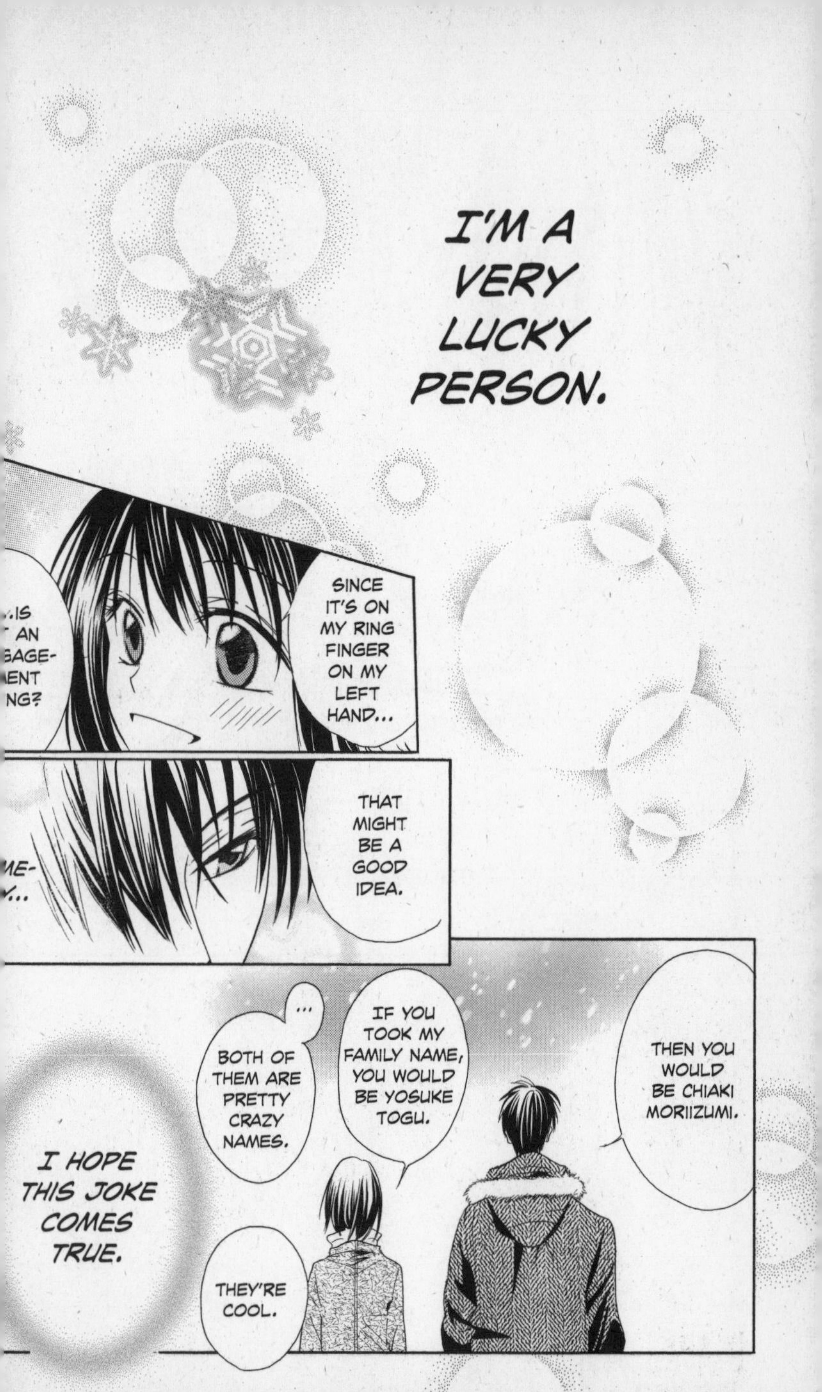
I'M A VERY LUCKY PERSON.
SINCE IT'S ON MY RING FINGER ON MY LEFT HAND...
THAT MIGHT BE A GOOD IDEA.
THEN YOU WOULD BE CHIAKI MORIIZUMI.
IF YOU TOOK MY FAMILY NAME, YOU WOULD BE YOSUKE TOGU.
...
BOTH OF THEM ARE PRETTY CRAZY NAMES.
THEY'RE COOL.
I HOPE THIS JOKE COMES TRUE.

The Magic Touch, Part 48/The End

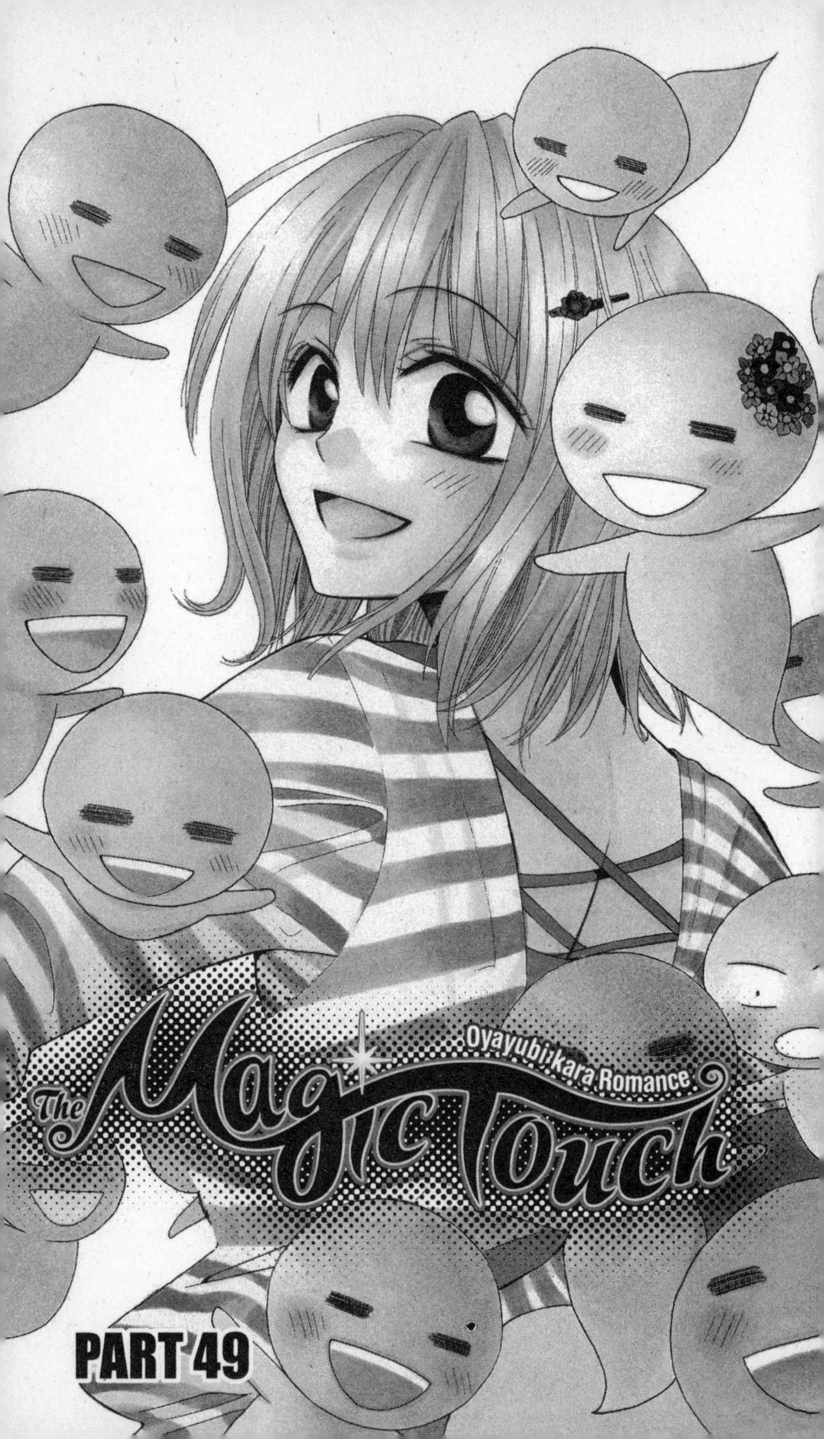
The Magic Touch
Oyayubi kara Romance
PART 49

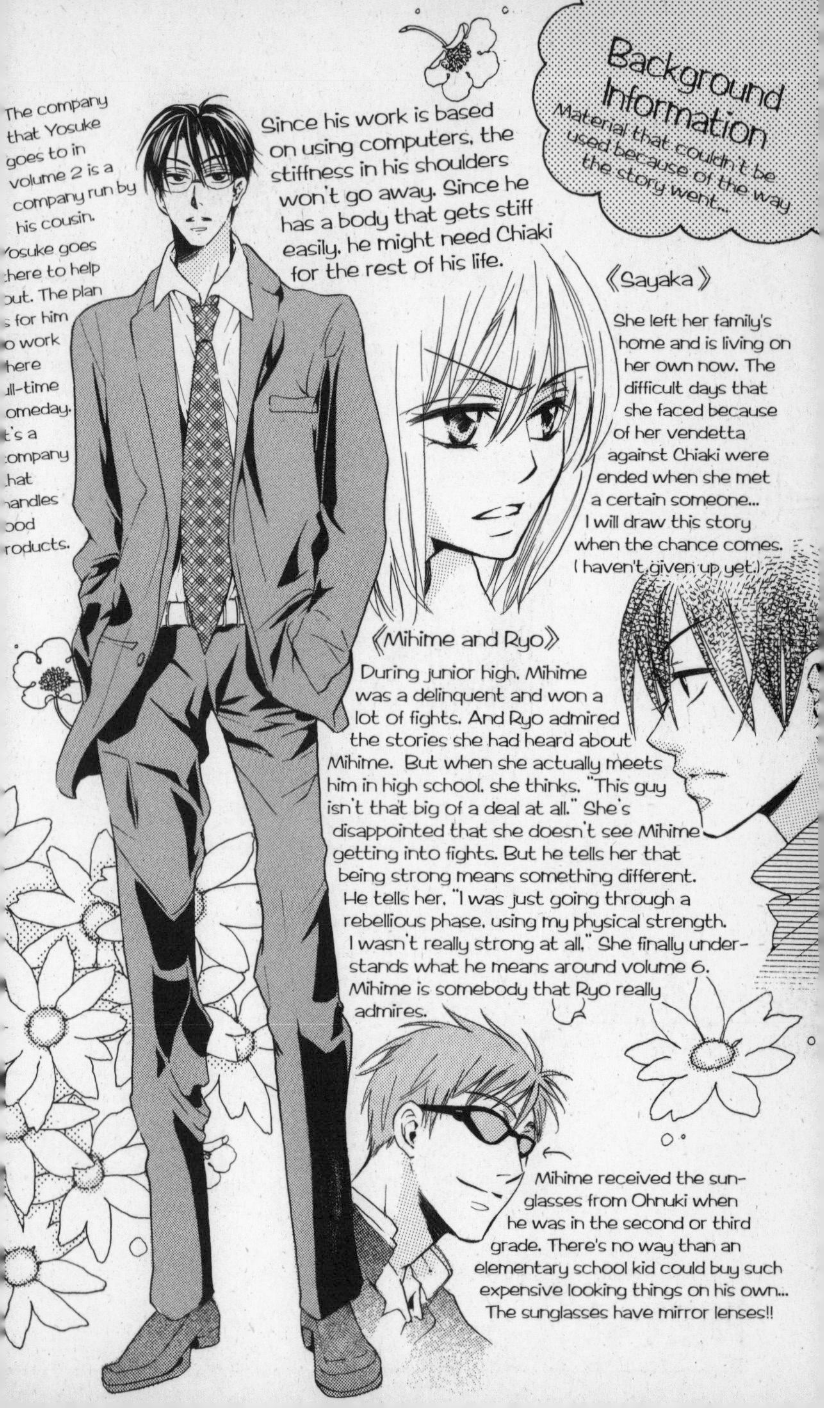

Background Information

Material that couldn't be used because of the way the story went...

Since his work is based on using computers, the stiffness in his shoulders won't go away. Since he has a body that gets stiff easily, he might need Chiaki for the rest of his life.

The company that Yosuke goes to in volume 2 is a company run by his cousin. Yosuke goes here to help out. The plan s for him o work here ll-time omeday. t's a ompany hat andles ood roducts.

《Sayaka》

She left her family's home and is living on her own now. The difficult days that she faced because of her vendetta against Chiaki were ended when she met a certain someone... I will draw this story when the chance comes. (I haven't given up yet.)

《Mihime and Ryo》

During junior high, Mihime was a delinquent and won a lot of fights. And Ryo admired the stories she had heard about Mihime. But when she actually meets him in high school, she thinks, "This guy isn't that big of a deal at all." She's disappointed that she doesn't see Mihime getting into fights. But he tells her that being strong means something different. He tells her, "I was just going through a rebellious phase, using my physical strength. I wasn't really strong at all." She finally understands what he means around volume 6. Mihime is somebody that Ryo really admires.

Mihime received the sunglasses from Ohnuki when he was in the second or third grade. There's no way than an elementary school kid could buy such expensive looking things on his own... The sunglasses have mirror lenses!!

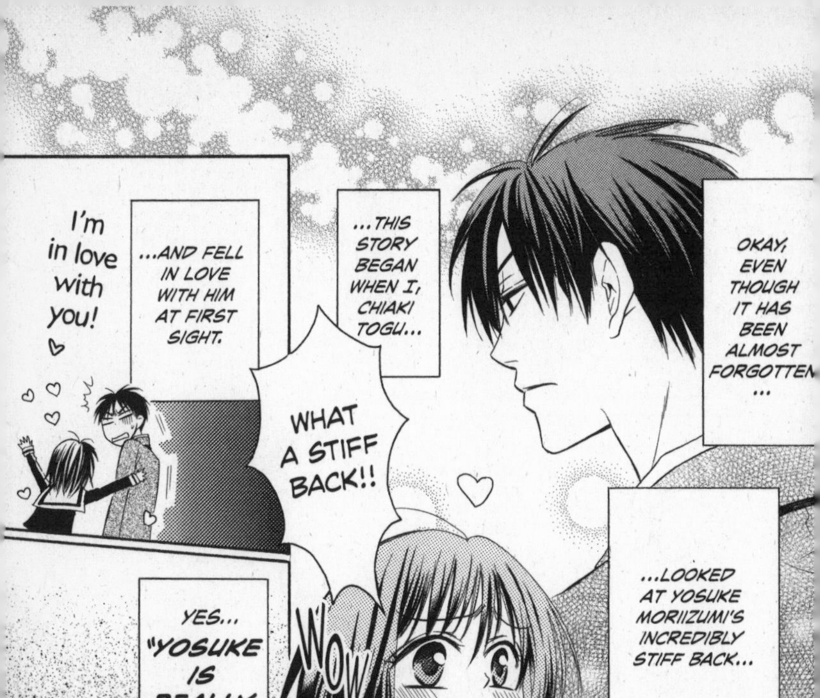
OKAY, EVEN THOUGH IT HAS BEEN ALMOST FORGOTTEN...
...THIS STORY BEGAN WHEN I, CHIAKI TOGU...
...LOOKED AT YOSUKE MORIIZUMI'S INCREDIBLY STIFF BACK...
WHAT A STIFF BACK!!
WOW
...AND FELL IN LOVE WITH HIM AT FIRST SIGHT.
I'm in love with you!
YES... "YOSUKE IS REALLY STIFF."
THOSE WERE THE WORDS TO DESCRIBE YOSUKE.

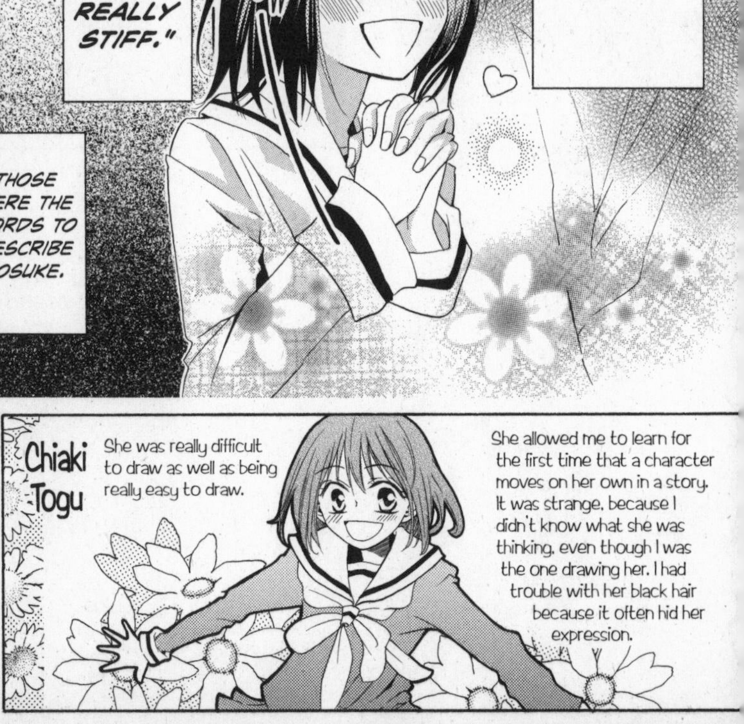
Chiaki Togu
She was really difficult to draw as well as being really easy to draw.
She allowed me to learn for the first time that a character moves on her own in a story. It was strange, because I didn't know what she was thinking, even though I was the one drawing her. I had trouble with her black hair because it often hid her expression.

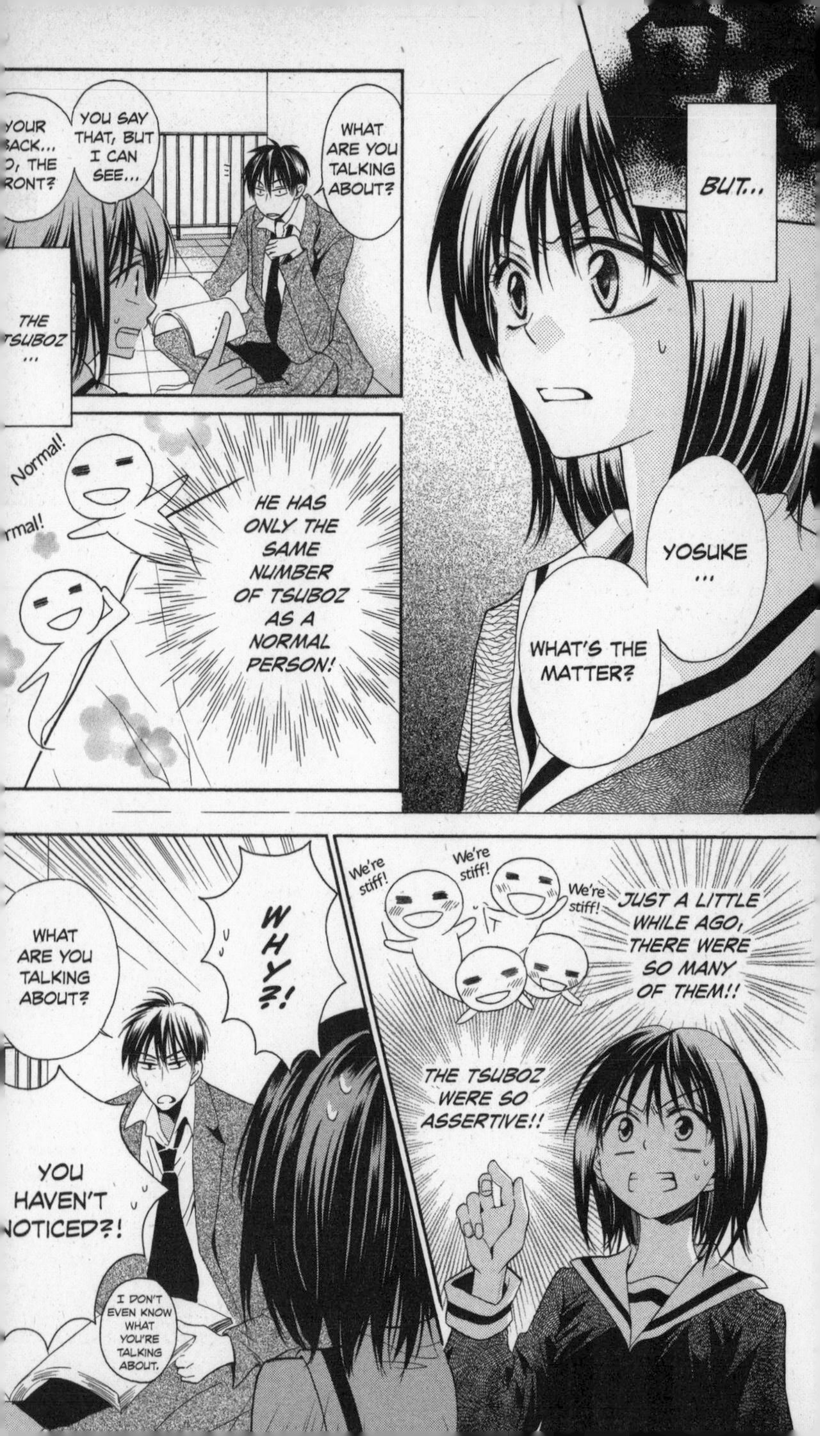
BUT...
YOSUKE ...
WHAT'S THE MATTER?
WHAT ARE YOU TALKING ABOUT?
YOU SAY THAT, BUT I CAN SEE...
YOUR BACK... O, THE RONT?
THE TSUBOZ ...
HE HAS ONLY THE SAME NUMBER OF TSUBOZ AS A NORMAL PERSON!
Normal!
rmal!
JUST A LITTLE WHILE AGO, THERE WERE SO MANY OF THEM!!
We're stiff!
We're stiff!
We're stiff!
THE TSUBOZ WERE SO ASSERTIVE!!
WHY?!
WHAT ARE YOU TALKING ABOUT?
YOU HAVEN'T NOTICED?!
I DON'T EVEN KNOW WHAT YOU'RE TALKING ABOUT.

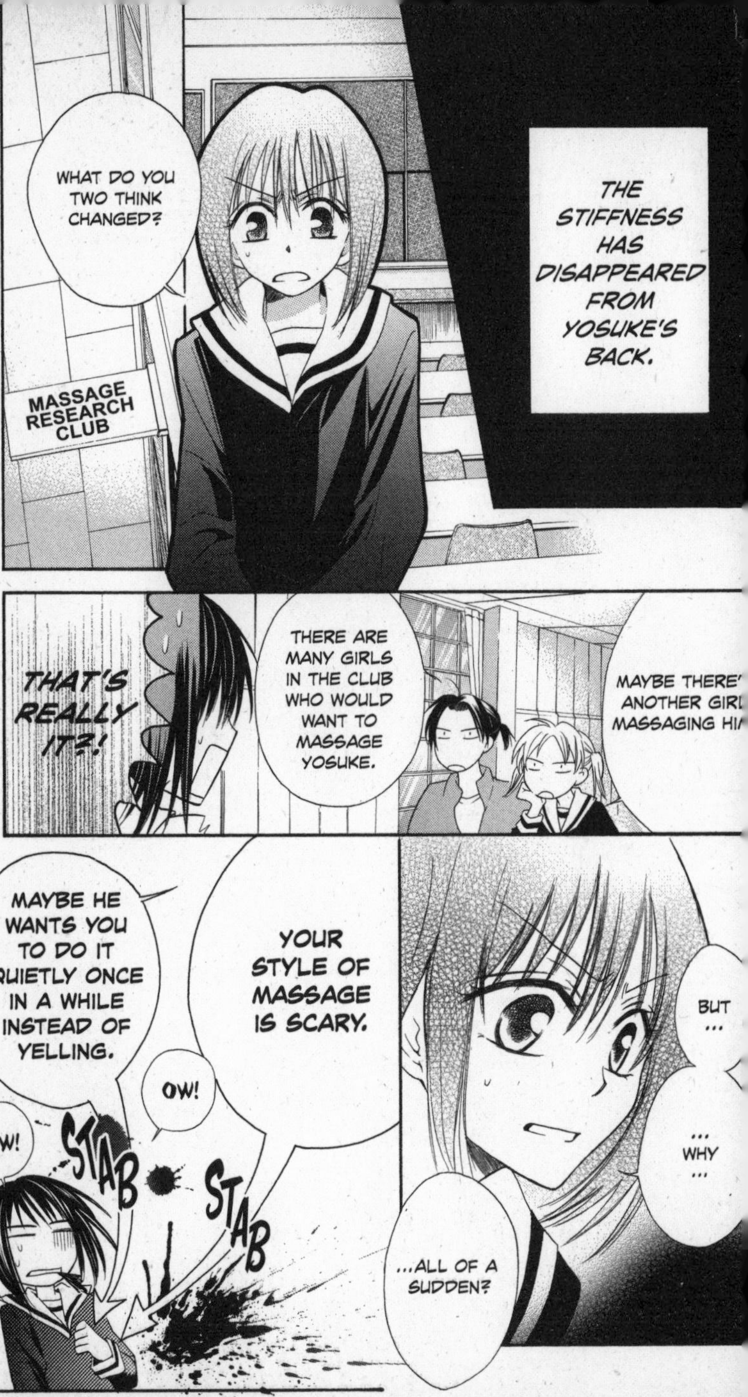
THE STIFFNESS HAS DISAPPEARED FROM YOSUKE'S BACK.
WHAT DO YOU TWO THINK CHANGED?
MASSAGE RESEARCH CLUB
MAYBE THERE' ANOTHER GIRL MASSAGING HI
THERE ARE MANY GIRLS IN THE CLUB WHO WOULD WANT TO MASSAGE YOSUKE.
THAT'S REALLY IT?!
BUT ...
... WHY ...
...ALL OF A SUDDEN?
YOUR STYLE OF MASSAGE IS SCARY.
MAYBE HE WANTS YOU TO DO IT QUIETLY ONCE IN A WHILE INSTEAD OF YELLING.
OW!
STAB
OW!
STAB

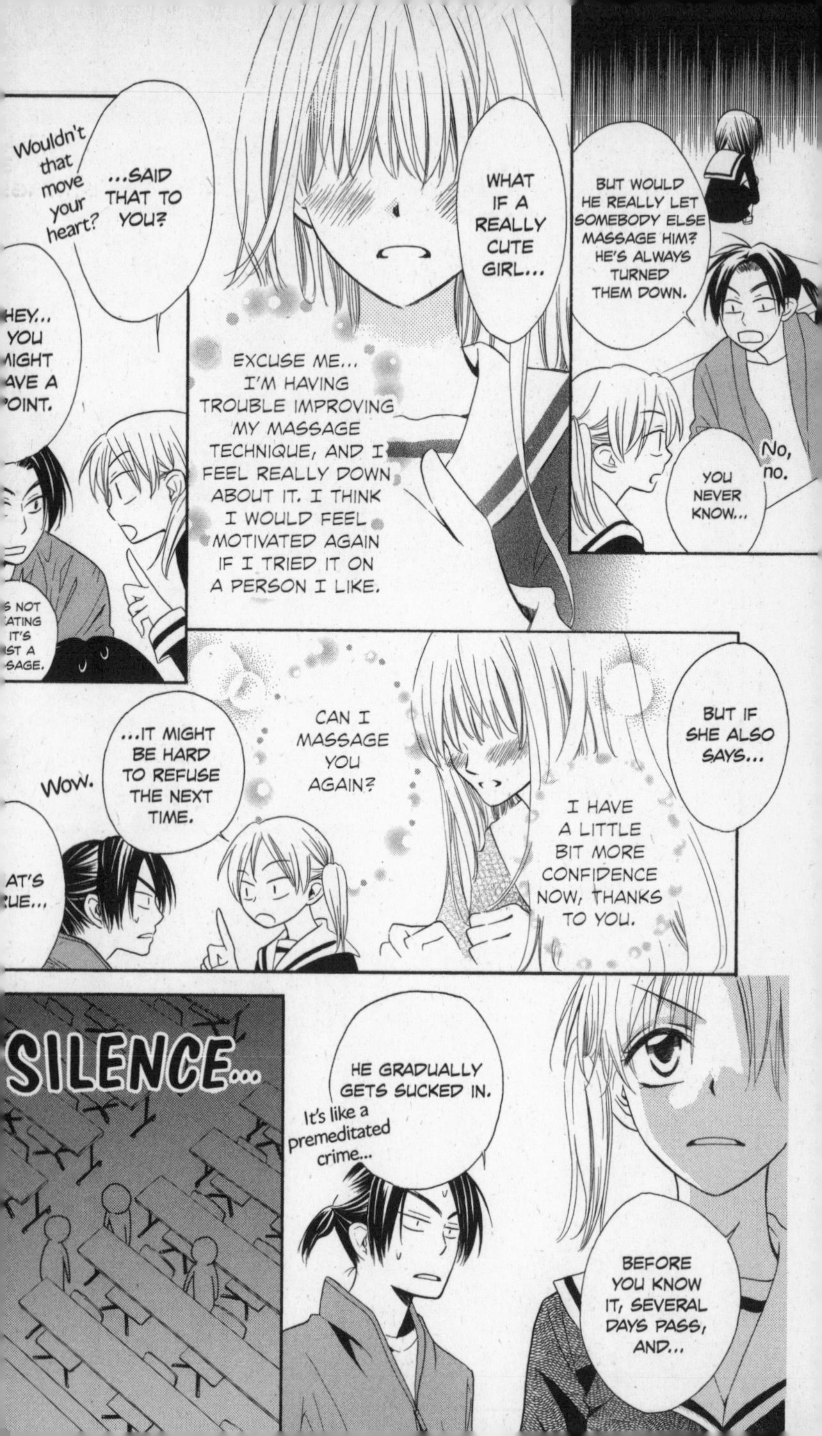
BUT WOULD HE REALLY LET SOMEBODY ELSE MASSAGE HIM? HE'S ALWAYS TURNED THEM DOWN.
YOU NEVER KNOW...
No, no.
WHAT IF A REALLY CUTE GIRL...
EXCUSE ME... I'M HAVING TROUBLE IMPROVING MY MASSAGE TECHNIQUE, AND I FEEL REALLY DOWN ABOUT IT. I THINK I WOULD FEEL MOTIVATED AGAIN IF I TRIED IT ON A PERSON I LIKE.
...SAID THAT TO YOU?
Wouldn't that move your heart?
HEY... YOU IGHT AVE A OINT.
S NOT ATING IT'S ST A SAGE.
BUT IF SHE ALSO SAYS...
I HAVE A LITTLE BIT MORE CONFIDENCE NOW, THANKS TO YOU.
CAN I MASSAGE YOU AGAIN?
...IT MIGHT BE HARD TO REFUSE THE NEXT TIME.
Wow.
AT'S UE...
BEFORE YOU KNOW IT, SEVERAL DAYS PASS, AND...
HE GRADUALLY GETS SUCKED IN.
It's like a premeditated crime...
SILENCE...

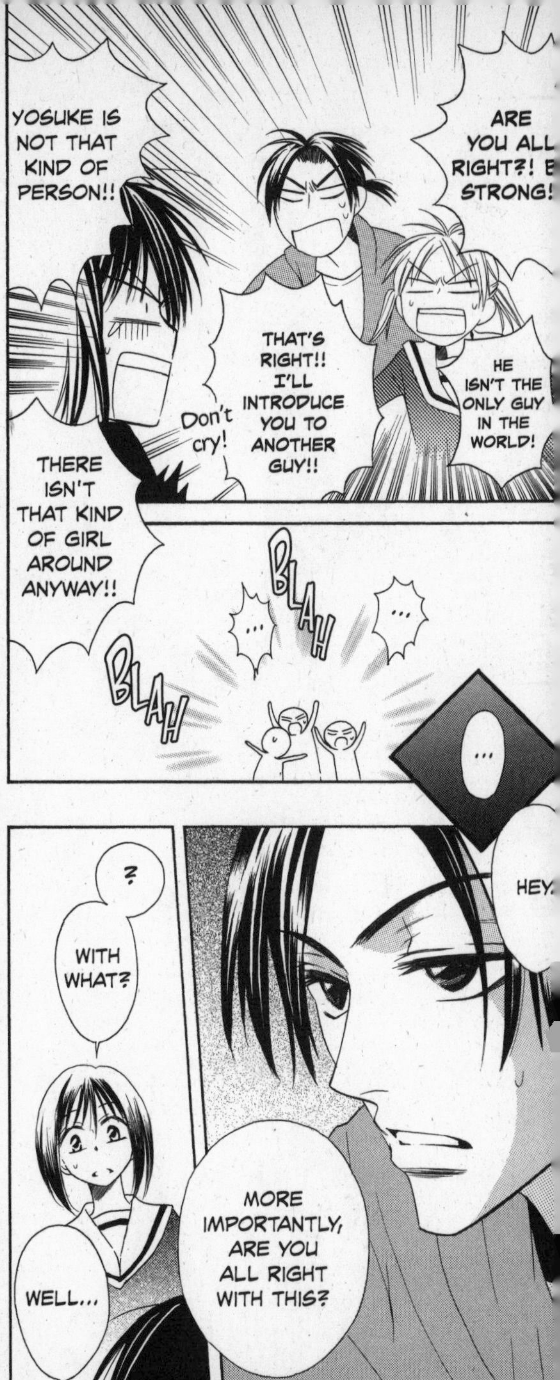
ARE YOU ALL RIGHT?! BE STRONG!
HE ISN'T THE ONLY GUY IN THE WORLD!
THAT'S RIGHT!! I'LL INTRODUCE YOU TO ANOTHER GUY!!
Don't cry!
YOSUKE IS NOT THAT KIND OF PERSON!!
THERE ISN'T THAT KIND OF GIRL AROUND ANYWAY!!
...
BLAH
...
BLAH
...
HEY.
?
WITH WHAT?
MORE IMPORTANTLY, ARE YOU ALL RIGHT WITH THIS?
WELL...

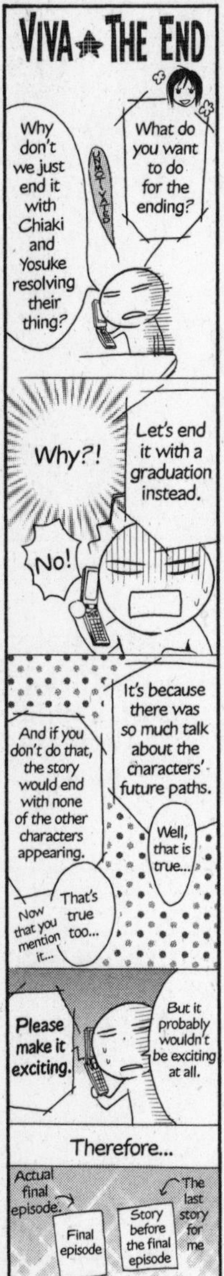
VIVA ☆ THE END
What do you want to do for the ending?
Why don't we just end it with Chiaki and Yosuke resolving their thing?
Let's end it with a graduation instead.
Why?!
No!
It's because there was so much talk about the characters' future paths.
And if you don't do that, the story would end with none of the other characters appearing.
Well, that is true...
That's true too...
Now that you mention it...
But it probably wouldn't be exciting at all.
Please make it exciting.
Therefore...
The last story for me
Story before the final episode
Actual final episode
Final episode
I wonder which was really better...

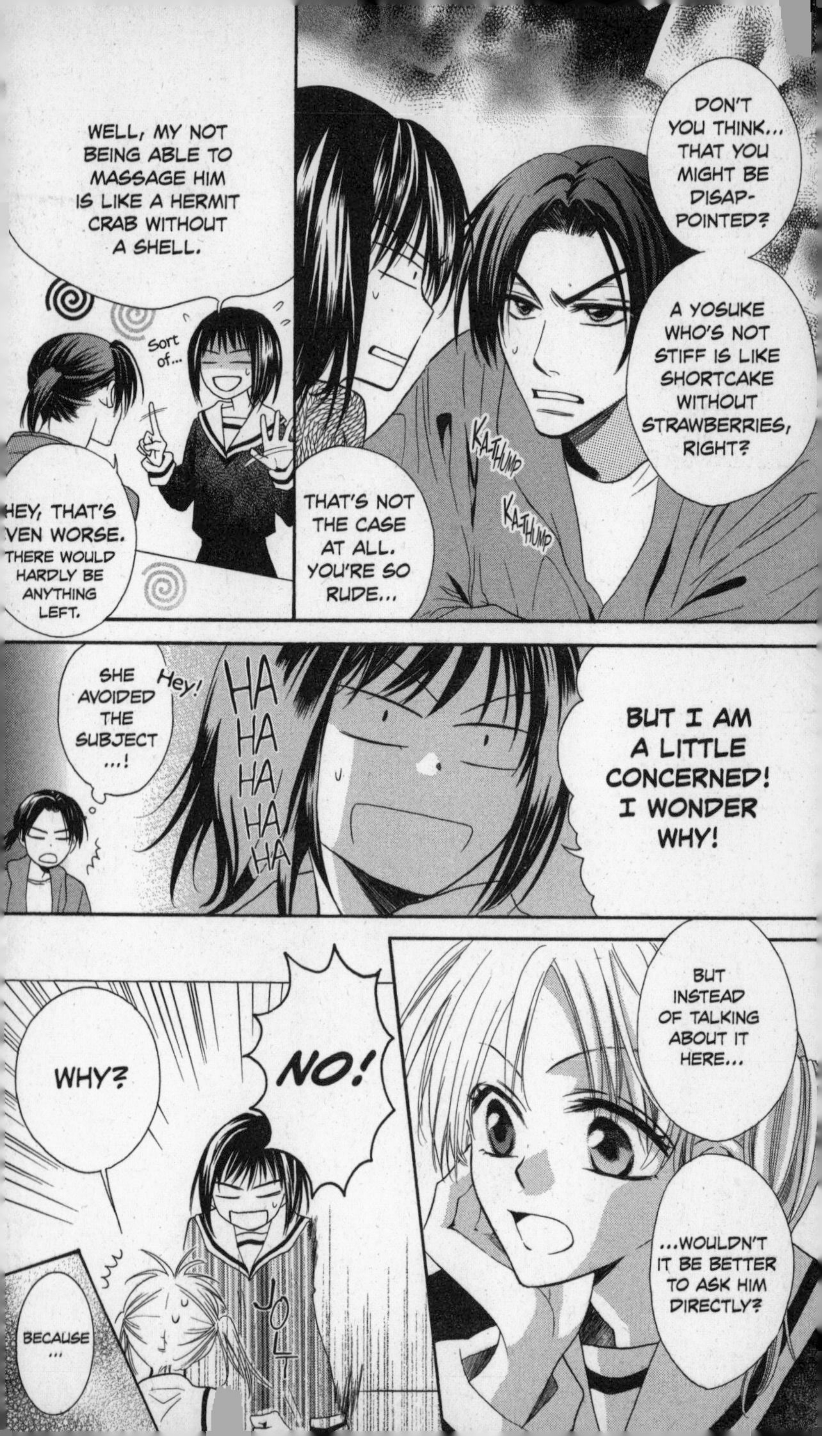
DON'T YOU THINK... THAT YOU MIGHT BE DISAPPOINTED?
A YOSUKE WHO'S NOT STIFF IS LIKE SHORTCAKE WITHOUT STRAWBERRIES, RIGHT?
KA-THUMP
KA-THUMP
THAT'S NOT THE CASE AT ALL. YOU'RE SO RUDE...
WELL, MY NOT BEING ABLE TO MASSAGE HIM IS LIKE A HERMIT CRAB WITHOUT A SHELL.
Sort of...
HEY, THAT'S VEN WORSE. THERE WOULD HARDLY BE ANYTHING LEFT.
BUT I AM A LITTLE CONCERNED! I WONDER WHY!
HA HA HA HA HA HA
SHE AVOIDED THE SUBJECT...!
Hey!
BUT INSTEAD OF TALKING ABOUT IT HERE...
...WOULDN'T IT BE BETTER TO ASK HIM DIRECTLY?
NO!
JOLT
WHY?
BECAUSE...

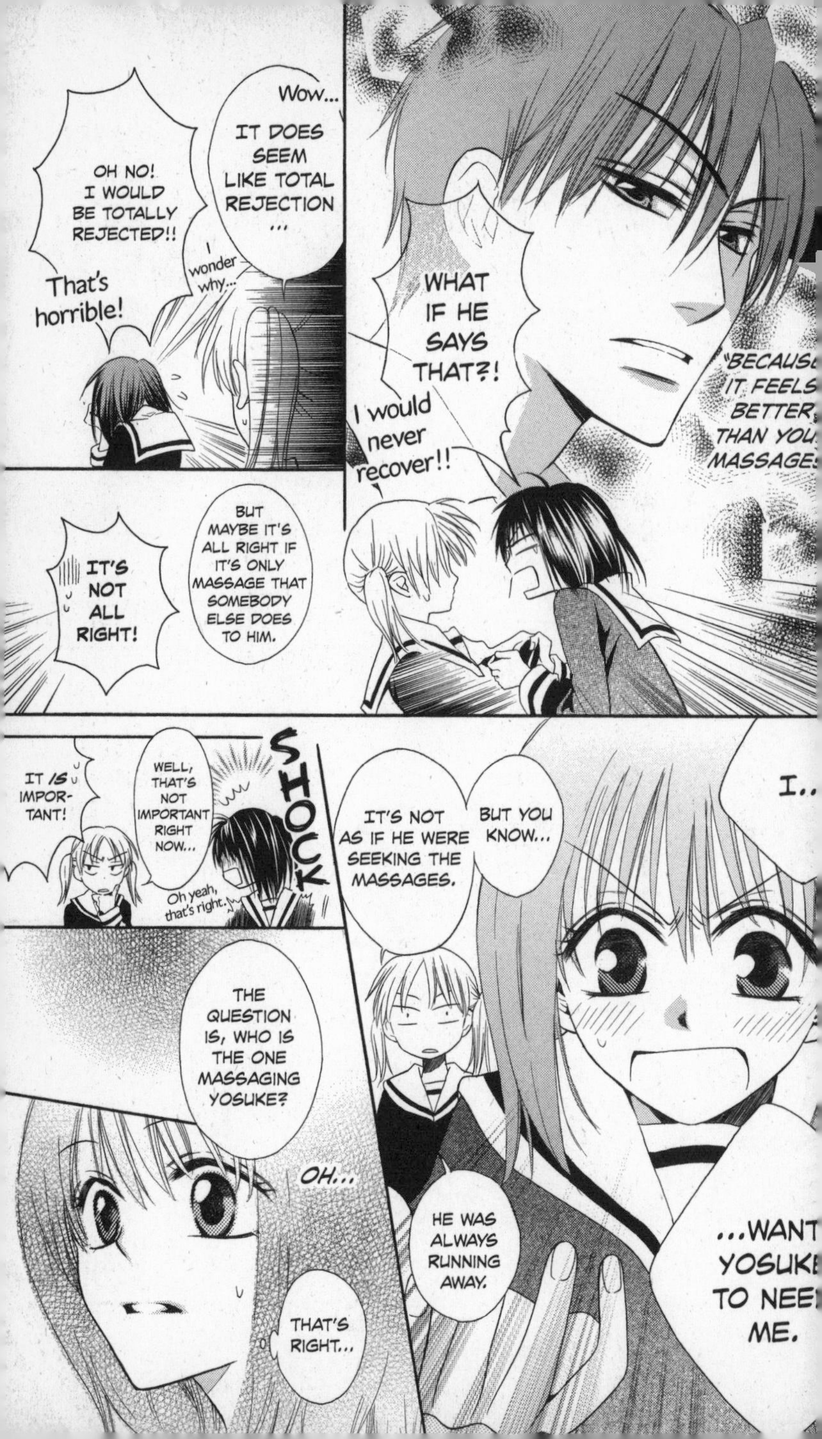
"BECAUSE IT FEELS BETTER THAN YOUR MASSAGES"
WHAT IF HE SAYS THAT?!
I would never recover!!
Wow...
IT DOES SEEM LIKE TOTAL REJECTION ...
I wonder why...
OH NO! I WOULD BE TOTALLY REJECTED!!
That's horrible!
BUT MAYBE IT'S ALL RIGHT IF IT'S ONLY MASSAGE THAT SOMEBODY ELSE DOES TO HIM.
IT'S NOT ALL RIGHT!
I...
...WANT YOSUKE TO NEED ME.
BUT YOU KNOW...
IT'S NOT AS IF HE WERE SEEKING THE MASSAGES.
HE WAS ALWAYS RUNNING AWAY.
SHOCK
WELL, THAT'S NOT IMPORTANT RIGHT NOW...
Oh yeah, that's right.
IT *IS* IMPORTANT!
THE QUESTION IS, WHO IS THE ONE MASSAGING YOSUKE?
OH...
THAT'S RIGHT...

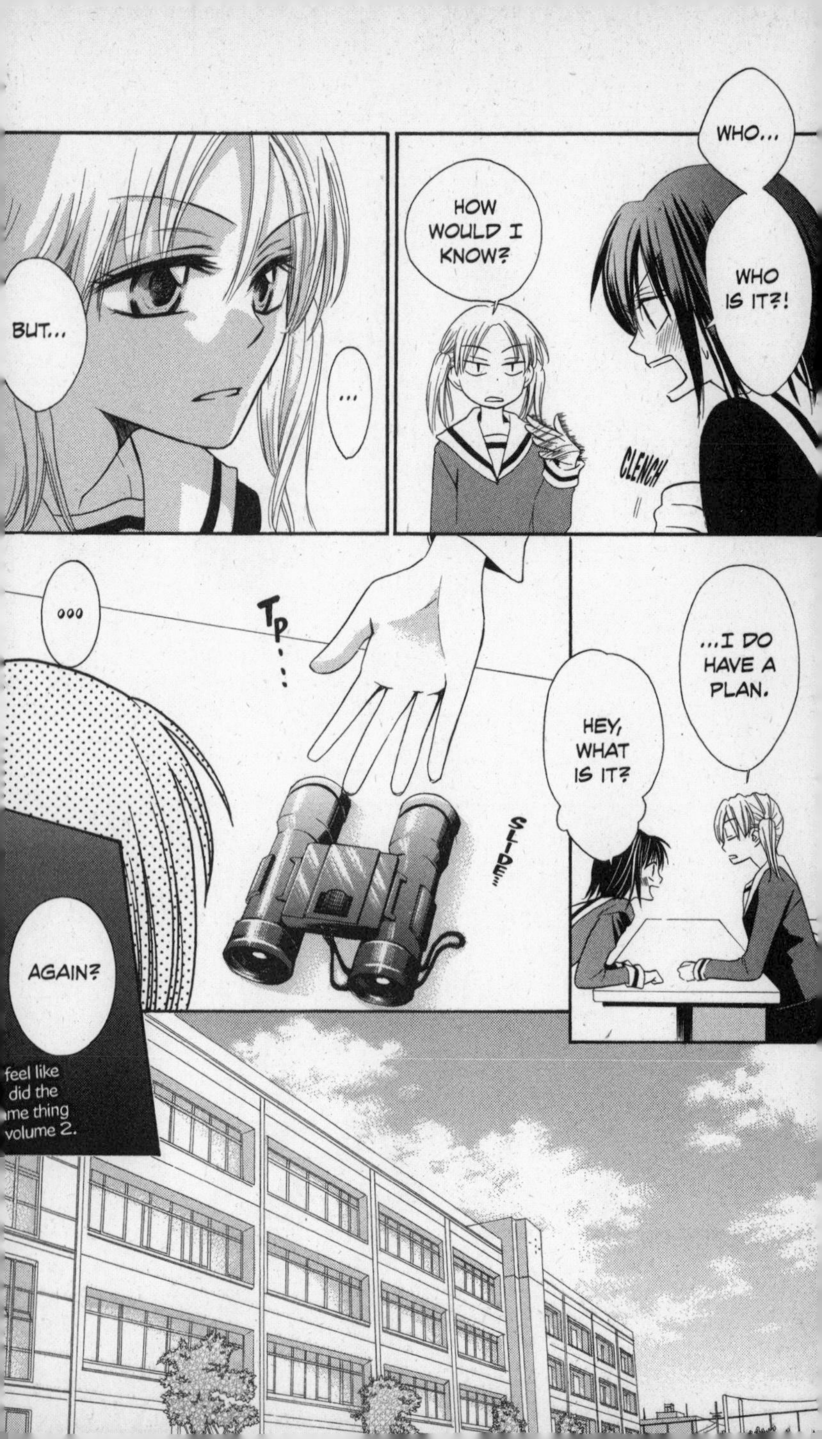
WHO...
WHO IS IT?!
HOW WOULD I KNOW?
CLENCH
...
BUT...
...I DO HAVE A PLAN.
HEY, WHAT IS IT?
SLIDE...
TP...
ooo
AGAIN?
feel like
did the
me thing
volume 2.

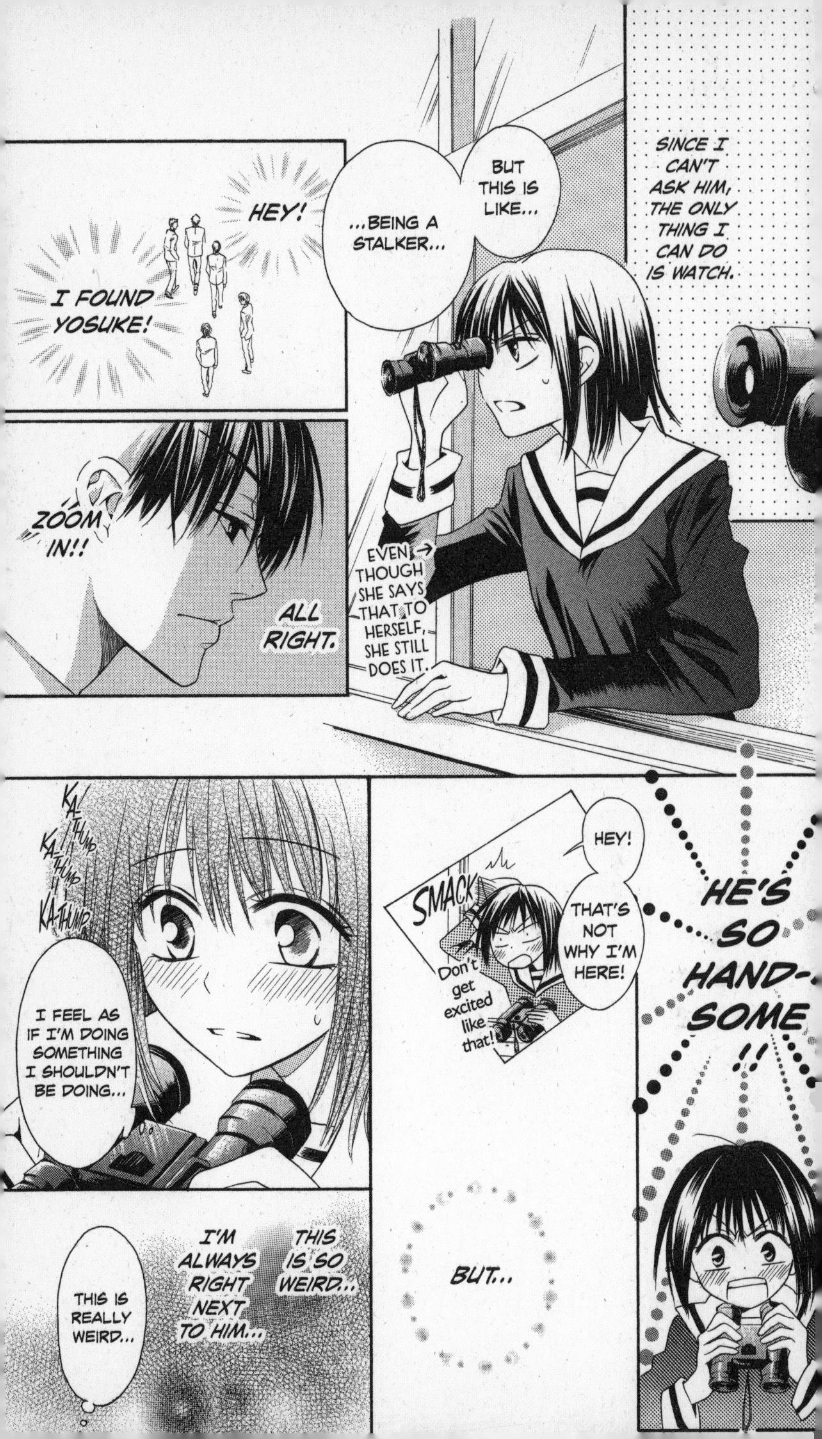
SINCE I CAN'T ASK HIM, THE ONLY THING I CAN DO IS WATCH.
BUT THIS IS LIKE...
...BEING A STALKER...
EVEN THOUGH SHE SAYS THAT TO HERSELF, SHE STILL DOES IT.
HEY!
I FOUND YOSUKE!
ZOOM IN!!
ALL RIGHT.
HE'S SO HAND-SOME!!
HEY!
THAT'S NOT WHY I'M HERE!
SMACK
Don't get excited like that!
BUT...
KA-THUMP KA-THUMP KA-THUMP
I FEEL AS IF I'M DOING SOMETHING I SHOULDN'T BE DOING...
THIS IS SO WEIRD...
I'M ALWAYS RIGHT NEXT TO HIM...
THIS IS REALLY WEIRD...

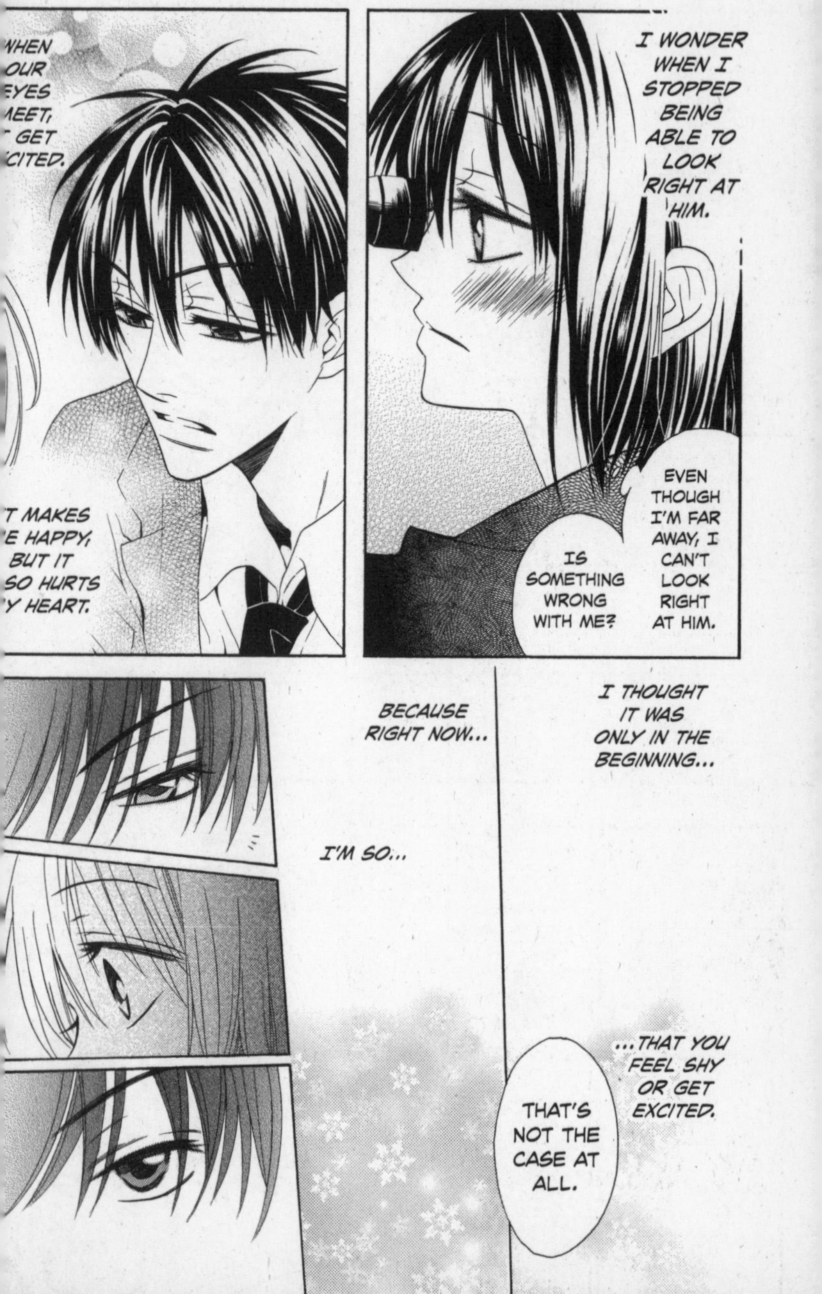
I WONDER WHEN I STOPPED BEING ABLE TO LOOK RIGHT AT HIM.
EVEN THOUGH I'M FAR AWAY, I CAN'T LOOK RIGHT AT HIM.
IS SOMETHING WRONG WITH ME?
HEN OUR EYES MEET, GET CITED.
T MAKES E HAPPY, BUT IT SO HURTS Y HEART.
I THOUGHT IT WAS ONLY IN THE BEGINNING...
...THAT YOU FEEL SHY OR GET EXCITED.
THAT'S NOT THE CASE AT ALL.
BECAUSE RIGHT NOW...
I'M SO...

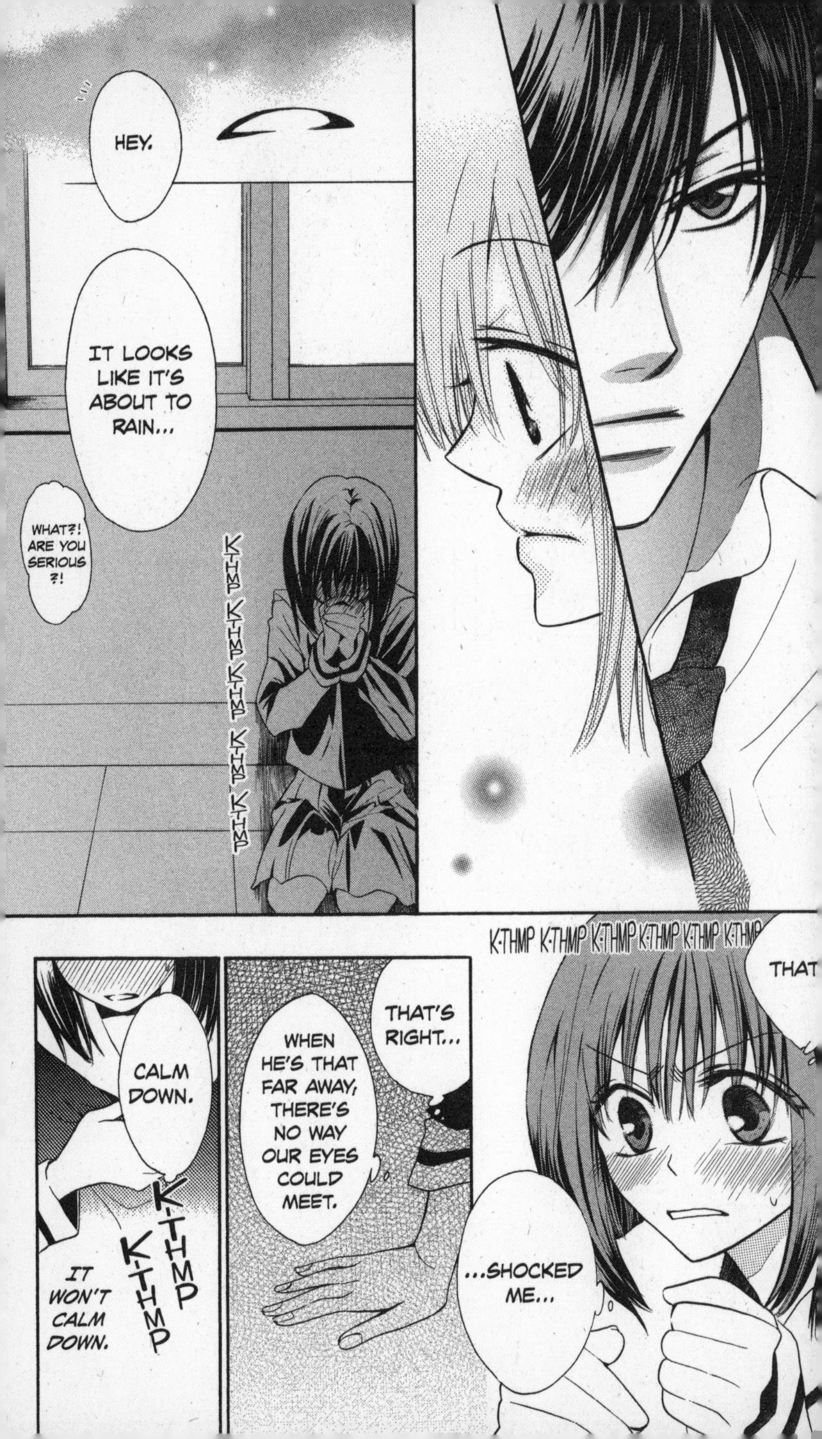
HEY.
IT LOOKS LIKE IT'S ABOUT TO RAIN...
WHAT?! ARE YOU SERIOUS?!
K-THMP K-THMP K-THMP K-THMP K-THMP
K-THMP K-THMP K-THMP K-THMP K-THMP K-THM
THAT
...SHOCKED ME...
THAT'S RIGHT...
WHEN HE'S THAT FAR AWAY, THERE'S NO WAY OUR EYES COULD MEET.
CALM DOWN.
K-THMP K-THMP
IT WON'T CALM DOWN.

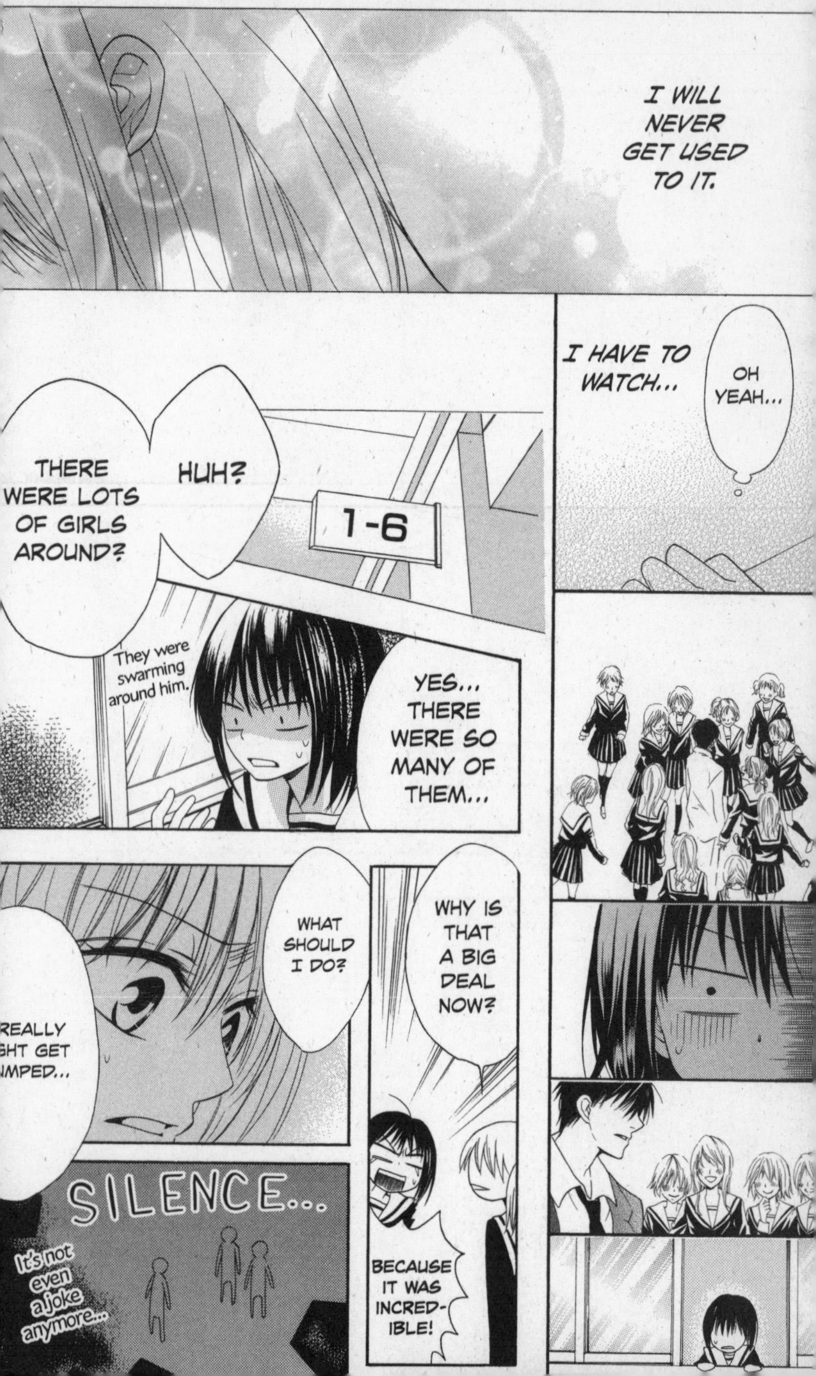

I WILL NEVER GET USED TO IT.
I HAVE TO WATCH...
OH YEAH...
HUH?
THERE WERE LOTS OF GIRLS AROUND?
YES... THERE WERE SO MANY OF THEM...
They were swarming around him.
1-6
WHY IS THAT A BIG DEAL NOW?
BECAUSE IT WAS INCRED-IBLE!
WHAT SHOULD I DO?
REALLY
GHT GET
MPED...
SILENCE...
It's not even a joke anymore...

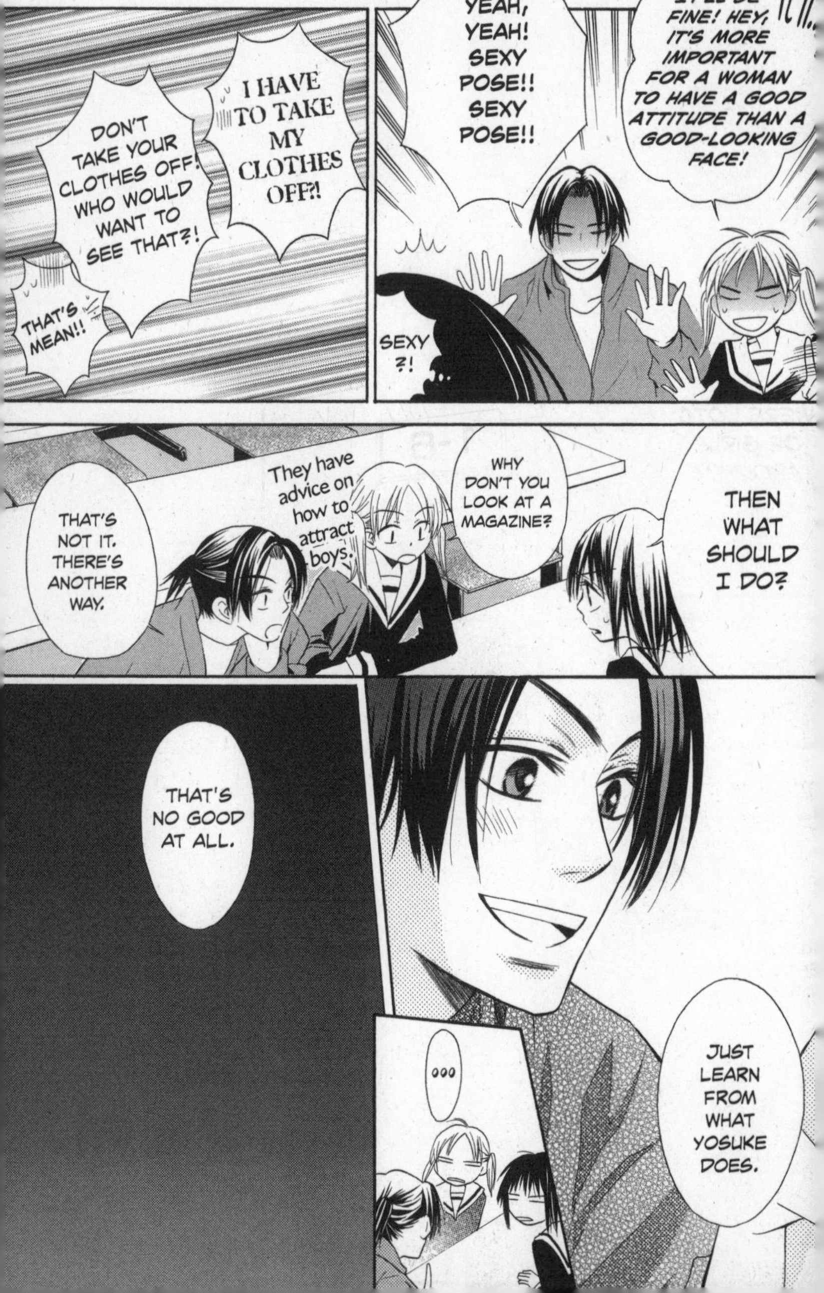
IT'LL BE FINE! HEY, IT'S MORE IMPORTANT FOR A WOMAN TO HAVE A GOOD ATTITUDE THAN A GOOD-LOOKING FACE!
YEAH, YEAH! SEXY POSE!! SEXY POSE!!
SEXY?!
I HAVE TO TAKE MY CLOTHES OFF?!
DON'T TAKE YOUR CLOTHES OFF! WHO WOULD WANT TO SEE THAT?!
THAT'S MEAN!!
THEN WHAT SHOULD I DO?
WHY DON'T YOU LOOK AT A MAGAZINE?
They have advice on how to attract boys.
THAT'S NOT IT. THERE'S ANOTHER WAY.
THAT'S NO GOOD AT ALL.
JUST LEARN FROM WHAT YOSUKE DOES.
...

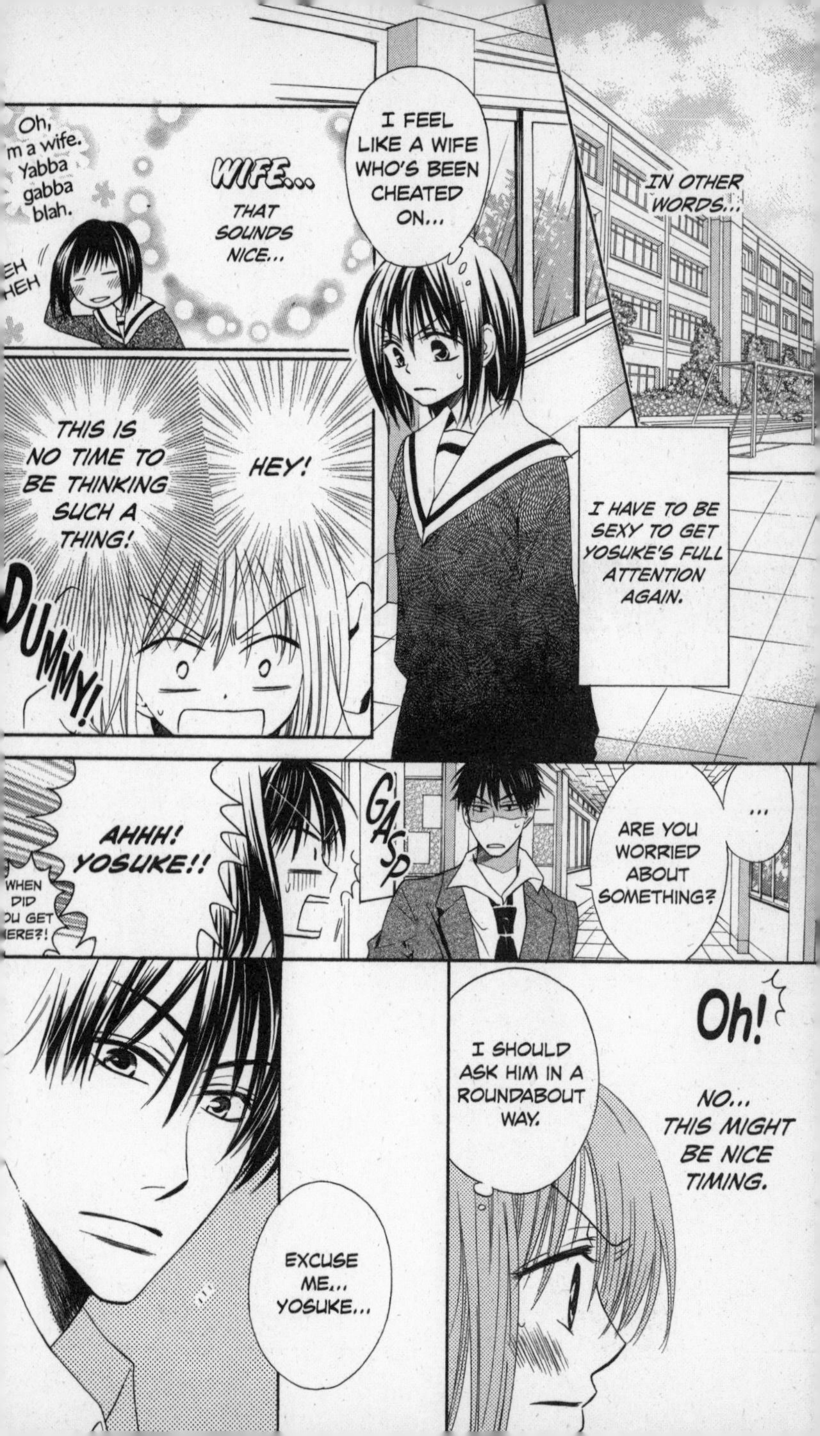
IN OTHER WORDS...
I FEEL LIKE A WIFE WHO'S BEEN CHEATED ON...
I HAVE TO BE SEXY TO GET YOSUKE'S FULL ATTENTION AGAIN.
WIFE...
THAT SOUNDS NICE...
Oh, m a wife. Yabba gabba blah.
EH HEH
HEY!
THIS IS NO TIME TO BE THINKING SUCH A THING!
DUMMY!
...
ARE YOU WORRIED ABOUT SOMETHING?
GASP
AHHH! YOSUKE!!
WHEN DID OU GET ERE?!
Oh!
NO... THIS MIGHT BE NICE TIMING.
I SHOULD ASK HIM IN A ROUNDABOUT WAY.
EXCUSE ME... YOSUKE...

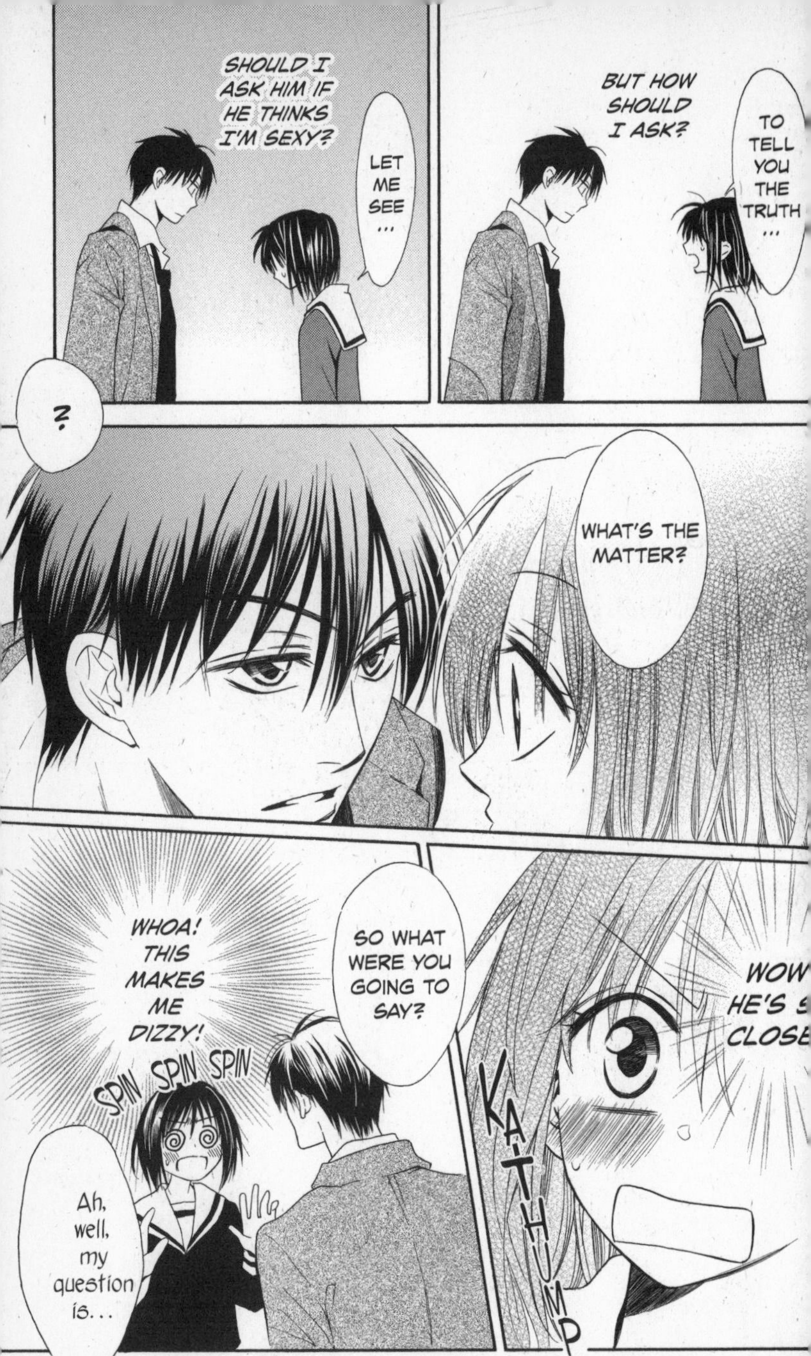
TO TELL YOU THE TRUTH...
BUT HOW SHOULD I ASK?
LET ME SEE...
SHOULD I ASK HIM IF HE THINKS I'M SEXY?
?
WHAT'S THE MATTER?
WOW HE'S S CLOSE
KATHUMP
SO WHAT WERE YOU GOING TO SAY?
WHOA! THIS MAKES ME DIZZY!
SPIN SPIN SPIN
Ah, well, my question is...

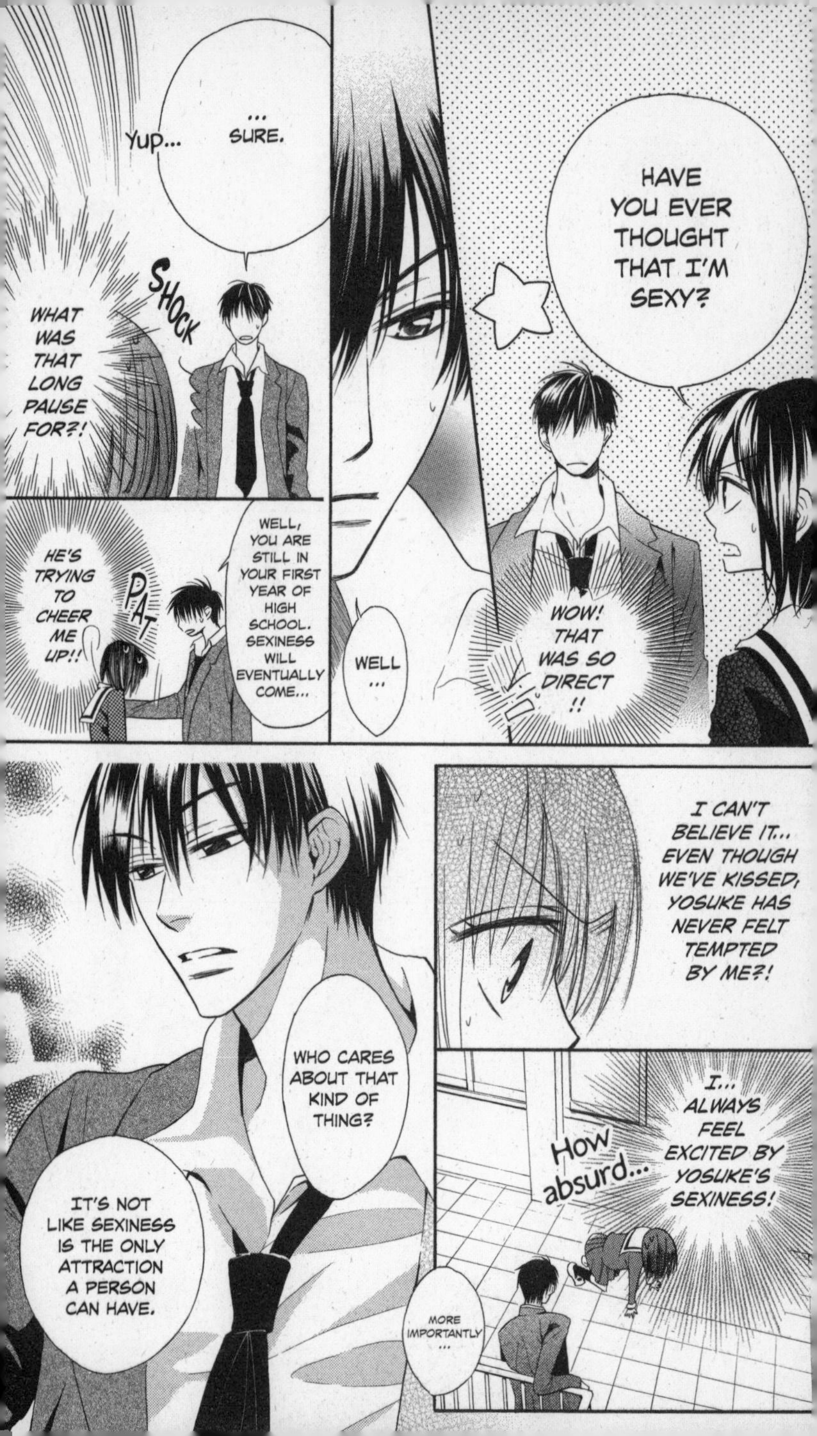
HAVE YOU EVER THOUGHT THAT I'M SEXY?
WOW! THAT WAS SO DIRECT!!
WELL ...
Yup... ... SURE.
SHOCK
WHAT WAS THAT LONG PAUSE FOR?!
WELL, YOU ARE STILL IN YOUR FIRST YEAR OF HIGH SCHOOL. SEXINESS WILL EVENTUALLY COME...
PAT
HE'S TRYING TO CHEER ME UP!!
I CAN'T BELIEVE IT... EVEN THOUGH WE'VE KISSED, YOSUKE HAS NEVER FELT TEMPTED BY ME?!
I... ALWAYS FEEL EXCITED BY YOSUKE'S SEXINESS!
How absurd...
MORE IMPORTANTLY ...
WHO CARES ABOUT THAT KIND OF THING?
IT'S NOT LIKE SEXINESS IS THE ONLY ATTRACTION A PERSON CAN HAVE.

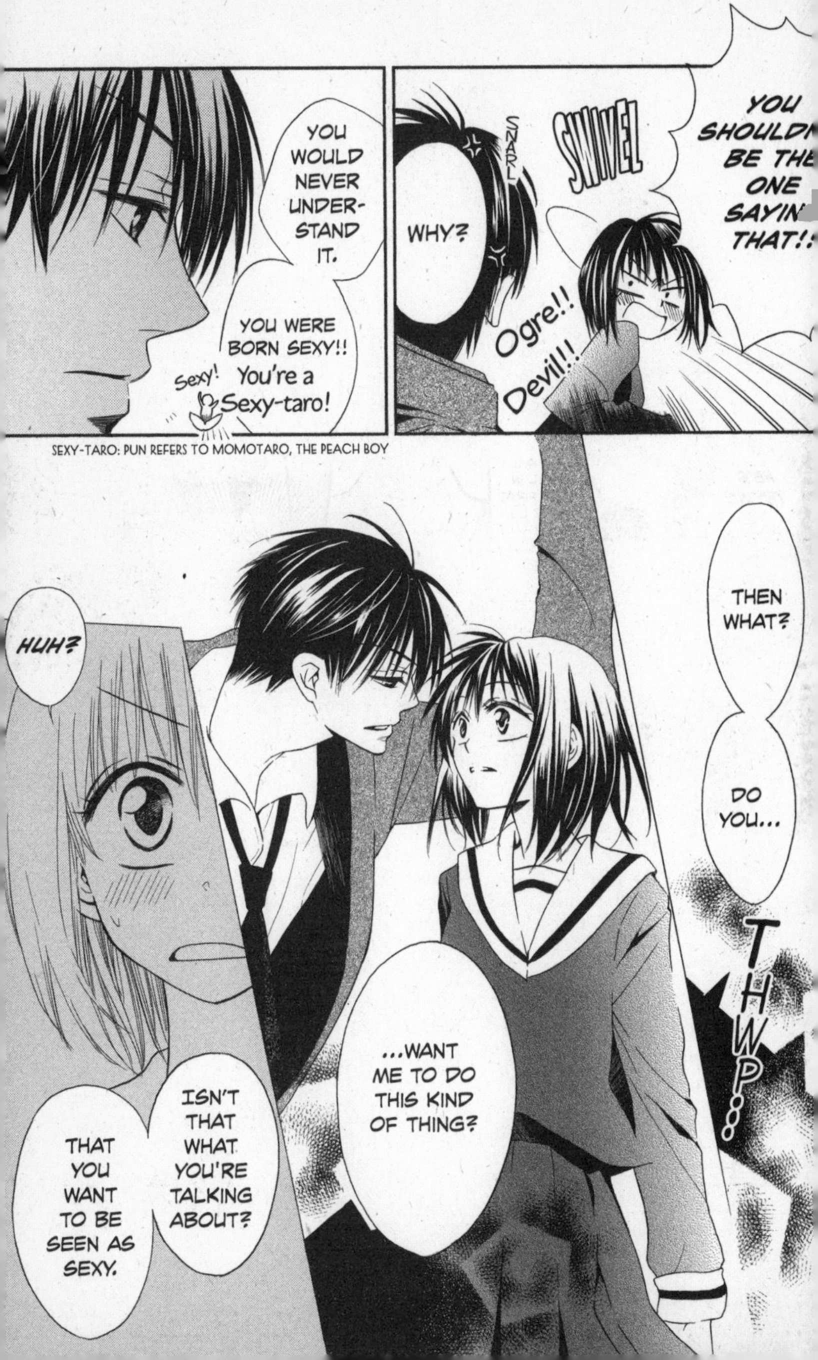
YOU SHOULDN BE THE ONE SAYIN THAT!!
SWIVEL
SNARL
Ogre!! Devil!!
WHY?
YOU WOULD NEVER UNDER-STAND IT.
YOU WERE BORN SEXY!! You're a Sexy-taro!
Sexy!
THEN WHAT?
DO YOU...
THWP...
...WANT ME TO DO THIS KIND OF THING?
ISN'T THAT WHAT YOU'RE TALKING ABOUT?
THAT YOU WANT TO BE SEEN AS SEXY.
HUH?

SEXY-TARO: PUN REFERS TO MOMOTARO, THE PEACH BOY

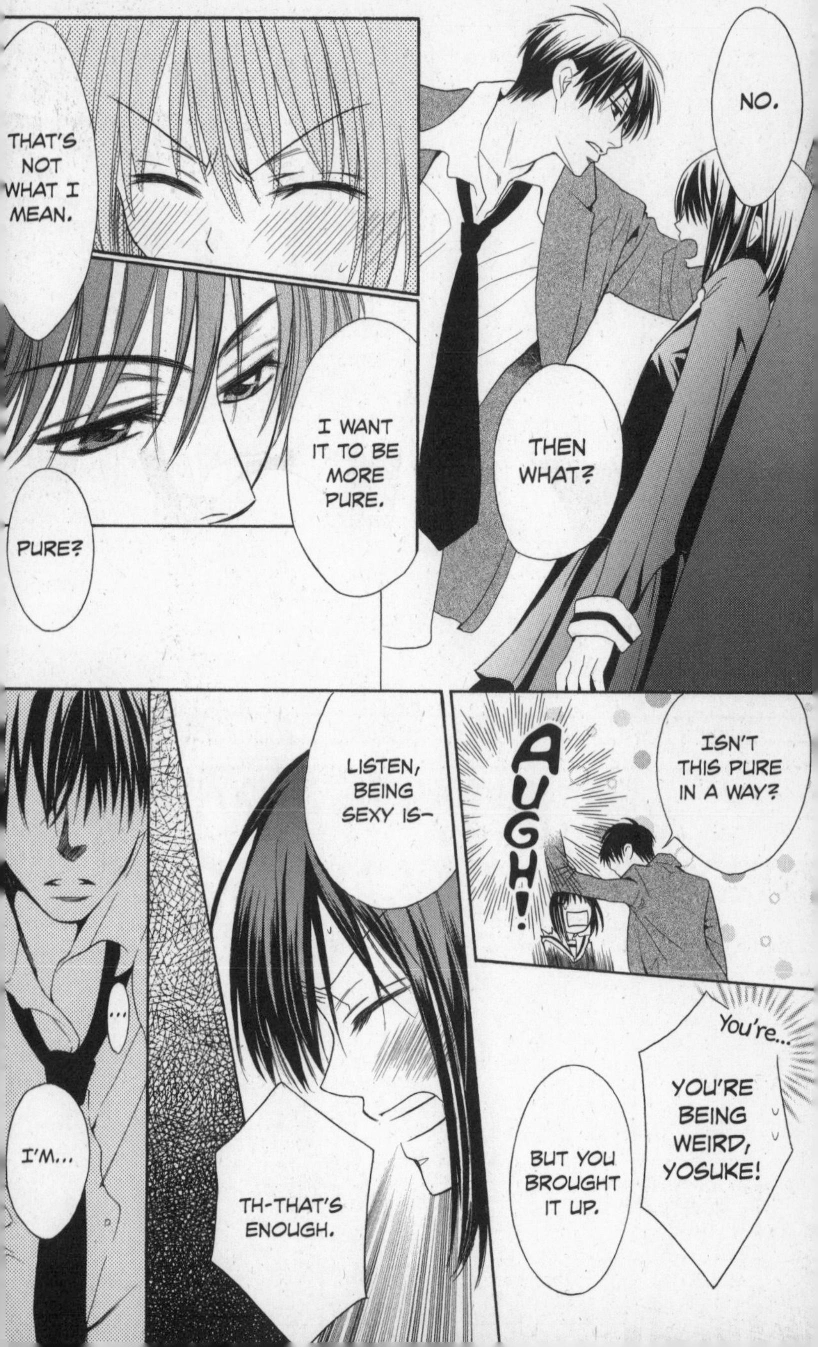
NO.
THEN WHAT?
THAT'S NOT WHAT I MEAN.
I WANT IT TO BE MORE PURE.
PURE?
ISN'T THIS PURE IN A WAY?
AUGH!
You're...
YOU'RE BEING WEIRD, YOSUKE!
BUT YOU BROUGHT IT UP.
LISTEN, BEING SEXY IS–
TH-THAT'S ENOUGH.
...
I'M...

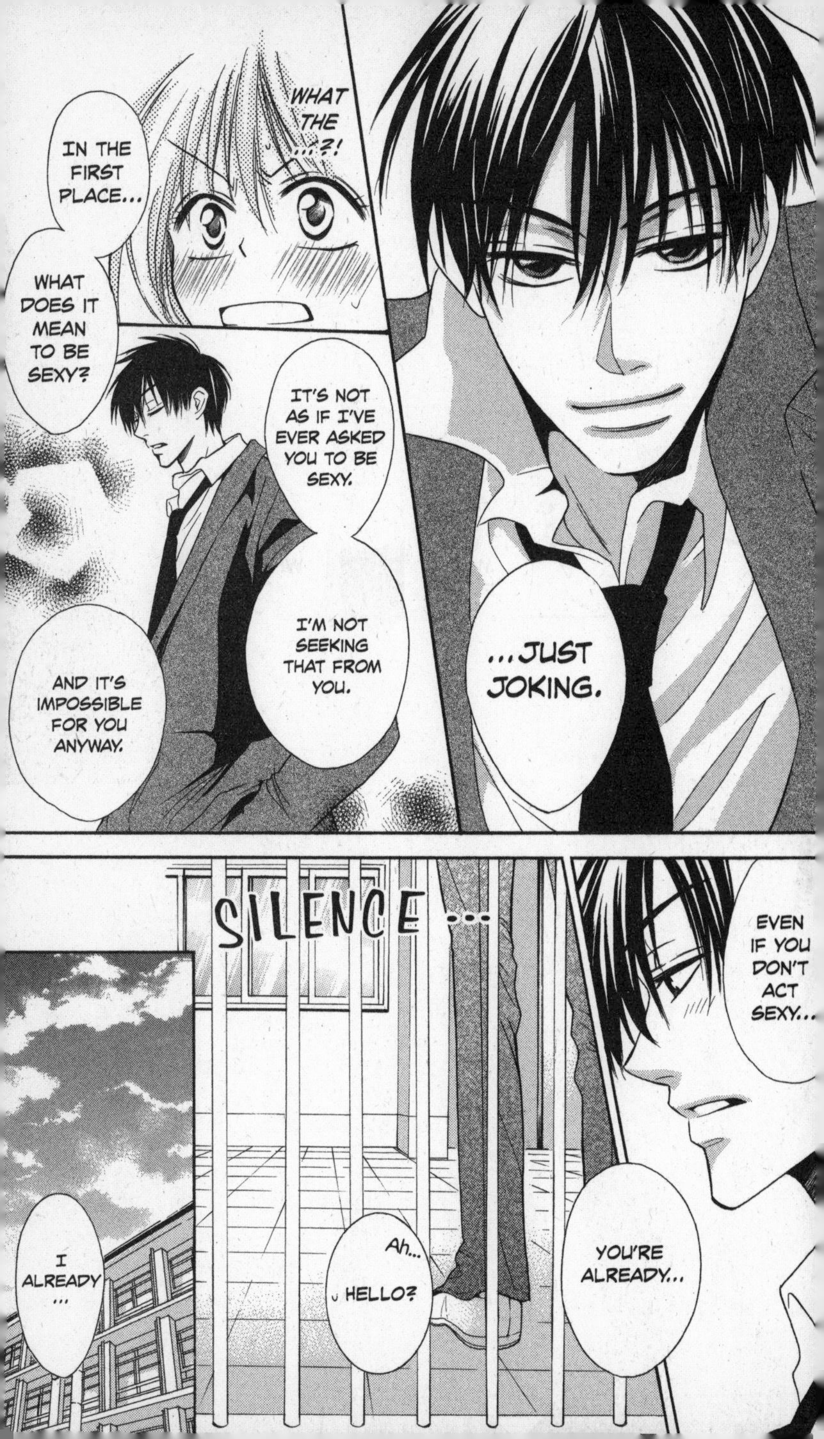
...JUST JOKING.
WHAT THE ...?!
IN THE FIRST PLACE...
WHAT DOES IT MEAN TO BE SEXY?
IT'S NOT AS IF I'VE EVER ASKED YOU TO BE SEXY.
I'M NOT SEEKING THAT FROM YOU.
AND IT'S IMPOSSIBLE FOR YOU ANYWAY.
EVEN IF YOU DON'T ACT SEXY...
YOU'RE ALREADY...
SILENCE ...
Ah...
HELLO?
I ALREADY ...

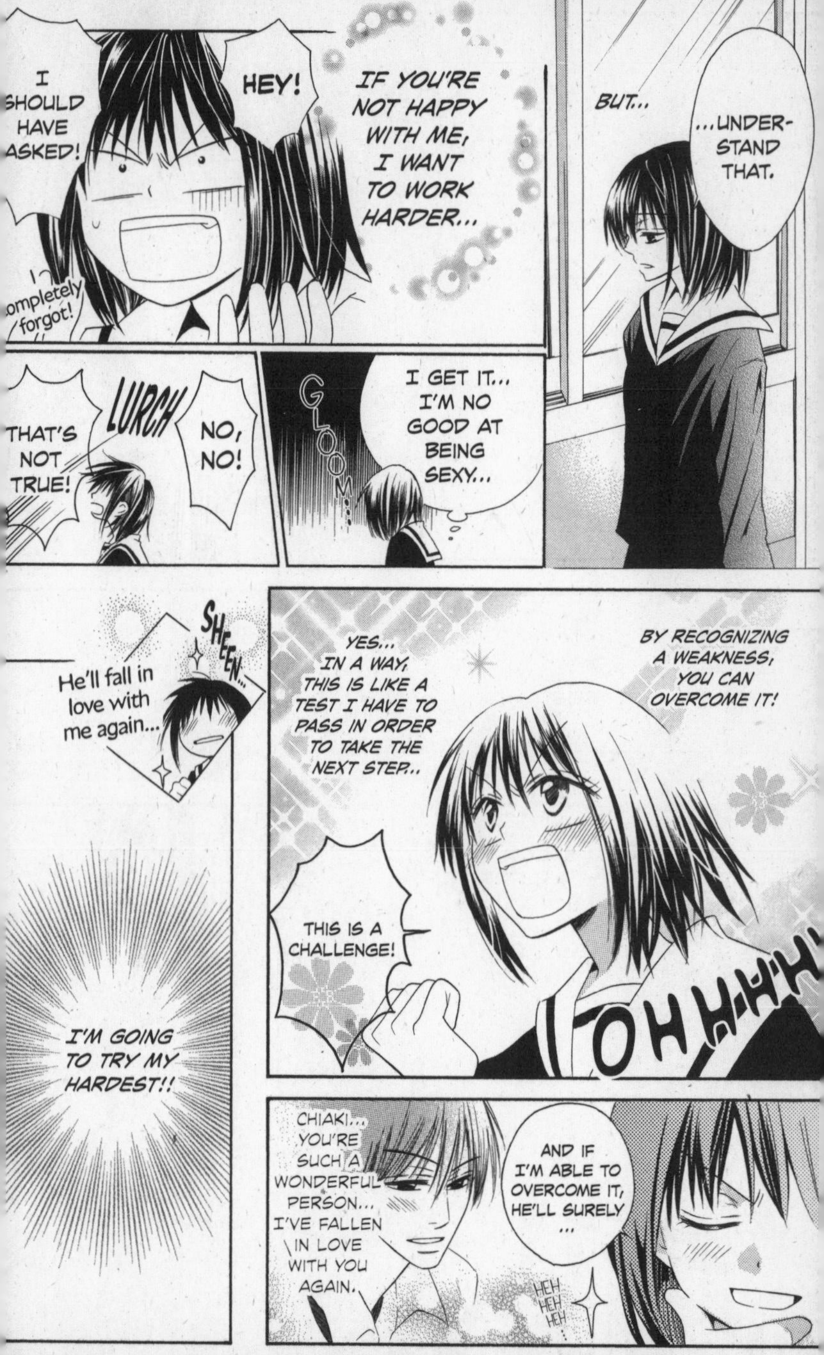
...UNDER-STAND THAT.
BUT...
IF YOU'RE NOT HAPPY WITH ME, I WANT TO WORK HARDER...
HEY!
I SHOULD HAVE ASKED!
I ompletely forgot!
GLOOM...
I GET IT... I'M NO GOOD AT BEING SEXY...
NO, NO!
LURCH
THAT'S NOT TRUE!
BY RECOGNIZING A WEAKNESS, YOU CAN OVERCOME IT!
YES... IN A WAY, THIS IS LIKE A TEST I HAVE TO PASS IN ORDER TO TAKE THE NEXT STEP...
OHHHHH
THIS IS A CHALLENGE!
AND IF I'M ABLE TO OVERCOME IT, HE'LL SURELY ...
HEH HEH HEH
CHIAKI... YOU'RE SUCH A WONDERFUL PERSON... I'VE FALLEN IN LOVE WITH YOU AGAIN.
SHEEN...
He'll fall in love with me again...
I'M GOING TO TRY MY HARDEST!!

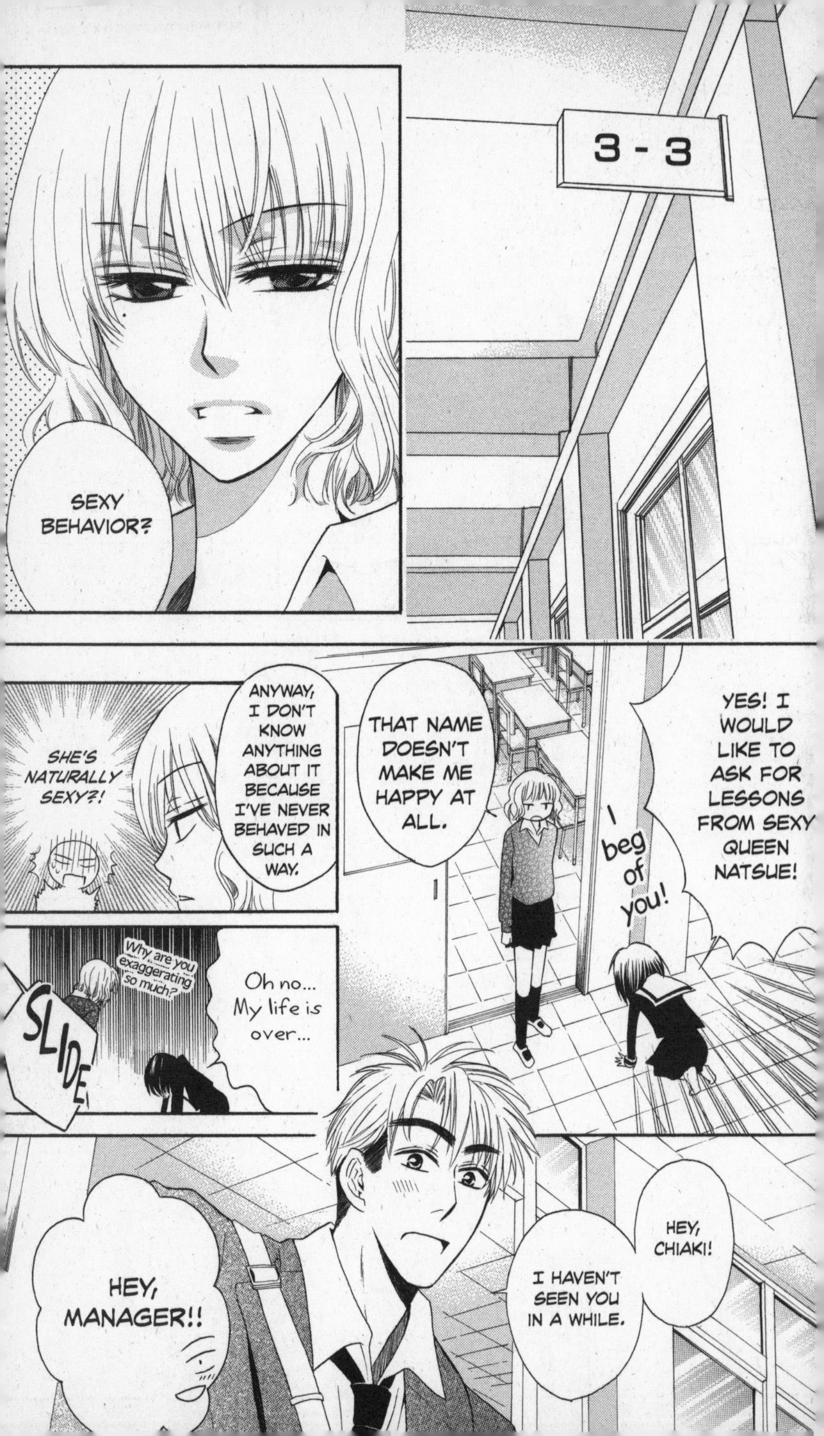
3 - 3
SEXY BEHAVIOR?
YES! I WOULD LIKE TO ASK FOR LESSONS FROM SEXY QUEEN NATSUE!
I beg of you!
THAT NAME DOESN'T MAKE ME HAPPY AT ALL.
ANYWAY, I DON'T KNOW ANYTHING ABOUT IT BECAUSE I'VE NEVER BEHAVED IN SUCH A WAY.
SHE'S NATURALLY SEXY?!
Oh no... My life is over...
Why are you exaggerating so much?
SLIDE
HEY, CHIAKI!
I HAVEN'T SEEN YOU IN A WHILE.
HEY, MANAGER!!

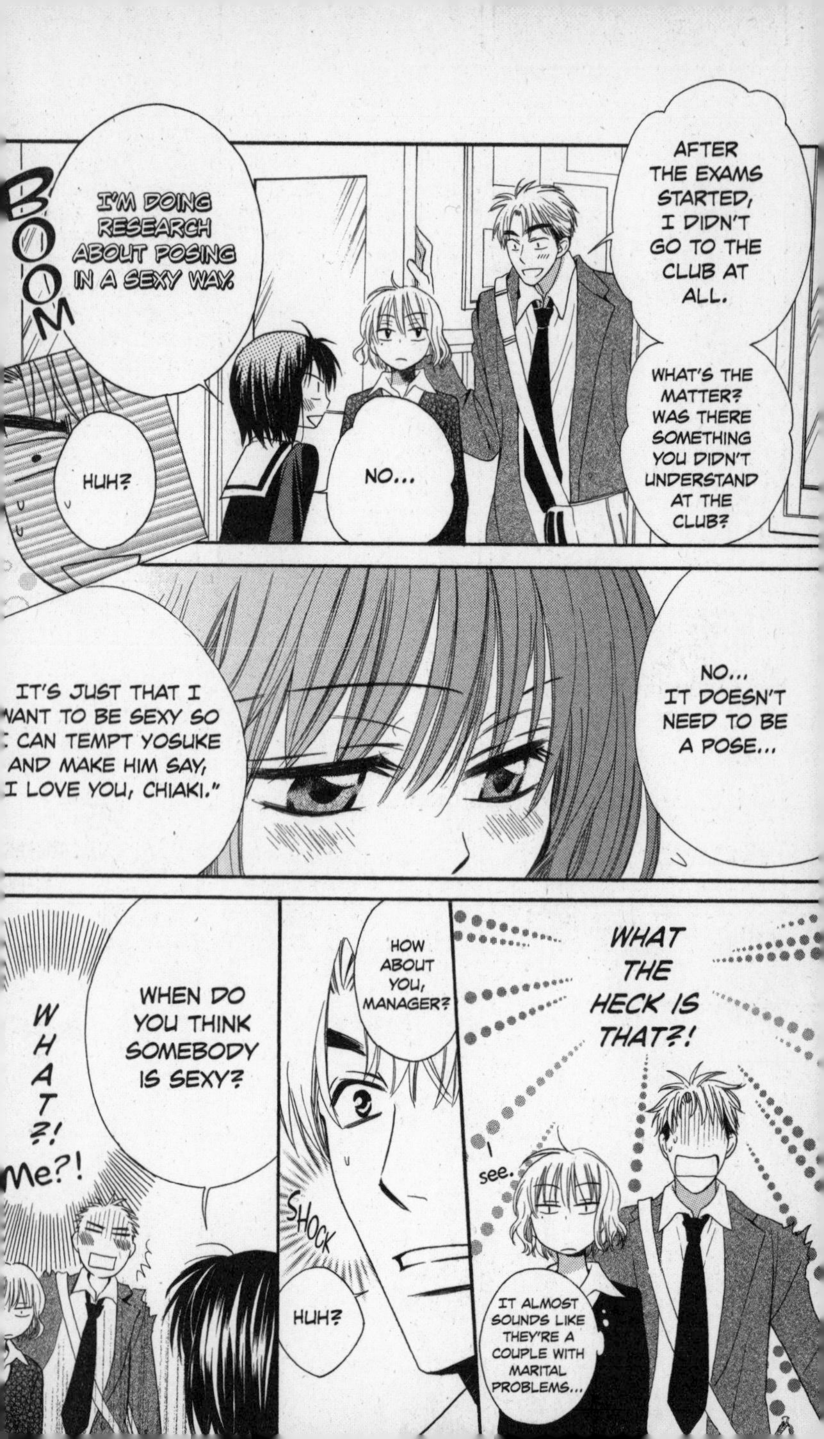
AFTER THE EXAMS STARTED, I DIDN'T GO TO THE CLUB AT ALL.
WHAT'S THE MATTER? WAS THERE SOMETHING YOU DIDN'T UNDERSTAND AT THE CLUB?
NO...
I'M DOING RESEARCH ABOUT POSING IN A SEXY WAY.
BOOM
HUH?
NO... IT DOESN'T NEED TO BE A POSE...
IT'S JUST THAT I WANT TO BE SEXY SO I CAN TEMPT YOSUKE AND MAKE HIM SAY, I LOVE YOU, CHIAKI."
WHAT THE HECK IS THAT?!
I see.
IT ALMOST SOUNDS LIKE THEY'RE A COUPLE WITH MARITAL PROBLEMS...
HOW ABOUT YOU, MANAGER?
SHOCK
HUH?
WHEN DO YOU THINK SOMEBODY IS SEXY?
WHAT?! Me?!

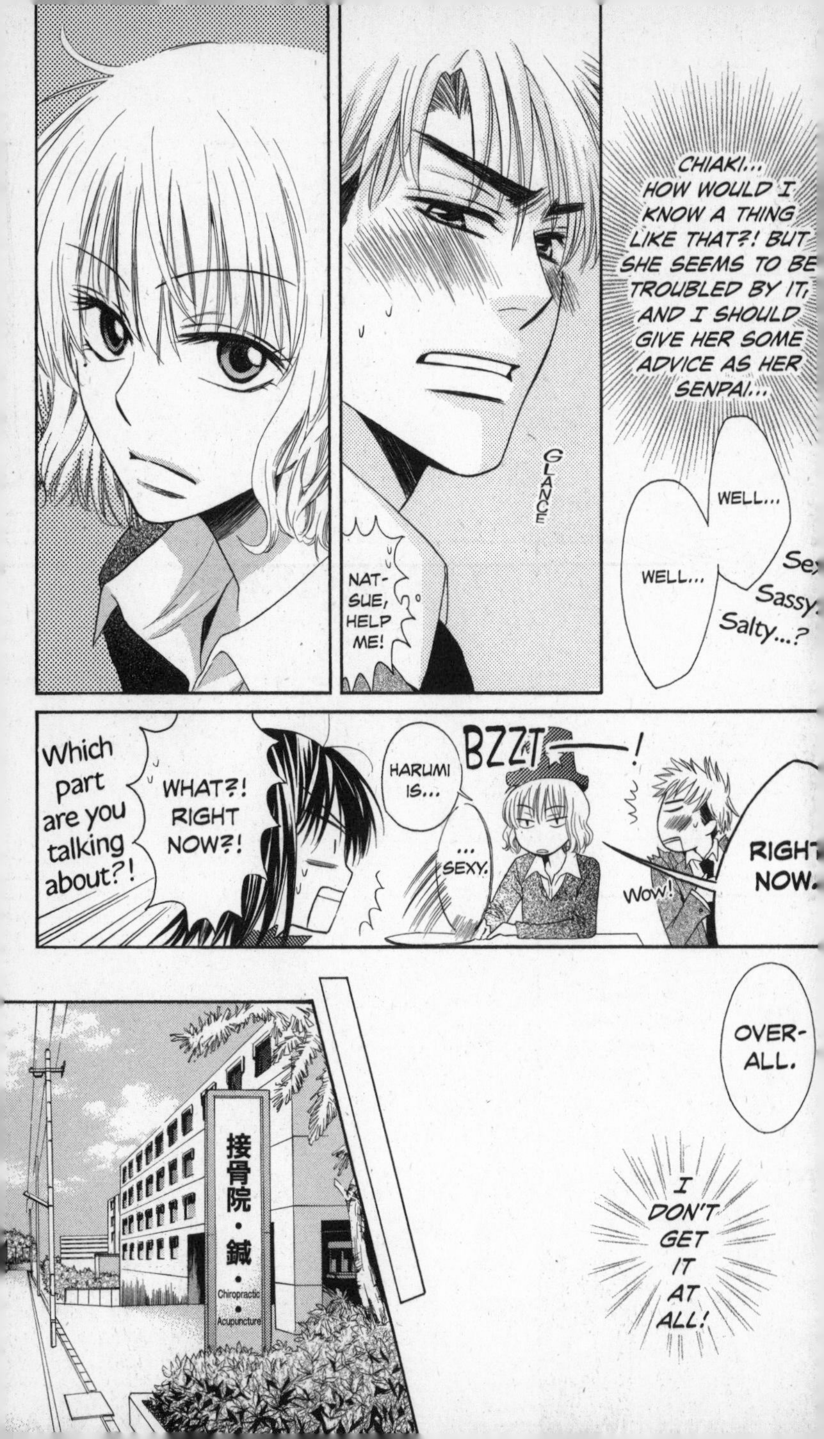
CHIAKI... HOW WOULD I KNOW A THING LIKE THAT?! BUT SHE SEEMS TO BE TROUBLED BY IT, AND I SHOULD GIVE HER SOME ADVICE AS HER SENPAI...
WELL...
WELL...
Se
Sassy.
Salty...?
GLANCE
NAT-SUE, HELP ME!
RIGHT NOW.
Wow!
BZZT—!
HARUMI IS...
...SEXY.
WHAT?! RIGHT NOW?!
Which part are you talking about?!
OVER-ALL.
I DON'T GET IT AT ALL!
接骨院・鍼・
Chiropractic
•
Acupuncture

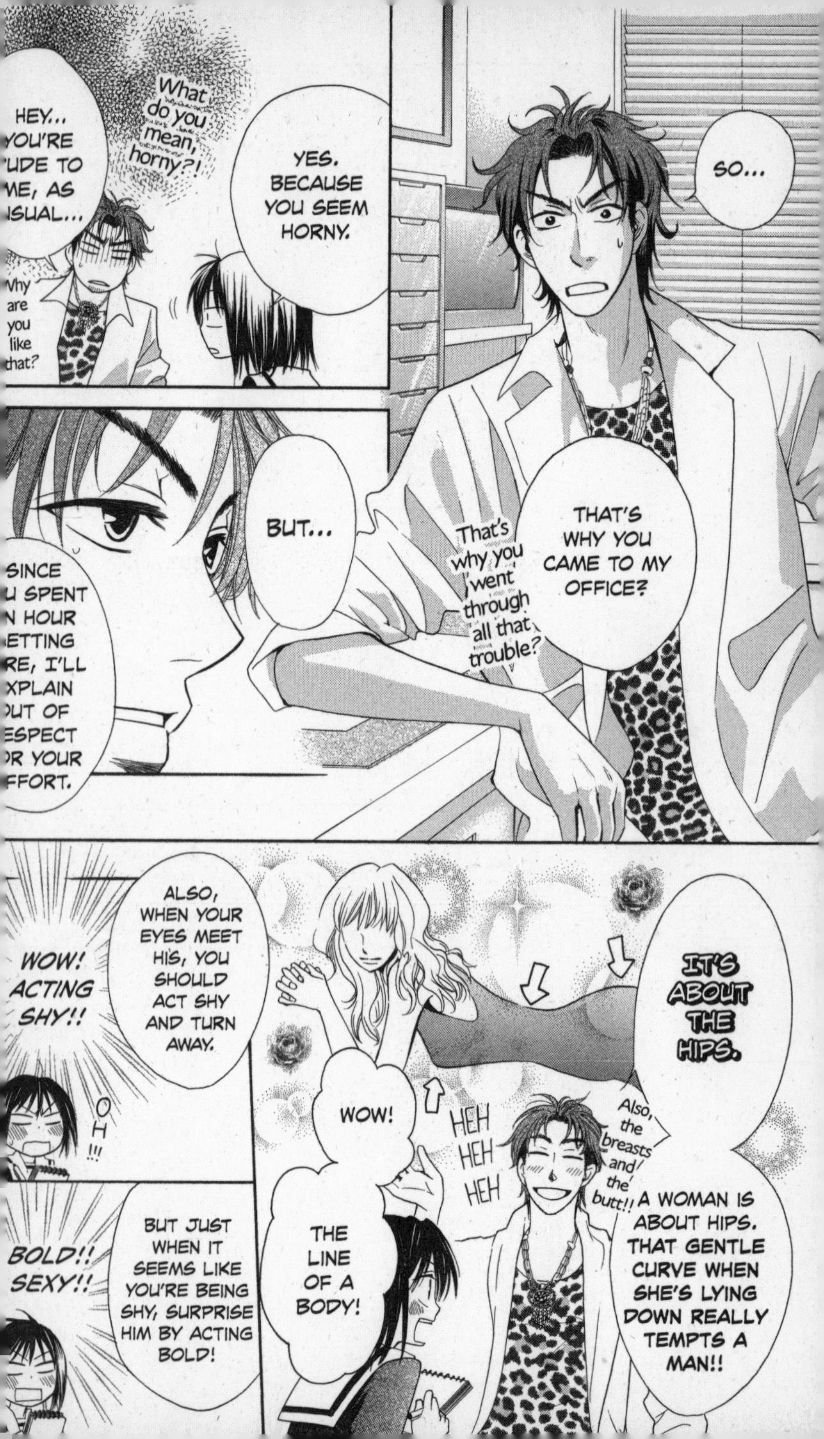
SO...
THAT'S WHY YOU CAME TO MY OFFICE?
That's why you went through all that trouble?
YES. BECAUSE YOU SEEM HORNY.
What do you mean, horny?!
HEY... YOU'RE UDE TO ME, AS SUAL...
Why are you like that?
BUT...
SINCE U SPENT N HOUR ETTING RE, I'LL XPLAIN UT OF ESPECT R YOUR FFORT.
IT'S ABOUT THE HIPS.
A WOMAN IS ABOUT HIPS. THAT GENTLE CURVE WHEN SHE'S LYING DOWN REALLY TEMPTS A MAN!!
Also, the breasts and the butt!!
HEH HEH HEH
WOW!
THE LINE OF A BODY!
ALSO, WHEN YOUR EYES MEET HIS, YOU SHOULD ACT SHY AND TURN AWAY.
WOW! ACTING SHY!!
OH!!!
BUT JUST WHEN IT SEEMS LIKE YOU'RE BEING SHY, SURPRISE HIM BY ACTING BOLD!
BOLD!! SEXY!!

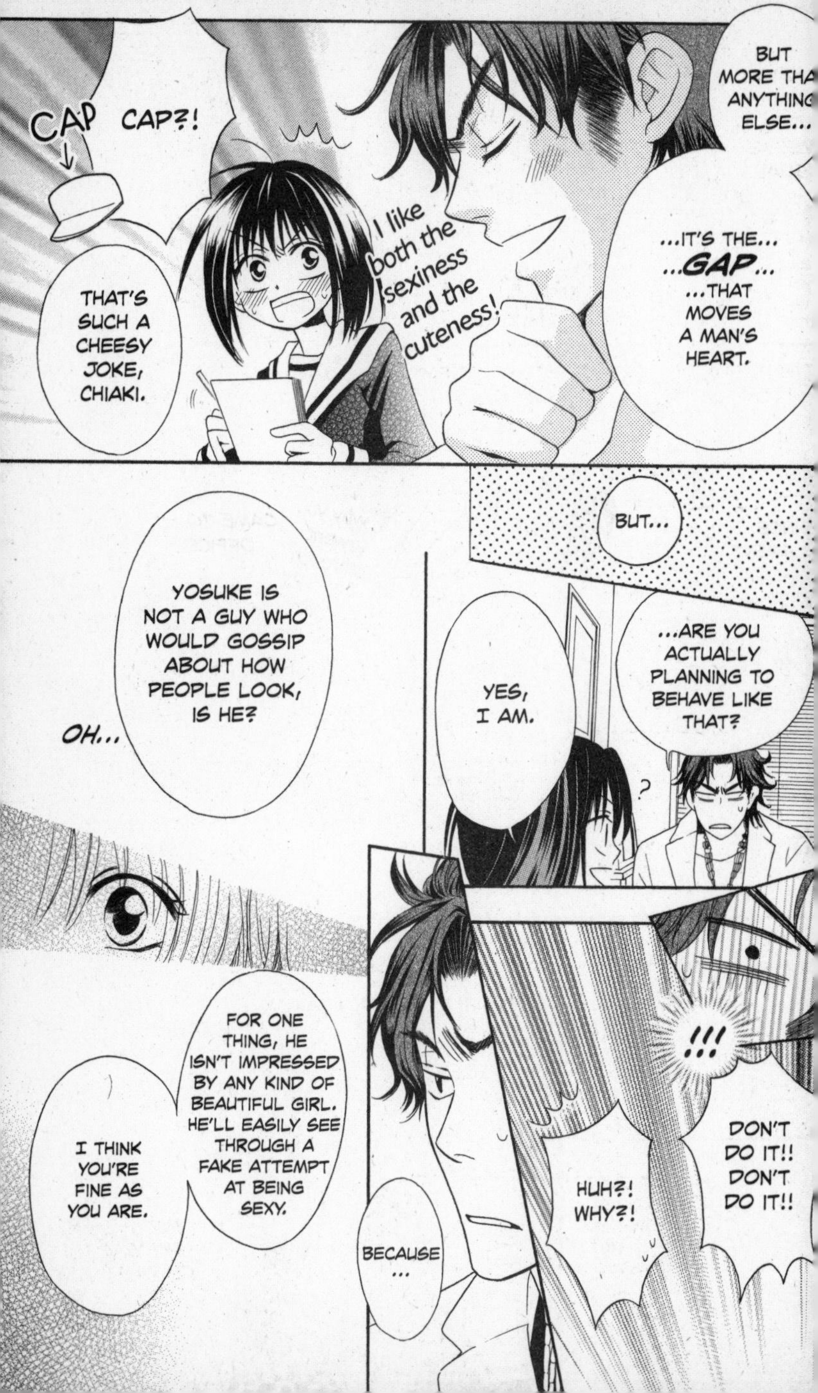
BUT MORE THA ANYTHING ELSE...
...IT'S THE... ...GAP... ...THAT MOVES A MAN'S HEART.
I like both the sexiness and the cuteness!
CAP
CAP?!
THAT'S SUCH A CHEESY JOKE, CHIAKI.
BUT...
...ARE YOU ACTUALLY PLANNING TO BEHAVE LIKE THAT?
YES, I AM.
?
!!!
DON'T DO IT!! DON'T DO IT!!
HUH?! WHY?!
BECAUSE ...
YOSUKE IS NOT A GUY WHO WOULD GOSSIP ABOUT HOW PEOPLE LOOK, IS HE?
OH...
FOR ONE THING, HE ISN'T IMPRESSED BY ANY KIND OF BEAUTIFUL GIRL. HE'LL EASILY SEE THROUGH A FAKE ATTEMPT AT BEING SEXY.
I THINK YOU'RE FINE AS YOU ARE.

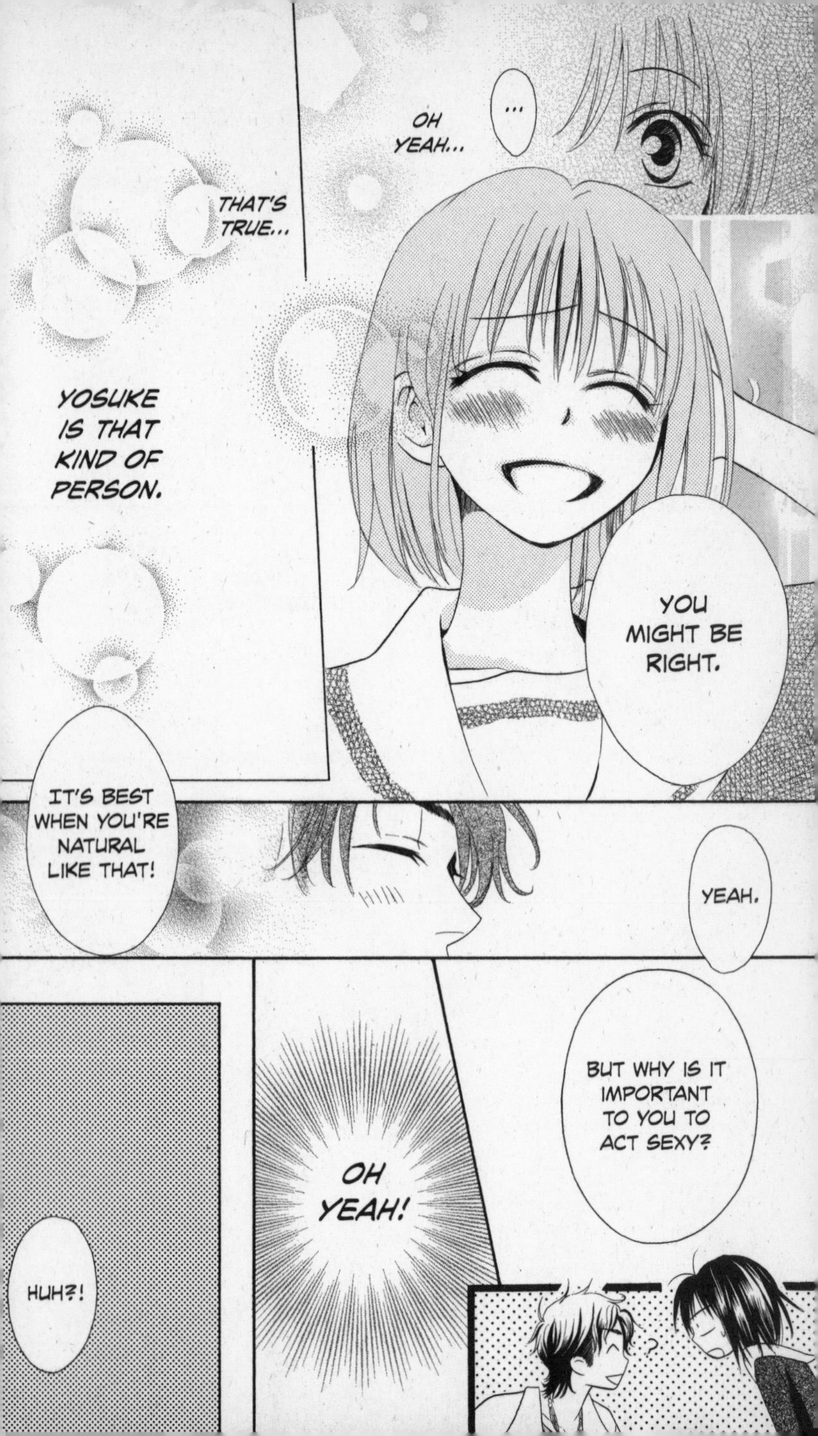
...
OH YEAH...
YOU MIGHT BE RIGHT.
THAT'S TRUE...
YOSUKE IS THAT KIND OF PERSON.
IT'S BEST WHEN YOU'RE NATURAL LIKE THAT!
YEAH.
BUT WHY IS IT IMPORTANT TO YOU TO ACT SEXY?
?
OH YEAH!
HUH?!

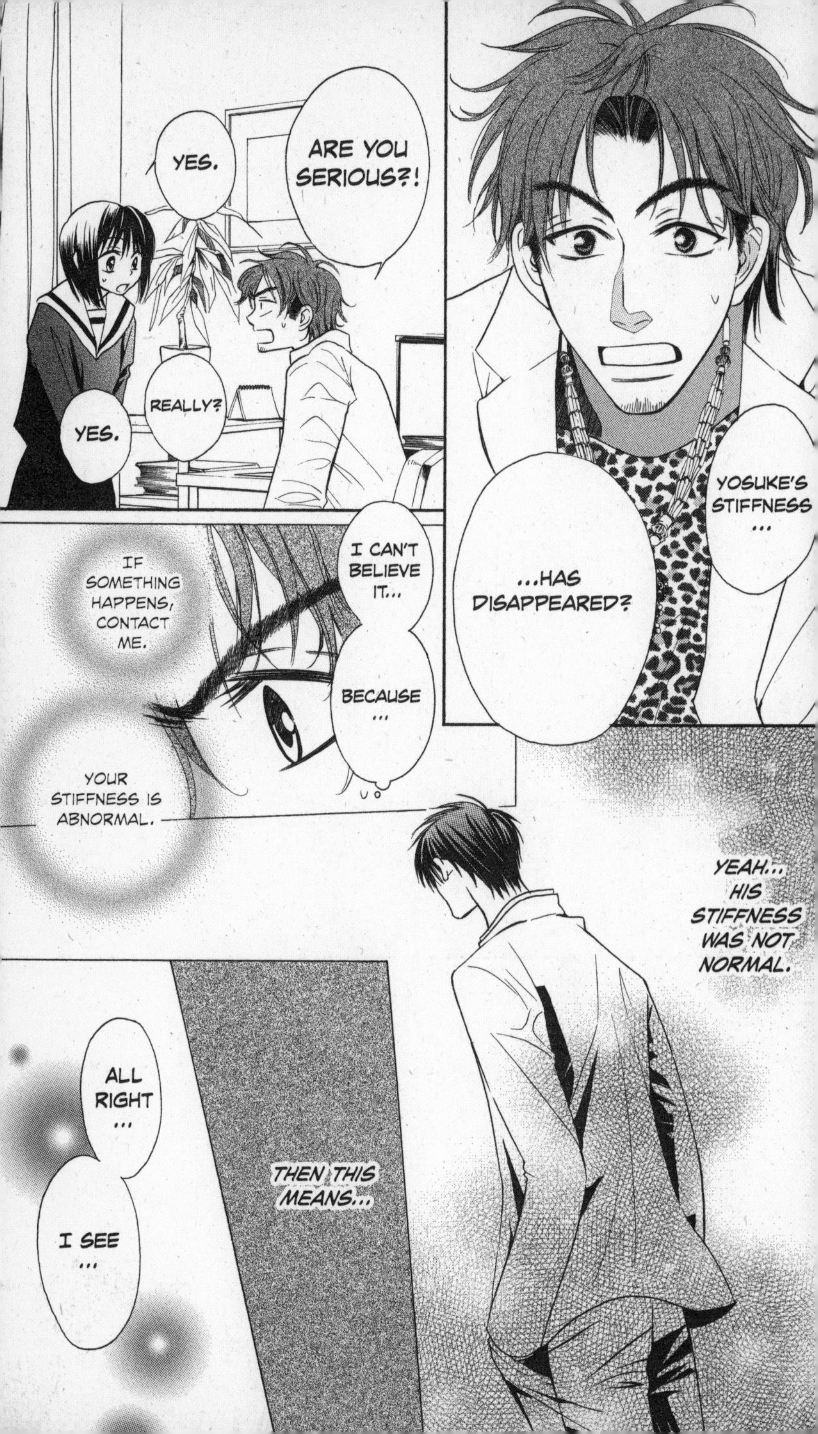
YOSUKE'S STIFFNESS ...
...HAS DISAPPEARED?
ARE YOU SERIOUS?!
YES.
REALLY?
YES.
I CAN'T BELIEVE IT...
BECAUSE ...
IF SOMETHING HAPPENS, CONTACT ME.
YOUR STIFFNESS IS ABNORMAL.
YEAH... HIS STIFFNESS WAS NOT NORMAL.
THEN THIS MEANS...
ALL RIGHT ...
I SEE ...

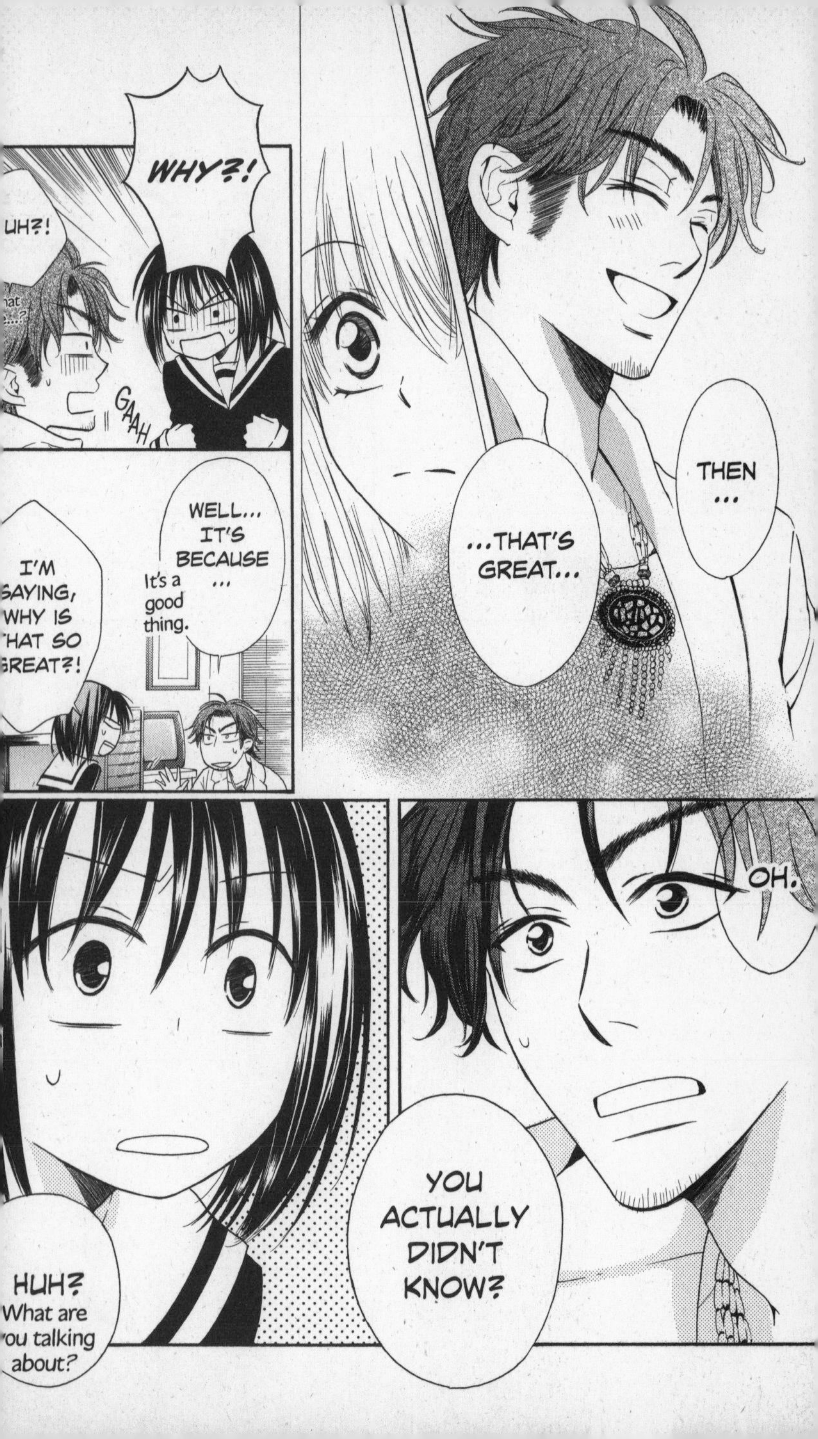
THEN...
...THAT'S GREAT...
WHY?!
UH?!
GAAH
WELL... IT'S BECAUSE...
It's a good thing.
I'M SAYING, WHY IS THAT SO GREAT?!
OH.
YOU ACTUALLY DIDN'T KNOW?
HUH? What are you talking about?

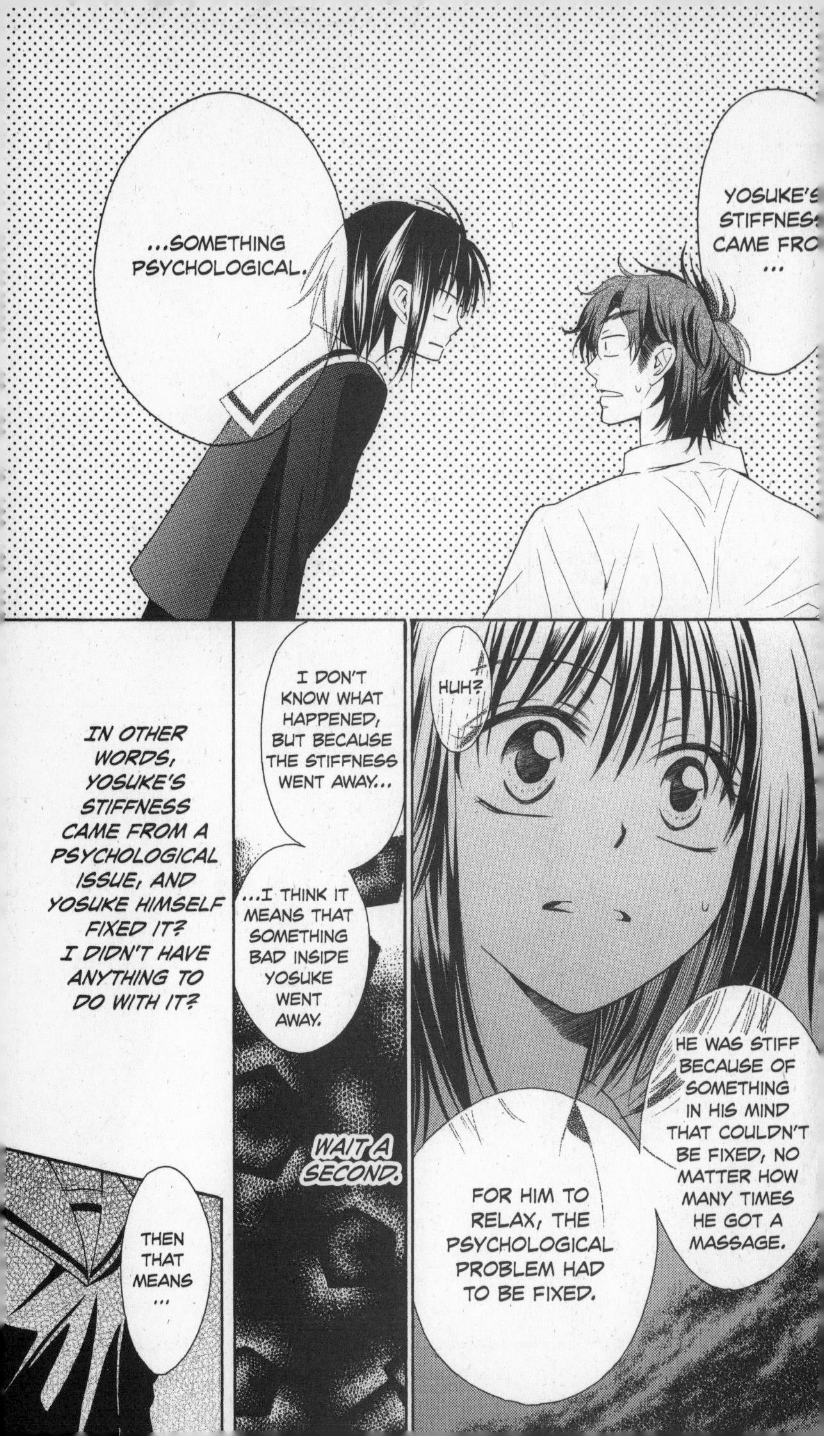

YOSUKE'S STIFFNESS CAME FRO ...
...SOMETHING PSYCHOLOGICAL.
HUH?
HE WAS STIFF BECAUSE OF SOMETHING IN HIS MIND THAT COULDN'T BE FIXED, NO MATTER HOW MANY TIMES HE GOT A MASSAGE.
FOR HIM TO RELAX, THE PSYCHOLOGICAL PROBLEM HAD TO BE FIXED.
I DON'T KNOW WHAT HAPPENED, BUT BECAUSE THE STIFFNESS WENT AWAY...
...I THINK IT MEANS THAT SOMETHING BAD INSIDE YOSUKE WENT AWAY.
WAIT A SECOND.
IN OTHER WORDS, YOSUKE'S STIFFNESS CAME FROM A PSYCHOLOGICAL ISSUE, AND YOSUKE HIMSELF FIXED IT? I DIDN'T HAVE ANYTHING TO DO WITH IT?
THEN THAT MEANS ...

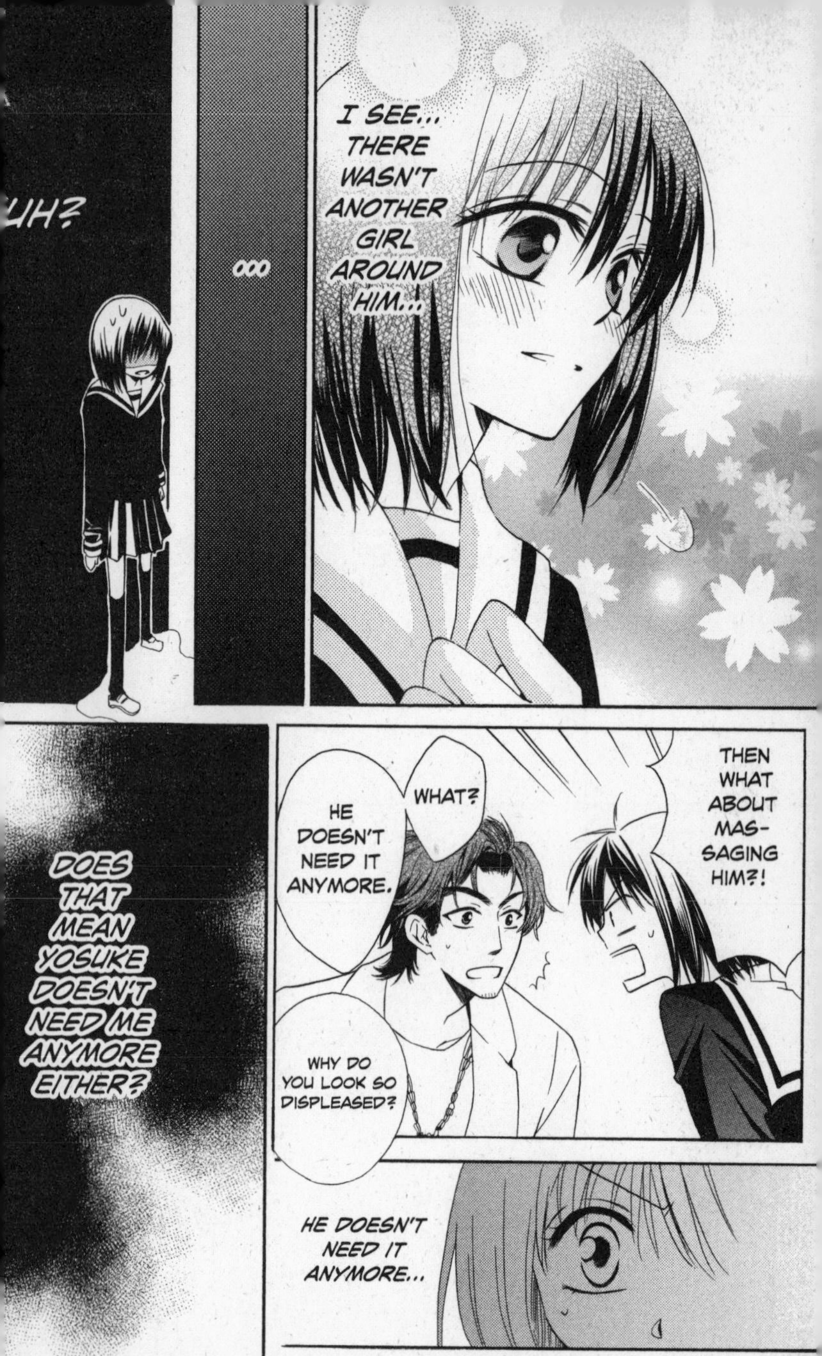

I SEE... THERE WASN'T ANOTHER GIRL AROUND HIM...
...
UH?
THEN WHAT ABOUT MAS-SAGING HIM?!
WHAT?
HE DOESN'T NEED IT ANYMORE.
WHY DO YOU LOOK SO DISPLEASED?
HE DOESN'T NEED IT ANYMORE...
DOES THAT MEAN YOSUKE DOESN'T NEED ME ANYMORE EITHER?

The Magic Touch, Part 49/The End

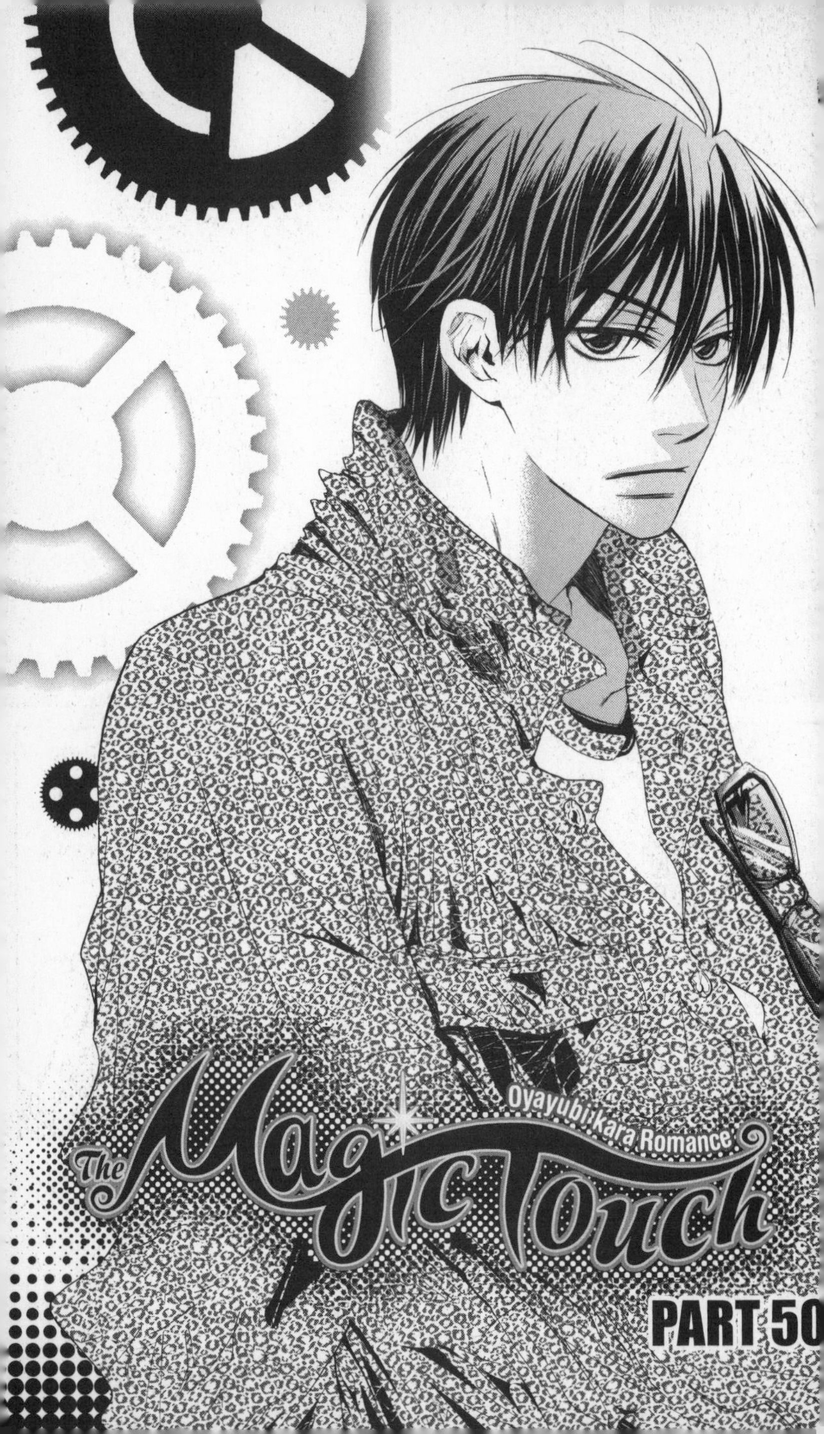

The Magic Touch
Oyayubi kara Romance
PART 50

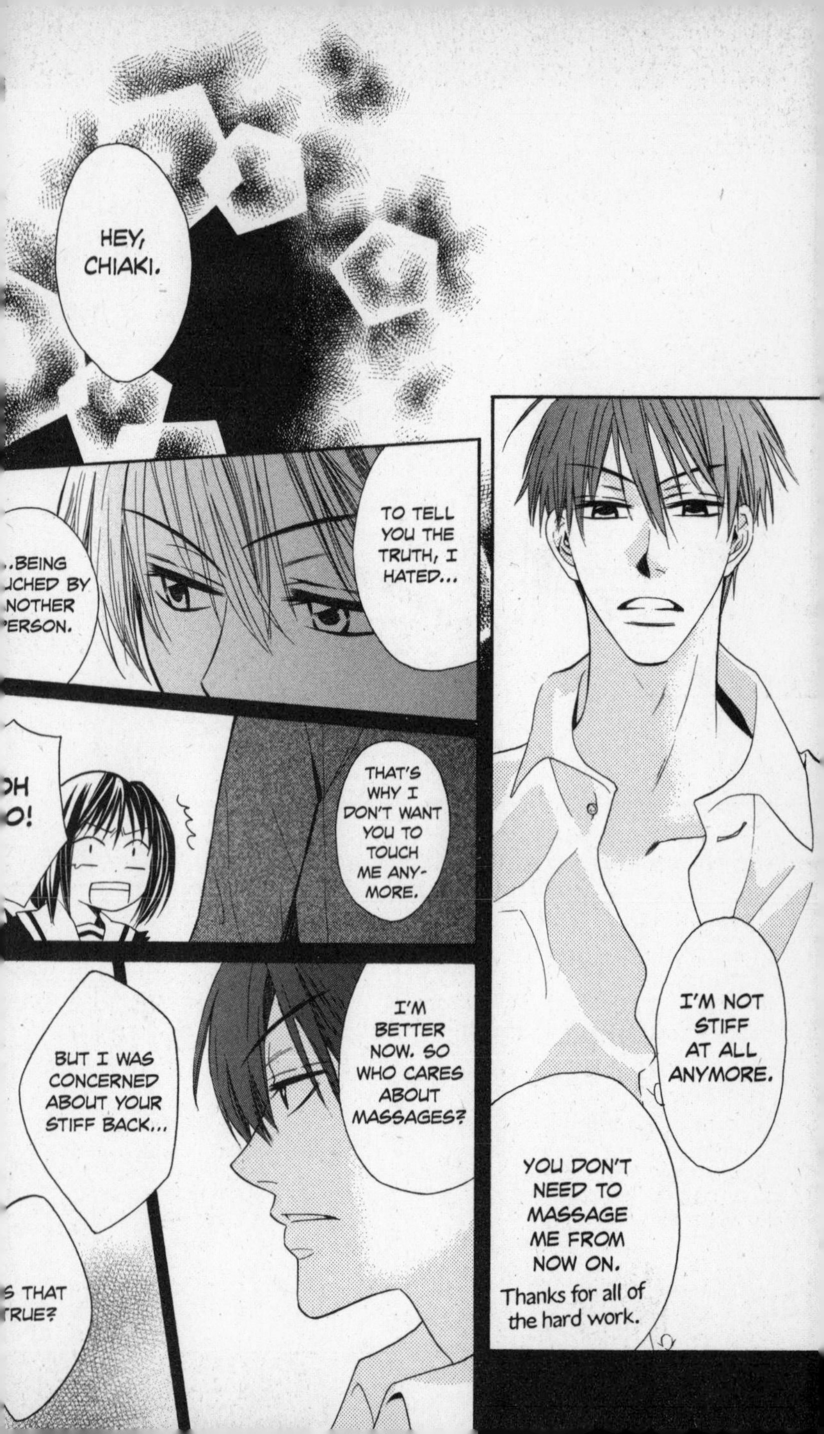
HEY, CHIAKI.
I'M NOT STIFF AT ALL ANYMORE.
YOU DON'T NEED TO MASSAGE ME FROM NOW ON.
Thanks for all of the hard work.
TO TELL YOU THE TRUTH, I HATED...
..BEING UCHED BY NOTHER ERSON.
THAT'S WHY I DON'T WANT YOU TO TOUCH ME ANY-MORE.
H O!
I'M BETTER NOW. SO WHO CARES ABOUT MASSAGES?
BUT I WAS CONCERNED ABOUT YOUR STIFF BACK...
S THAT TRUE?

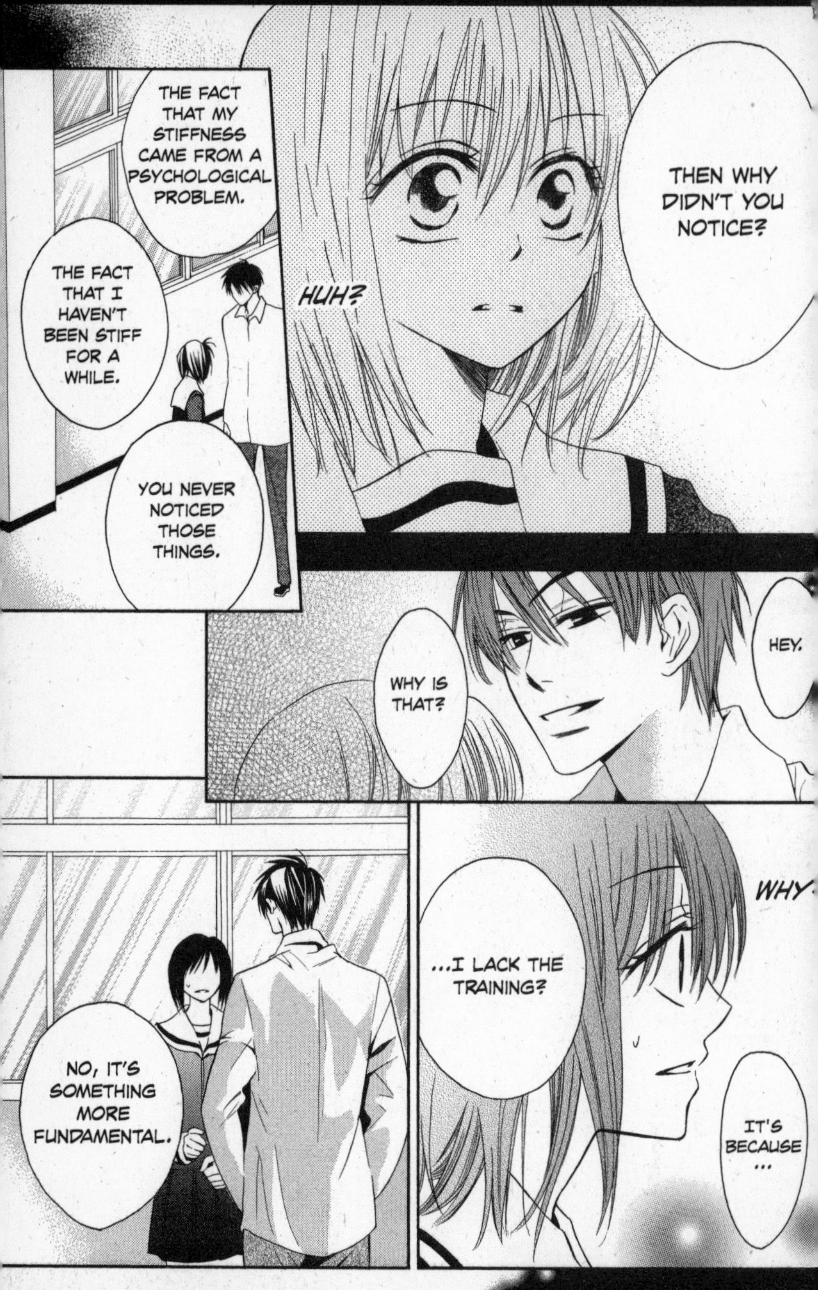
THEN WHY DIDN'T YOU NOTICE?
HUH?
THE FACT THAT MY STIFFNESS CAME FROM A PSYCHOLOGICAL PROBLEM.
THE FACT THAT I HAVEN'T BEEN STIFF FOR A WHILE.
YOU NEVER NOTICED THOSE THINGS.
HEY.
WHY IS THAT?
WHY...
...I LACK THE TRAINING?
IT'S BECAUSE...
NO, IT'S SOMETHING MORE FUNDAMENTAL.

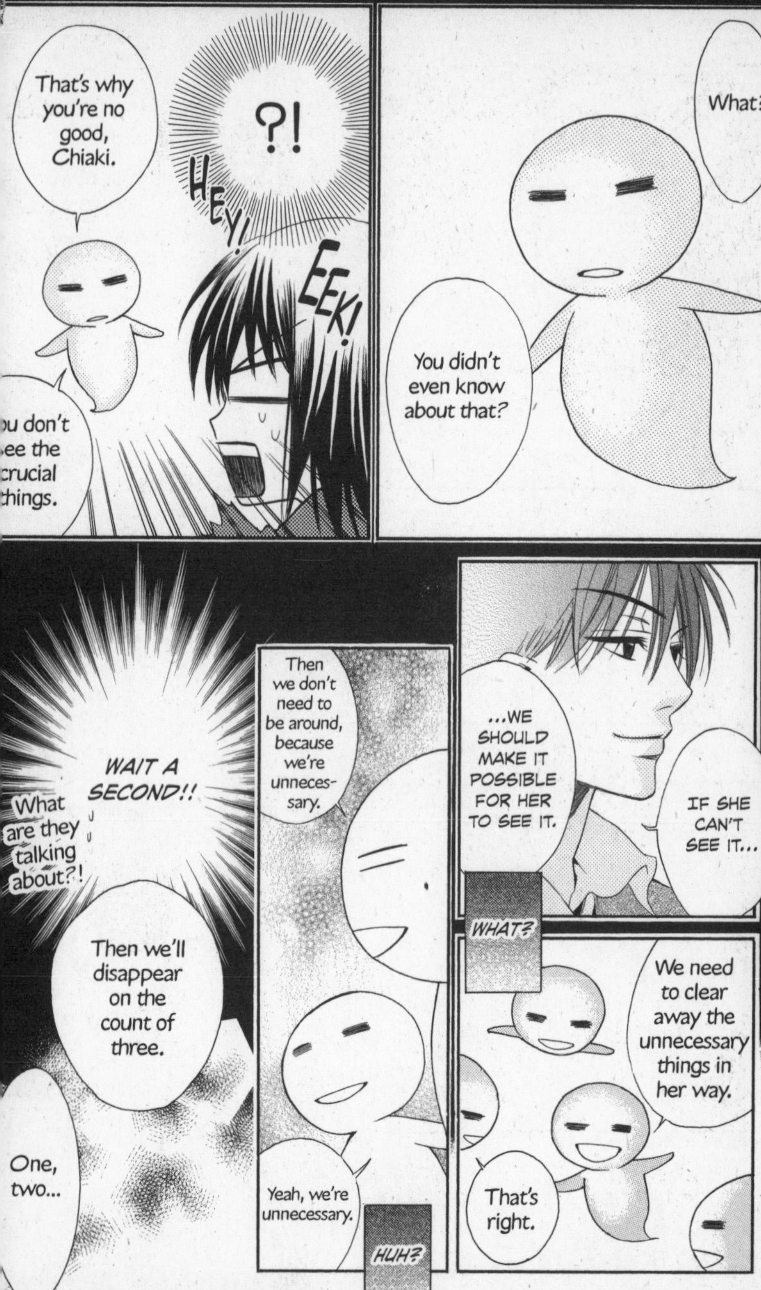

What?
You didn't even know about that?
That's why you're no good, Chiaki.
?!
HEY!
EEK!
u don't ee the rucial hings.
IF SHE CAN'T SEE IT...
...WE SHOULD MAKE IT POSSIBLE FOR HER TO SEE IT.
WHAT?
We need to clear away the unnecessary things in her way.
That's right.
Then we don't need to be around, because we're unnecessary.
Yeah, we're unnecessary.
HUH?
WAIT A SECOND!!
What are they talking about?!
Then we'll disappear on the count of three.
One, two...

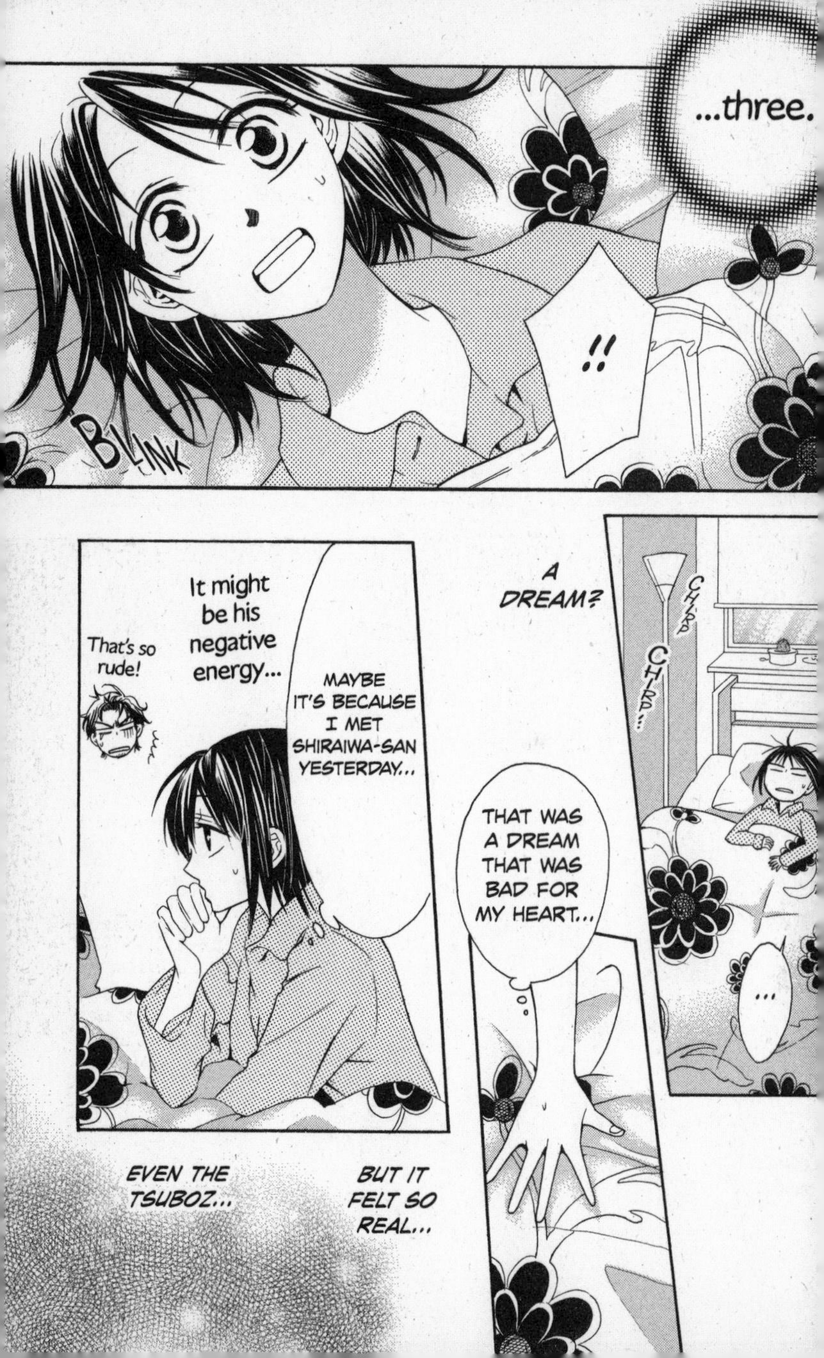
...three.
!!
BLINK
CHIRP
CHIRP...
...
A DREAM?
THAT WAS A DREAM THAT WAS BAD FOR MY HEART...
BUT IT FELT SO REAL...
MAYBE IT'S BECAUSE I MET SHIRAIWA-SAN YESTERDAY...
It might be his negative energy...
That's so rude!
EVEN THE TSUBOZ...

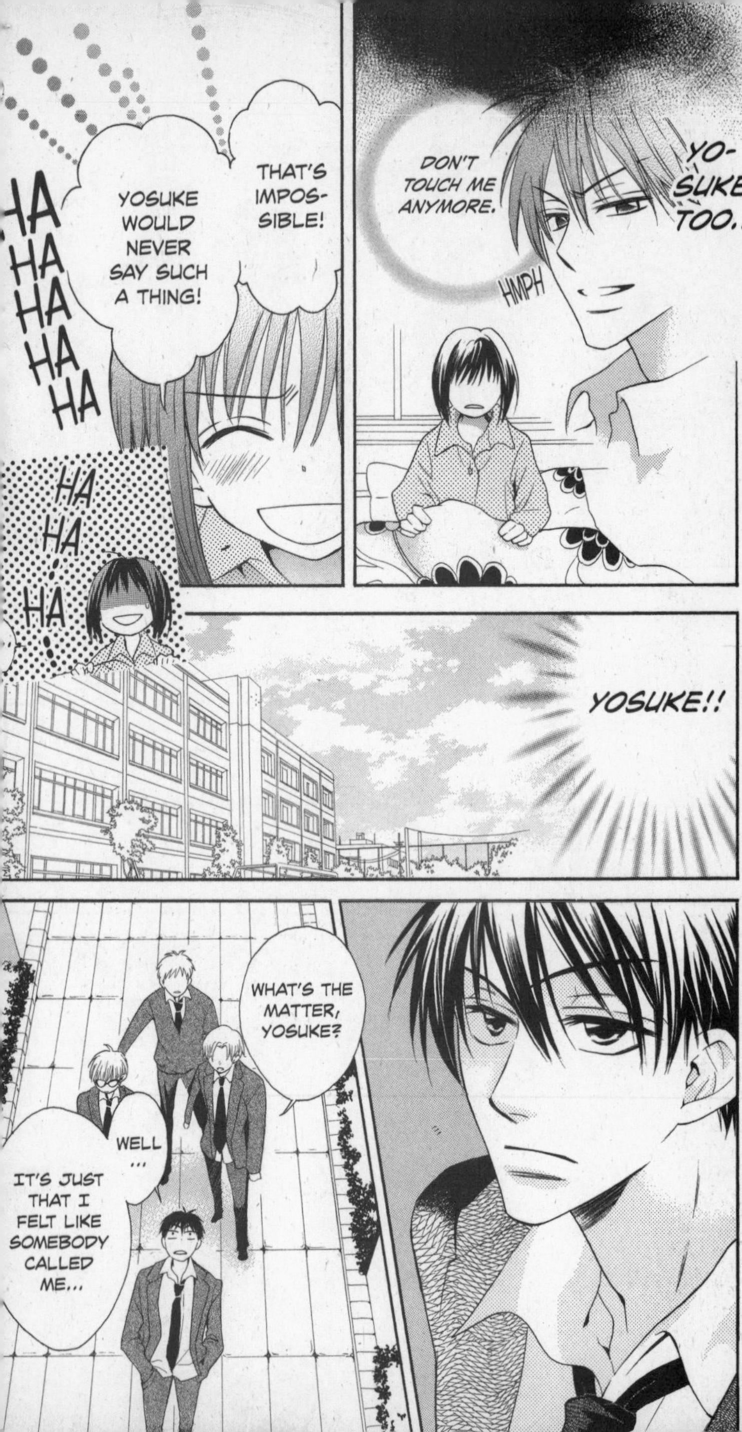
YO-SUKE TOO...
DON'T TOUCH ME ANYMORE.
HMPH
THAT'S IMPOS-SIBLE!
YOSUKE WOULD NEVER SAY SUCH A THING!
HA HA HA HA HA HA
HA HA HA
YOSUKE!!
WHAT'S THE MATTER, YOSUKE?
WELL...
IT'S JUST THAT I FELT LIKE SOMEBODY CALLED ME...

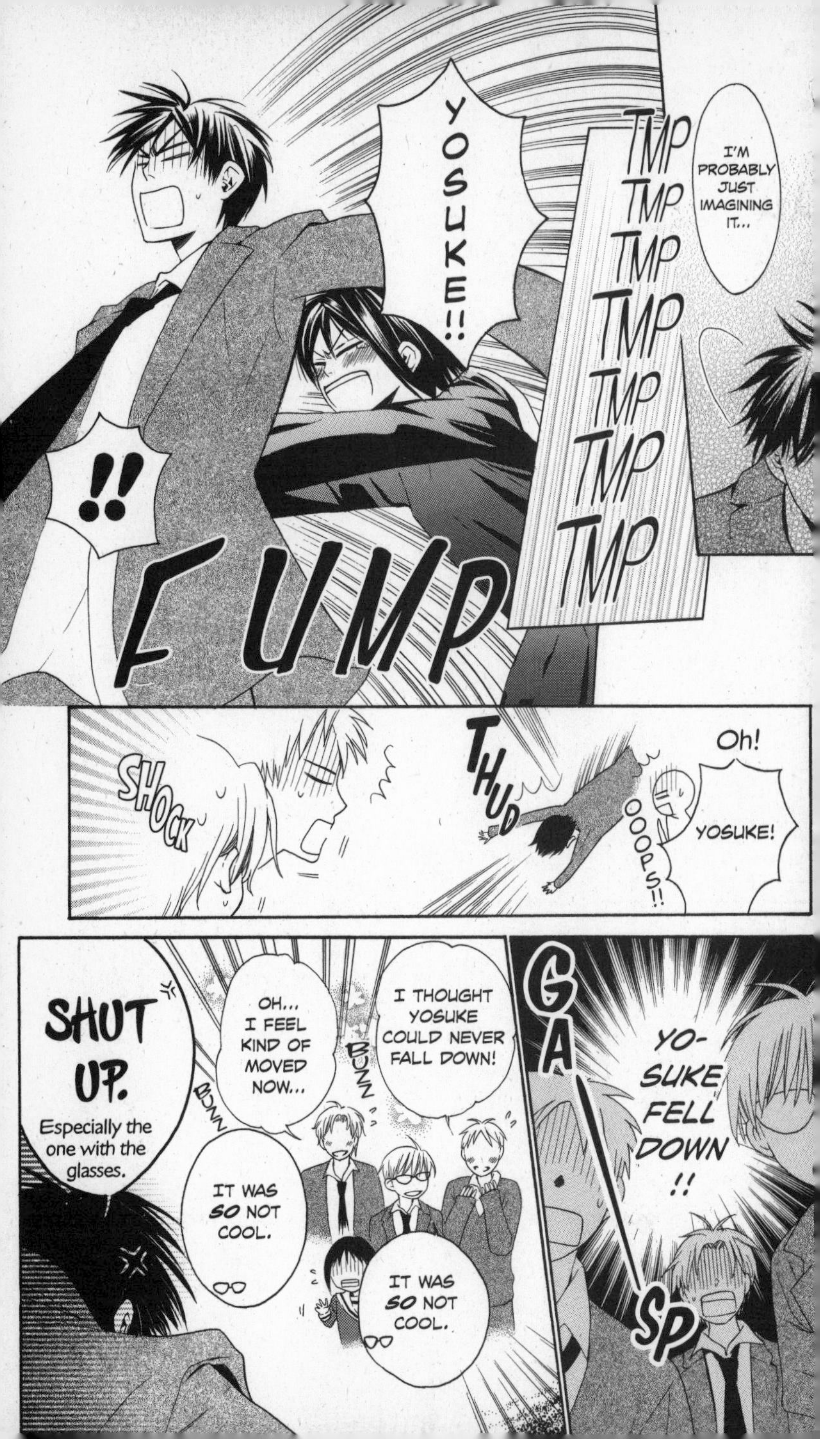
I'M PROBABLY JUST IMAGINING IT...
TMP TMP TMP TMP TMP TMP TMP
YOSUKE!!
!!
FUMP
Oh!
YOSUKE!
OOOPS!!
THUD
SHOCK
GA
YO-SUKE FELL DOWN!!
SP
I THOUGHT YOSUKE COULD NEVER FALL DOWN!
OH... I FEEL KIND OF MOVED NOW...
BUZZ
BUZZ
SHUT UP.
Especially the one with the glasses.
IT WAS SO NOT COOL.
IT WAS SO NOT COOL.

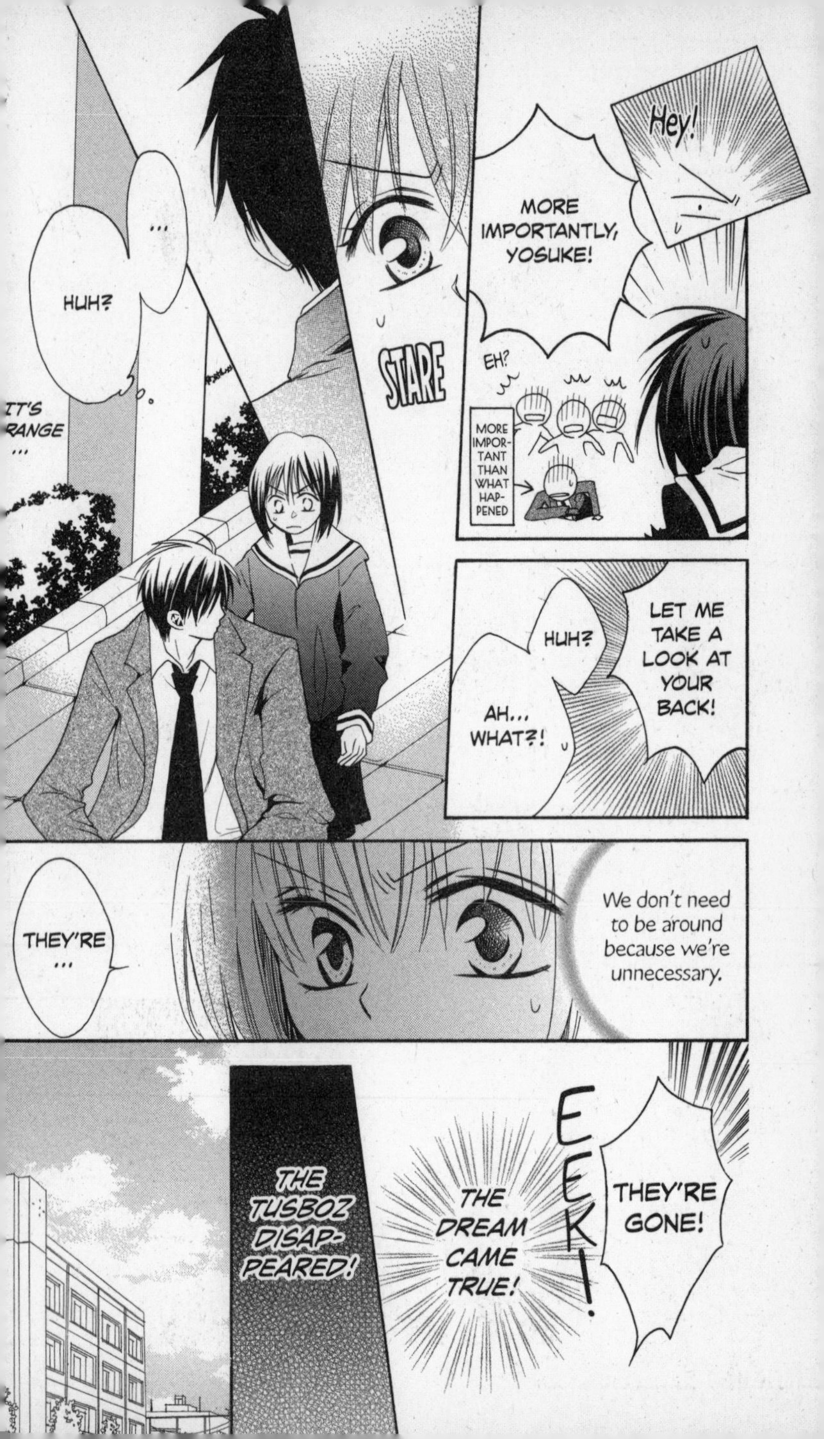
Hey!
MORE IMPORTANTLY, YOSUKE!
EH?
MORE IMPOR-TANT THAN WHAT HAP-PENED
LET ME TAKE A LOOK AT YOUR BACK!
HUH?
AH... WHAT?!
STARE
...
HUH?
IT'S RANGE ...
We don't need to be around because we're unnecessary.
THEY'RE ...
THEY'RE GONE!
EEK!
THE DREAM CAME TRUE!
THE TUSBOZ DISAP-PEARED!

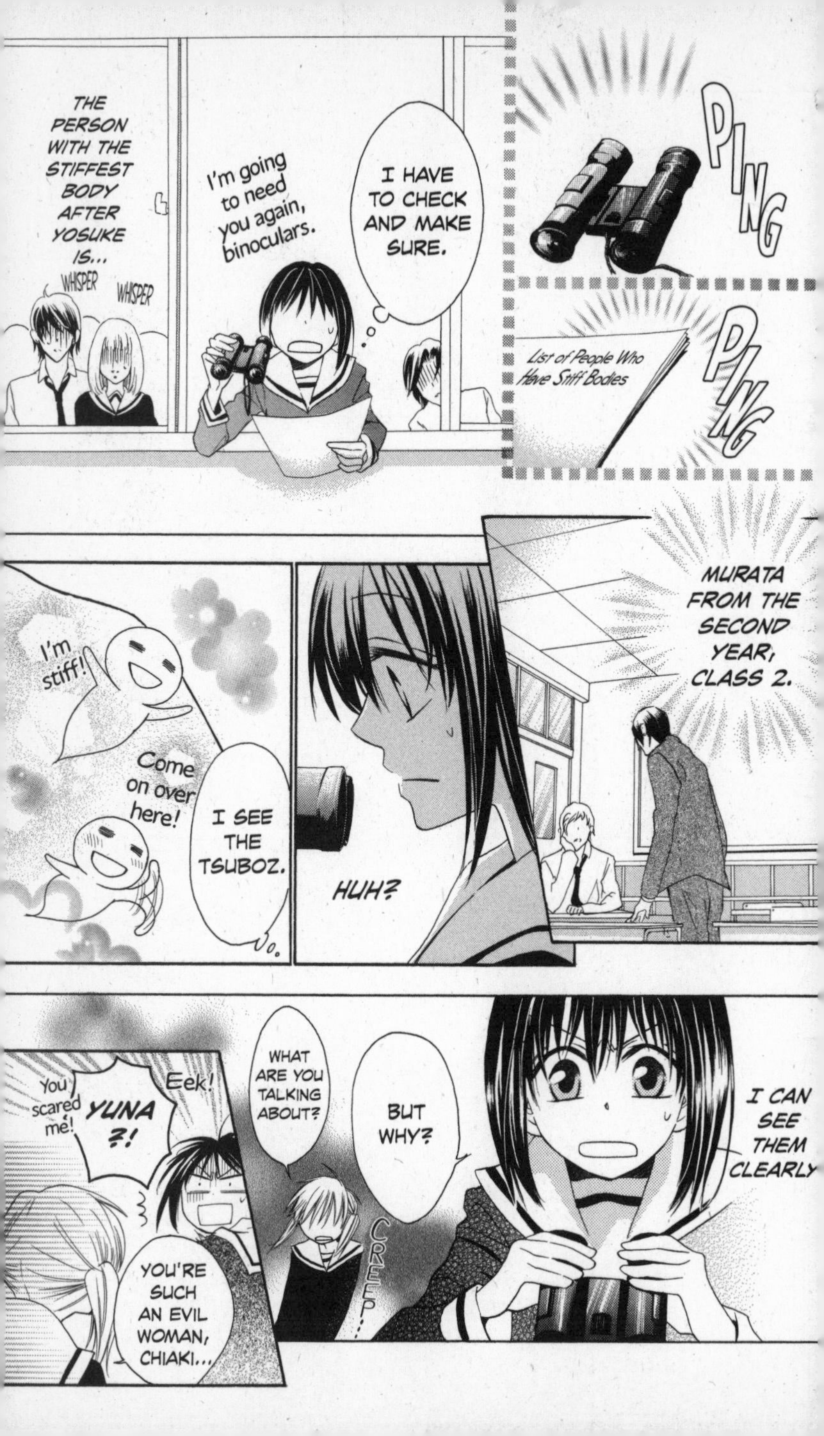
PING
List of People Who Have Stiff Bodies
PING
I HAVE TO CHECK AND MAKE SURE.
I'm going to need you again, binoculars.
THE PERSON WITH THE STIFFEST BODY AFTER YOSUKE IS...
WHISPER
WHISPER
MURATA FROM THE SECOND YEAR, CLASS 2.
HUH?
I SEE THE TSUBOZ.
Come on over here!
I'm stiff!
I CAN SEE THEM CLEARLY
BUT WHY?
WHAT ARE YOU TALKING ABOUT?
Eek!
YUNA ?!
You scared me!
CREEP...
YOU'RE SUCH AN EVIL WOMAN, CHIAKI...

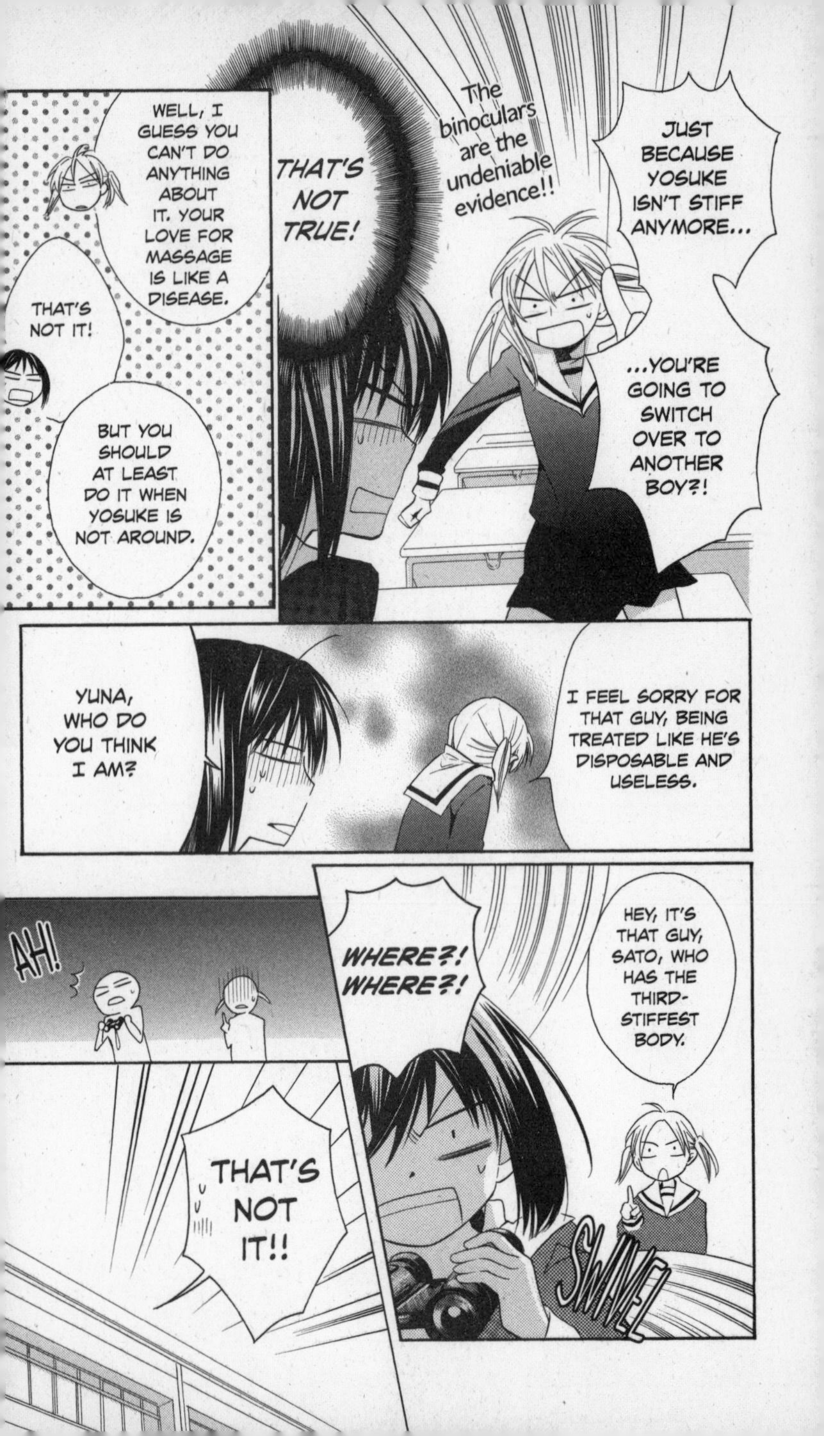
JUST BECAUSE YOSUKE ISN'T STIFF ANYMORE...
...YOU'RE GOING TO SWITCH OVER TO ANOTHER BOY?!
The binoculars are the undeniable evidence!!
THAT'S NOT TRUE!
WELL, I GUESS YOU CAN'T DO ANYTHING ABOUT IT. YOUR LOVE FOR MASSAGE IS LIKE A DISEASE.
THAT'S NOT IT!
BUT YOU SHOULD AT LEAST DO IT WHEN YOSUKE IS NOT AROUND.
I FEEL SORRY FOR THAT GUY, BEING TREATED LIKE HE'S DISPOSABLE AND USELESS.
YUNA, WHO DO YOU THINK I AM?
HEY, IT'S THAT GUY, SATO, WHO HAS THE THIRD-STIFFEST BODY.
WHERE?! WHERE?!
SWIVEL
AH!
THAT'S NOT IT!!

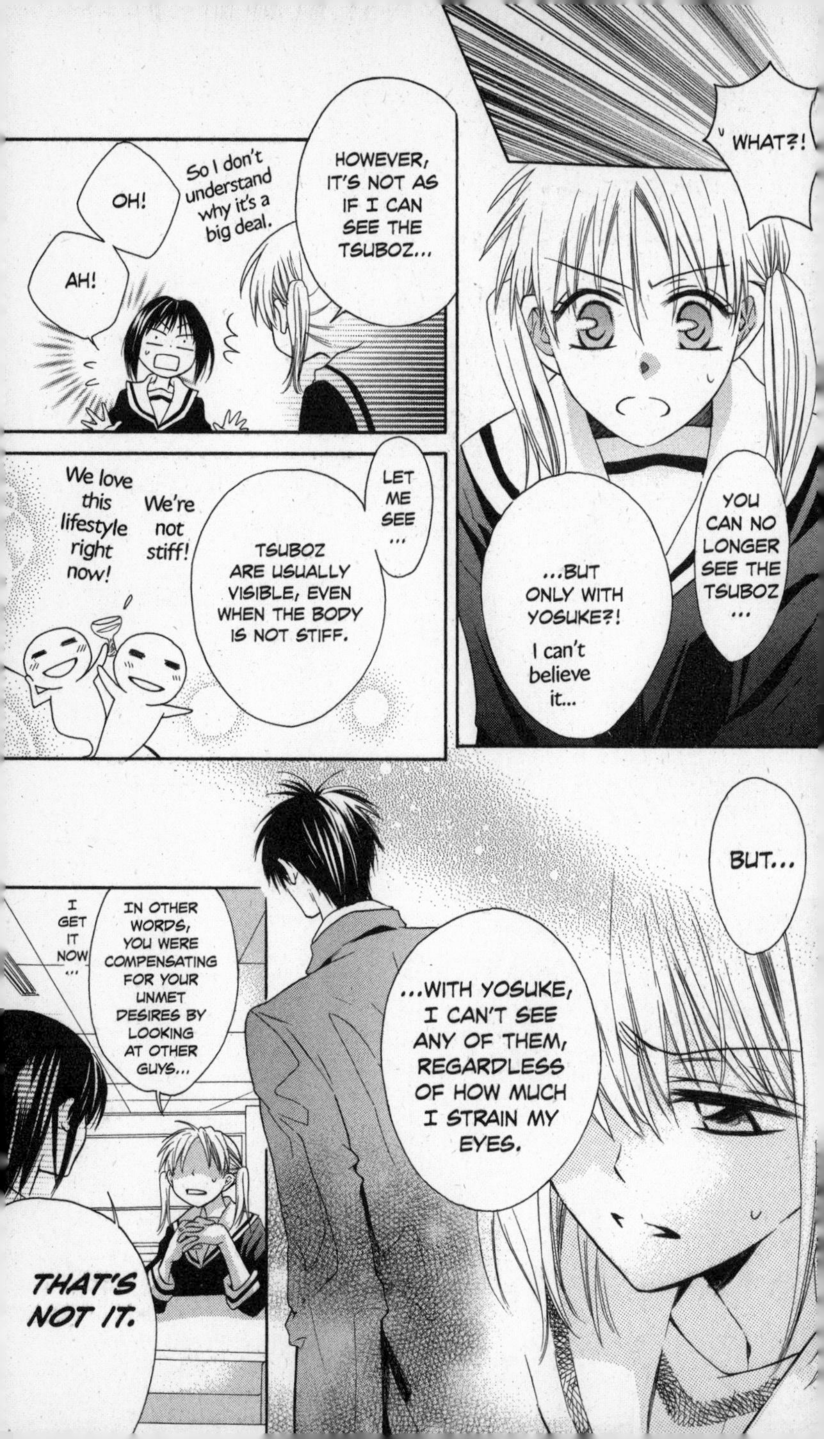
WHAT?!
YOU CAN NO LONGER SEE THE TSUBOZ...
...BUT ONLY WITH YOSUKE?!
I can't believe it...
HOWEVER, IT'S NOT AS IF I CAN SEE THE TSUBOZ...
So I don't understand why it's a big deal.
OH!
AH!
LET ME SEE...
TSUBOZ ARE USUALLY VISIBLE, EVEN WHEN THE BODY IS NOT STIFF.
We're not stiff!
We love this lifestyle right now!
BUT...
...WITH YOSUKE, I CAN'T SEE ANY OF THEM, REGARDLESS OF HOW MUCH I STRAIN MY EYES.
IN OTHER WORDS, YOU WERE COMPENSATING FOR YOUR UNMET DESIRES BY LOOKING AT OTHER GUYS...
I GET IT NOW...
THAT'S NOT IT.

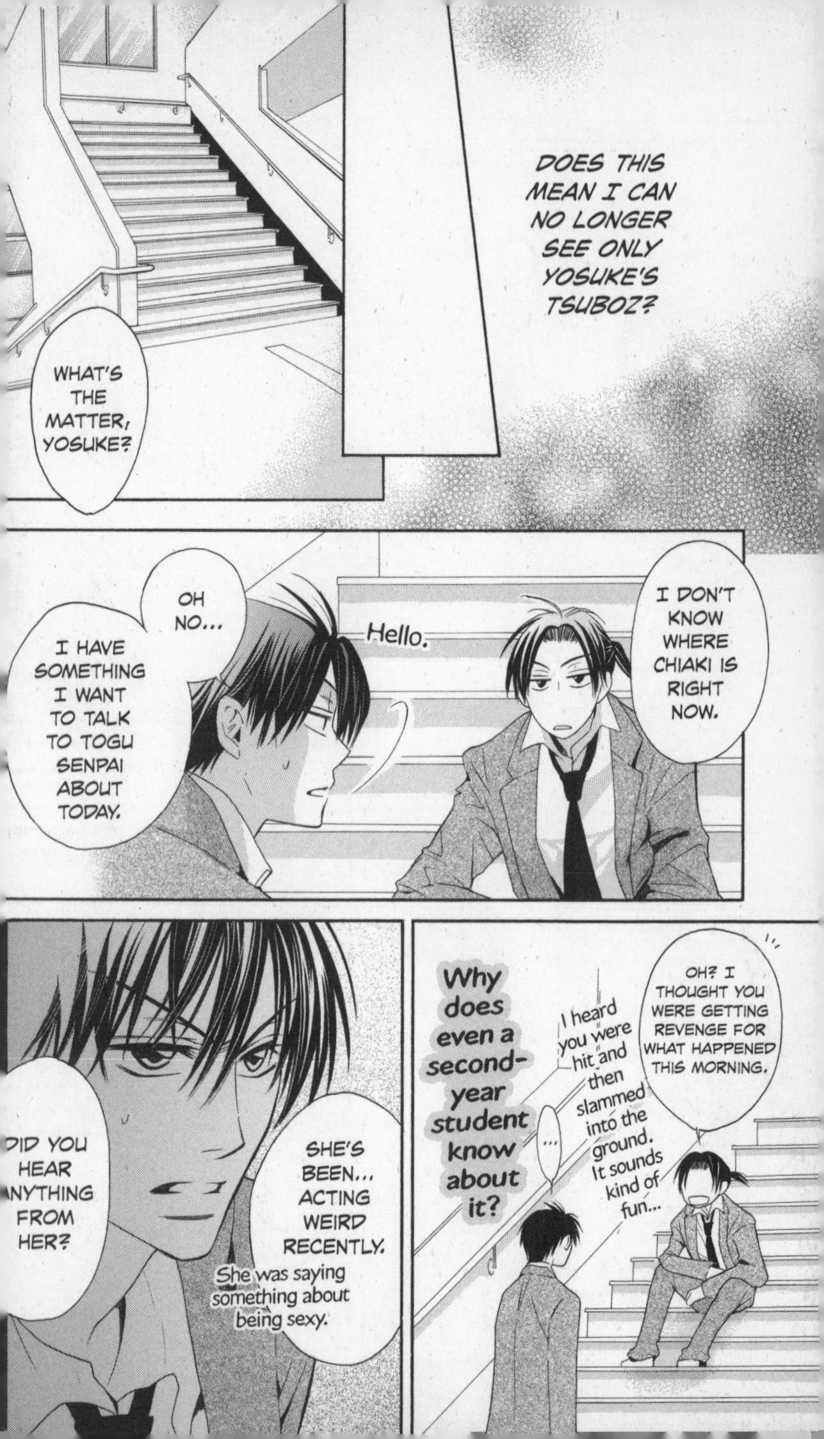

DOES THIS MEAN I CAN NO LONGER SEE ONLY YOSUKE'S TSUBOZ?
WHAT'S THE MATTER, YOSUKE?
I DON'T KNOW WHERE CHIAKI IS RIGHT NOW.
OH NO...
Hello.
I HAVE SOMETHING I WANT TO TALK TO TOGU SENPAI ABOUT TODAY.
OH? I THOUGHT YOU WERE GETTING REVENGE FOR WHAT HAPPENED THIS MORNING.
I heard you were hit and then slammed into the ground. It sounds kind of fun...
...
Why does even a second-year student know about it?
SHE'S BEEN... ACTING WEIRD RECENTLY.
She was saying something about being sexy.
DID YOU HEAR ANYTHING FROM HER?

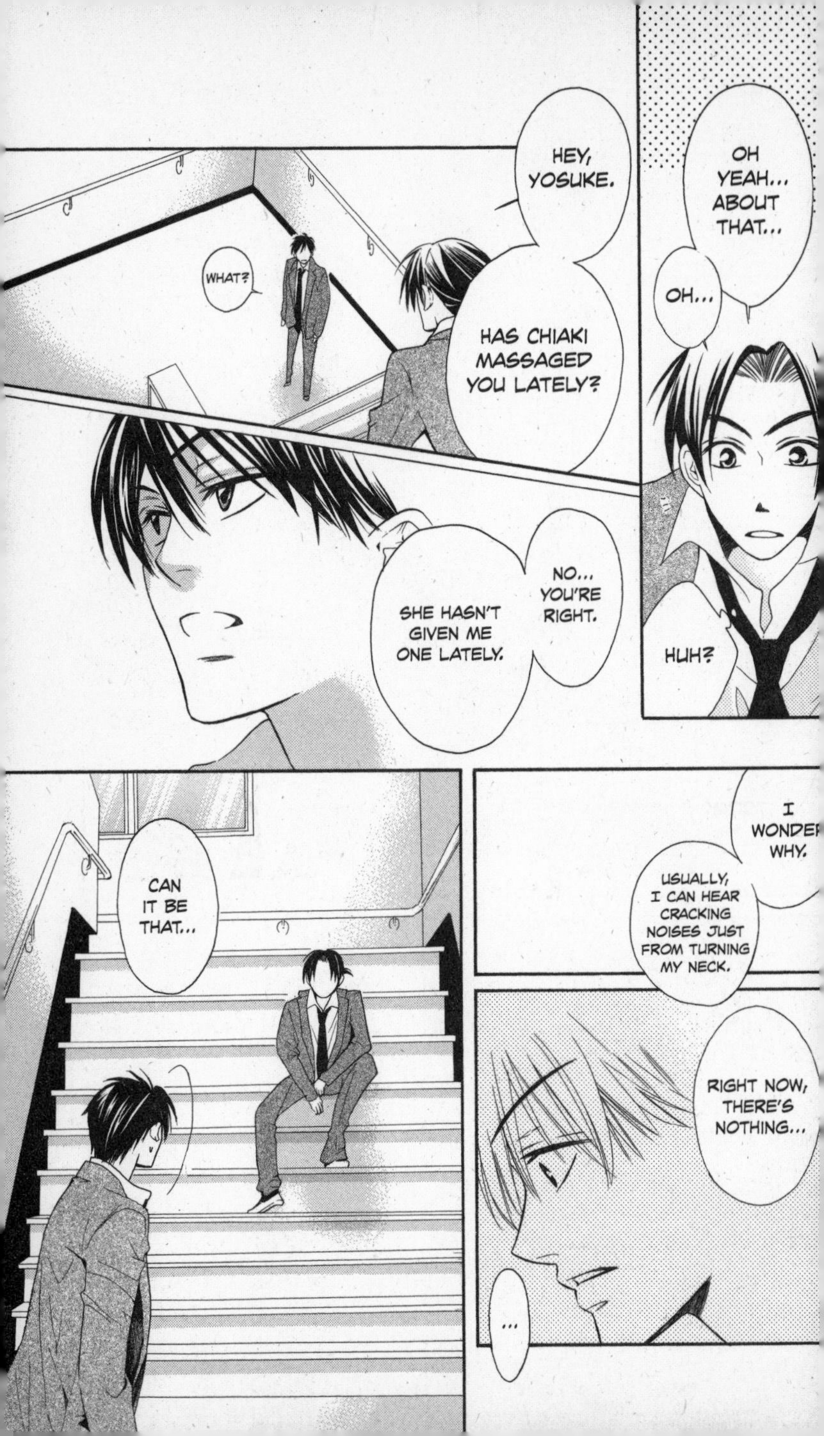
OH YEAH... ABOUT THAT...
OH...
HUH?
HEY, YOSUKE.
WHAT?
HAS CHIAKI MASSAGED YOU LATELY?
NO... YOU'RE RIGHT.
SHE HASN'T GIVEN ME ONE LATELY.
I WONDER WHY.
USUALLY, I CAN HEAR CRACKING NOISES JUST FROM TURNING MY NECK.
RIGHT NOW, THERE'S NOTHING...
...
CAN IT BE THAT...

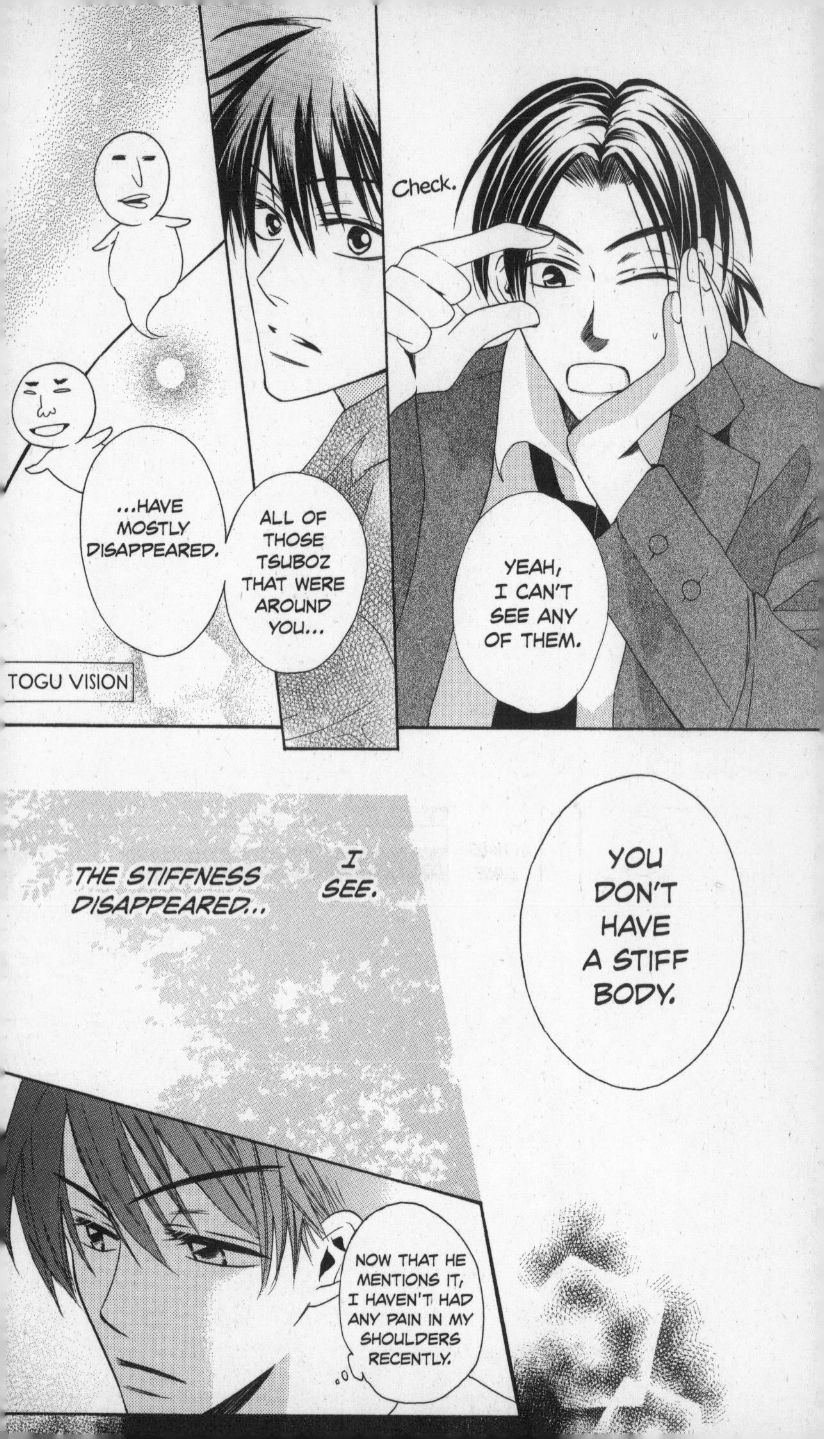
Check.
YEAH, I CAN'T SEE ANY OF THEM.
ALL OF THOSE TSUBOZ THAT WERE AROUND YOU...
...HAVE MOSTLY DISAPPEARED.
TOGU VISION
YOU DON'T HAVE A STIFF BODY.
I SEE.
THE STIFFNESS DISAPPEARED...
NOW THAT HE MENTIONS IT, I HAVEN'T HAD ANY PAIN IN MY SHOULDERS RECENTLY.

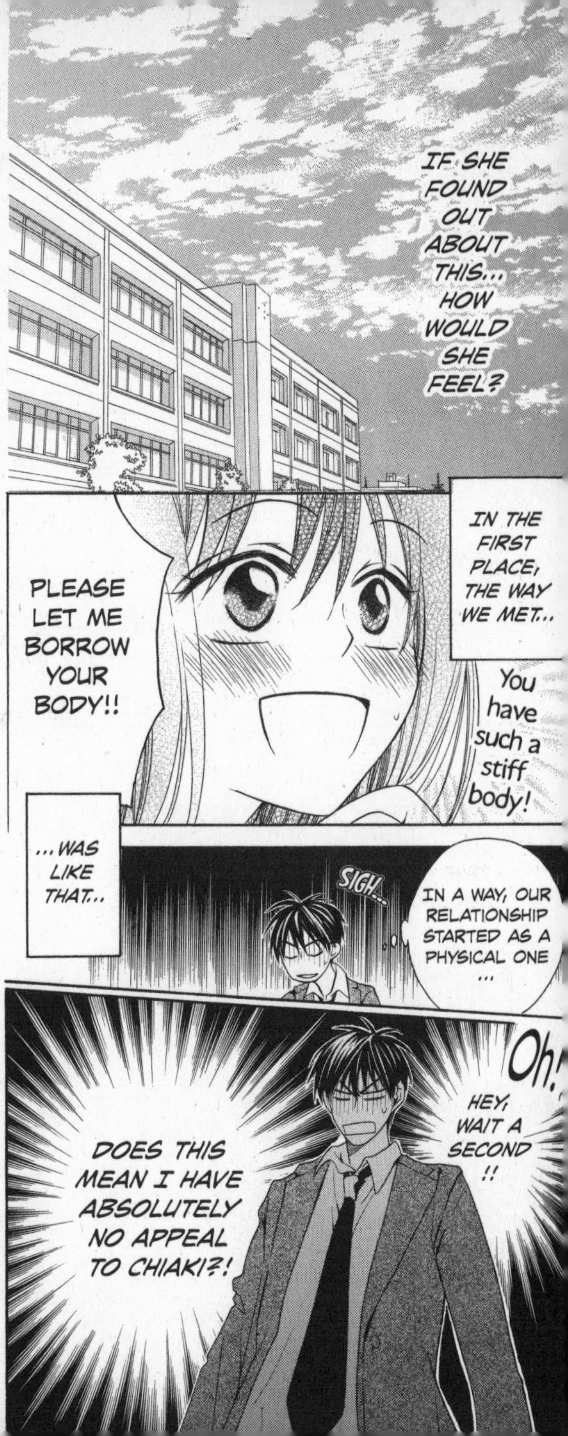
IF SHE FOUND OUT ABOUT THIS... HOW WOULD SHE FEEL?
IN THE FIRST PLACE, THE WAY WE MET...
You have such a stiff body!
PLEASE LET ME BORROW YOUR BODY!!
...WAS LIKE THAT...
IN A WAY, OUR RELATIONSHIP STARTED AS A PHYSICAL ONE...
SIGH...
Oh!
HEY, WAIT A SECOND!!
DOES THIS MEAN I HAVE ABSOLUTELY NO APPEAL TO CHIAKI?!

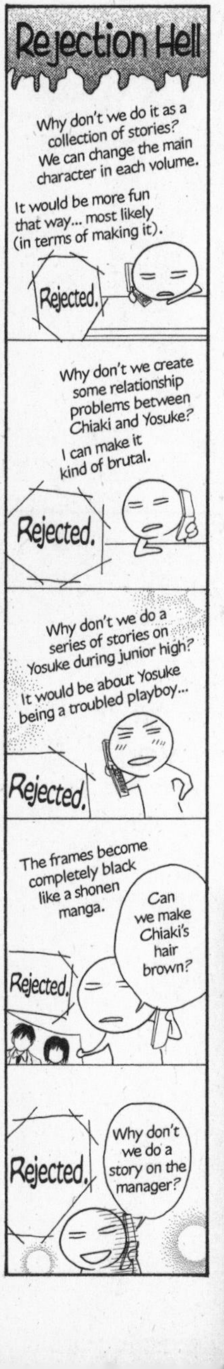
Rejection Hell
Why don't we do it as a collection of stories? We can change the main character in each volume.
It would be more fun that way... most likely (in terms of making it).
Rejected.
Why don't we create some relationship problems between Chiaki and Yosuke?
I can make it kind of brutal.
Rejected.
Why don't we do a series of stories on Yosuke during junior high?
It would be about Yosuke being a troubled playboy...
Rejected.
The frames become completely black like a shonen manga.
Can we make Chiaki's hair brown?
Rejected.
Why don't we do a story on the manager?
Rejected.

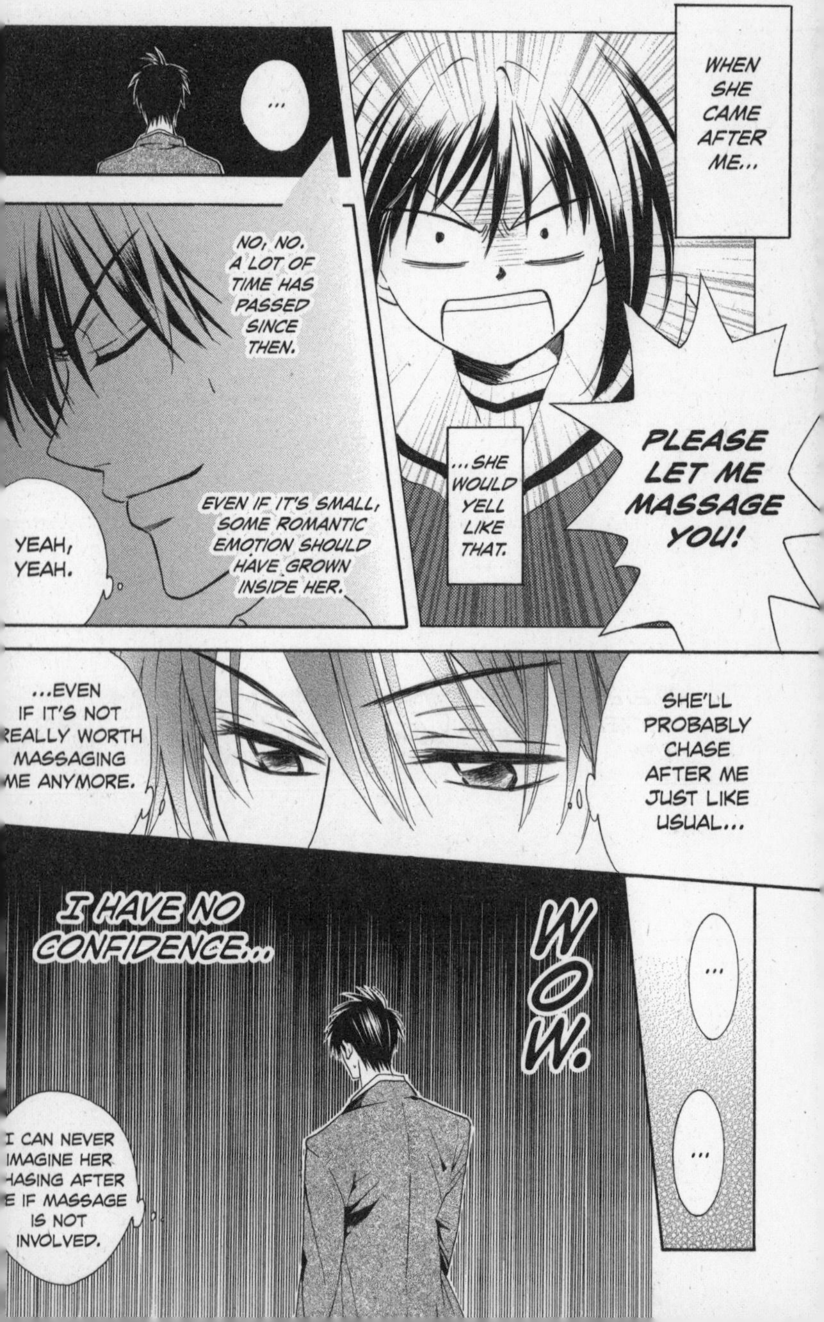
WHEN SHE CAME AFTER ME...
PLEASE LET ME MASSAGE YOU!
...SHE WOULD YELL LIKE THAT.
...
NO, NO. A LOT OF TIME HAS PASSED SINCE THEN.
EVEN IF IT'S SMALL, SOME ROMANTIC EMOTION SHOULD HAVE GROWN INSIDE HER.
YEAH, YEAH.
SHE'LL PROBABLY CHASE AFTER ME JUST LIKE USUAL...
...EVEN IF IT'S NOT REALLY WORTH MASSAGING ME ANYMORE.
...
...
WOW.
I HAVE NO CONFIDENCE...
I CAN NEVER IMAGINE HER HASING AFTER E IF MASSAGE IS NOT INVOLVED.

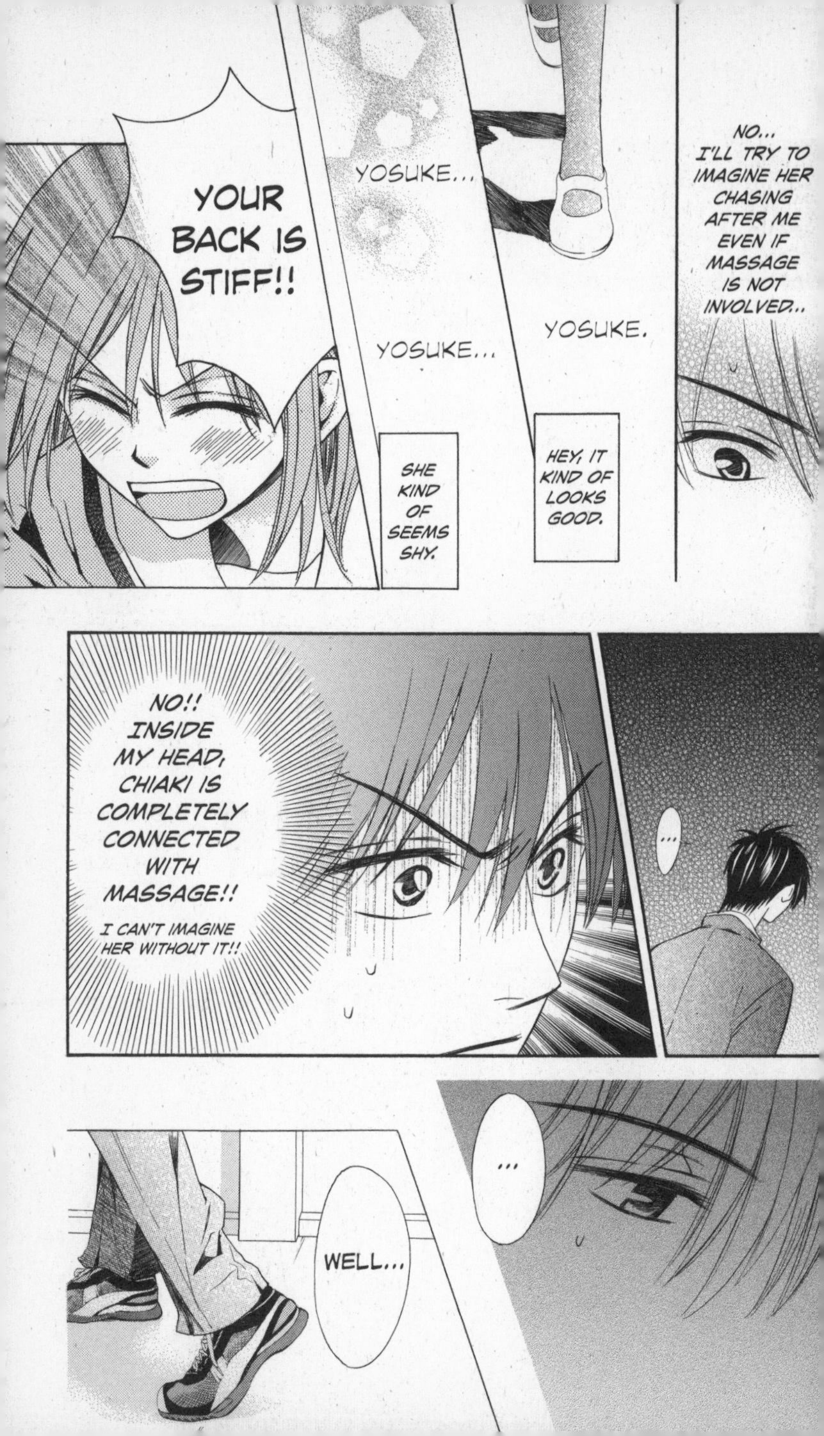
NO... I'LL TRY TO IMAGINE HER CHASING AFTER ME EVEN IF MASSAGE IS NOT INVOLVED...
YOSUKE.
HEY, IT KIND OF LOOKS GOOD.
YOSUKE...
YOSUKE...
SHE KIND OF SEEMS SHY.
YOUR BACK IS STIFF!!
...
NO!! INSIDE MY HEAD, CHIAKI IS COMPLETELY CONNECTED WITH MASSAGE!!
I CAN'T IMAGINE HER WITHOUT IT!!
...
WELL...

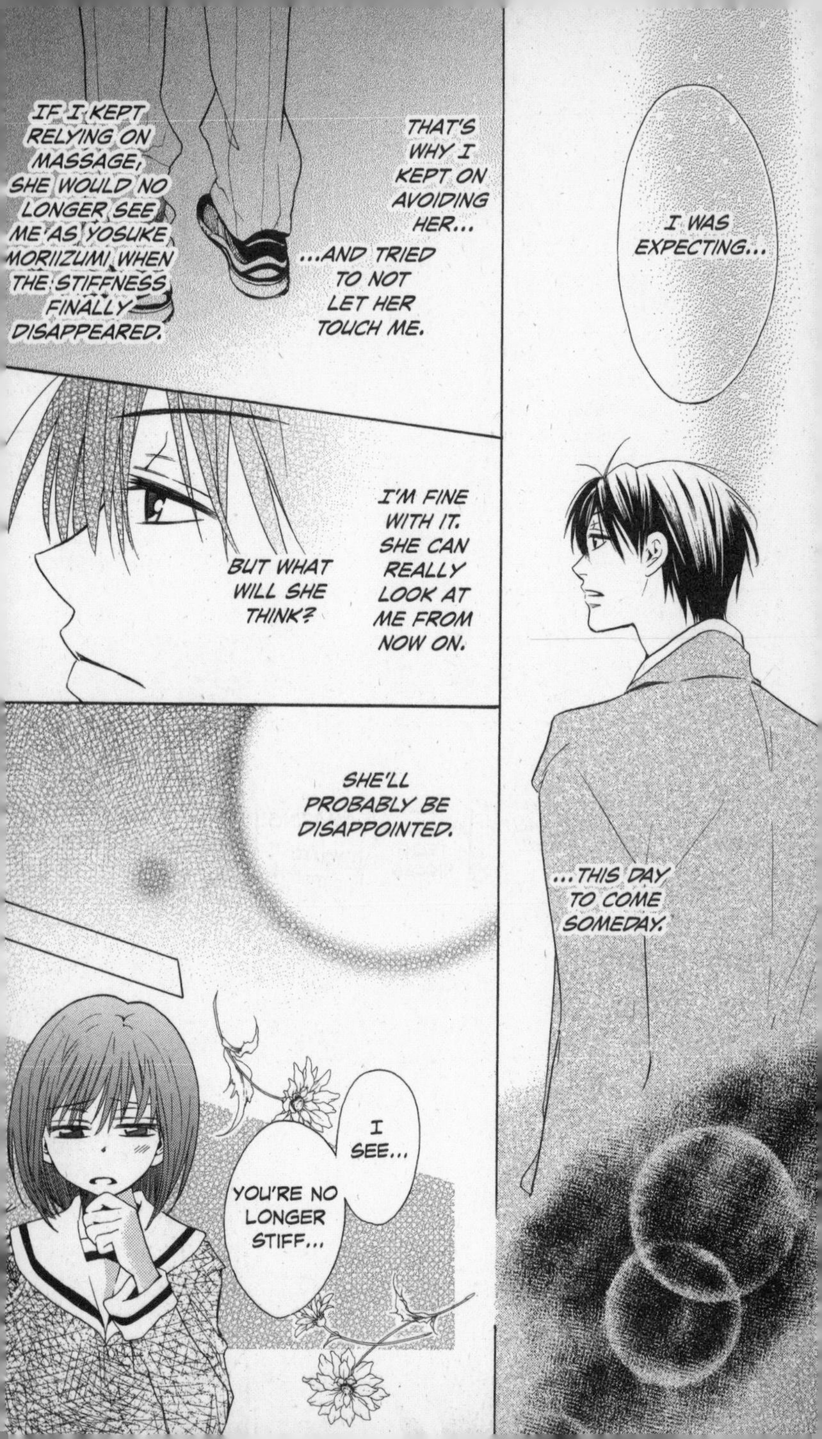

I WAS EXPECTING...
...THIS DAY TO COME SOMEDAY.
IF I KEPT RELYING ON MASSAGE, SHE WOULD NO LONGER SEE ME AS YOSUKE MORIIZUMI WHEN THE STIFFNESS FINALLY DISAPPEARED.
THAT'S WHY I KEPT ON AVOIDING HER...
...AND TRIED TO NOT LET HER TOUCH ME.
I'M FINE WITH IT. SHE CAN REALLY LOOK AT ME FROM NOW ON.
BUT WHAT WILL SHE THINK?
SHE'LL PROBABLY BE DISAPPOINTED.
I SEE...
YOU'RE NO LONGER STIFF...

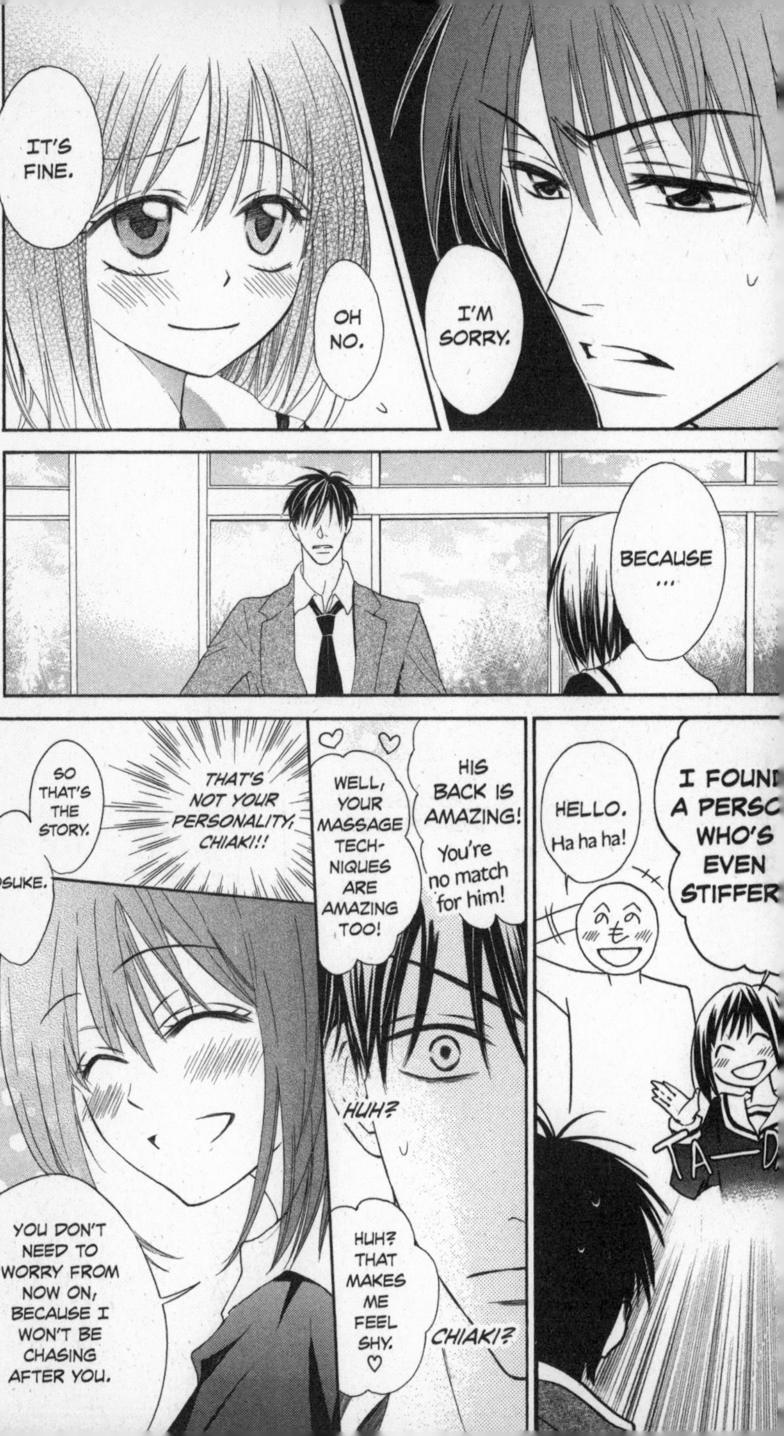
I'M SORRY.
OH NO.
IT'S FINE.
BECAUSE ...
I FOUND A PERSO WHO'S EVEN STIFFER
HELLO. Ha ha ha!
TA—D
HIS BACK IS AMAZING! You're no match for him!
WELL, YOUR MASSAGE TECH-NIQUES ARE AMAZING TOO!
HUH?
HUH? THAT MAKES ME FEEL SHY. ♡
CHIAKI!?
THAT'S NOT YOUR PERSONALITY, CHIAKI!!
SO THAT'S THE STORY.
YOSUKE.
YOU DON'T NEED TO WORRY FROM NOW ON, BECAUSE I WON'T BE CHASING AFTER YOU.

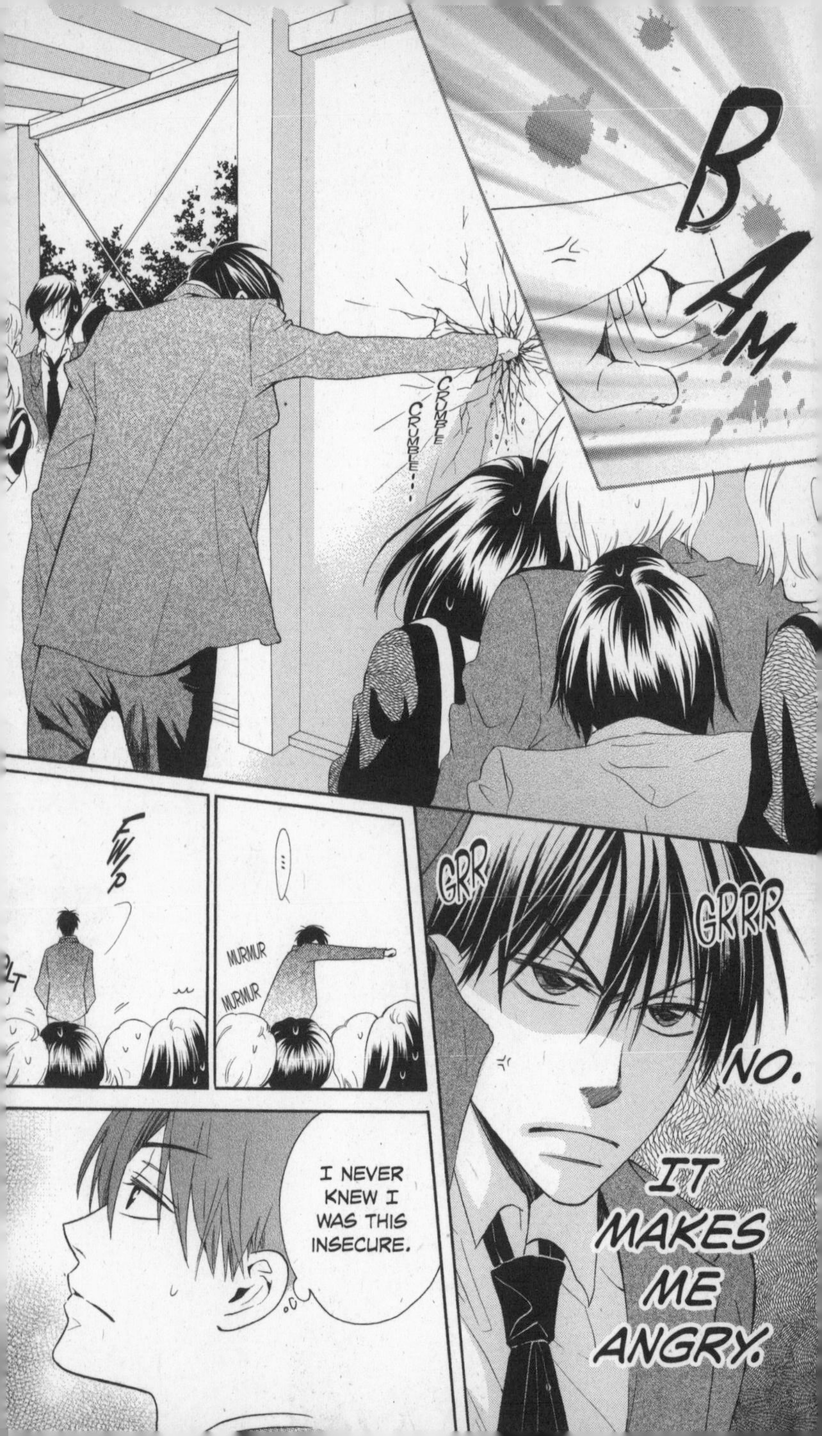
BAM
CRUMBLE
CRUMBLE...
GRR
GRRR
NO.
IT MAKES ME ANGRY.
...
MURMUR
MURMUR
FWP
I NEVER KNEW I WAS THIS INSECURE.

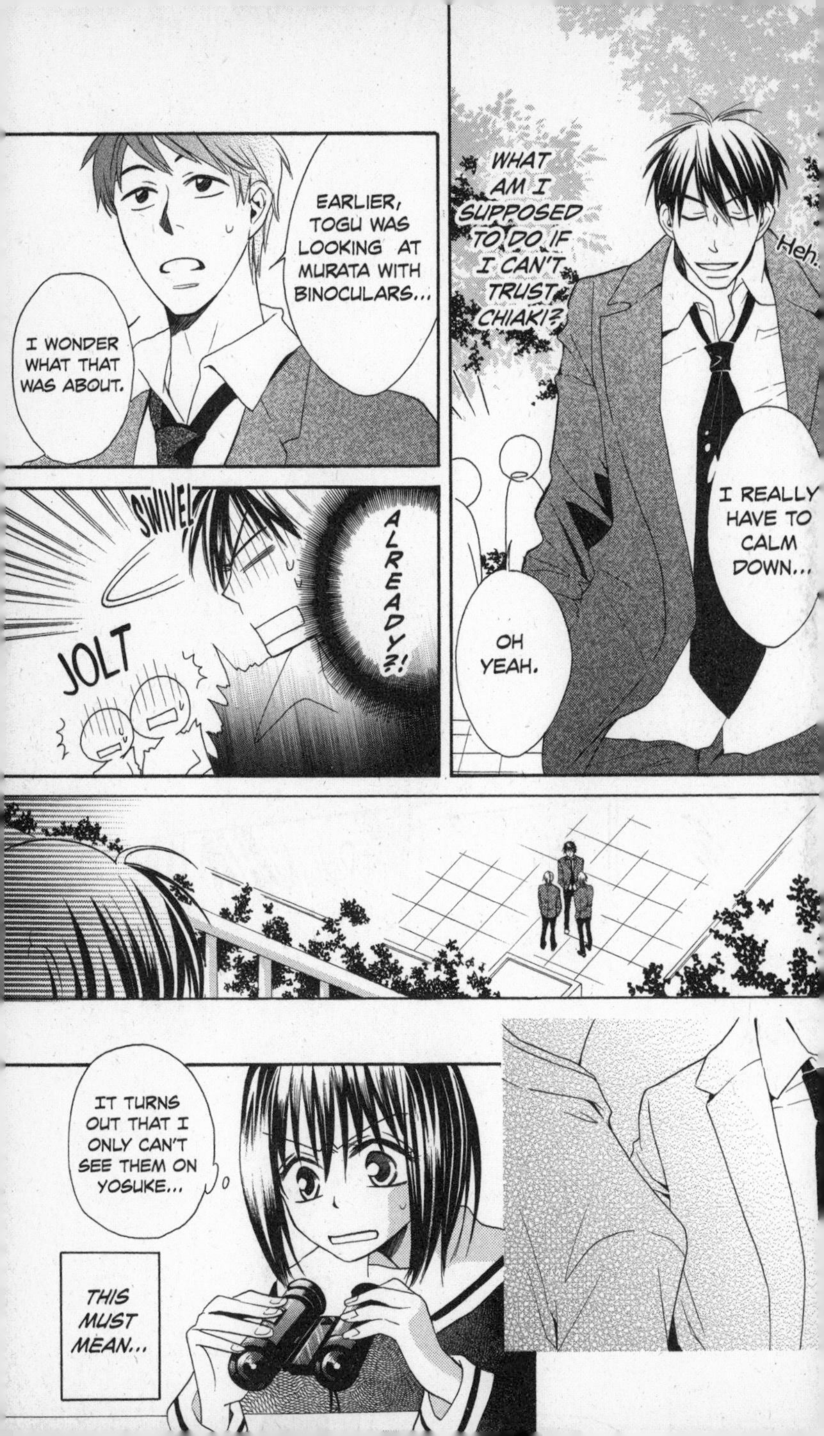
Heh.
WHAT AM I SUPPOSED TO DO IF I CAN'T TRUST CHIAKI?
I REALLY HAVE TO CALM DOWN...
OH YEAH.
EARLIER, TOGU WAS LOOKING AT MURATA WITH BINOCULARS...
I WONDER WHAT THAT WAS ABOUT.
ALREADY?!
SWIVEL
JOLT
IT TURNS OUT THAT I ONLY CAN'T SEE THEM ON YOSUKE...
THIS MUST MEAN...

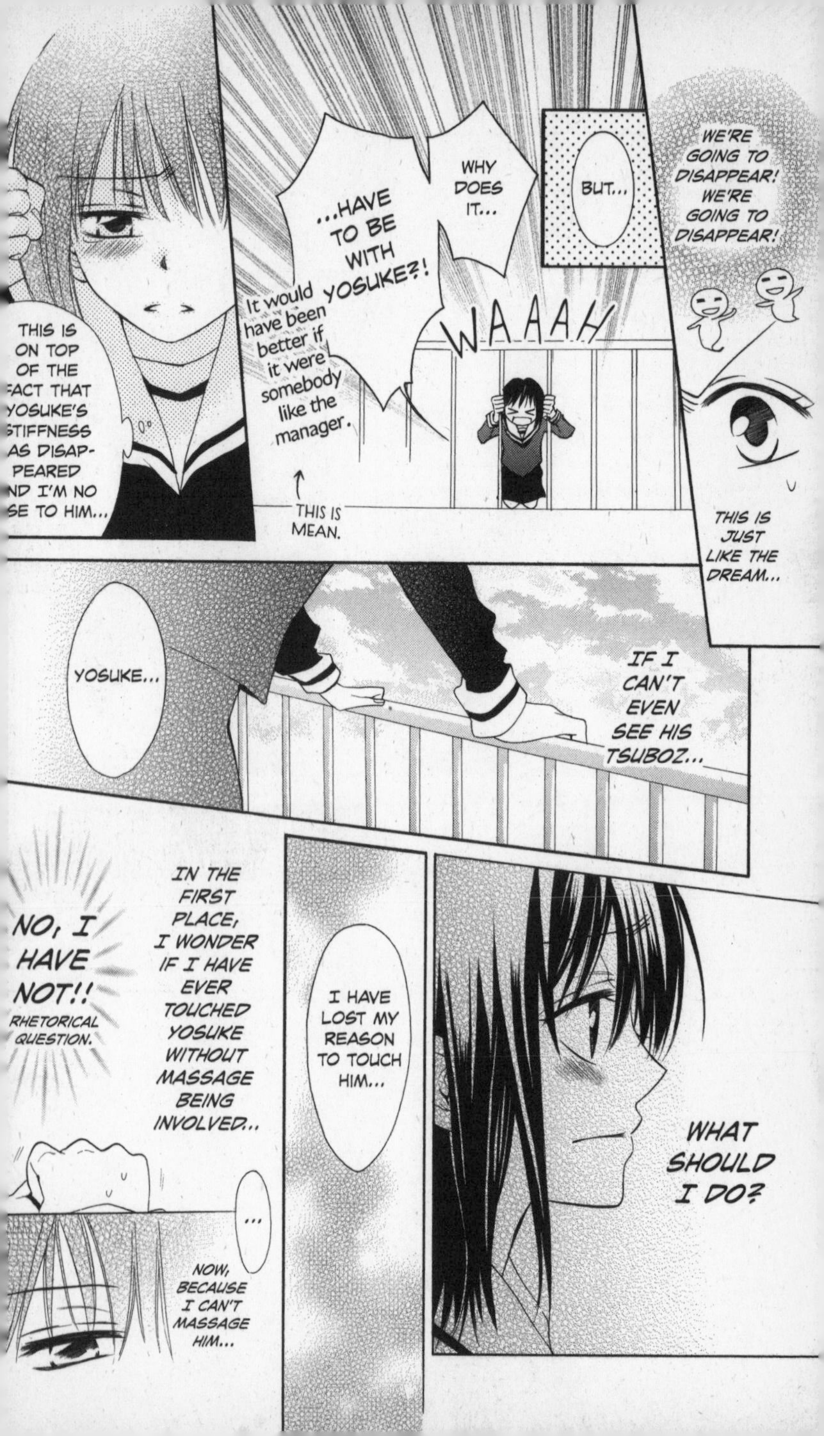
WE'RE GOING TO DISAPPEAR! WE'RE GOING TO DISAPPEAR!
THIS IS JUST LIKE THE DREAM...
BUT...
WHY DOES IT...
...HAVE TO BE WITH YOSUKE?!
It would have been better if it were somebody like the manager.
WAAAH
THIS IS MEAN.
THIS IS ON TOP OF THE FACT THAT YOSUKE'S STIFFNESS AS DISAP-PEARED ND I'M NO SE TO HIM...
IF I CAN'T EVEN SEE HIS TSUBOZ...
YOSUKE...
WHAT SHOULD I DO?
I HAVE LOST MY REASON TO TOUCH HIM...
IN THE FIRST PLACE, I WONDER IF I HAVE EVER TOUCHED YOSUKE WITHOUT MASSAGE BEING INVOLVED...
NO, I HAVE NOT!!
RHETORICAL QUESTION.
...
NOW, BECAUSE I CAN'T MASSAGE HIM...

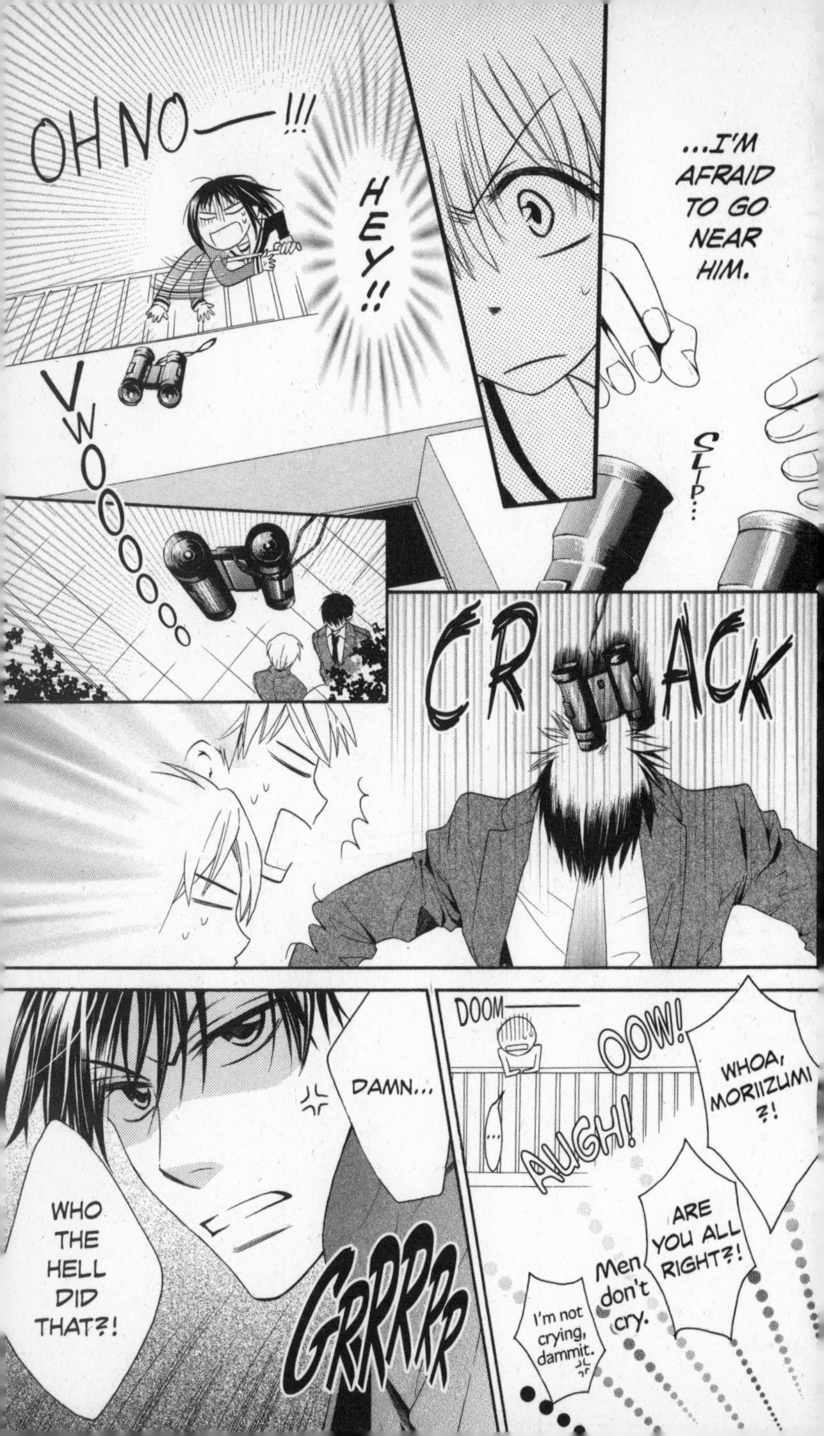
...I'M AFRAID TO GO NEAR HIM.
SLIP...
OH NO—!!!
HEY!!
VWOOOOOOOO
CRACK
DOOM—
OOW!
AUGH!
...
WHOA, MORIIZUMI?!
ARE YOU ALL RIGHT?!
Men don't cry.
I'm not crying, dammit.
DAMN...
WHO THE HELL DID THAT?!
GRRRRR

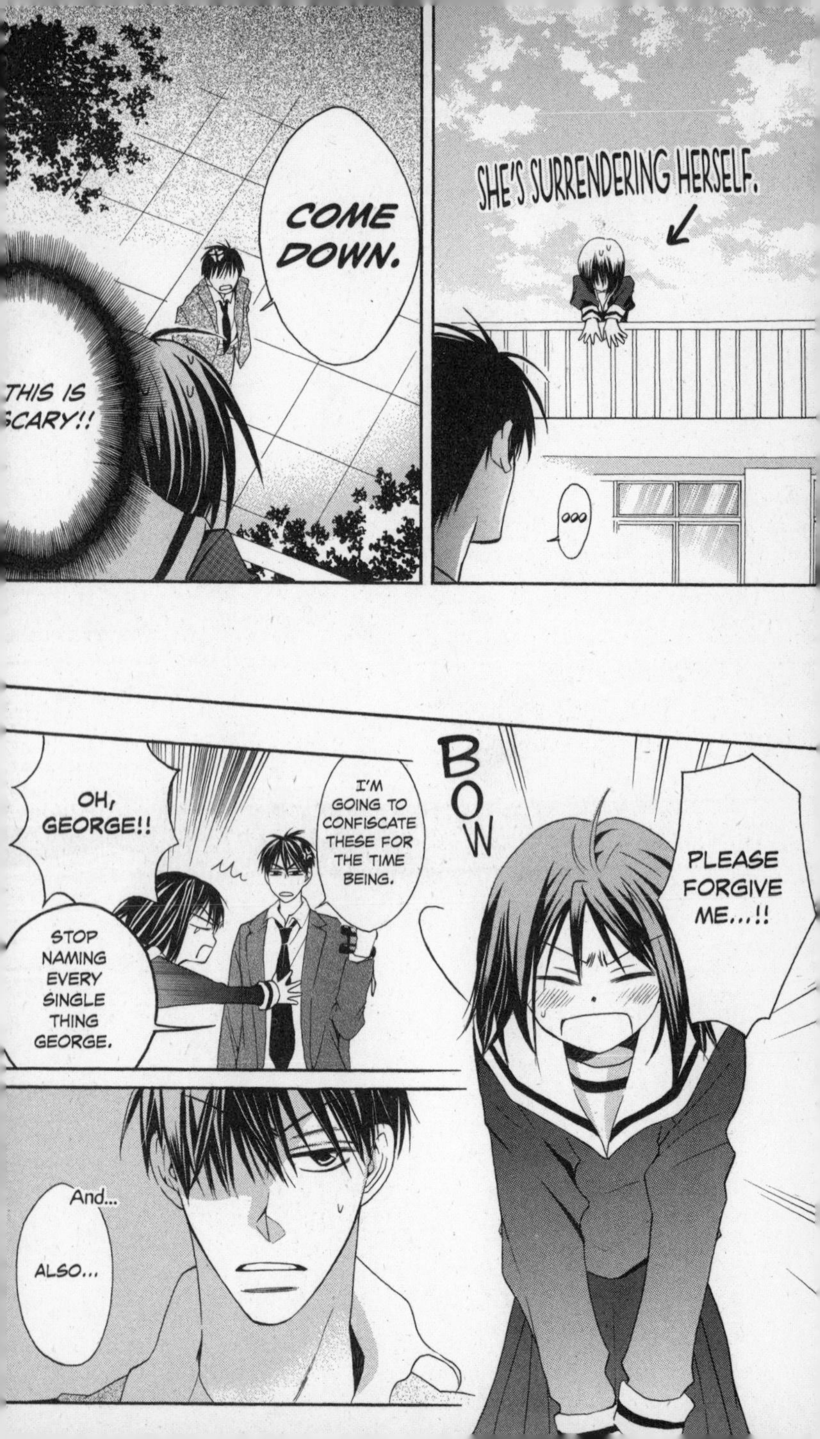
SHE'S SURRENDERING HERSELF.
ooo
COME DOWN.
THIS IS SCARY!!
BOW
PLEASE FORGIVE ME...!!
I'M GOING TO CONFISCATE THESE FOR THE TIME BEING.
OH, GEORGE!!
STOP NAMING EVERY SINGLE THING GEORGE.
And...
ALSO...

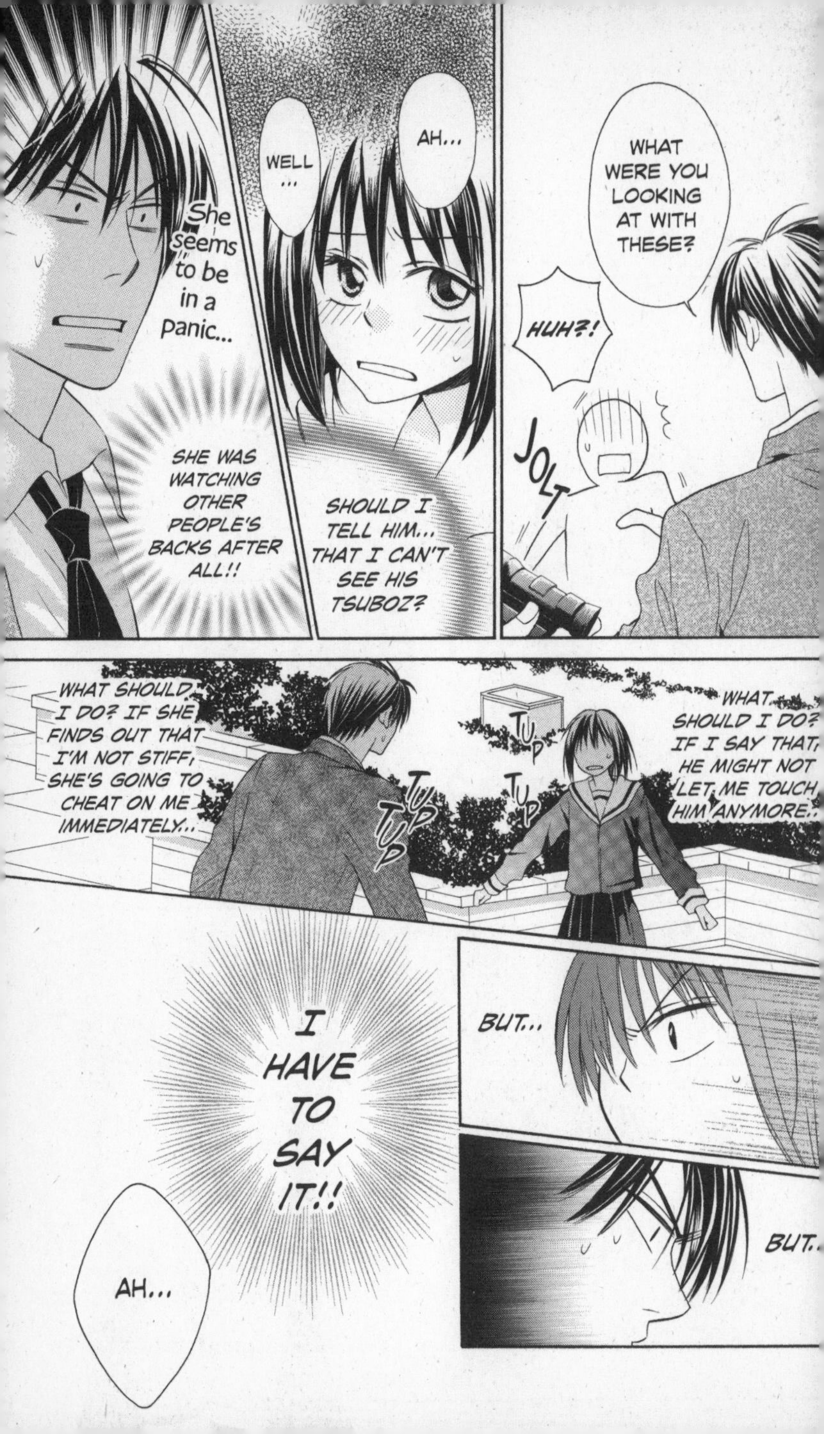
WHAT WERE YOU LOOKING AT WITH THESE?
HUH?!
JOLT
AH...
WELL ...
SHOULD I TELL HIM... THAT I CAN'T SEE HIS TSUBOZ?
She seems to be in a panic...
SHE WAS WATCHING OTHER PEOPLE'S BACKS AFTER ALL!!
WHAT SHOULD I DO? IF I SAY THAT, HE MIGHT NOT LET ME TOUCH HIM ANYMORE...
TUP
TUP
TUP
TUP
WHAT SHOULD I DO? IF SHE FINDS OUT THAT I'M NOT STIFF, SHE'S GOING TO CHEAT ON ME IMMEDIATELY...
BUT...
BUT...
I HAVE TO SAY IT!!
AH...

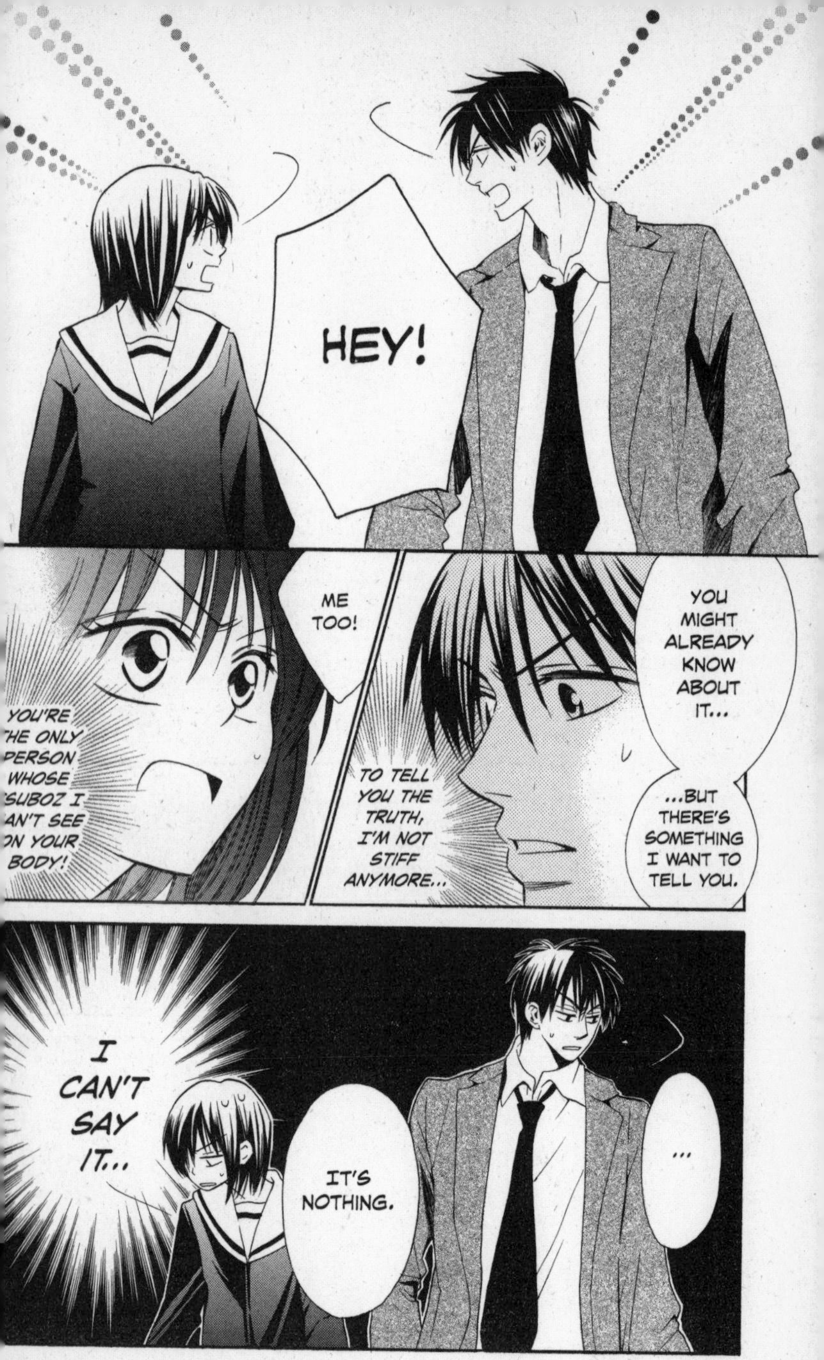
HEY!
YOU MIGHT ALREADY KNOW ABOUT IT...
...BUT THERE'S SOMETHING I WANT TO TELL YOU.
TO TELL YOU THE TRUTH, I'M NOT STIFF ANYMORE...
ME TOO!
YOU'RE THE ONLY PERSON WHOSE TSUBOZ I CAN'T SEE ON YOUR BODY!
...
IT'S NOTHING.
I CAN'T SAY IT...

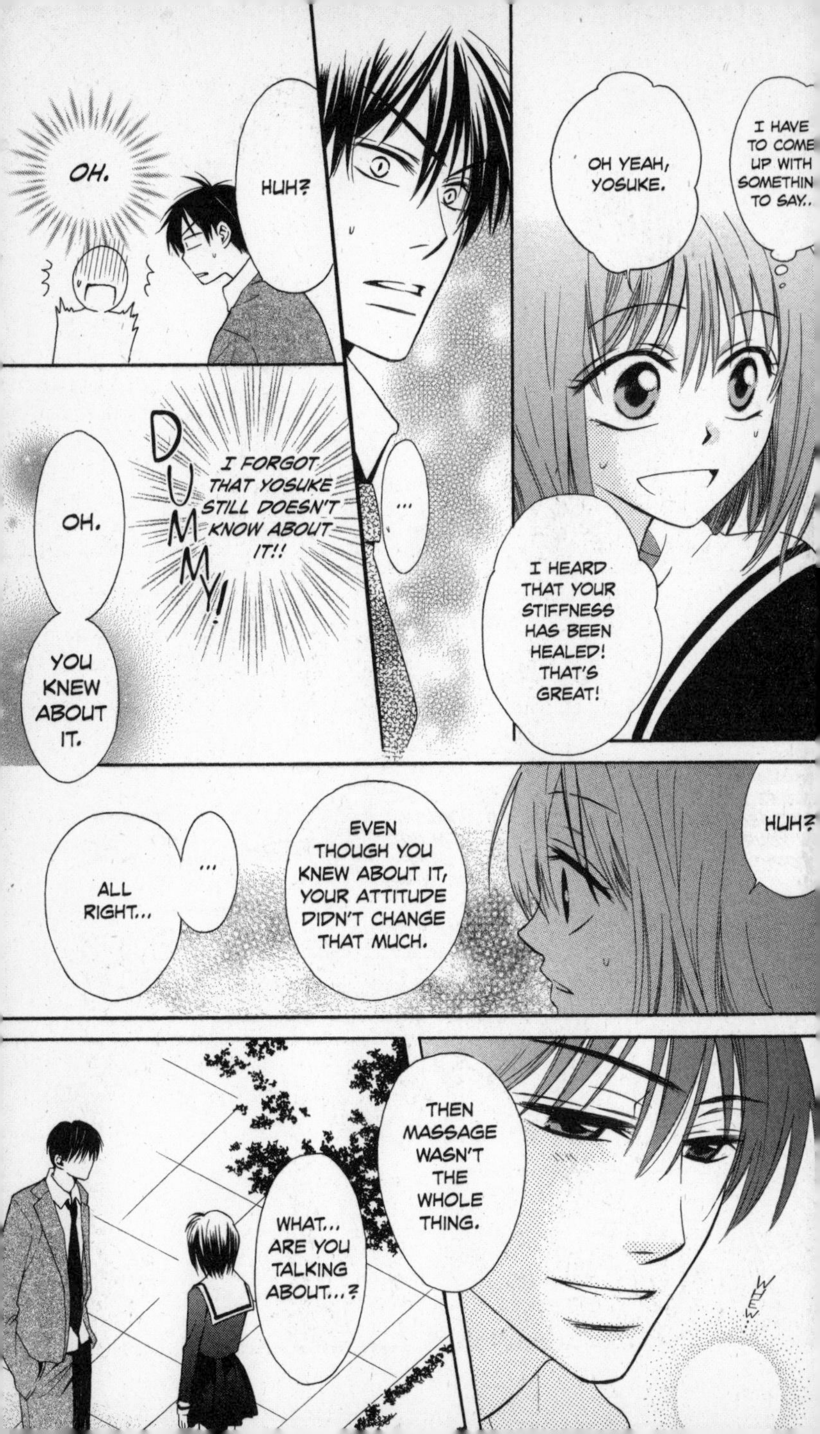
I HAVE TO COME UP WITH SOMETHIN TO SAY..
OH YEAH, YOSUKE.
I HEARD THAT YOUR STIFFNESS HAS BEEN HEALED! THAT'S GREAT!
...
HUH?
OH.
I FORGOT THAT YOSUKE STILL DOESN'T KNOW ABOUT IT!!
DUMMY!
OH.
YOU KNEW ABOUT IT.
HUH?
EVEN THOUGH YOU KNEW ABOUT IT, YOUR ATTITUDE DIDN'T CHANGE THAT MUCH.
...
ALL RIGHT...
WHEW...
THEN MASSAGE WASN'T THE WHOLE THING.
WHAT... ARE YOU TALKING ABOUT...?

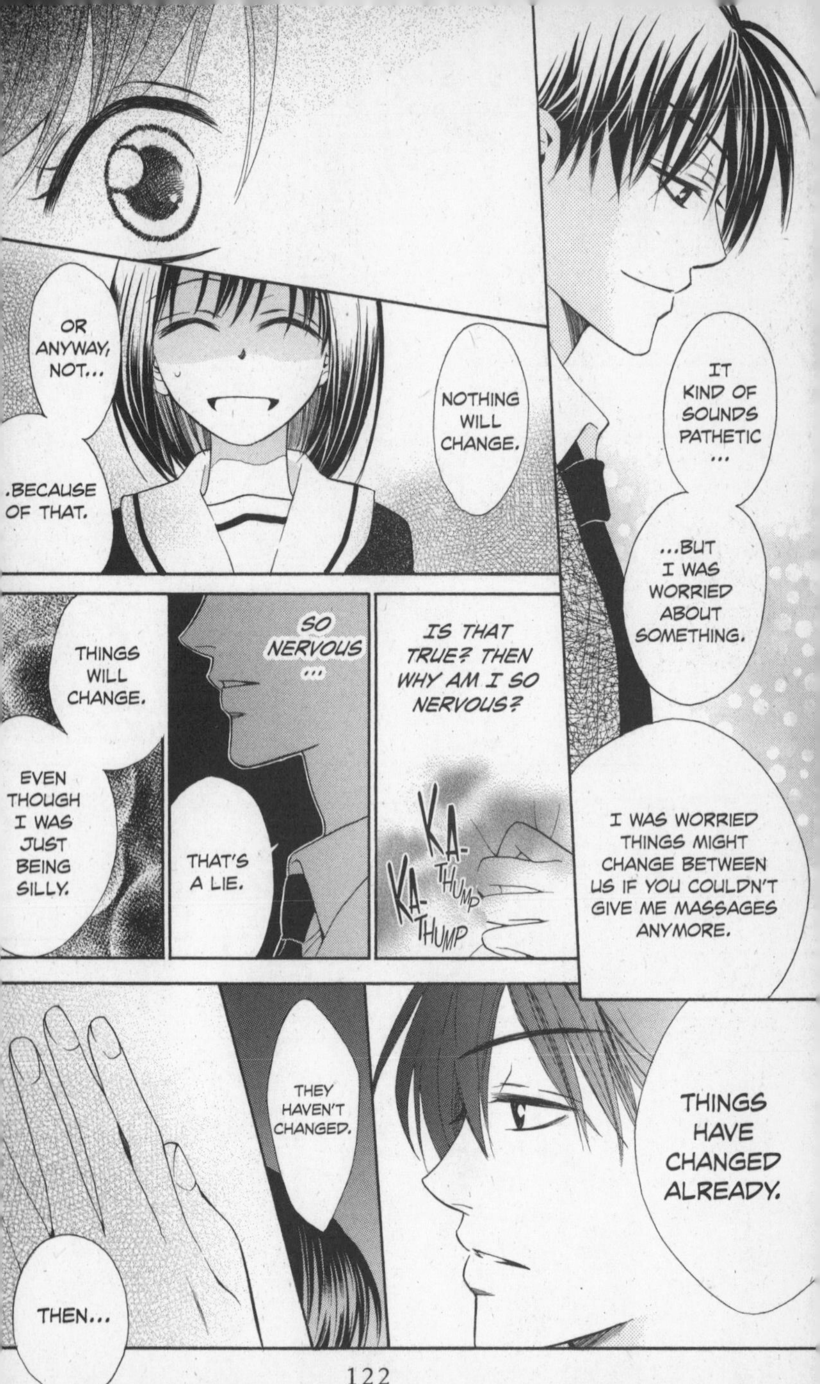
IT KIND OF SOUNDS PATHETIC...
...BUT I WAS WORRIED ABOUT SOMETHING.
I WAS WORRIED THINGS MIGHT CHANGE BETWEEN US IF YOU COULDN'T GIVE ME MASSAGES ANYMORE.
NOTHING WILL CHANGE.
OR ANYWAY, NOT...
...BECAUSE OF THAT.
IS THAT TRUE? THEN WHY AM I SO NERVOUS?
KA-THUMP
KA-THUMP
SO NERVOUS...
THAT'S A LIE.
THINGS WILL CHANGE.
EVEN THOUGH I WAS JUST BEING SILLY.
THINGS HAVE CHANGED ALREADY.
THEY HAVEN'T CHANGED.
THEN...

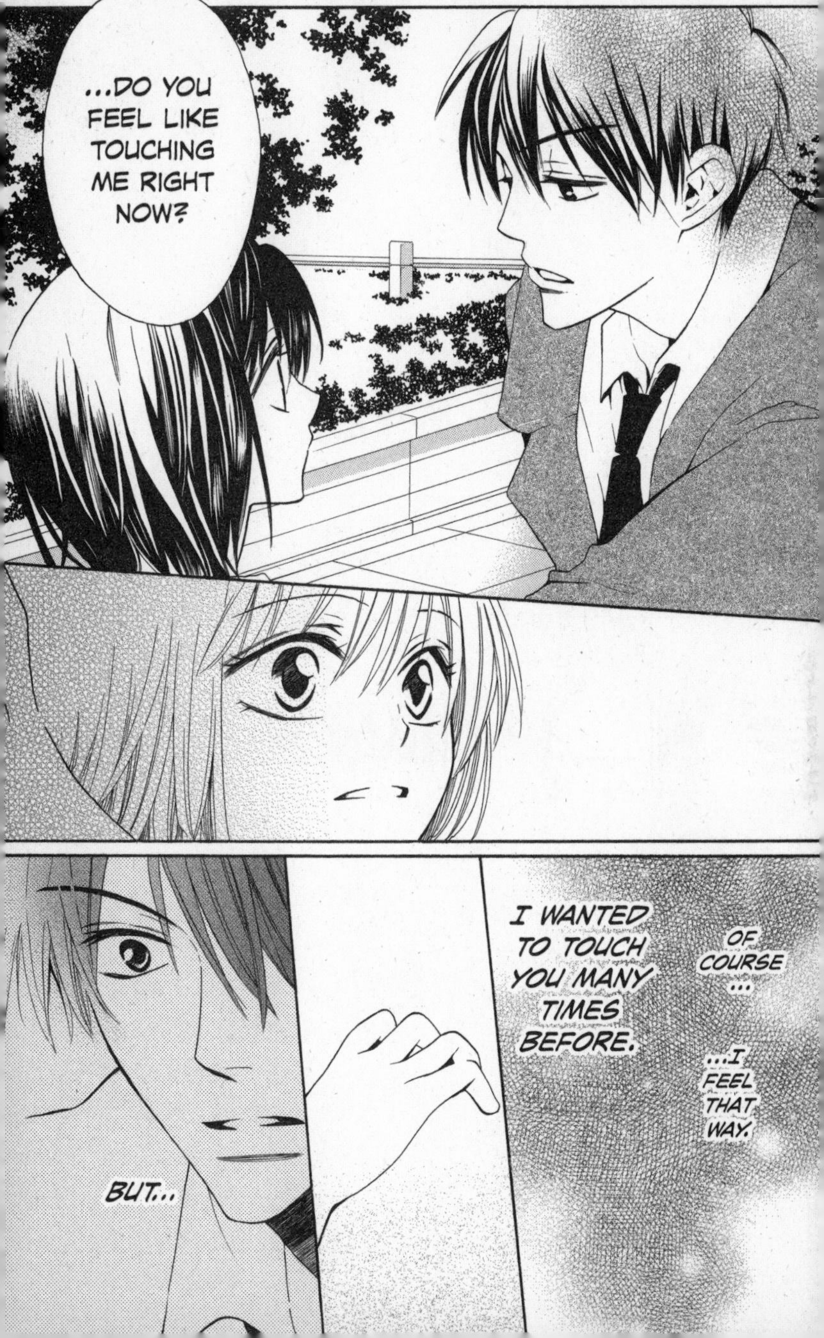
...DO YOU FEEL LIKE TOUCHING ME RIGHT NOW?
OF COURSE...
...I FEEL THAT WAY.
I WANTED TO TOUCH YOU MANY TIMES BEFORE.
BUT...

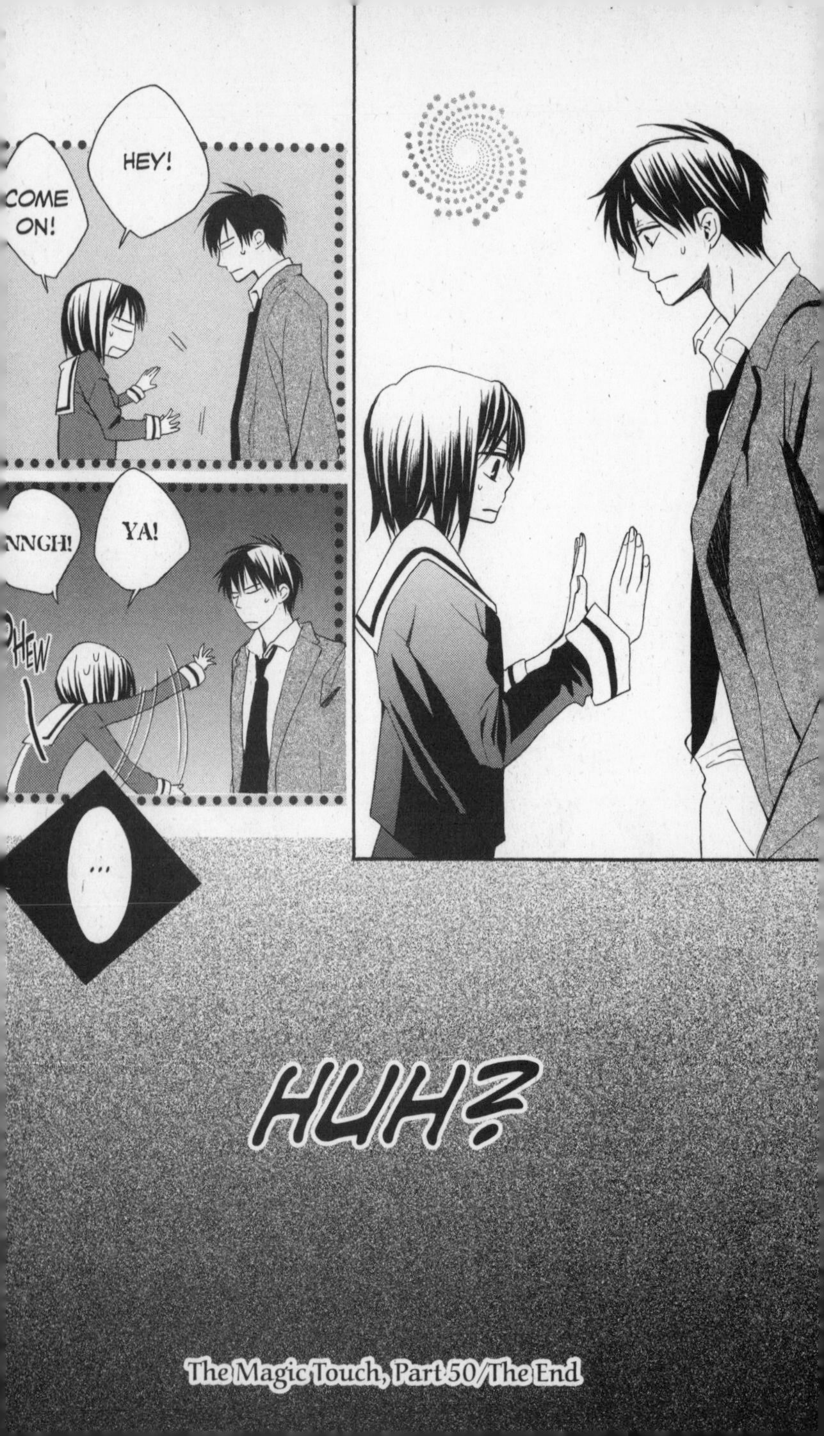
HEY!
COME ON!
YA!
NNGH!
PHEW
...
HUH?
The Magic Touch, Part 50/The End

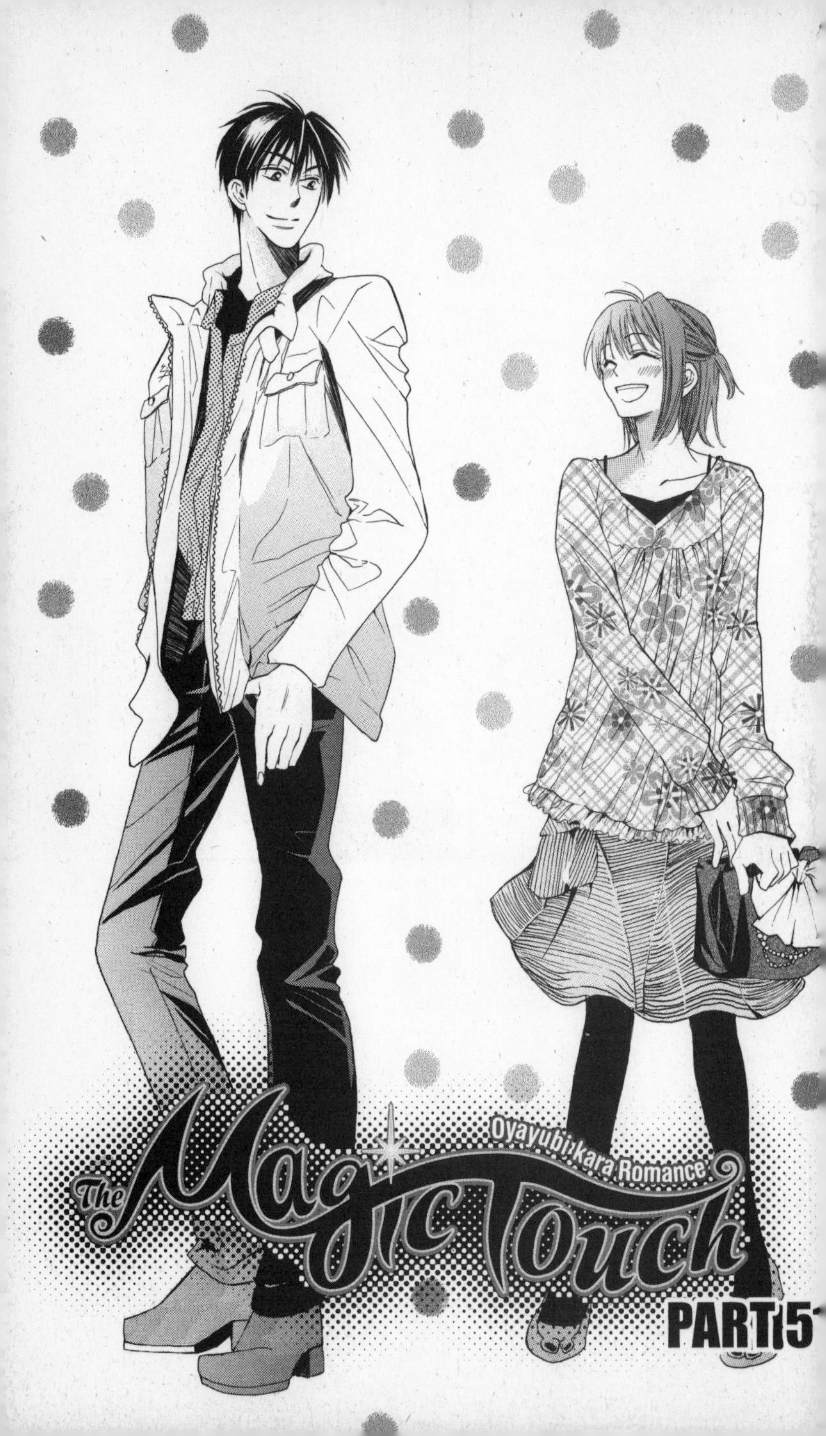
The Magic Touch
Oyayubi kara Romance
PART 5

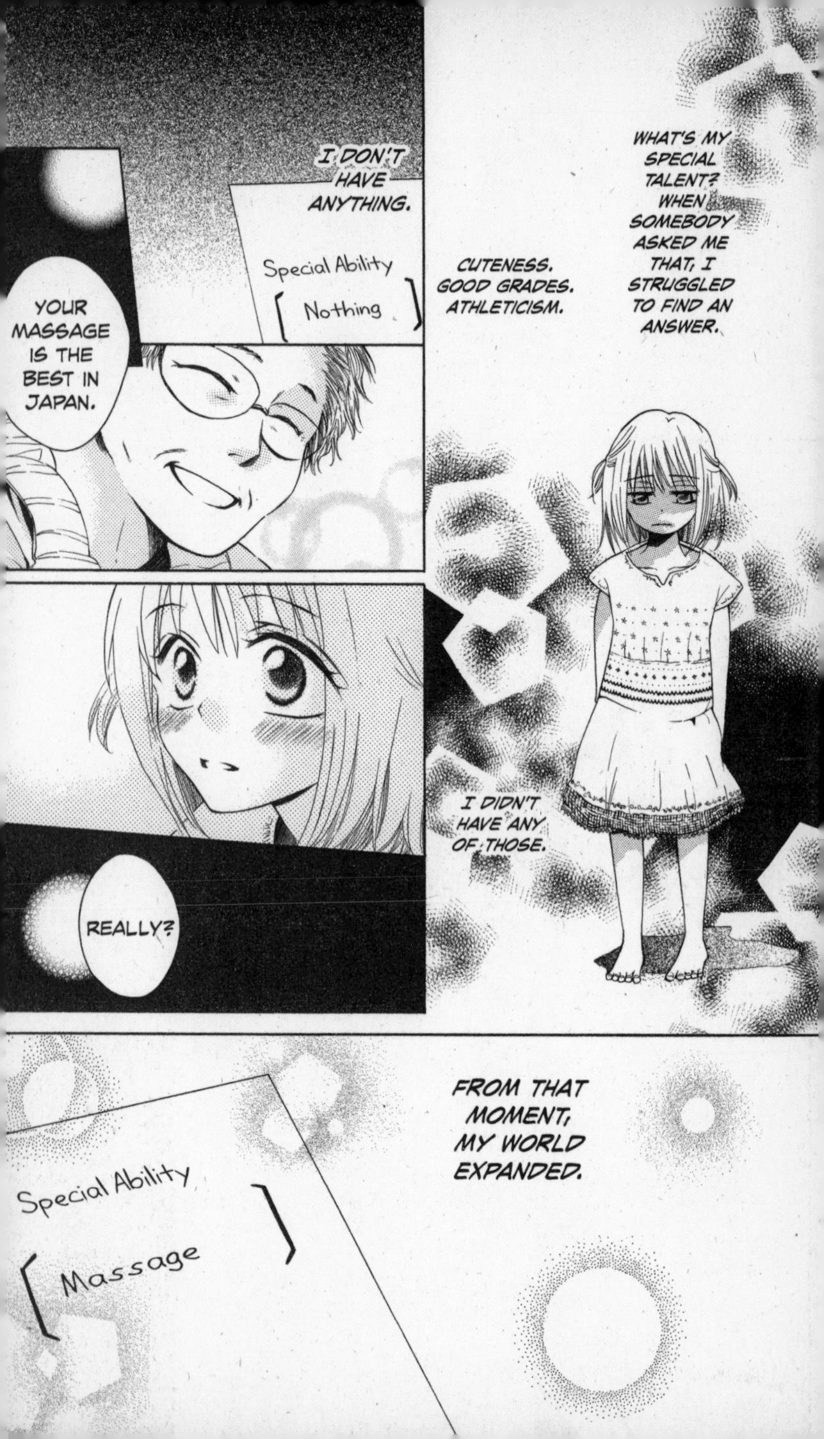
WHAT'S MY SPECIAL TALENT? WHEN SOMEBODY ASKED ME THAT, I STRUGGLED TO FIND AN ANSWER.
CUTENESS. GOOD GRADES. ATHLETICISM.
I DIDN'T HAVE ANY OF THOSE.
I DON'T HAVE ANYTHING.
Special Ability
[Nothing]
YOUR MASSAGE IS THE BEST IN JAPAN.
REALLY?
FROM THAT MOMENT, MY WORLD EXPANDED.
Special Ability
[Massage]

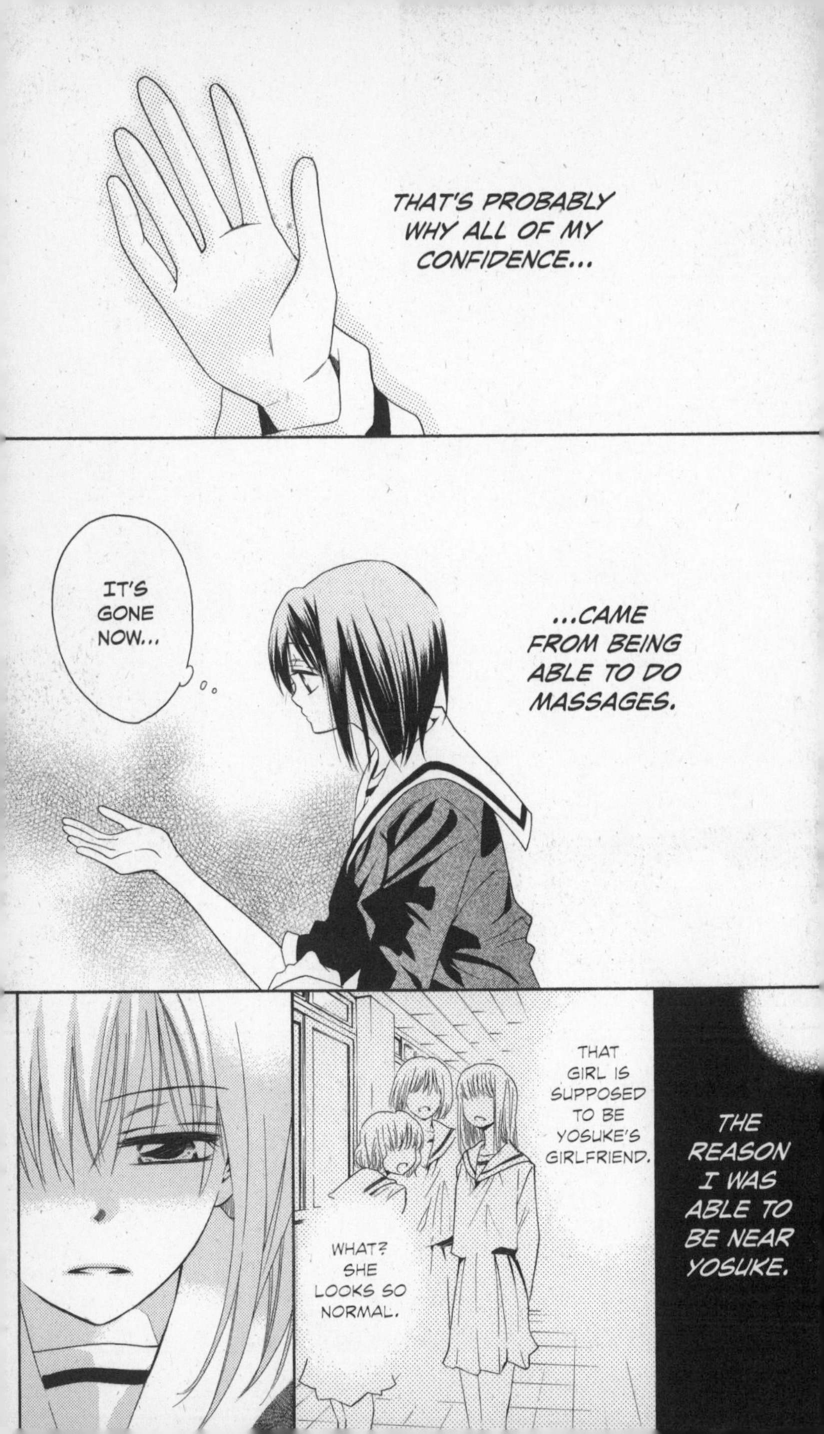
THAT'S PROBABLY WHY ALL OF MY CONFIDENCE...
...CAME FROM BEING ABLE TO DO MASSAGES.
IT'S GONE NOW...
THE REASON I WAS ABLE TO BE NEAR YOSUKE.
THAT GIRL IS SUPPOSED TO BE YOSUKE'S GIRLFRIEND.
WHAT? SHE LOOKS SO NORMAL.

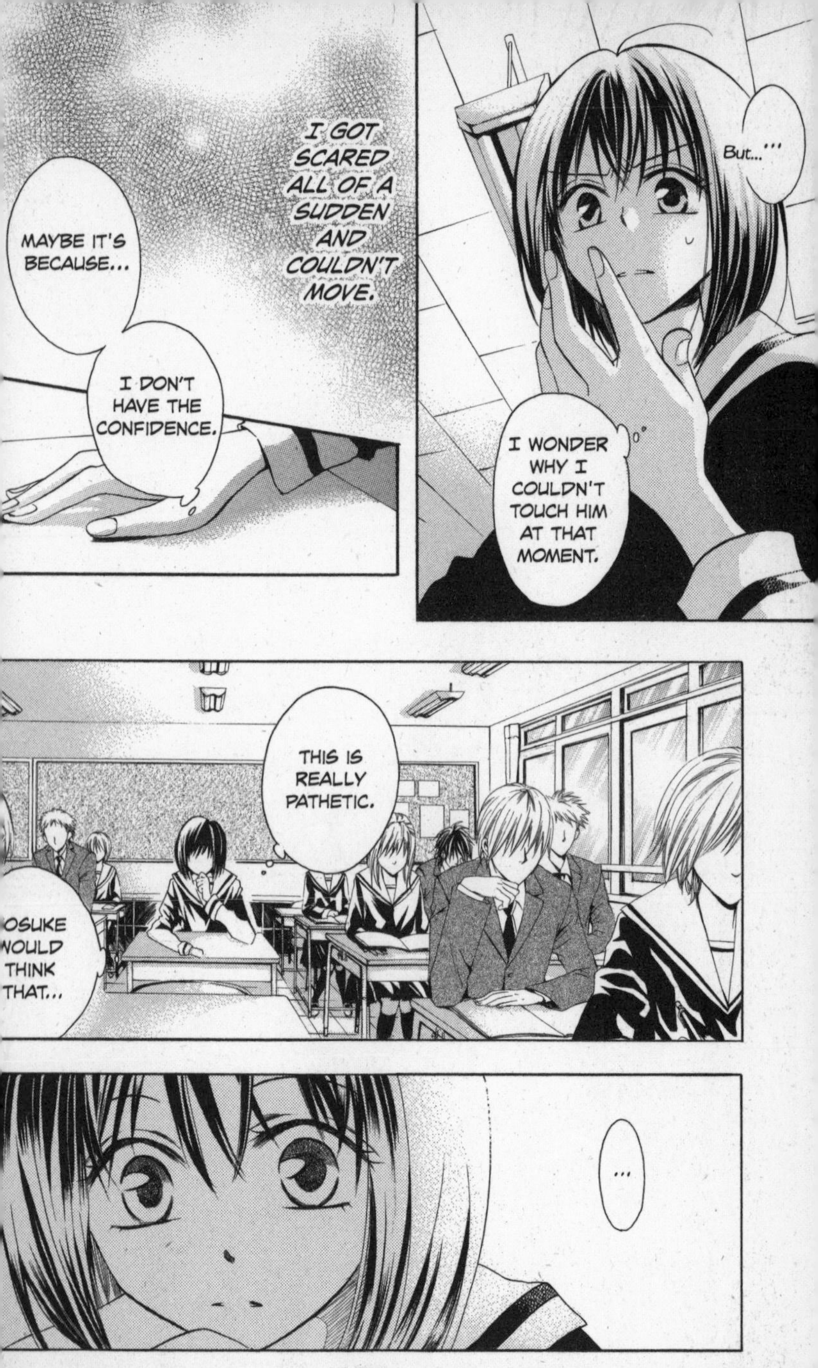
But...
I WONDER WHY I COULDN'T TOUCH HIM AT THAT MOMENT.
I GOT SCARED ALL OF A SUDDEN AND COULDN'T MOVE.
MAYBE IT'S BECAUSE...
I DON'T HAVE THE CONFIDENCE.
THIS IS REALLY PATHETIC.
OSUKE WOULD THINK THAT...
...

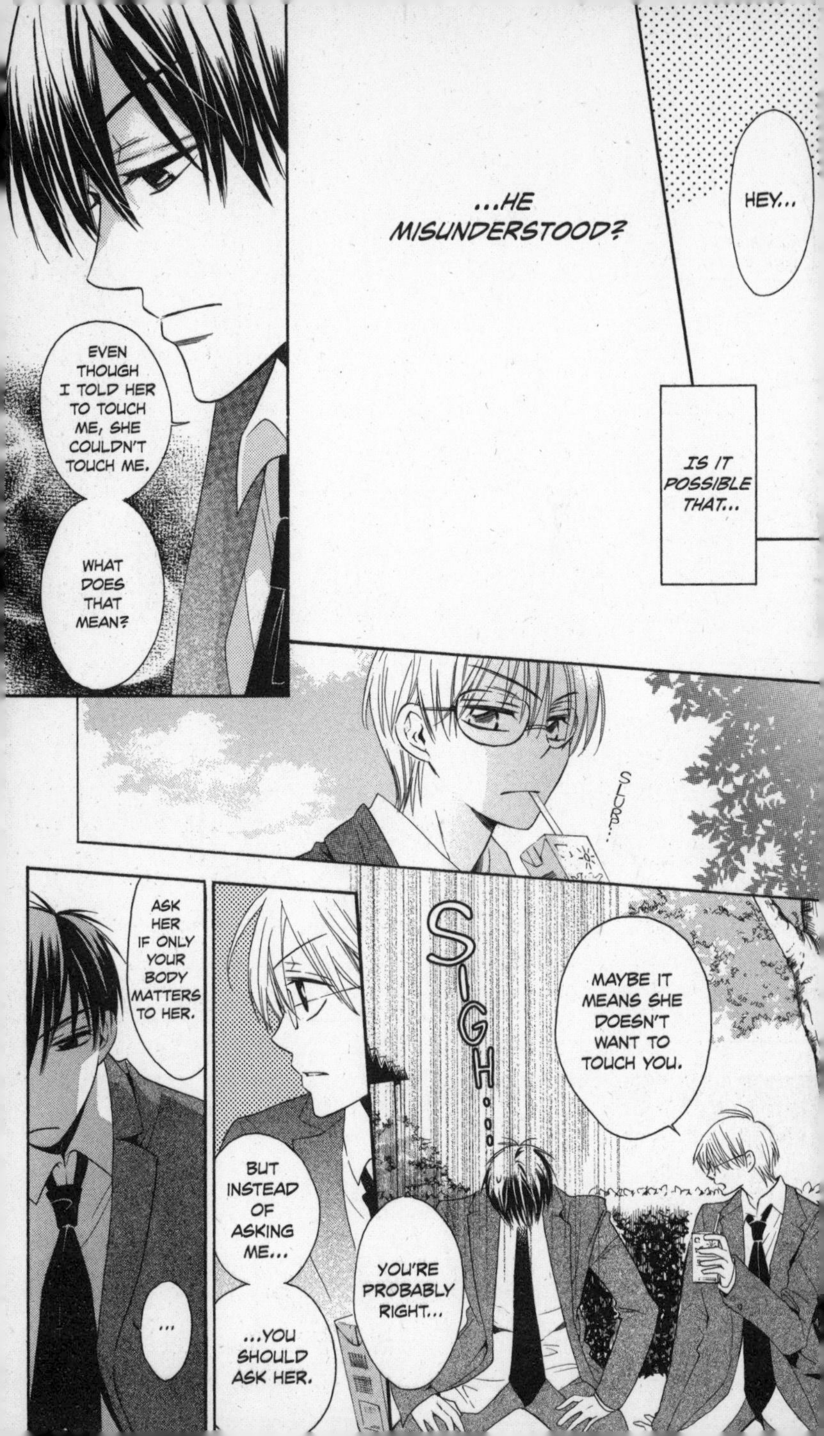
HEY...
IS IT POSSIBLE THAT...
...HE MISUNDERSTOOD?
EVEN THOUGH I TOLD HER TO TOUCH ME, SHE COULDN'T TOUCH ME.
WHAT DOES THAT MEAN?
SLURP...
SIGH...
MAYBE IT MEANS SHE DOESN'T WANT TO TOUCH YOU.
YOU'RE PROBABLY RIGHT...
BUT INSTEAD OF ASKING ME...
...YOU SHOULD ASK HER.
ASK HER IF ONLY YOUR BODY MATTERS TO HER.
...

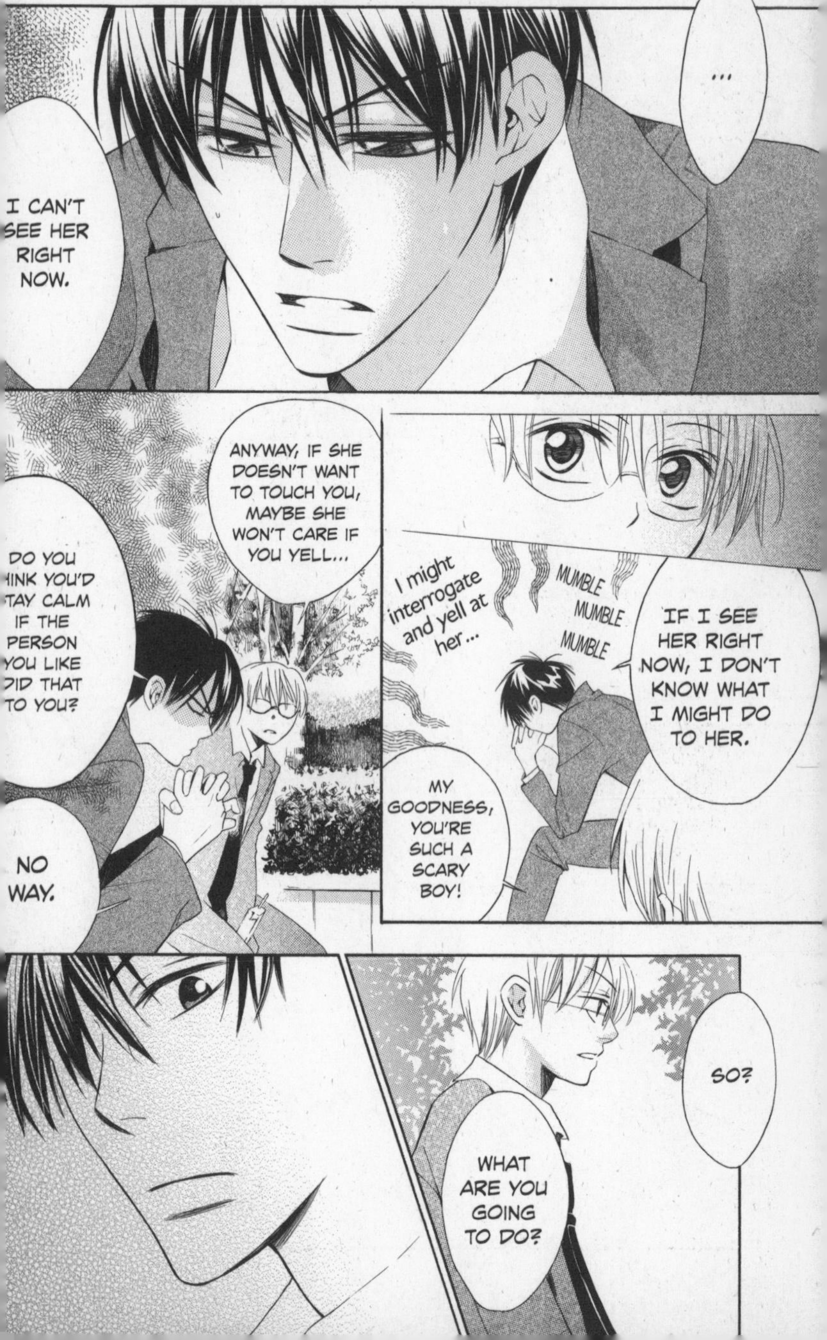
...
I CAN'T SEE HER RIGHT NOW.
IF I SEE HER RIGHT NOW, I DON'T KNOW WHAT I MIGHT DO TO HER.
MUMBLE MUMBLE MUMBLE
I might interrogate and yell at her...
MY GOODNESS, YOU'RE SUCH A SCARY BOY!
ANYWAY, IF SHE DOESN'T WANT TO TOUCH YOU, MAYBE SHE WON'T CARE IF YOU YELL...
DO YOU HINK YOU'D TAY CALM IF THE PERSON YOU LIKE ID THAT TO YOU?
NO WAY.
SO?
WHAT ARE YOU GOING TO DO?

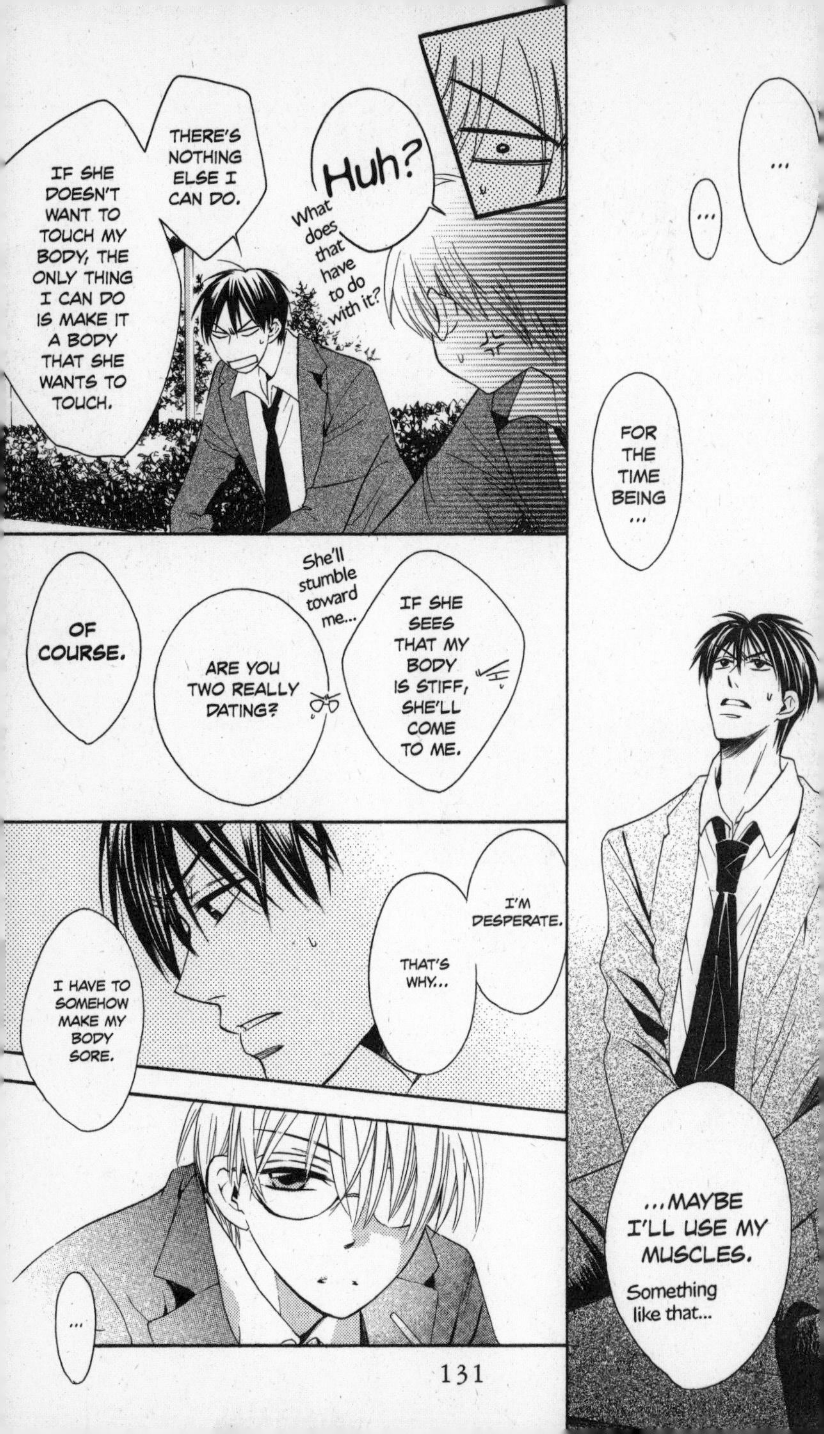
...
...
FOR THE TIME BEING...
...MAYBE I'LL USE MY MUSCLES.
Something like that...
Huh?
What does that have to do with it?
THERE'S NOTHING ELSE I CAN DO.
IF SHE DOESN'T WANT TO TOUCH MY BODY, THE ONLY THING I CAN DO IS MAKE IT A BODY THAT SHE WANTS TO TOUCH.
She'll stumble toward me...
IF SHE SEES THAT MY BODY IS STIFF, SHE'LL COME TO ME.
ARE YOU TWO REALLY DATING?
OF COURSE.
I'M DESPERATE.
THAT'S WHY...
I HAVE TO SOMEHOW MAKE MY BODY SORE.
...

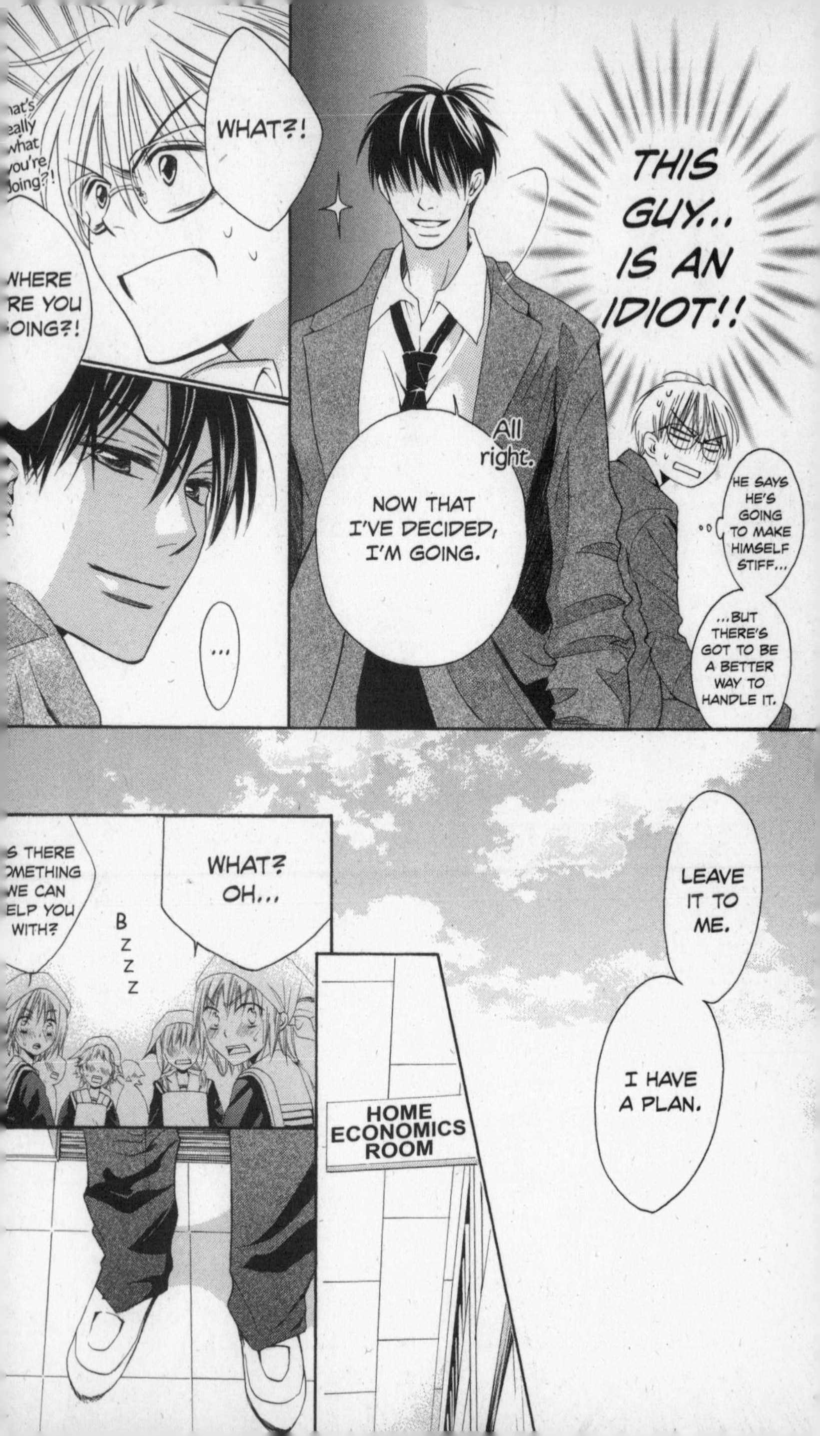
THIS GUY... IS AN IDIOT!!
HE SAYS HE'S GOING TO MAKE HIMSELF STIFF...
...BUT THERE'S GOT TO BE A BETTER WAY TO HANDLE IT.
All right.
NOW THAT I'VE DECIDED, I'M GOING.
WHAT?!
hat's eally what you're doing?!
WHERE RE YOU OING?!
...
LEAVE IT TO ME.
I HAVE A PLAN.
HOME ECONOMICS ROOM
WHAT? OH...
S THERE OMETHING WE CAN ELP YOU WITH?
BZZZ

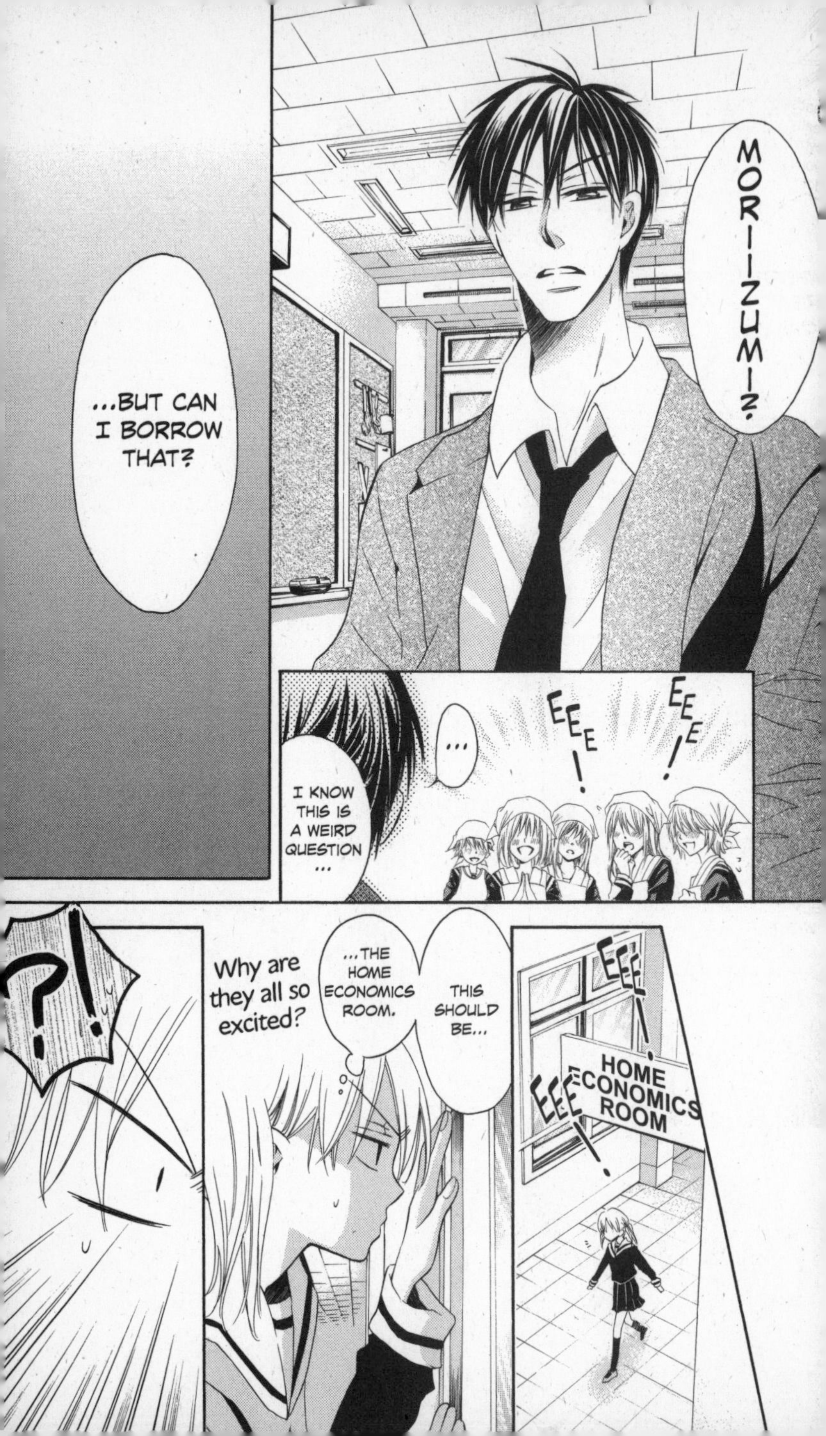
MORIIZUMI?
...
EEEE!
EEEE!
I KNOW THIS IS A WEIRD QUESTION...
...BUT CAN I BORROW THAT?
EEE!
HOME ECONOMICS ROOM
EEE!
THIS SHOULD BE...
...THE HOME ECONOMICS ROOM.
Why are they all so excited?
?!

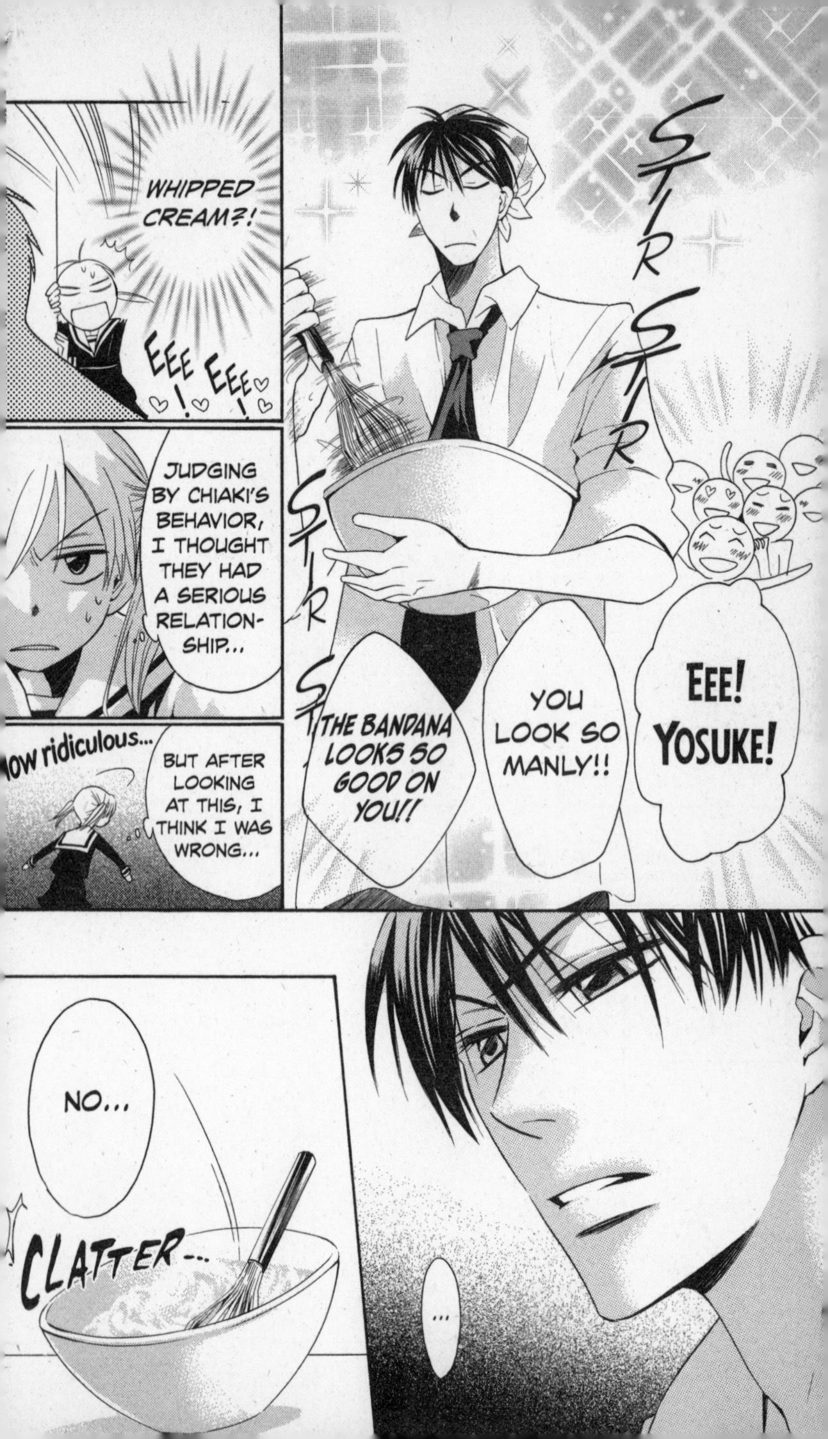
STIR STIR STIR
EEE! YOSUKE!
YOU LOOK SO MANLY!!
THE BANDANA LOOKS SO GOOD ON YOU!!
WHIPPED CREAM?!
EEE! EEE!
JUDGING BY CHIAKI'S BEHAVIOR, I THOUGHT THEY HAD A SERIOUS RELATIONSHIP...
ow ridiculous...
BUT AFTER LOOKING AT THIS, I THINK I WAS WRONG...
...
NO...
CLATTER...

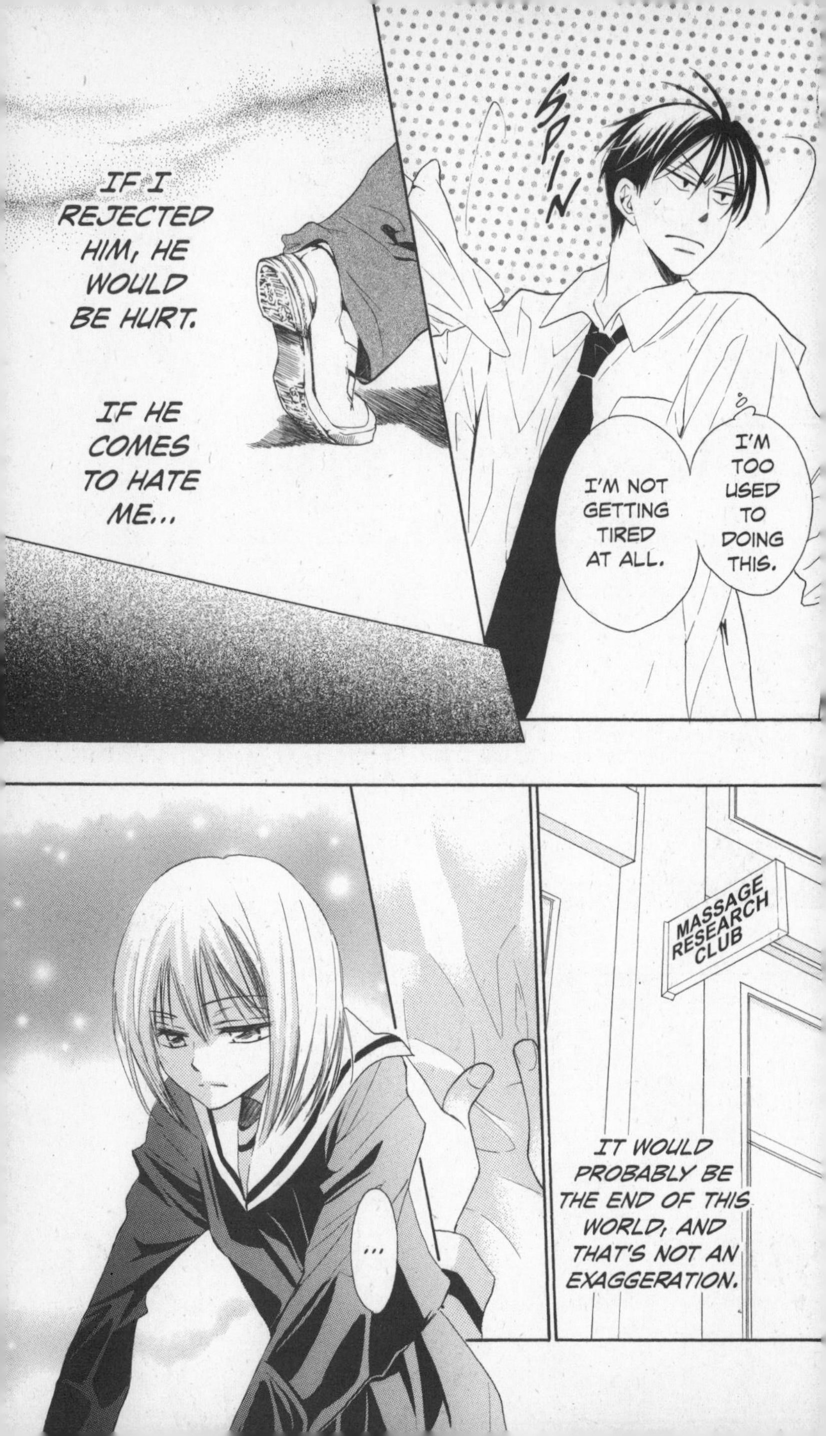
SPIN
I'M TOO USED TO DOING THIS.
I'M NOT GETTING TIRED AT ALL.
IF I REJECTED HIM, HE WOULD BE HURT.
IF HE COMES TO HATE ME...
MASSAGE RESEARCH CLUB
IT WOULD PROBABLY BE THE END OF THIS WORLD, AND THAT'S NOT AN EXAGGERATION.
...

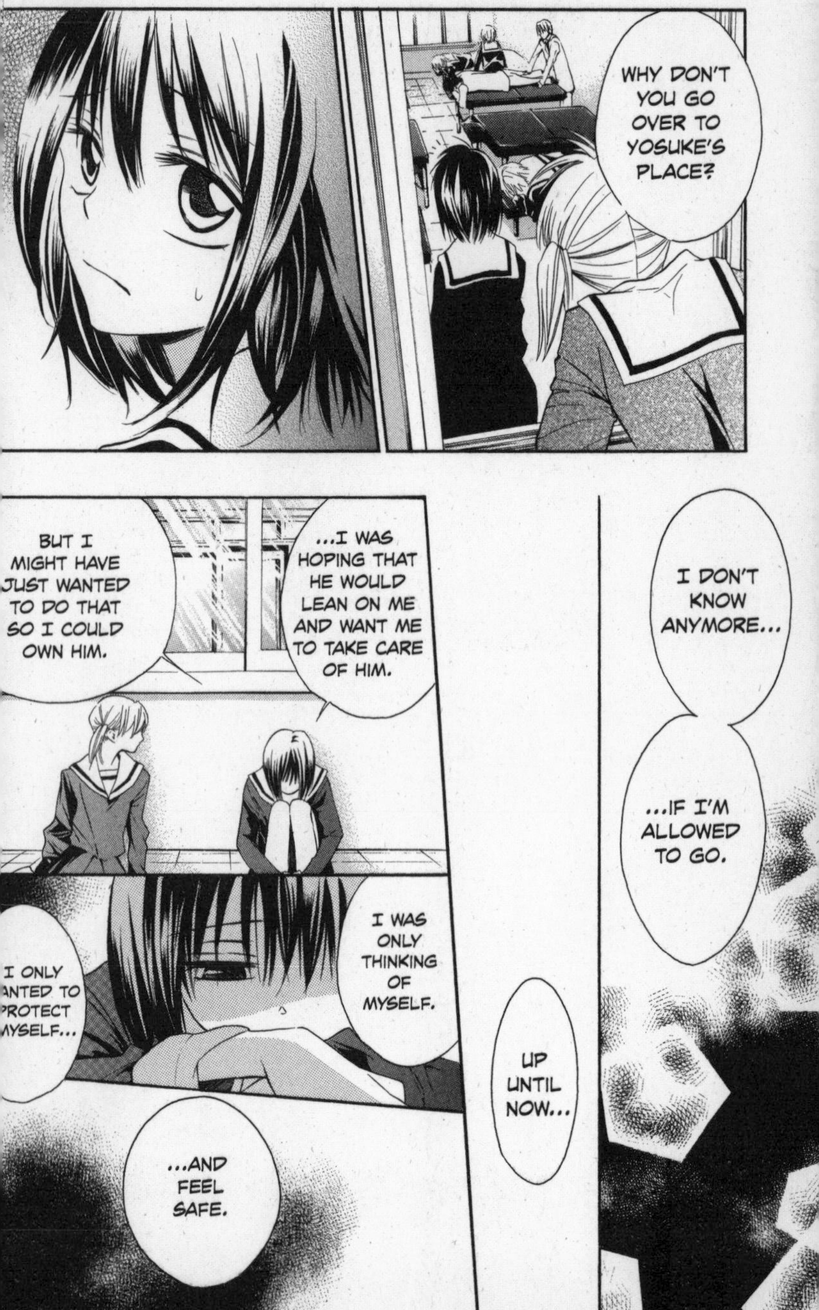
WHY DON'T YOU GO OVER TO YOSUKE'S PLACE?
I DON'T KNOW ANYMORE...
...IF I'M ALLOWED TO GO.
...I WAS HOPING THAT HE WOULD LEAN ON ME AND WANT ME TO TAKE CARE OF HIM.
BUT I MIGHT HAVE JUST WANTED TO DO THAT SO I COULD OWN HIM.
UP UNTIL NOW...
I WAS ONLY THINKING OF MYSELF.
I ONLY ANTED TO PROTECT MYSELF...
...AND FEEL SAFE.

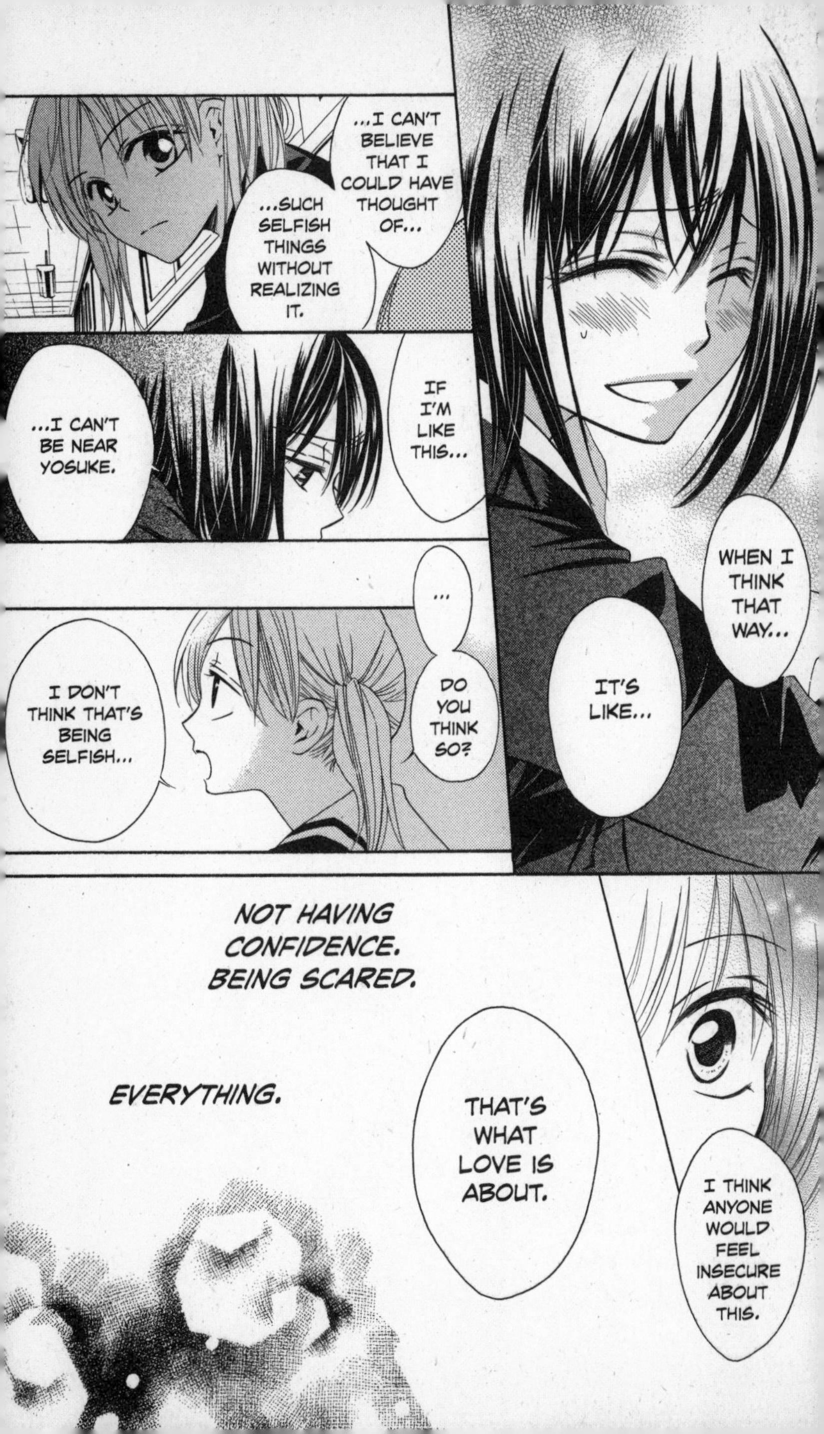
WHEN I THINK THAT WAY...
IT'S LIKE...
...I CAN'T BELIEVE THAT I COULD HAVE THOUGHT OF...
...SUCH SELFISH THINGS WITHOUT REALIZING IT.
IF I'M LIKE THIS...
...I CAN'T BE NEAR YOSUKE.
...
DO YOU THINK SO?
I DON'T THINK THAT'S BEING SELFISH...
I THINK ANYONE WOULD FEEL INSECURE ABOUT THIS.
THAT'S WHAT LOVE IS ABOUT.
NOT HAVING CONFIDENCE. BEING SCARED.
EVERYTHING.

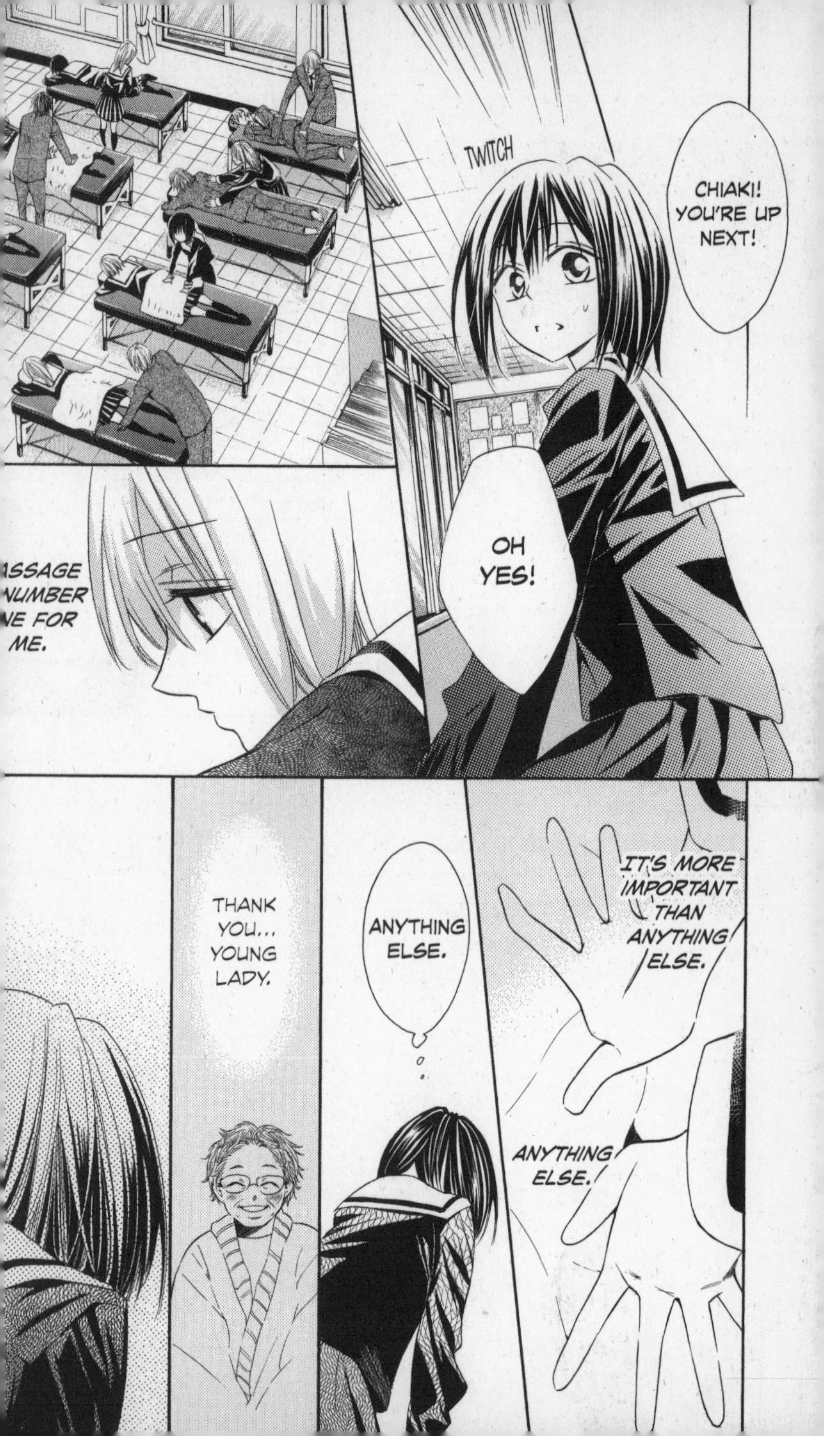
TWITCH
CHIAKI! YOU'RE UP NEXT!
OH YES!
SSAGE NUMBER NE FOR ME.
IT'S MORE IMPORTANT THAN ANYTHING ELSE.
ANYTHING ELSE.
ANYTHING ELSE.
THANK YOU... YOUNG LADY.

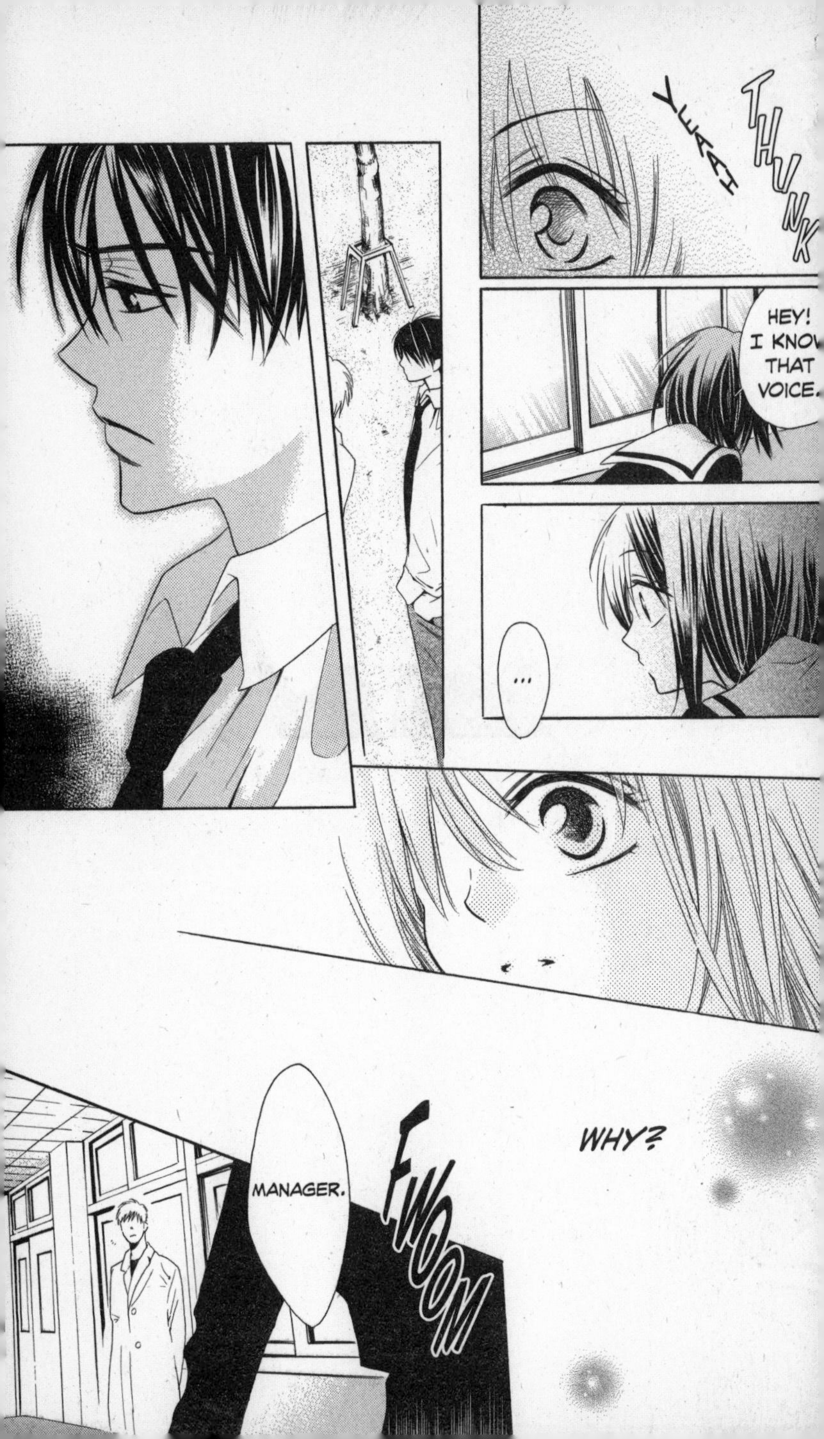
THUNK
YWAAH
HEY! I KNOW THAT VOICE.
...
WHY?
MANAGER.
FWOOM

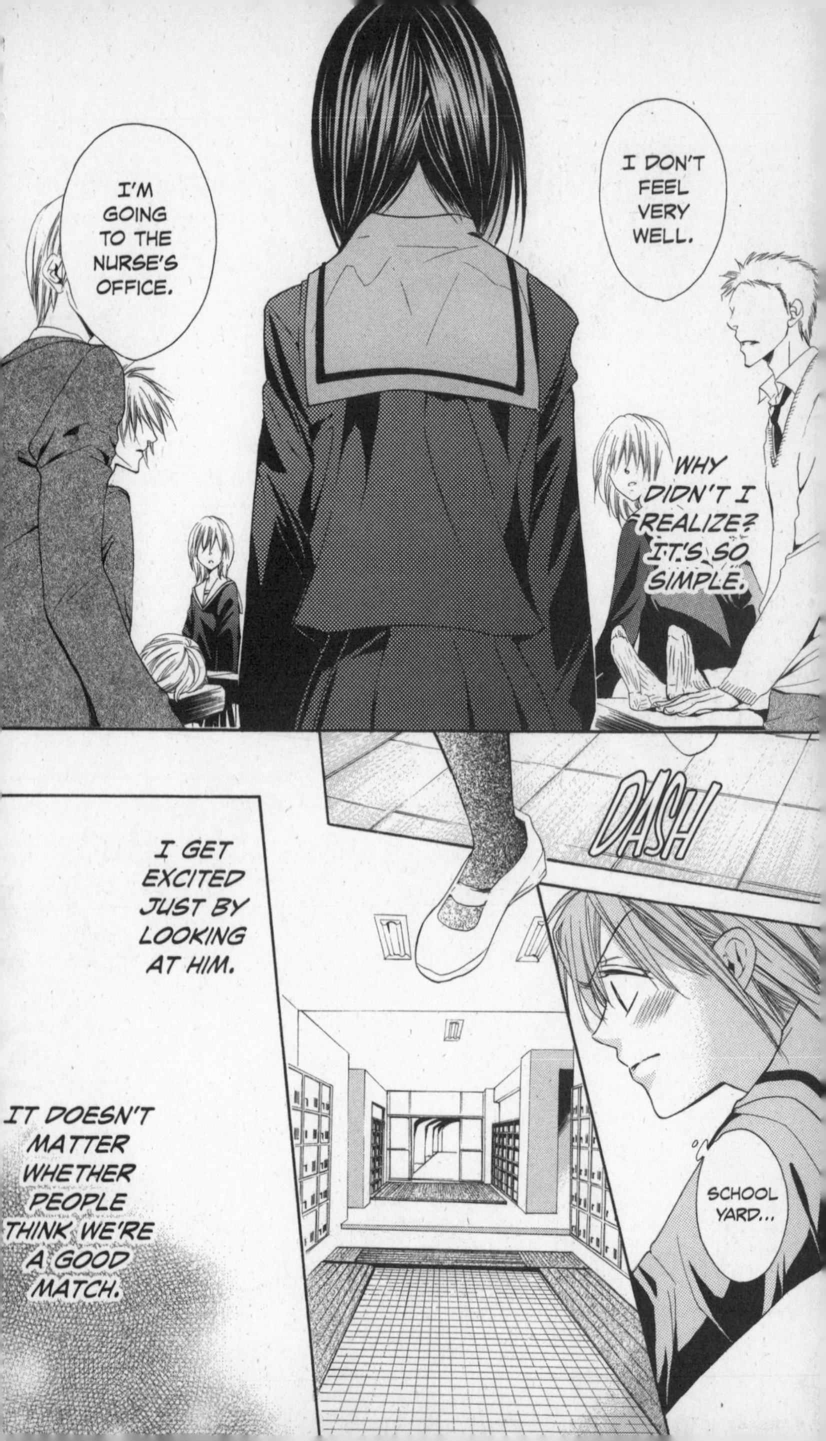
I DON'T FEEL VERY WELL.
I'M GOING TO THE NURSE'S OFFICE.
WHY DIDN'T I REALIZE? IT'S SO SIMPLE.
DASH
I GET EXCITED JUST BY LOOKING AT HIM.
SCHOOL YARD...
IT DOESN'T MATTER WHETHER PEOPLE THINK WE'RE A GOOD MATCH.

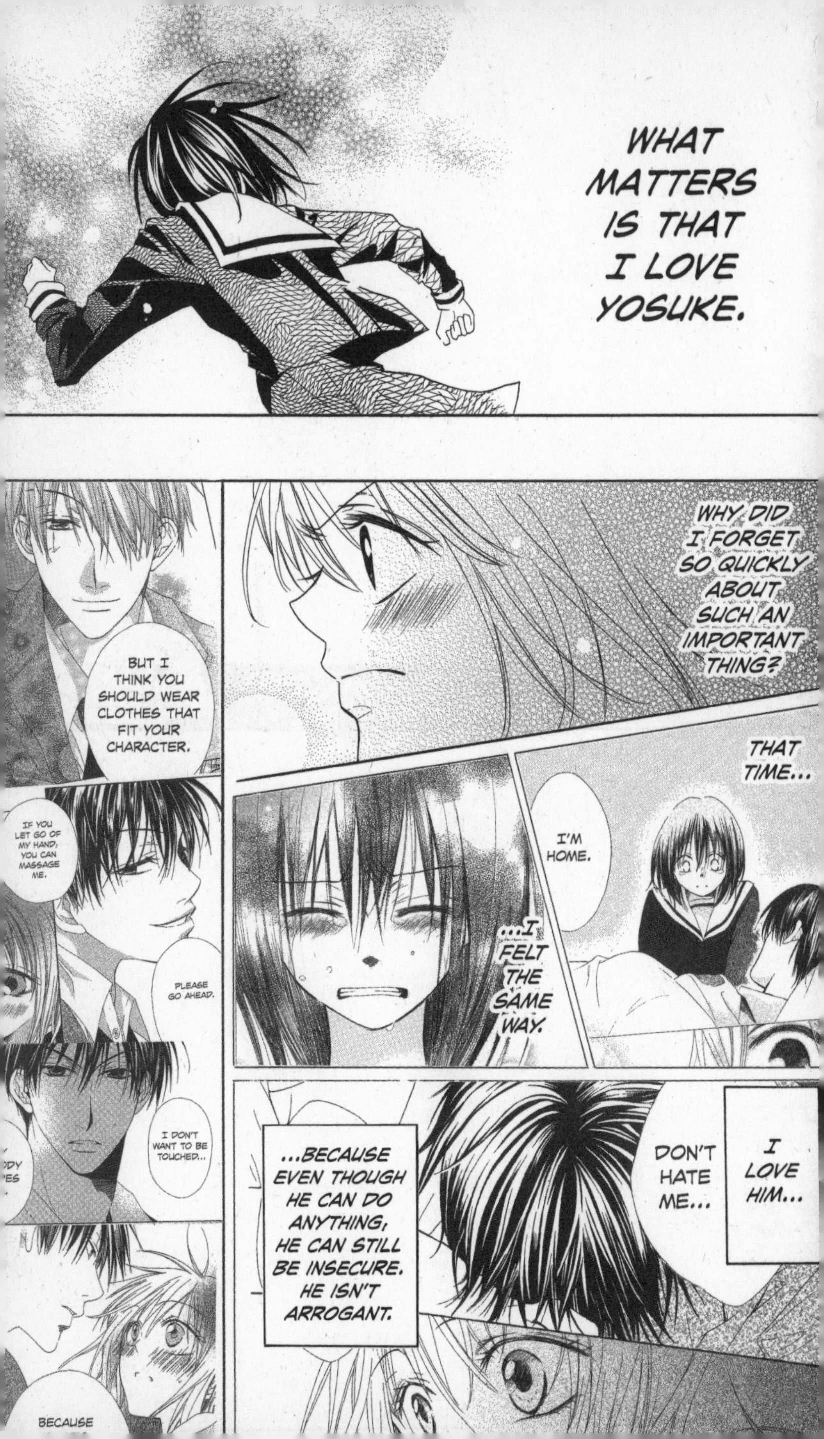
WHAT MATTERS IS THAT I LOVE YOSUKE.
WHY DID I FORGET SO QUICKLY ABOUT SUCH AN IMPORTANT THING?
THAT TIME...
I'M HOME.
...I FELT THE SAME WAY.
I LOVE HIM...
DON'T HATE ME...
...BECAUSE EVEN THOUGH HE CAN DO ANYTHING, HE CAN STILL BE INSECURE. HE ISN'T ARROGANT.
BUT I THINK YOU SHOULD WEAR CLOTHES THAT FIT YOUR CHARACTER.
IF YOU LET GO OF MY HAND, YOU CAN MASSAGE ME.
PLEASE GO AHEAD.
I DON'T WANT TO BE TOUCHED...
BECAUSE

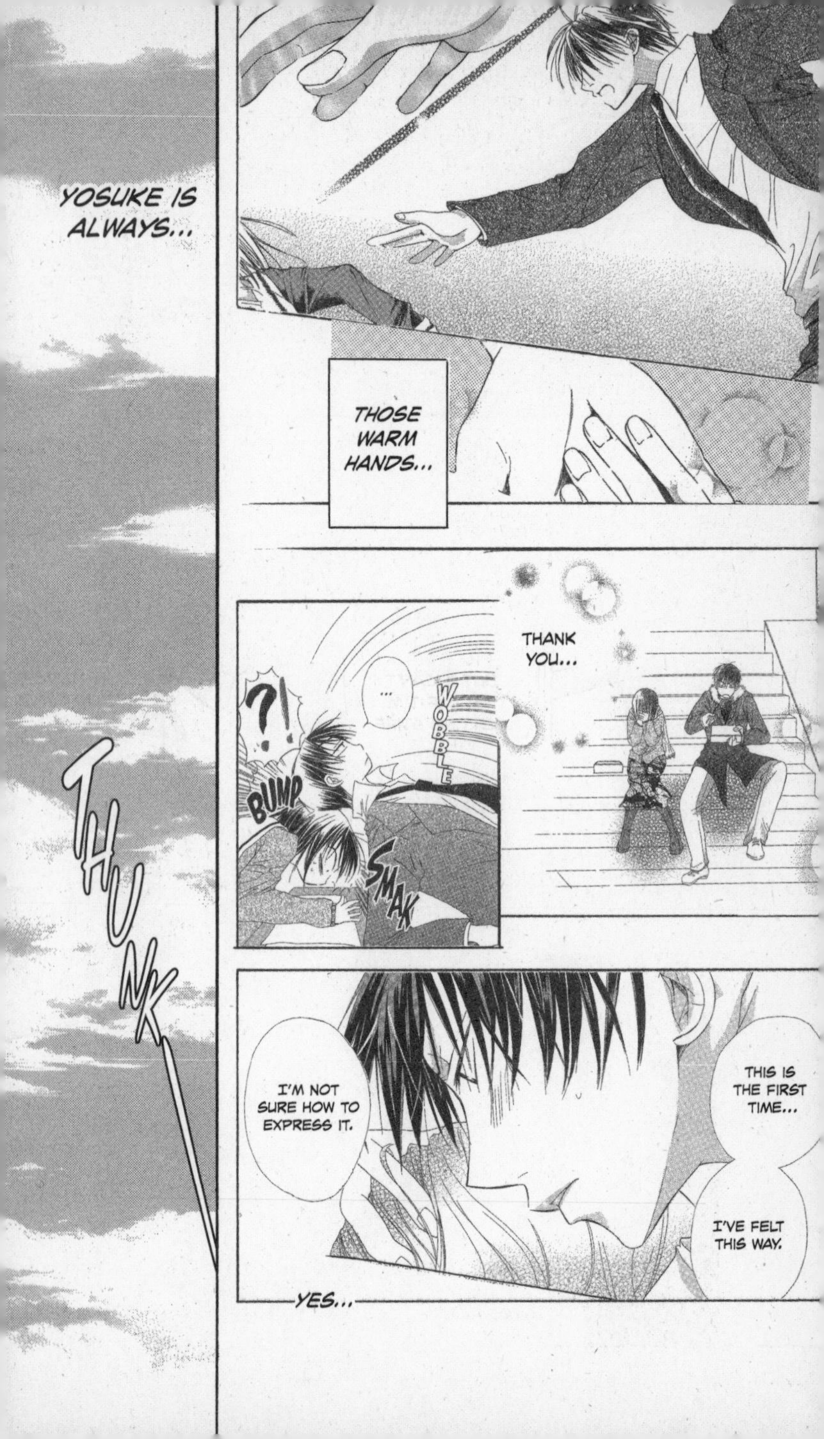
THOSE WARM HANDS...
THANK YOU...
...
WOBBLE
?!
BUMP
SMAK
THIS IS THE FIRST TIME...
I'VE FELT THIS WAY.
I'M NOT SURE HOW TO EXPRESS IT.
YES...
YOSUKE IS ALWAYS...
THUNK

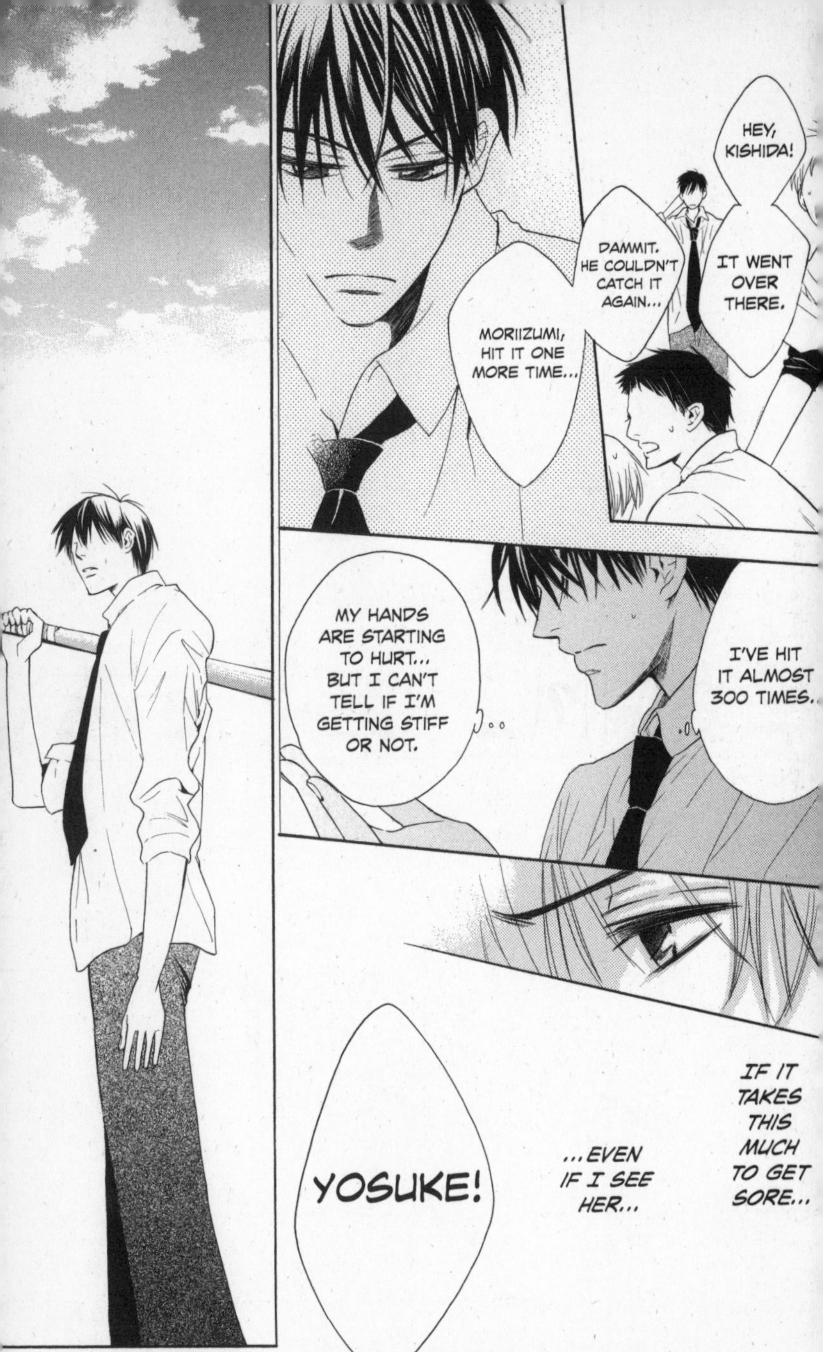
HEY, KISHIDA!
IT WENT OVER THERE.
DAMMIT. HE COULDN'T CATCH IT AGAIN...
MORIIZUMI, HIT IT ONE MORE TIME...
I'VE HIT IT ALMOST 300 TIMES.
MY HANDS ARE STARTING TO HURT... BUT I CAN'T TELL IF I'M GETTING STIFF OR NOT.
IF IT TAKES THIS MUCH TO GET SORE...
...EVEN IF I SEE HER...
YOSUKE!

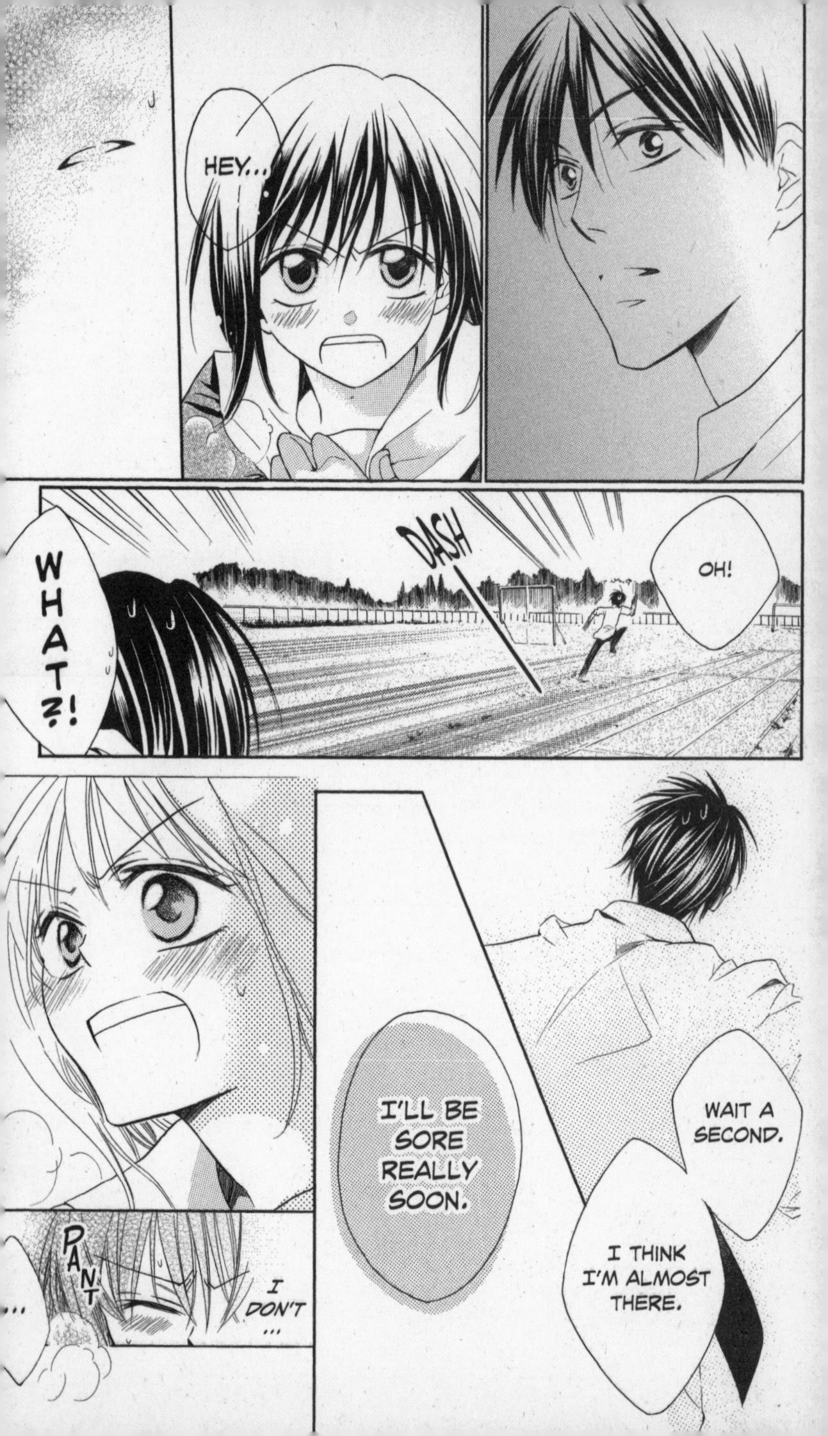
HEY...
OH!
DASH
WHAT?!
WAIT A SECOND.
I THINK I'M ALMOST THERE.
I'LL BE SORE REALLY SOON.
I DON'T ...
PANT
...

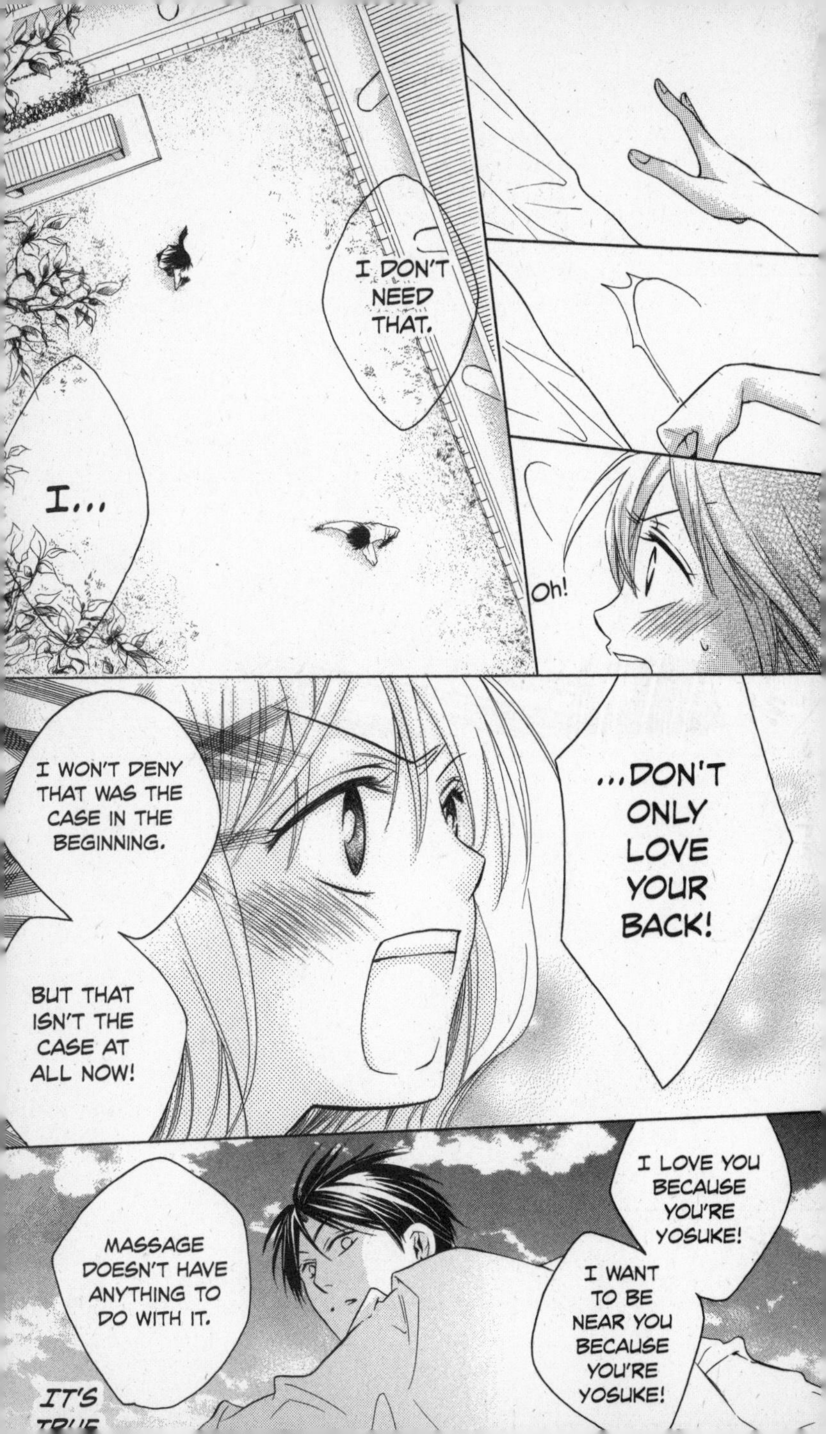
Oh!
I DON'T NEED THAT.
I...
...DON'T ONLY LOVE YOUR BACK!
I WON'T DENY THAT WAS THE CASE IN THE BEGINNING.
BUT THAT ISN'T THE CASE AT ALL NOW!
I LOVE YOU BECAUSE YOU'RE YOSUKE!
I WANT TO BE NEAR YOU BECAUSE YOU'RE YOSUKE!
MASSAGE DOESN'T HAVE ANYTHING TO DO WITH IT.
IT'S

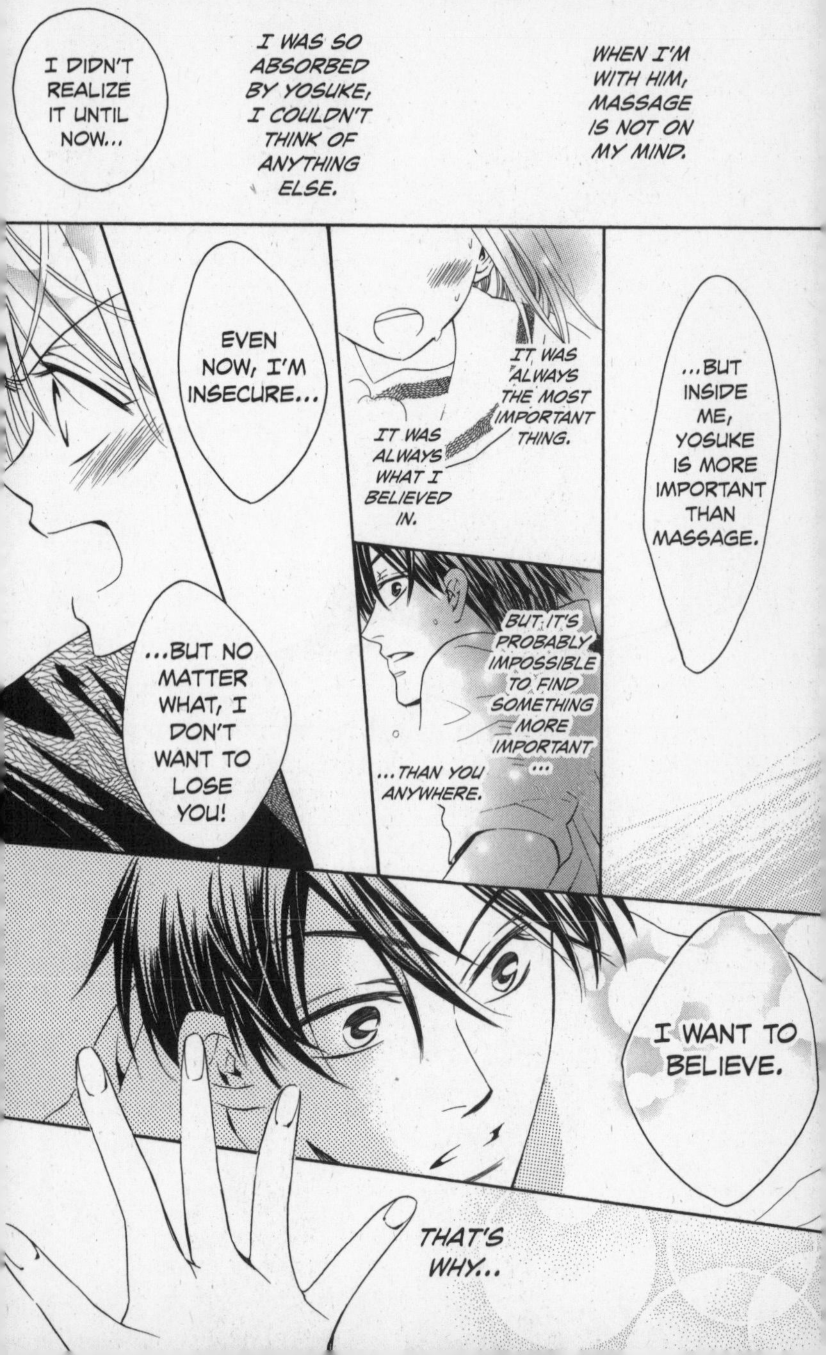
WHEN I'M WITH HIM, MASSAGE IS NOT ON MY MIND.
I WAS SO ABSORBED BY YOSUKE, I COULDN'T THINK OF ANYTHING ELSE.
I DIDN'T REALIZE IT UNTIL NOW...
...BUT INSIDE ME, YOSUKE IS MORE IMPORTANT THAN MASSAGE.
IT WAS ALWAYS THE MOST IMPORTANT THING.
IT WAS ALWAYS WHAT I BELIEVED IN.
BUT IT'S PROBABLY IMPOSSIBLE TO FIND SOMETHING MORE IMPORTANT...
...THAN YOU ANYWHERE.
EVEN NOW, I'M INSECURE...
...BUT NO MATTER WHAT, I DON'T WANT TO LOSE YOU!
I WANT TO BELIEVE.
THAT'S WHY...

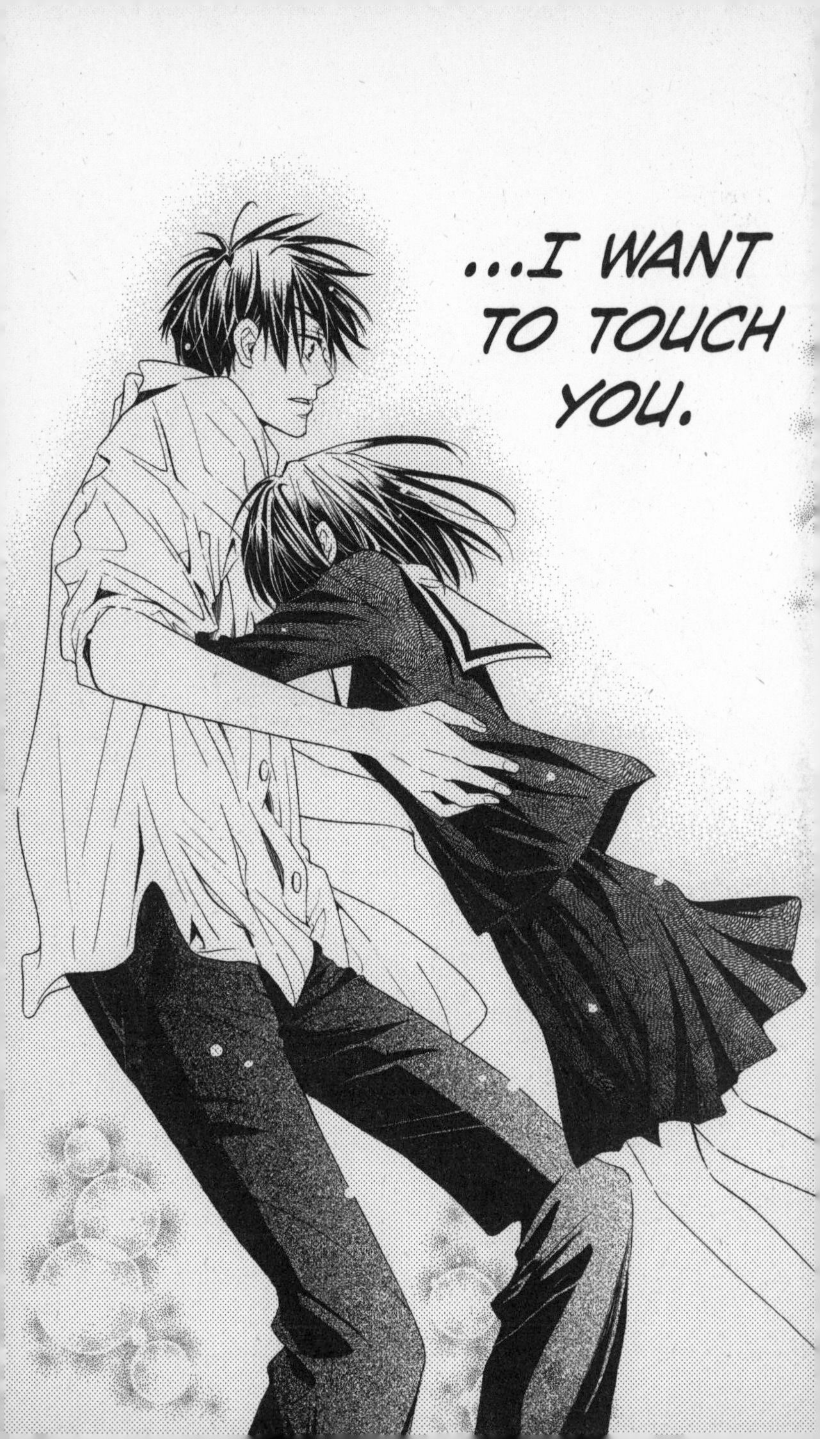
...I WANT TO TOUCH YOU.

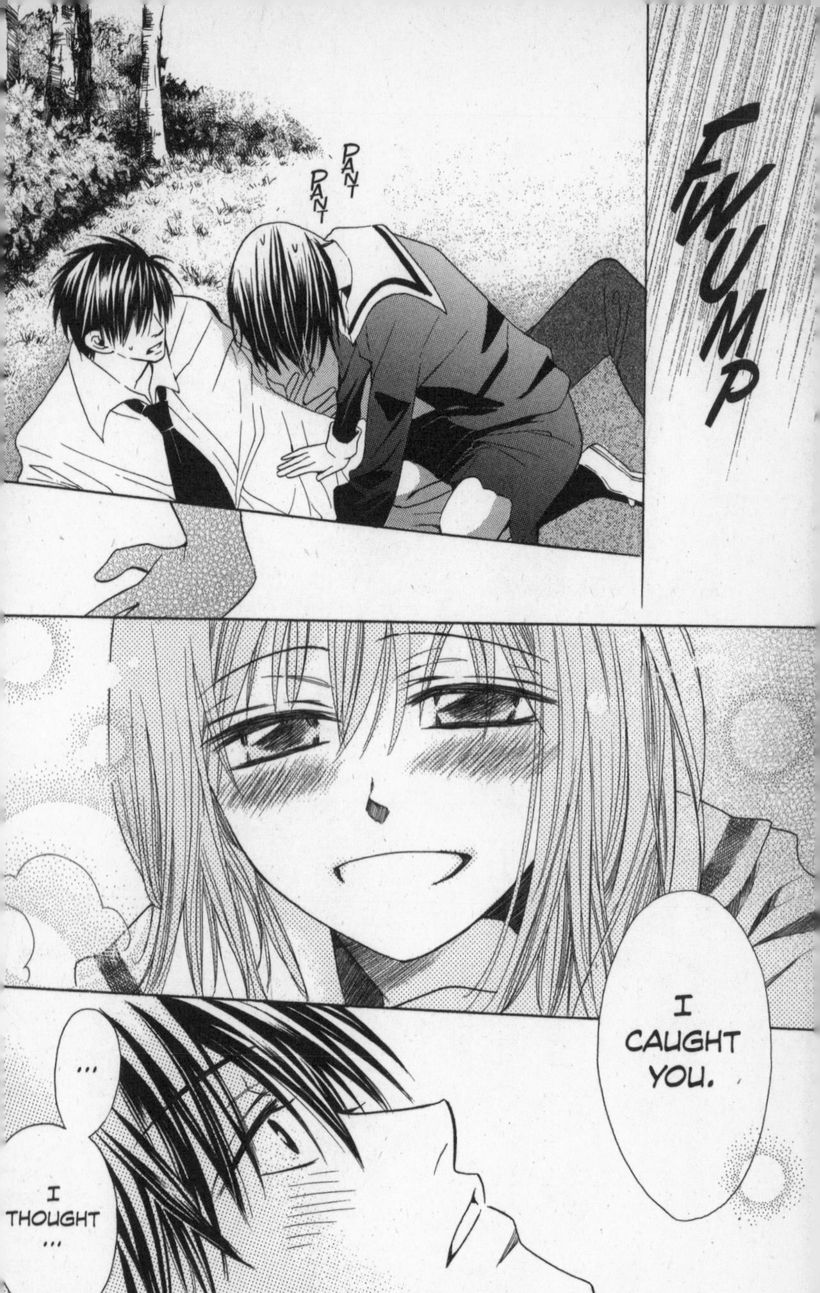
FWUMP
PANT PANT
I CAUGHT YOU.
...
I THOUGHT ...

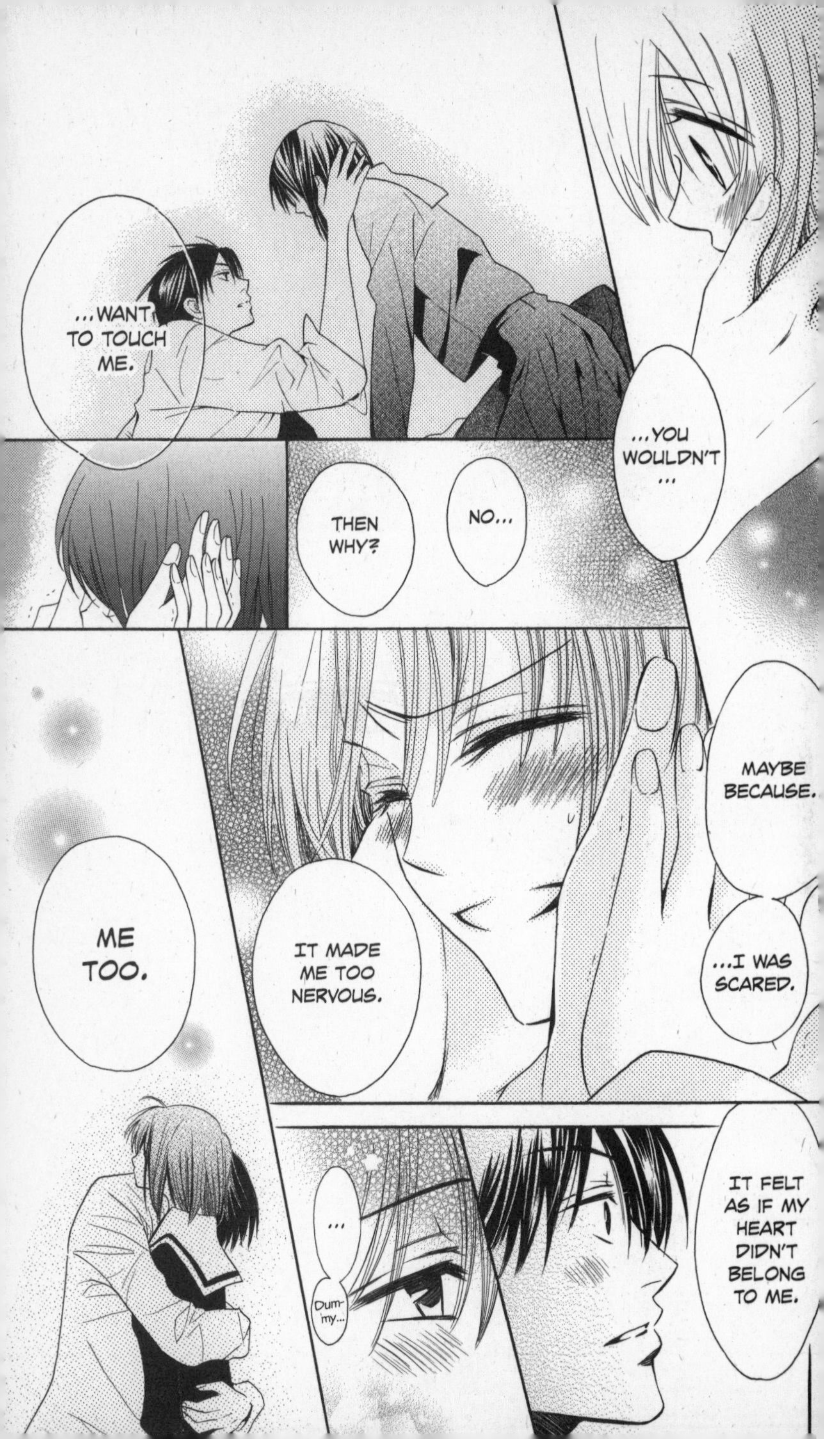
...YOU WOULDN'T ...
...WANT TO TOUCH ME.
NO...
THEN WHY?
MAYBE BECAUSE.
...I WAS SCARED.
IT MADE ME TOO NERVOUS.
ME TOO.
IT FELT AS IF MY HEART DIDN'T BELONG TO ME.
...
Dum-my...

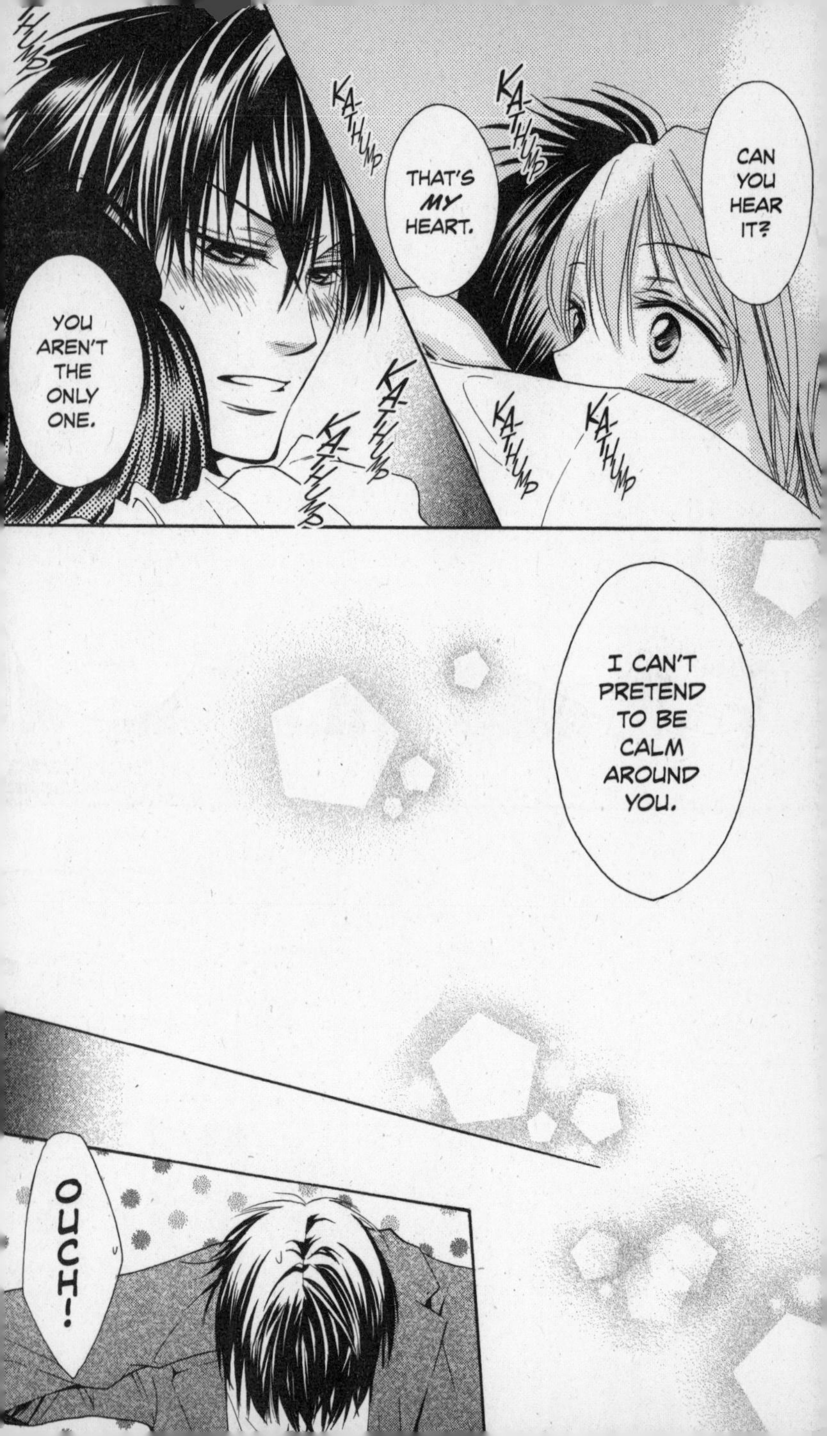
CAN YOU HEAR IT?
KA-THUMP
THAT'S MY HEART.
KA-THUMP
KA-THUMP
KA-THUMP
KA-THUMP
KA-THUMP
YOU AREN'T THE ONLY ONE.
I CAN'T PRETEND TO BE CALM AROUND YOU.
OUCH!

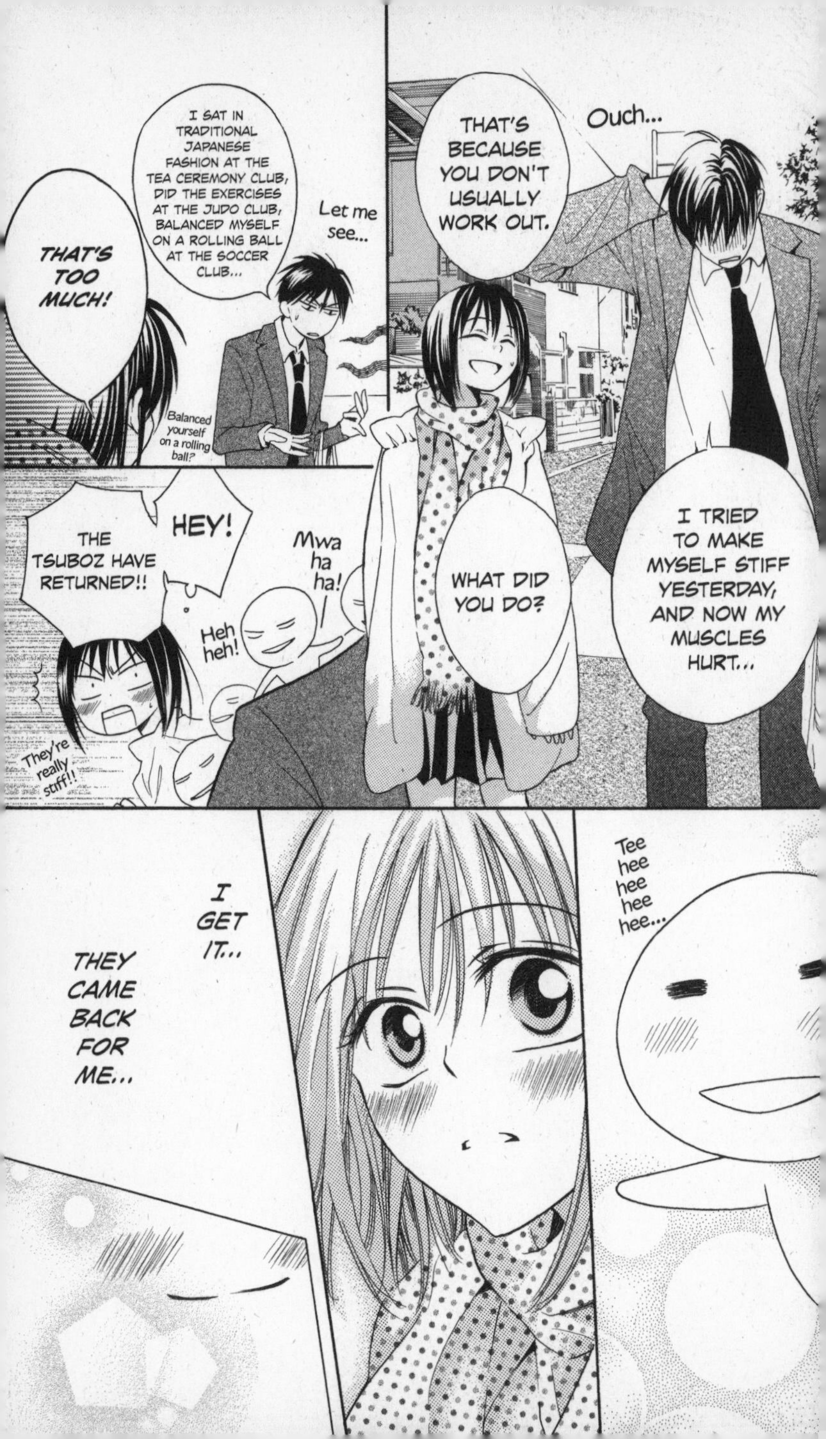
Ouch...
THAT'S BECAUSE YOU DON'T USUALLY WORK OUT.
WHAT DID YOU DO?
I TRIED TO MAKE MYSELF STIFF YESTERDAY, AND NOW MY MUSCLES HURT...
Let me see...
I SAT IN TRADITIONAL JAPANESE FASHION AT THE TEA CEREMONY CLUB, DID THE EXERCISES AT THE JUDO CLUB, BALANCED MYSELF ON A ROLLING BALL AT THE SOCCER CLUB...
THAT'S TOO MUCH!
Balanced yourself on a rolling ball?
HEY!
THE TSUBOZ HAVE RETURNED!!
Mwa ha ha!
Heh heh!
They're really stiff!!
Tee hee hee hee hee...
I GET IT...
THEY CAME BACK FOR ME...

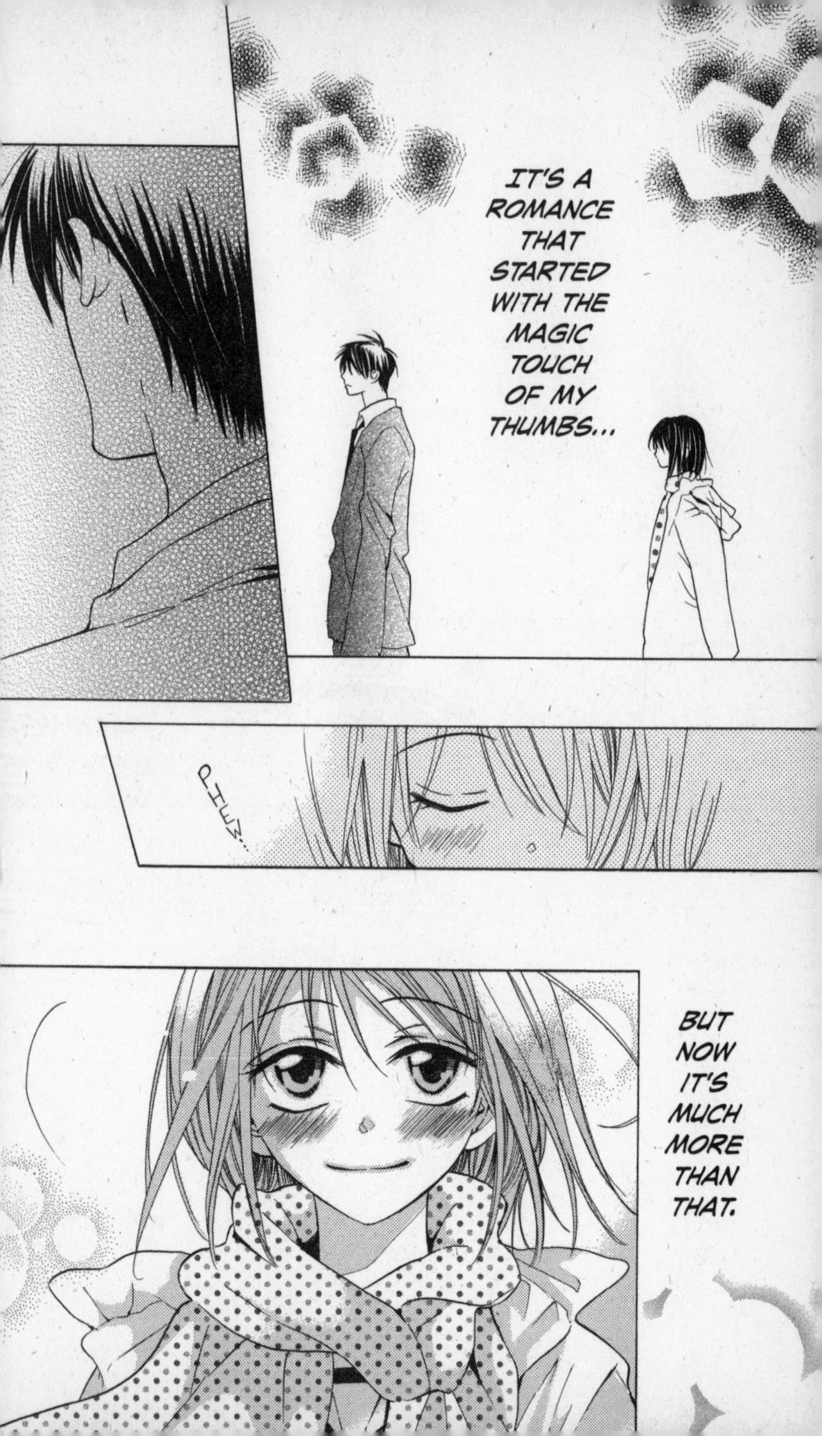
IT'S A ROMANCE THAT STARTED WITH THE MAGIC TOUCH OF MY THUMBS...
PHEW...
BUT NOW IT'S MUCH MORE THAN THAT.

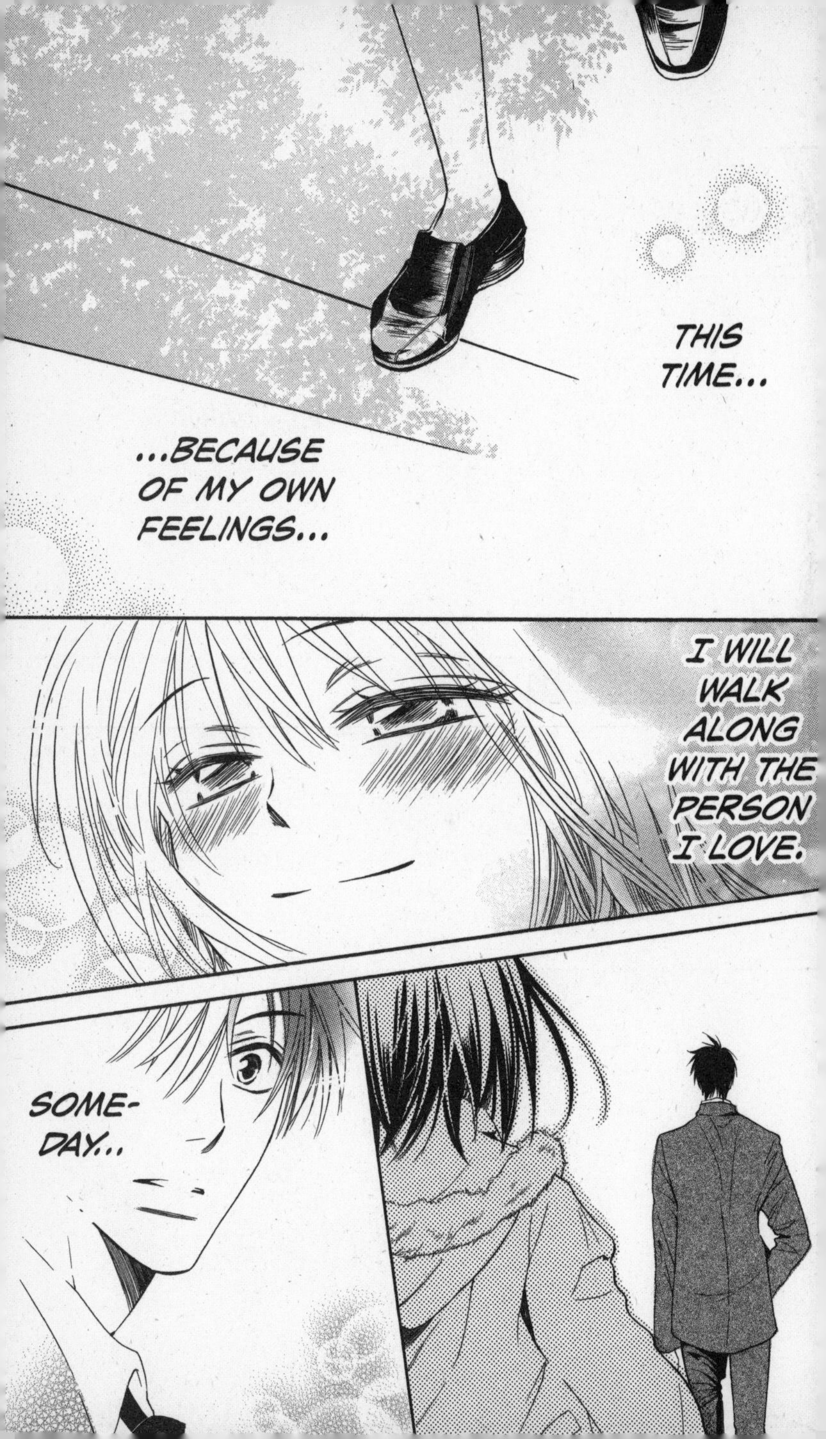
THIS TIME...
...BECAUSE OF MY OWN FEELINGS...
I WILL WALK ALONG WITH THE PERSON I LOVE.
SOME-DAY...

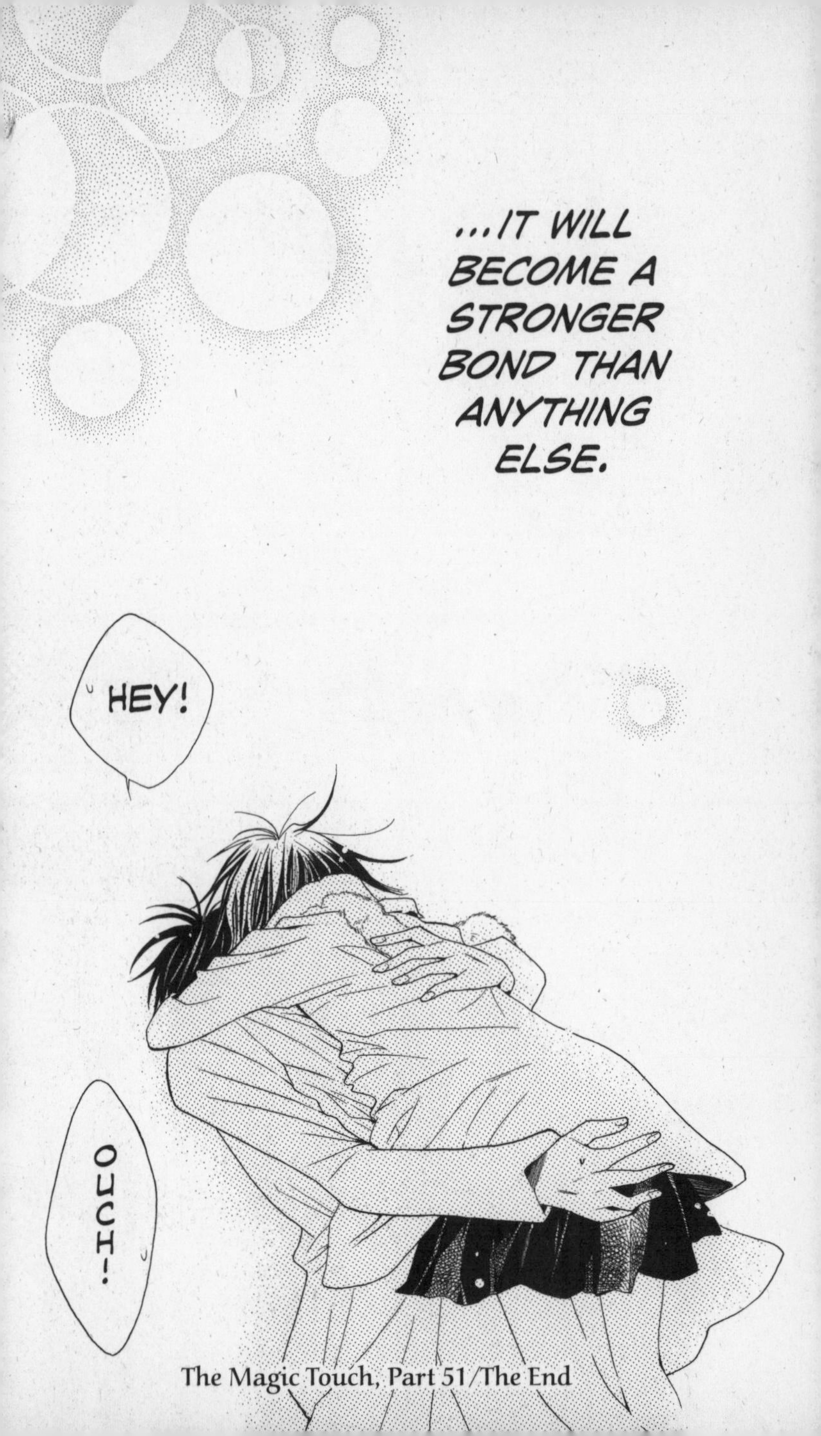
...IT WILL BECOME A STRONGER BOND THAN ANYTHING ELSE.
HEY!
OUCH!
The Magic Touch, Part 51/The End

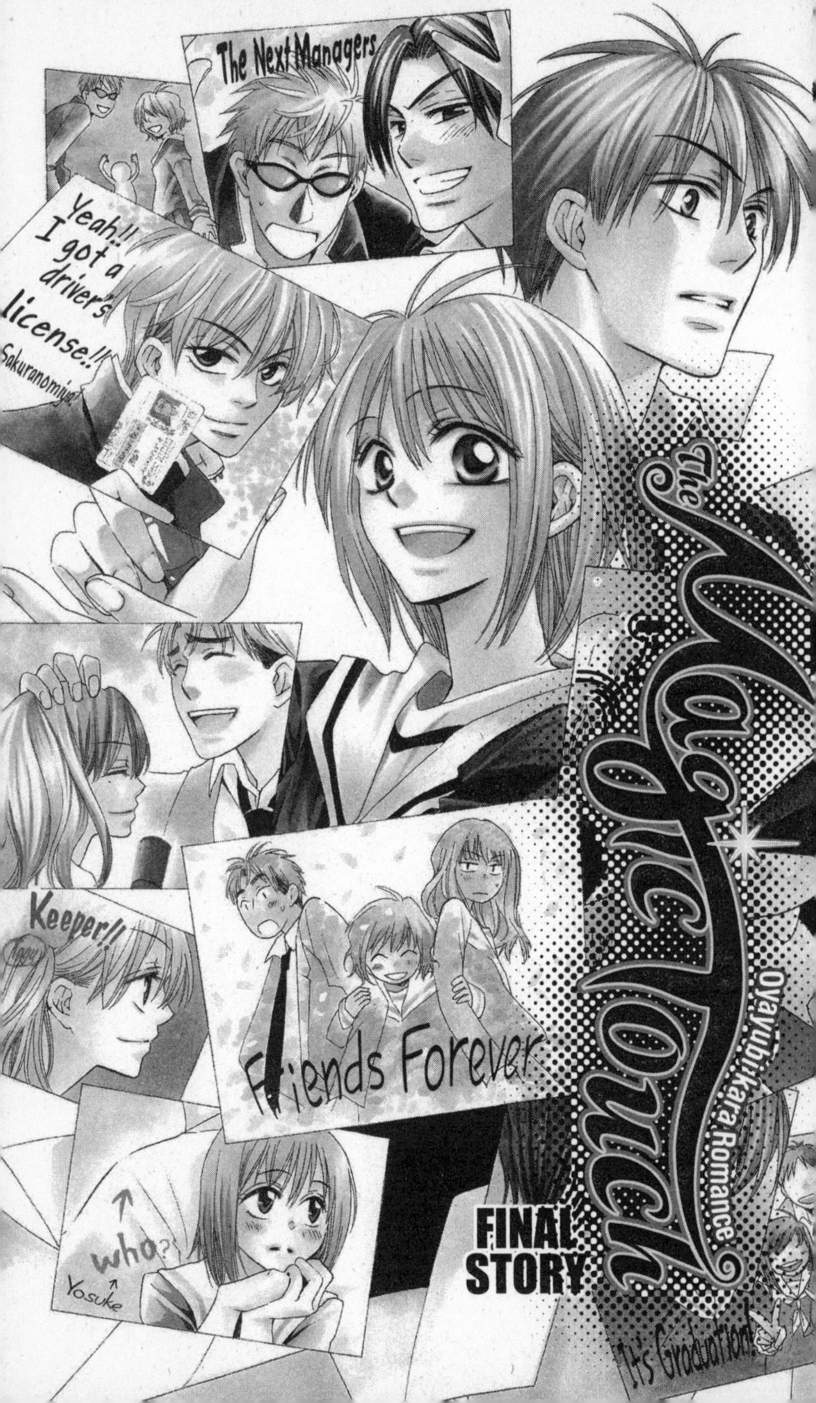
The Magic Touch
Oyayubi kara Romance
FINAL STORY
It's Graduation!
The Next Managers
Yeah!! I got a driver's license!!
Sakuranomiya
Friends Forever
Keeper!!
who?
Yosuke

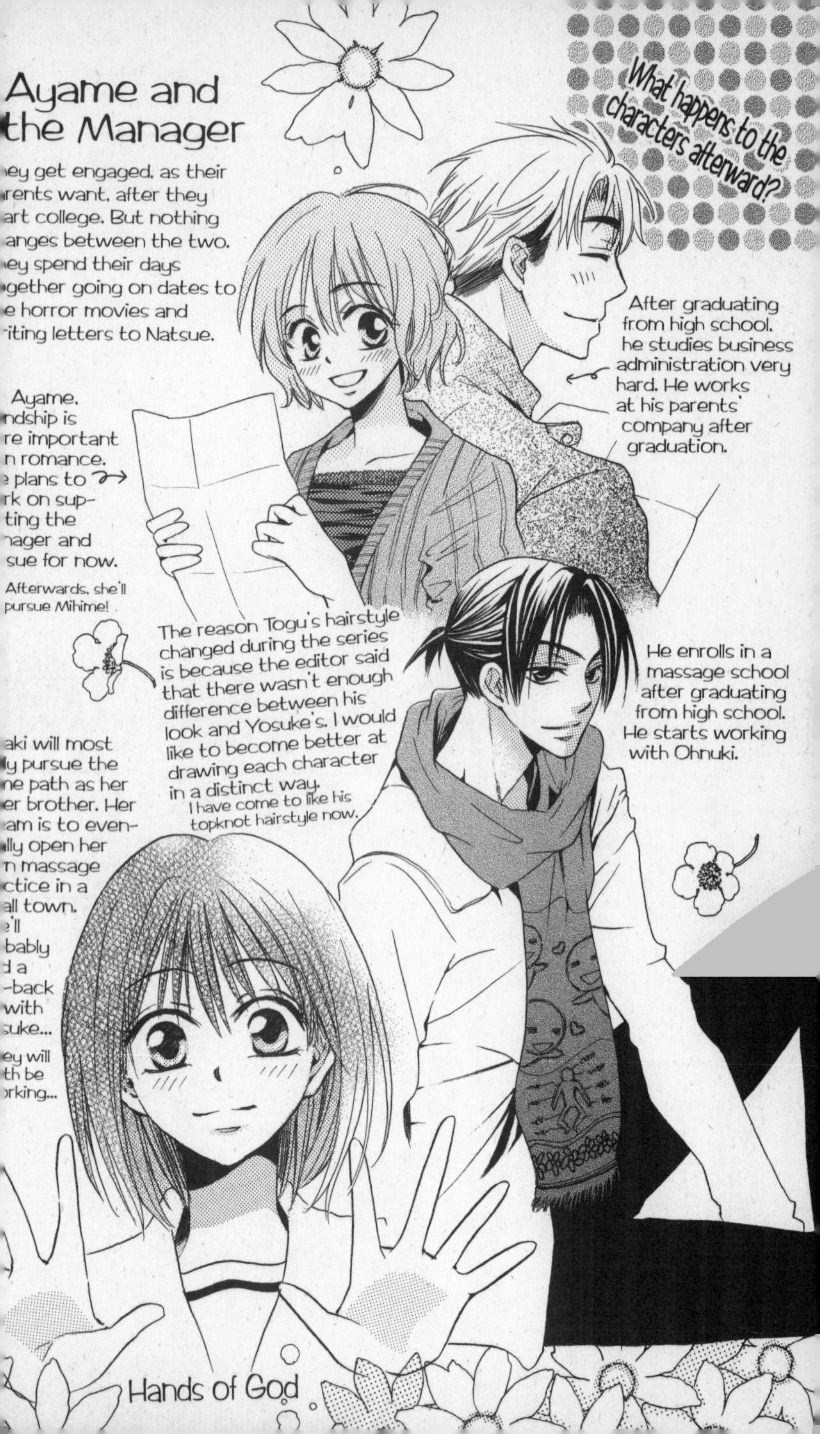
What happens to the characters afterward?
Ayame and the Manager
ıey get engaged, as their ırents want, after they art college. But nothing ıanges between the two. ıey spend their days ›gether going on dates to e horror movies and ·iting letters to Natsue.
After graduating from high school, he studies business administration very hard. He works at his parents' company after graduation.
Ayame, ndship is re important n romance. e plans to rk on sup- ting the ıager and sue for now.
Afterwards, she'll pursue Mihime!
The reason Togu's hairstyle changed during the series is because the editor said that there wasn't enough difference between his look and Yosuke's. I would like to become better at drawing each character in a distinct way.
I have come to like his topknot hairstyle now.
He enrolls in a massage school after graduating from high school. He starts working with Ohnuki.
aki will most ly pursue the ne path as her er brother. Her am is to even- ılly open her n massage ctice in a all town. e'll bably d a -back with suke...
ey will th be orking...
Hands of God

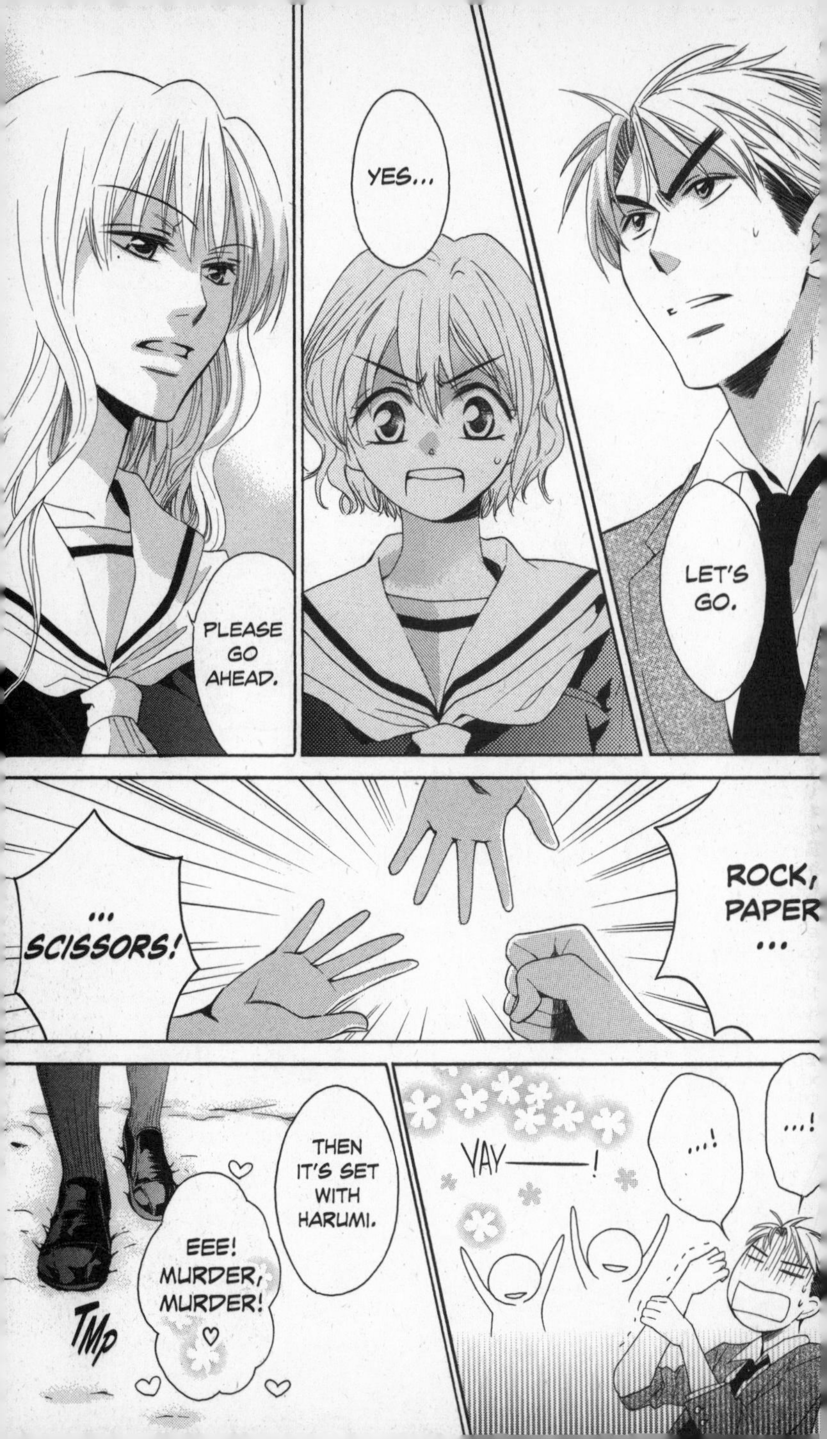
LET'S GO.
YES...
PLEASE GO AHEAD.
ROCK, PAPER ...
... SCISSORS!
...!
...!
YAY———!
THEN IT'S SET WITH HARUMI.
EEE! MURDER, MURDER!
TMP

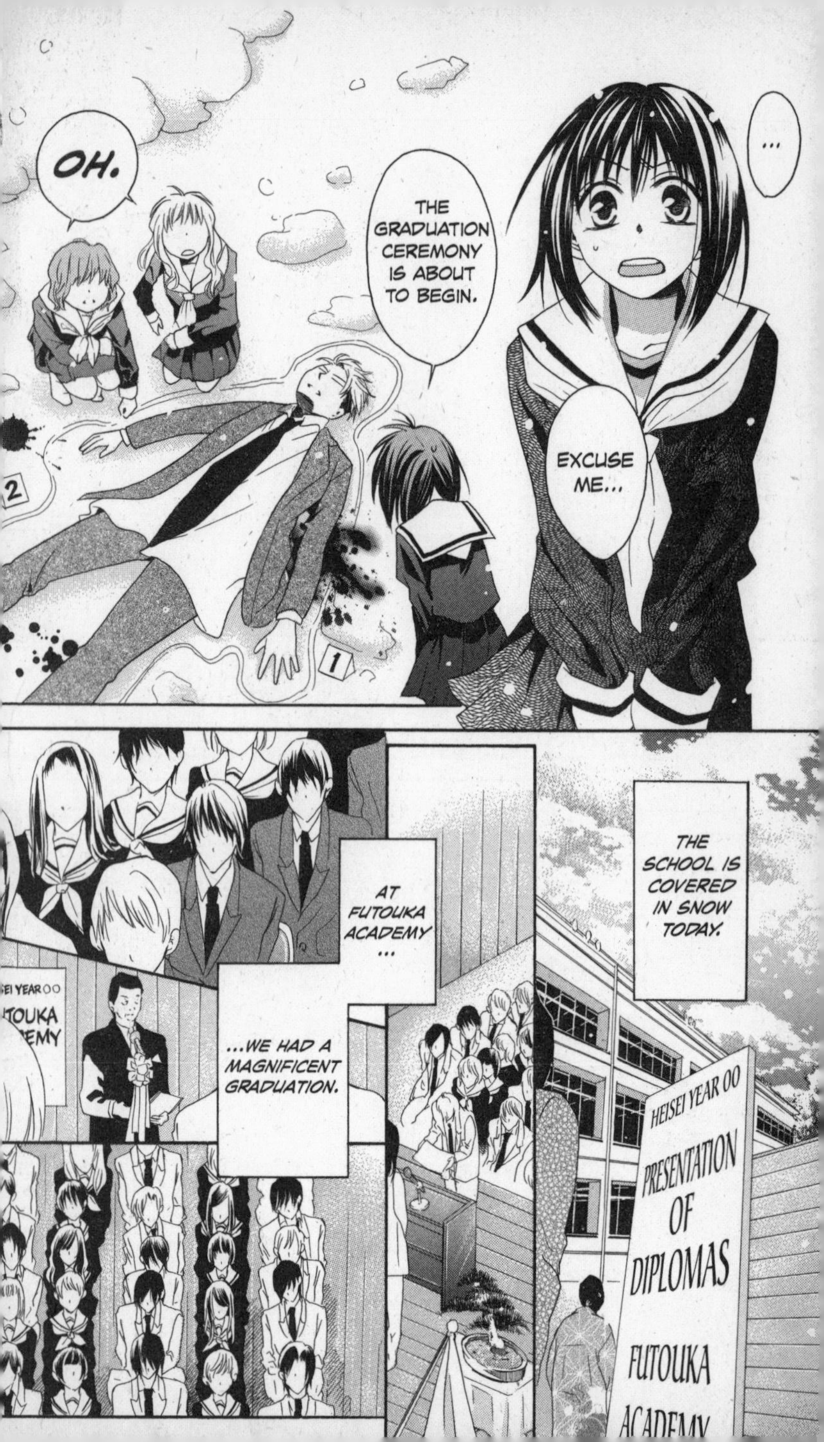
...
EXCUSE ME...
THE GRADUATION CEREMONY IS ABOUT TO BEGIN.
OH.
THE SCHOOL IS COVERED IN SNOW TODAY.
HEISEI YEAR OO
PRESENTATION OF DIPLOMAS
FUTOUKA ACADEMY
AT FUTOUKA ACADEMY...
...WE HAD A MAGNIFICENT GRADUATION.

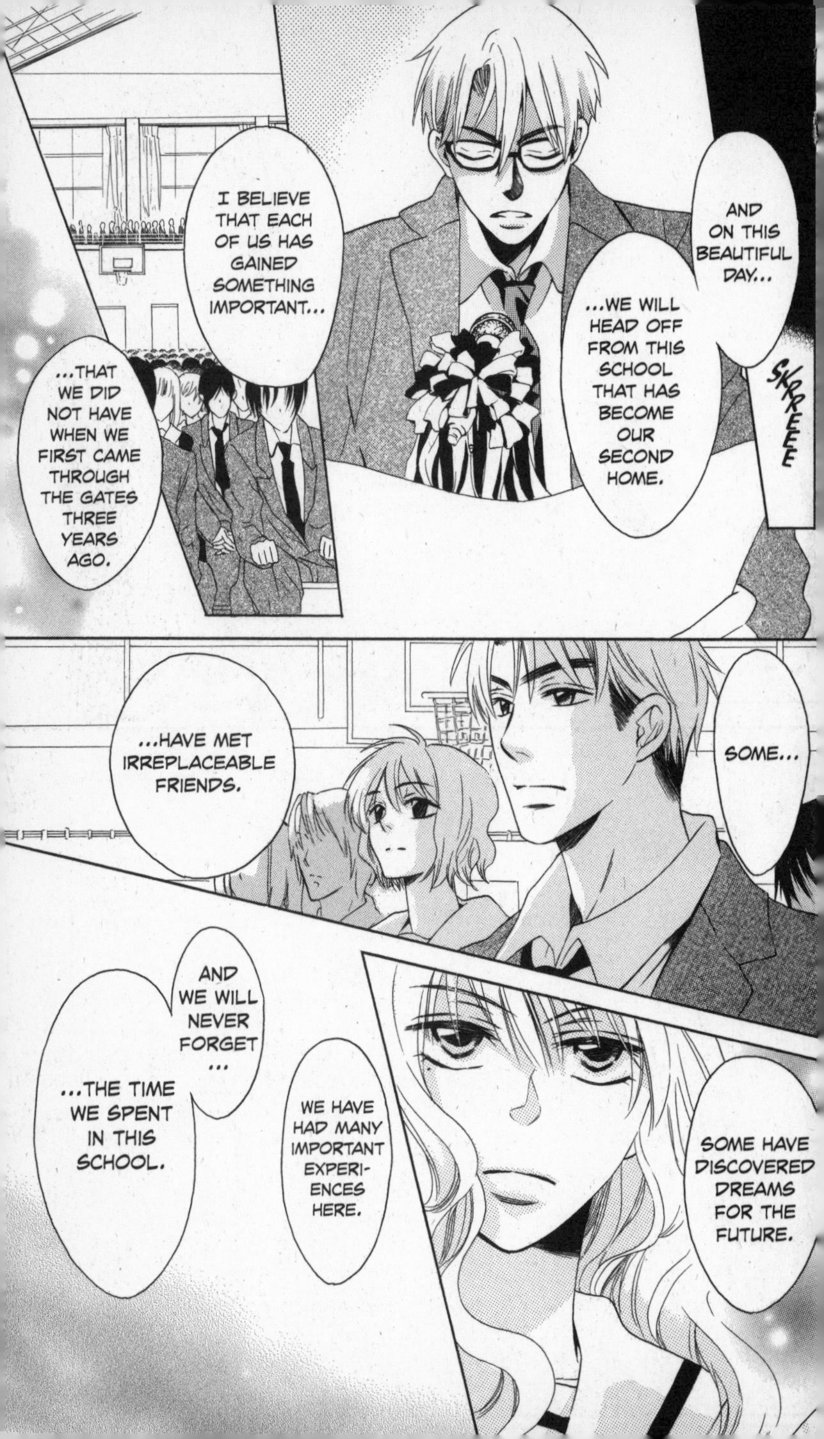
AND ON THIS BEAUTIFUL DAY...
...WE WILL HEAD OFF FROM THIS SCHOOL THAT HAS BECOME OUR SECOND HOME.
SKREEE
I BELIEVE THAT EACH OF US HAS GAINED SOMETHING IMPORTANT...
...THAT WE DID NOT HAVE WHEN WE FIRST CAME THROUGH THE GATES THREE YEARS AGO.
SOME...
...HAVE MET IRREPLACEABLE FRIENDS.
SOME HAVE DISCOVERED DREAMS FOR THE FUTURE.
WE HAVE HAD MANY IMPORTANT EXPERI-ENCES HERE.
AND WE WILL NEVER FORGET...
...THE TIME WE SPENT IN THIS SCHOOL.

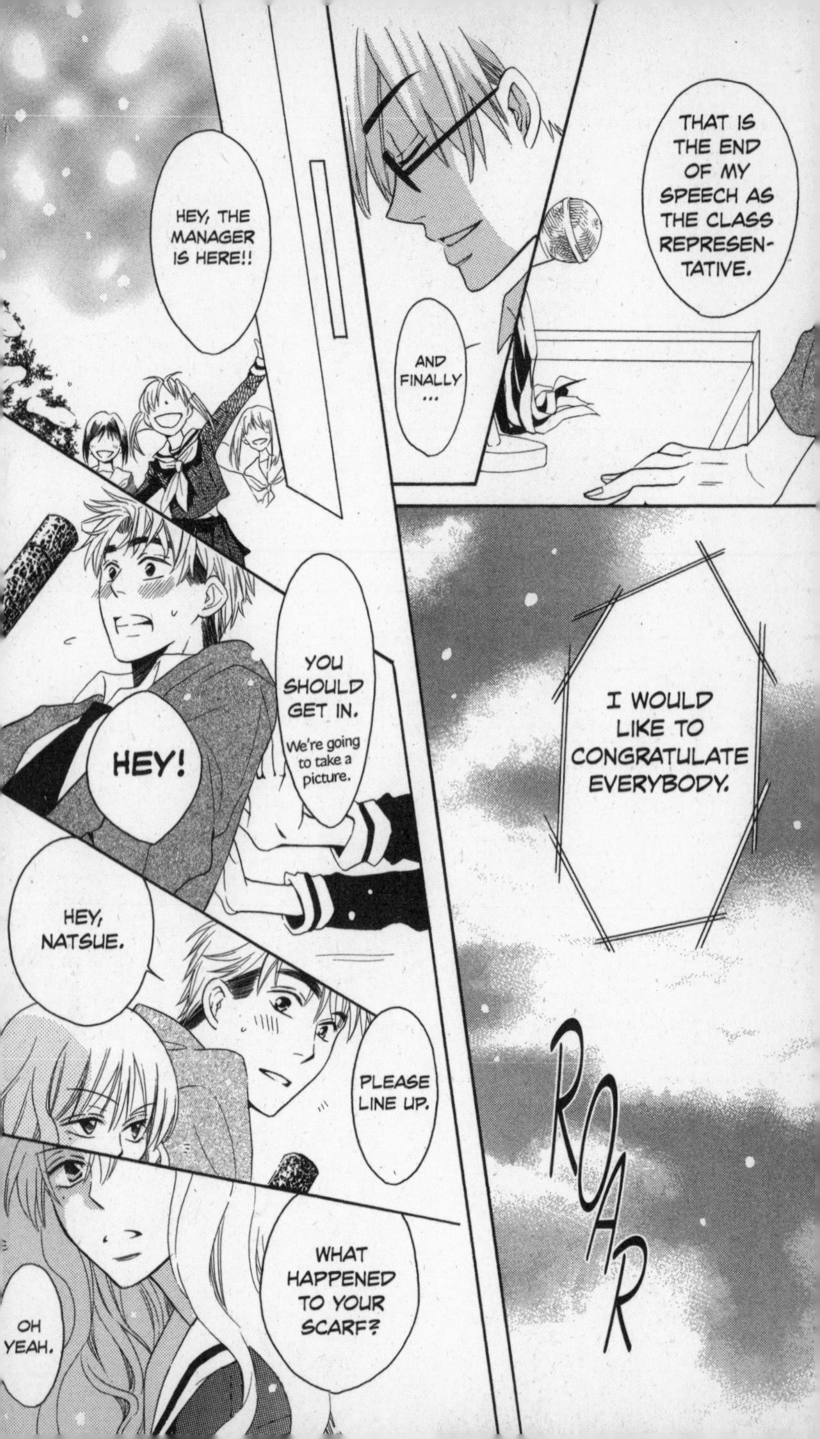
THAT IS THE END OF MY SPEECH AS THE CLASS REPRESENTATIVE.
AND FINALLY...
I WOULD LIKE TO CONGRATULATE EVERYBODY.
ROAR
HEY, THE MANAGER IS HERE!!
YOU SHOULD GET IN. We're going to take a picture.
HEY!
HEY, NATSUE.
PLEASE LINE UP.
WHAT HAPPENED TO YOUR SCARF?
OH YEAH.

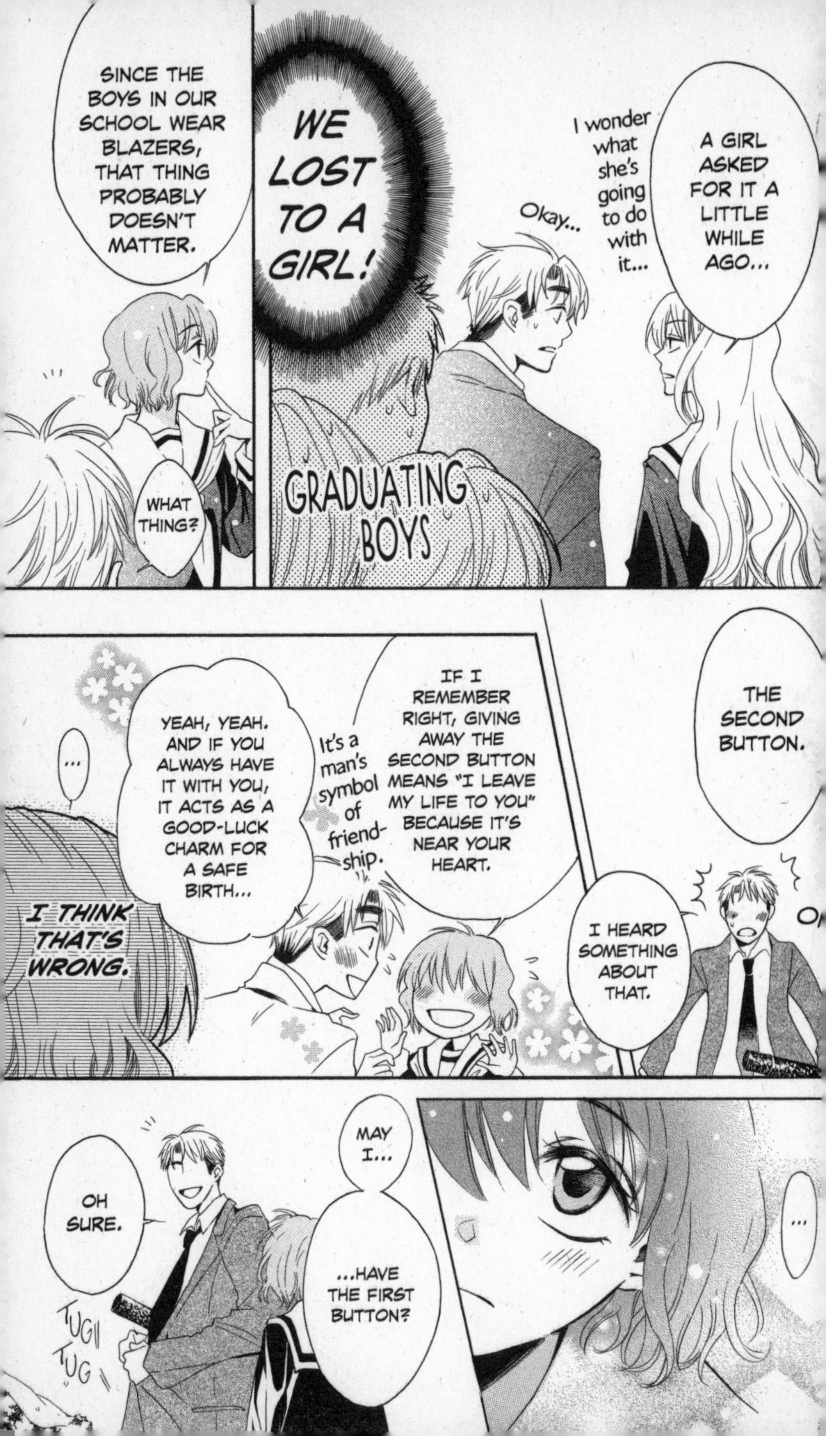
A GIRL ASKED FOR IT A LITTLE WHILE AGO...
I wonder what she's going to do with it...
Okay...
WE LOST TO A GIRL!
GRADUATING BOYS
SINCE THE BOYS IN OUR SCHOOL WEAR BLAZERS, THAT THING PROBABLY DOESN'T MATTER.
WHAT THING?
THE SECOND BUTTON.
I HEARD SOMETHING ABOUT THAT.
IF I REMEMBER RIGHT, GIVING AWAY THE SECOND BUTTON MEANS "I LEAVE MY LIFE TO YOU" BECAUSE IT'S NEAR YOUR HEART.
It's a man's symbol of friendship.
YEAH, YEAH. AND IF YOU ALWAYS HAVE IT WITH YOU, IT ACTS AS A GOOD-LUCK CHARM FOR A SAFE BIRTH...
...
I THINK THAT'S WRONG.
...
MAY I...
...HAVE THE FIRST BUTTON?
OH SURE.
TUG TUG

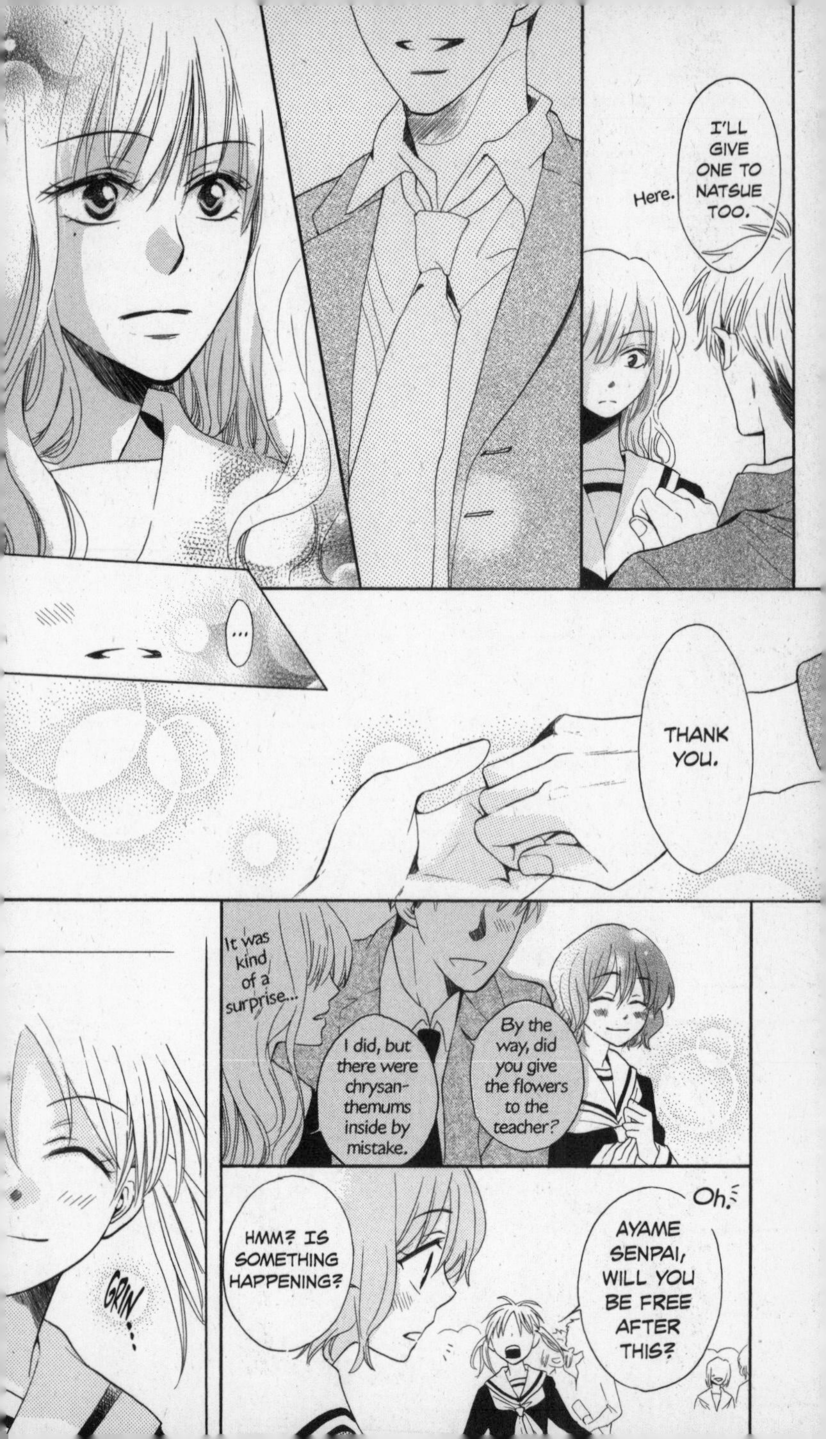

I'LL GIVE ONE TO NATSUE TOO.
Here.
...
THANK YOU.
By the way, did you give the flowers to the teacher?
I did, but there were chrysanthemums inside by mistake.
It was kind of a surprise...
Oh.
AYAME SENPAI, WILL YOU BE FREE AFTER THIS?
HMM? IS SOMETHING HAPPENING?
GRIN...

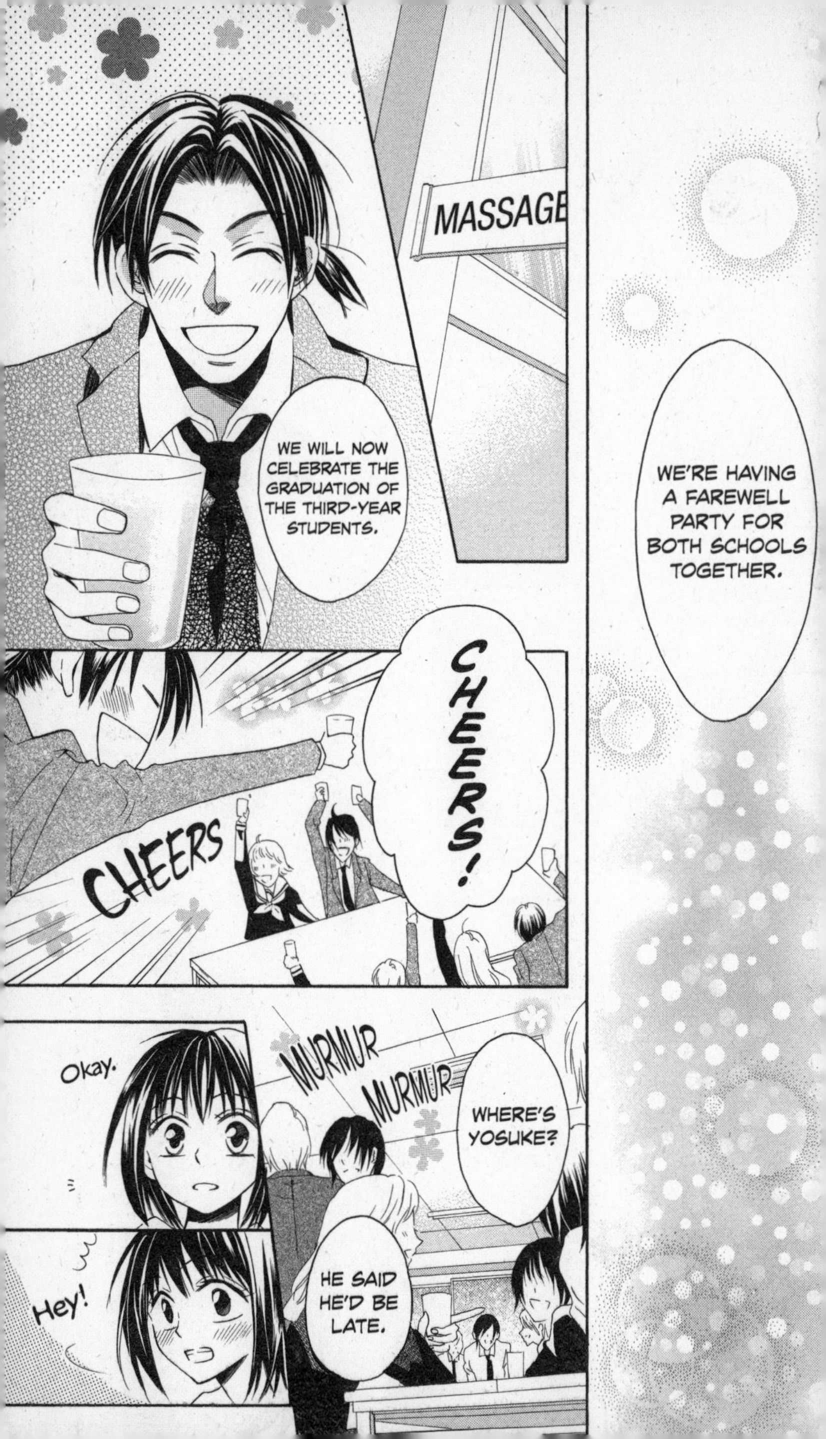
WE'RE HAVING A FAREWELL PARTY FOR BOTH SCHOOLS TOGETHER.
MASSAGE
WE WILL NOW CELEBRATE THE GRADUATION OF THE THIRD-YEAR STUDENTS.
CHEERS!
CHEERS
MURMUR
MURMUR
WHERE'S YOSUKE?
Okay.
HE SAID HE'D BE LATE.
Hey!

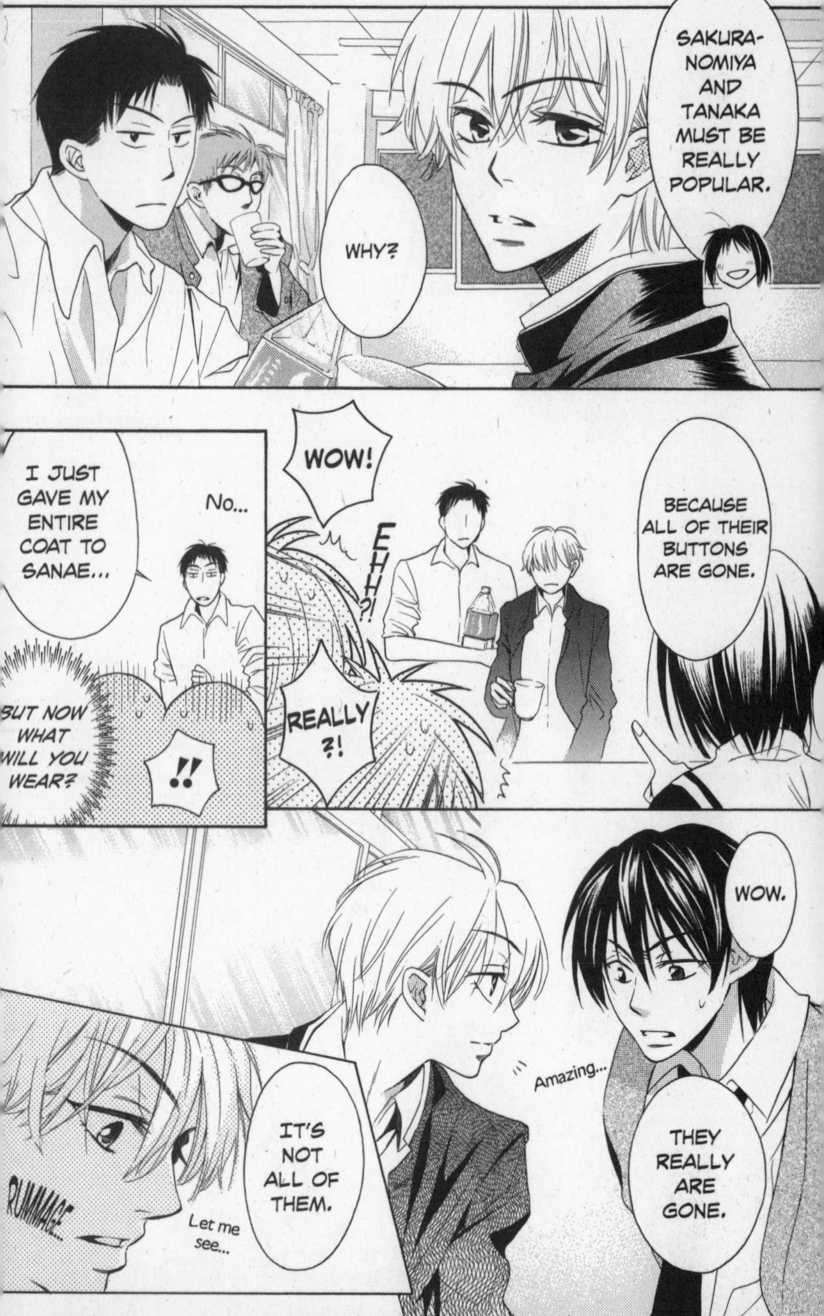
SAKURA-NOMIYA AND TANAKA MUST BE REALLY POPULAR.
WHY?
BECAUSE ALL OF THEIR BUTTONS ARE GONE.
WOW!
EHHH?!
REALLY?!
No...
I JUST GAVE MY ENTIRE COAT TO SANAE...
BUT NOW WHAT WILL YOU WEAR?
!!
WOW.
THEY REALLY ARE GONE.
Amazing...
IT'S NOT ALL OF THEM.
Let me see...
RUMMAGE...

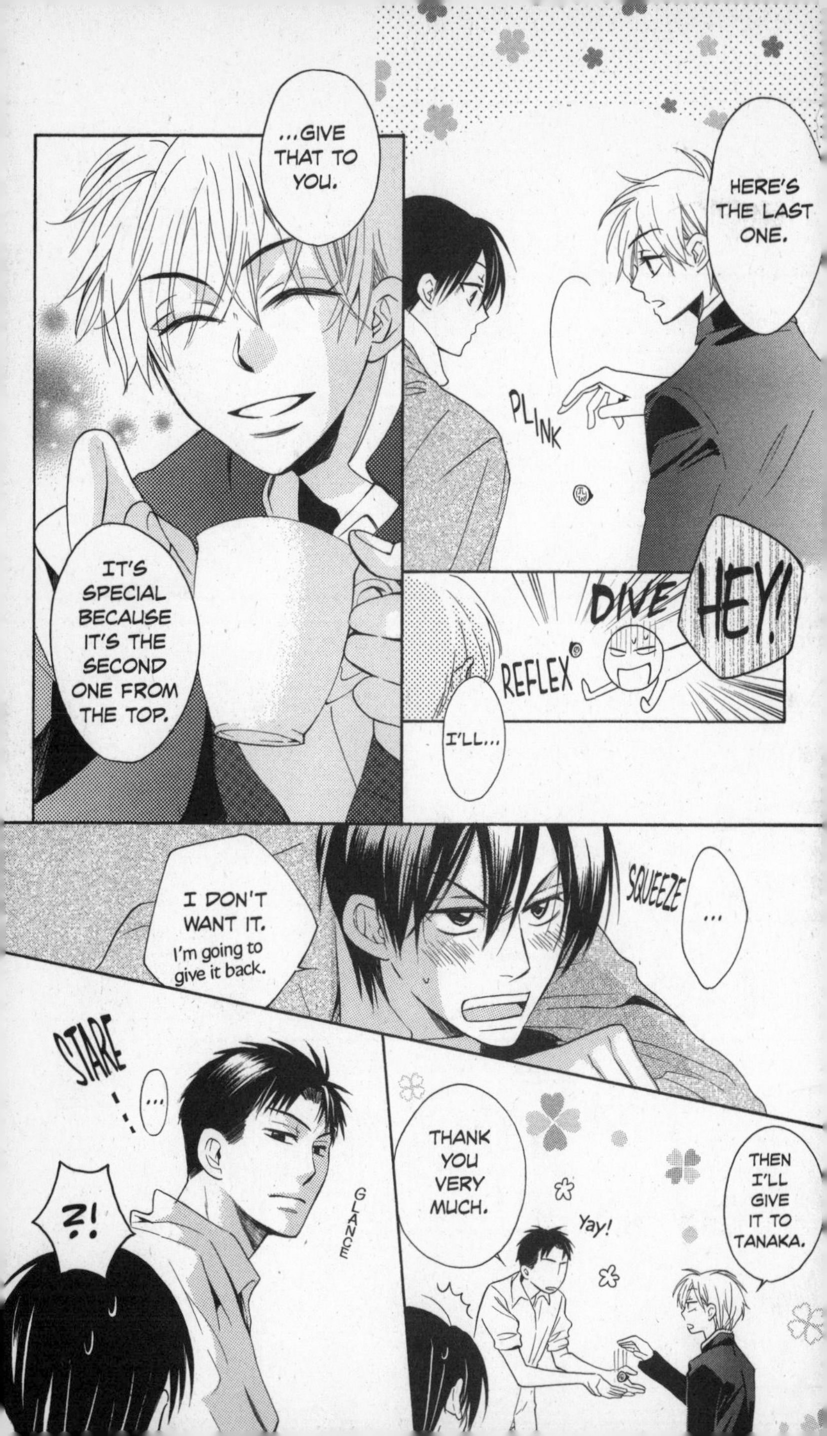
HERE'S THE LAST ONE.
PLINK
HEY!
DIVE
REFLEX
I'LL...
...GIVE THAT TO YOU.
IT'S SPECIAL BECAUSE IT'S THE SECOND ONE FROM THE TOP.
SQUEEZE
...
I DON'T WANT IT. I'm going to give it back.
THEN I'LL GIVE IT TO TANAKA.
Yay!
THANK YOU VERY MUCH.
STARE
...
GLANCE
?!

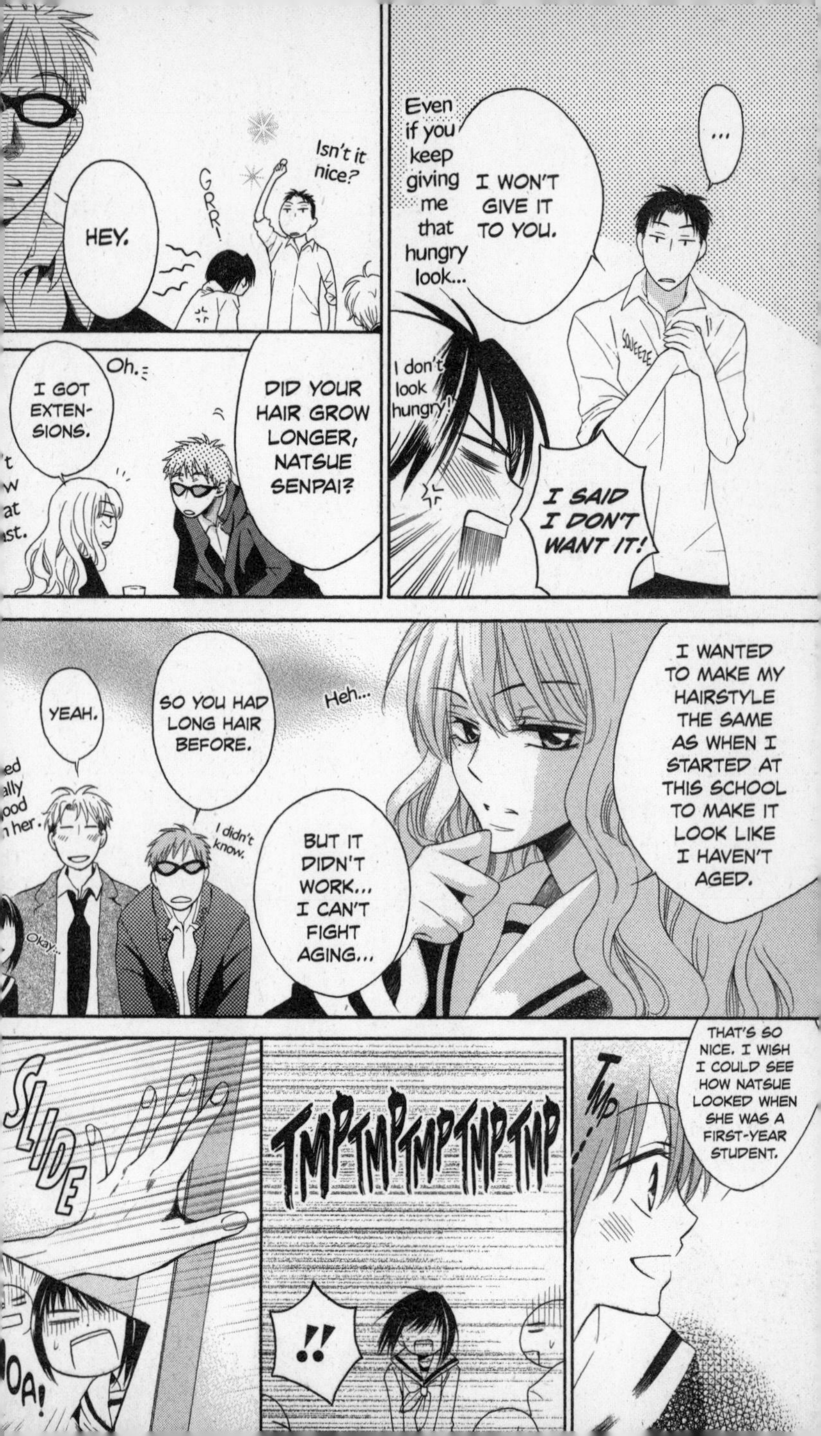
...
Even if you keep giving me that hungry look...
I WON'T GIVE IT TO YOU.
SQUEEZE
I don't look hungry!
I SAID I DON'T WANT IT!
Isn't it nice?
GRRR!
HEY.
DID YOUR HAIR GROW LONGER, NATSUE SENPAI?
Oh.
I GOT EXTEN- SIONS.
I WANTED TO MAKE MY HAIRSTYLE THE SAME AS WHEN I STARTED AT THIS SCHOOL TO MAKE IT LOOK LIKE I HAVEN'T AGED.
BUT IT DIDN'T WORK... I CAN'T FIGHT AGING...
Heh...
SO YOU HAD LONG HAIR BEFORE.
I didn't know.
YEAH.
Okay...
THAT'S SO NICE. I WISH I COULD SEE HOW NATSUE LOOKED WHEN SHE WAS A FIRST-YEAR STUDENT.
TMP
TMPTMPTMPTMPTMP
!!
SLIDE

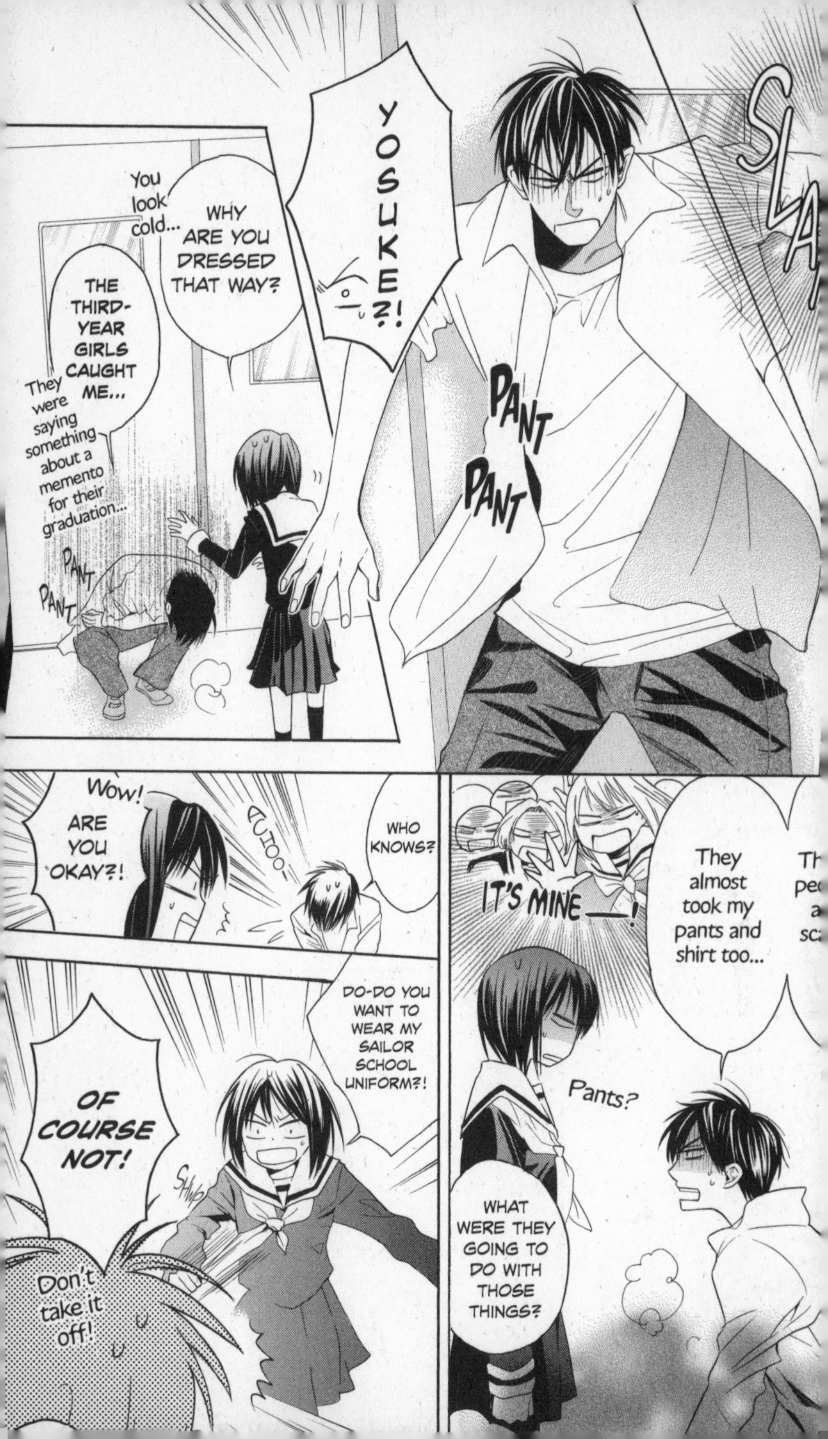
SLA
YOSUKE?!
PANT
PANT
WHY ARE YOU DRESSED THAT WAY?
You look cold...
THE THIRD-YEAR GIRLS CAUGHT ME...
They were saying something about a memento for their graduation...
PANT
PANT
IT'S MINE—!
They almost took my pants and shirt too...
Pants?
WHAT WERE THEY GOING TO DO WITH THOSE THINGS?
WHO KNOWS?
Wow!
ARE YOU OKAY?!
DO-DO YOU WANT TO WEAR MY SAILOR SCHOOL UNIFORM?!
OF COURSE NOT!
SHWP
Don't take it off!

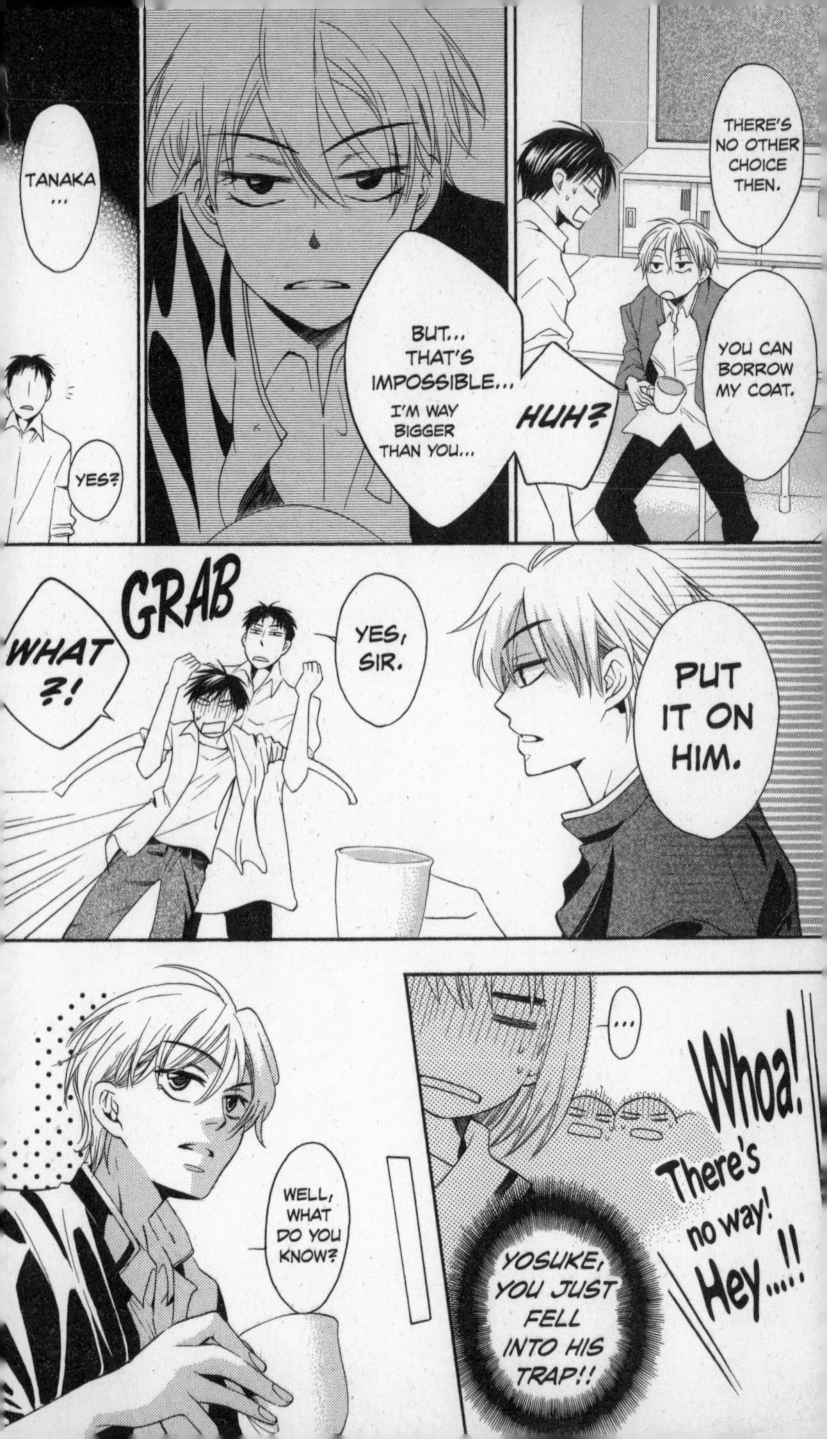
THERE'S NO OTHER CHOICE THEN.
YOU CAN BORROW MY COAT.
HUH?
BUT... THAT'S IMPOSSIBLE...
I'M WAY BIGGER THAN YOU...
TANAKA...
YES?
PUT IT ON HIM.
YES, SIR.
GRAB
WHAT?!
...
Whoa! There's no way! Hey...!!
YOSUKE, YOU JUST FELL INTO HIS TRAP!!
WELL, WHAT DO YOU KNOW?

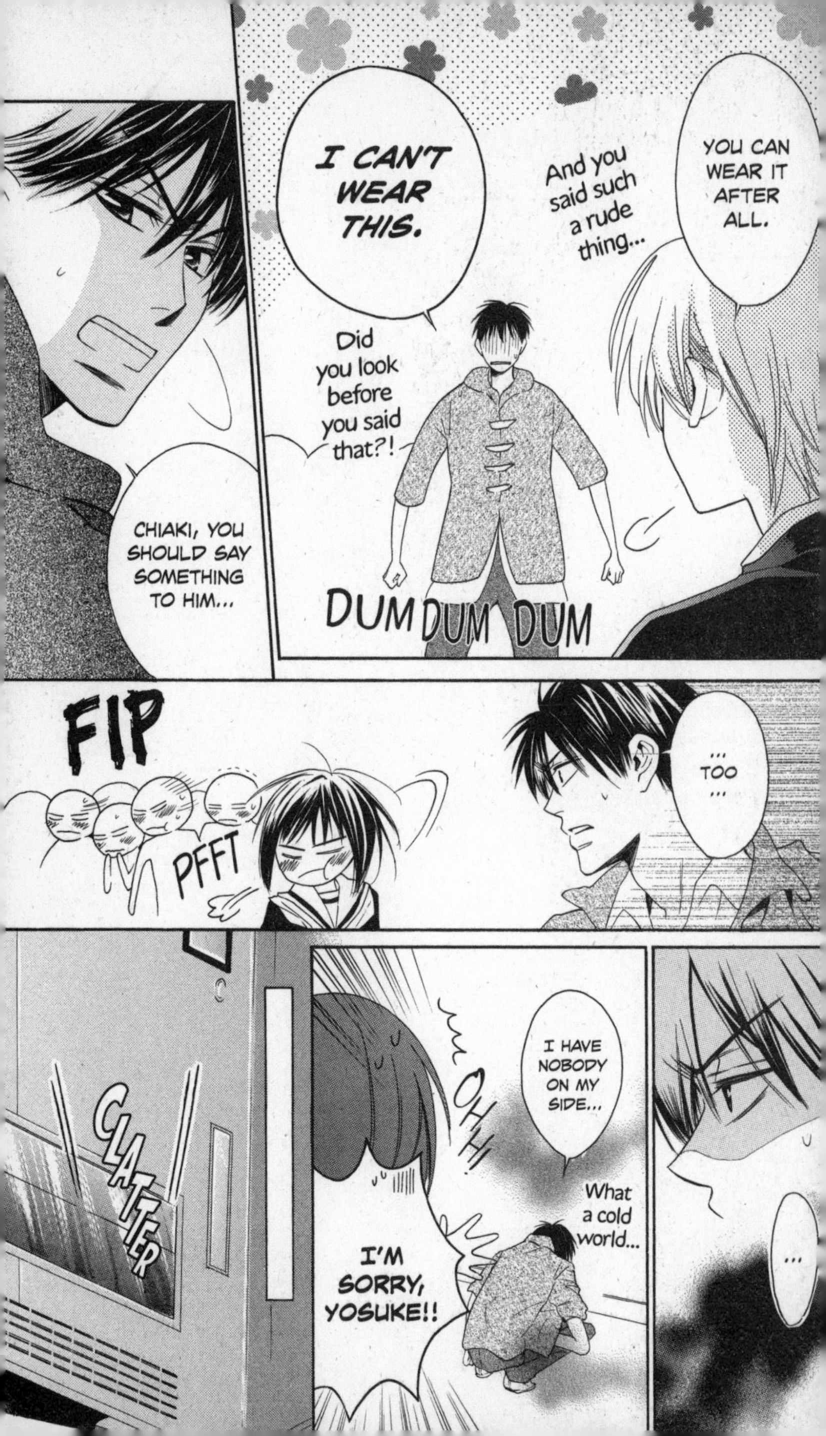
YOU CAN WEAR IT AFTER ALL.
And you said such a rude thing...
I CAN'T WEAR THIS.
Did you look before you said that?!
DUM DUM DUM
CHIAKI, YOU SHOULD SAY SOMETHING TO HIM...
... TOO ...
FIP
PFFT
...
I HAVE NOBODY ON MY SIDE...
What a cold world...
OHHH!
I'M SORRY, YOSUKE!!
CLATTER

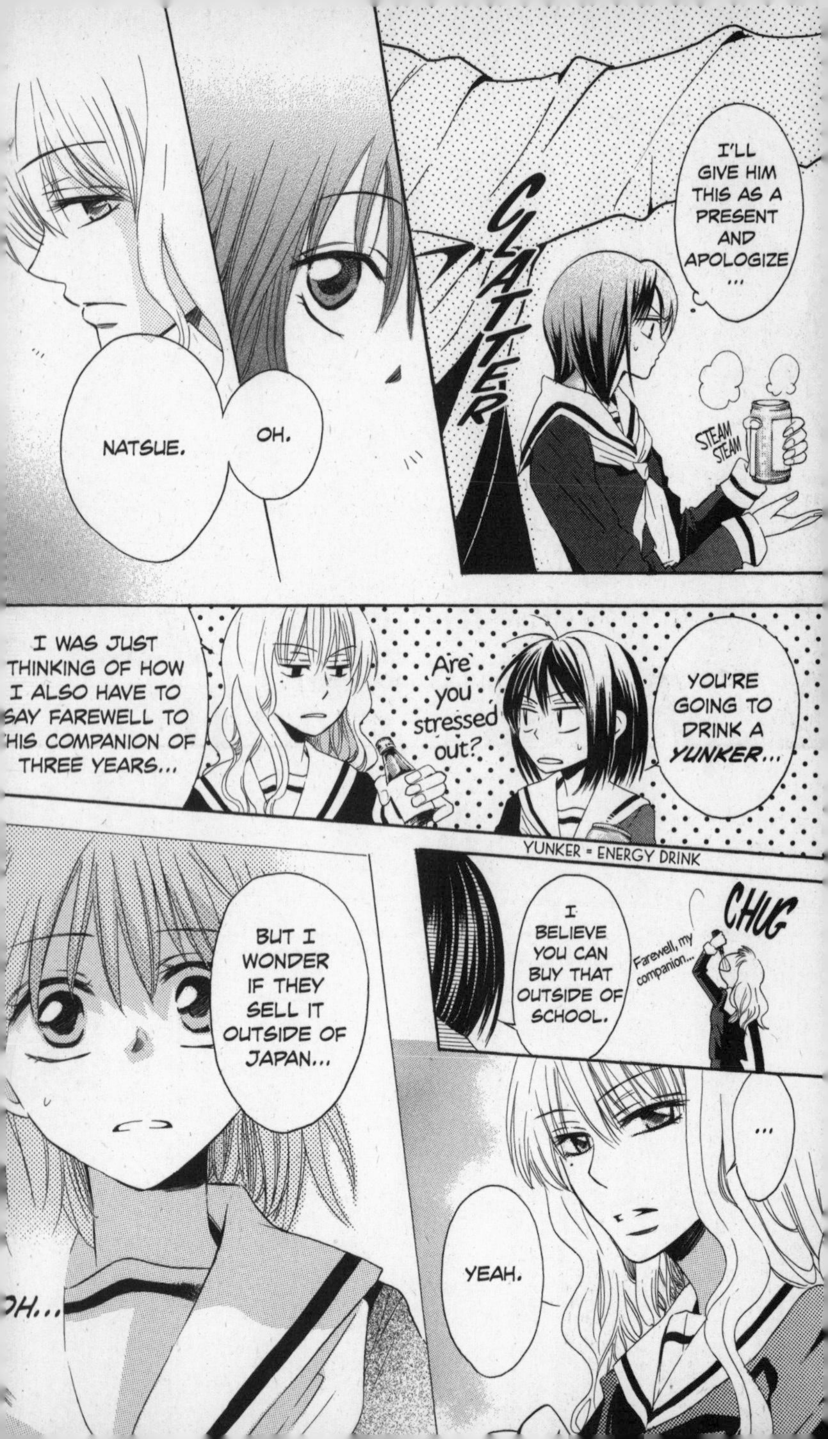

I'LL GIVE HIM THIS AS A PRESENT AND APOLOGIZE...
CLATTER
STEAM STEAM
OH.
NATSUE.
YOU'RE GOING TO DRINK A *YUNKER*...
Are you stressed out?
I WAS JUST THINKING OF HOW I ALSO HAVE TO SAY FAREWELL TO HIS COMPANION OF THREE YEARS...
YUNKER = ENERGY DRINK
I BELIEVE YOU CAN BUY THAT OUTSIDE OF SCHOOL.
CHUG
Farewell, my companion...
...
YEAH.
BUT I WONDER IF THEY SELL IT OUTSIDE OF JAPAN...
OH...

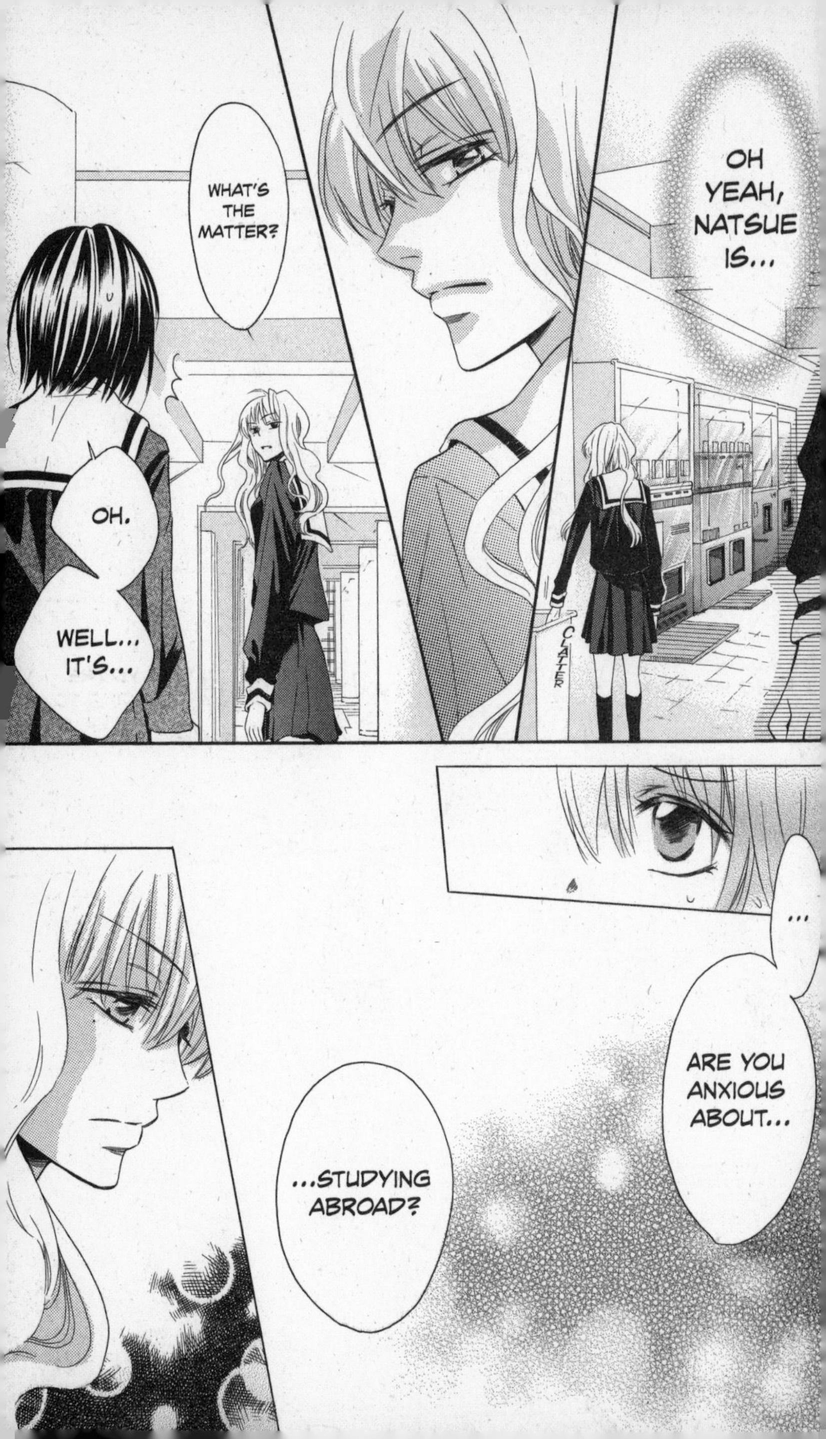
OH YEAH, NATSUE IS...
CLATTER
WHAT'S THE MATTER?
OH.
WELL... IT'S...
...
ARE YOU ANXIOUS ABOUT...
...STUDYING ABROAD?

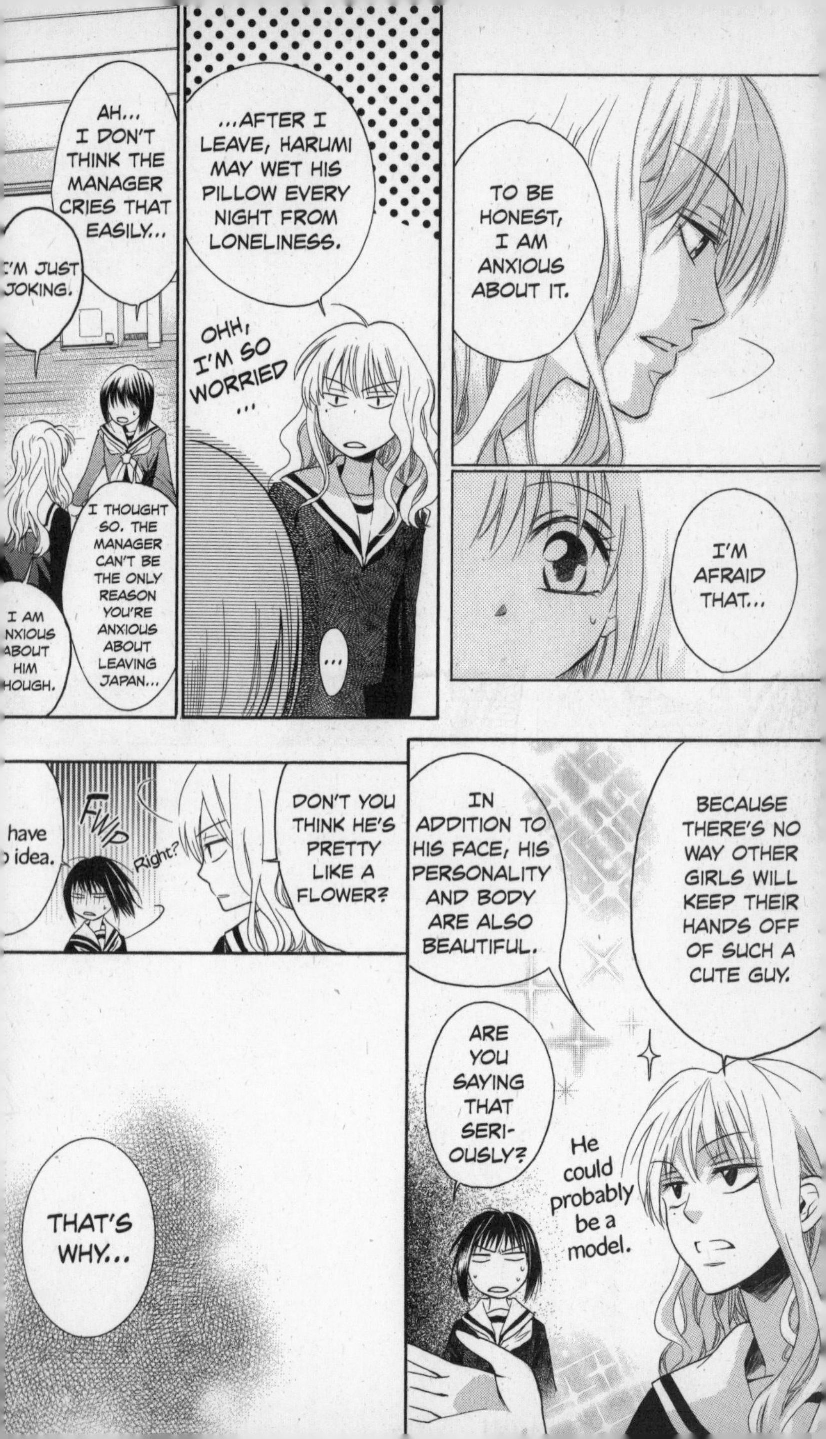
TO BE HONEST, I AM ANXIOUS ABOUT IT.
I'M AFRAID THAT...
...AFTER I LEAVE, HARUMI MAY WET HIS PILLOW EVERY NIGHT FROM LONELINESS.
OHH, I'M SO WORRIED...
...
AH... I DON'T THINK THE MANAGER CRIES THAT EASILY...
I'M JUST JOKING.
I THOUGHT SO. THE MANAGER CAN'T BE THE ONLY REASON YOU'RE ANXIOUS ABOUT LEAVING JAPAN...
I AM ANXIOUS ABOUT HIM THOUGH.
BECAUSE THERE'S NO WAY OTHER GIRLS WILL KEEP THEIR HANDS OFF OF SUCH A CUTE GUY.
IN ADDITION TO HIS FACE, HIS PERSONALITY AND BODY ARE ALSO BEAUTIFUL.
ARE YOU SAYING THAT SERIOUSLY?
He could probably be a model.
DON'T YOU THINK HE'S PRETTY LIKE A FLOWER?
FWIP
Right?
have no idea.
THAT'S WHY...

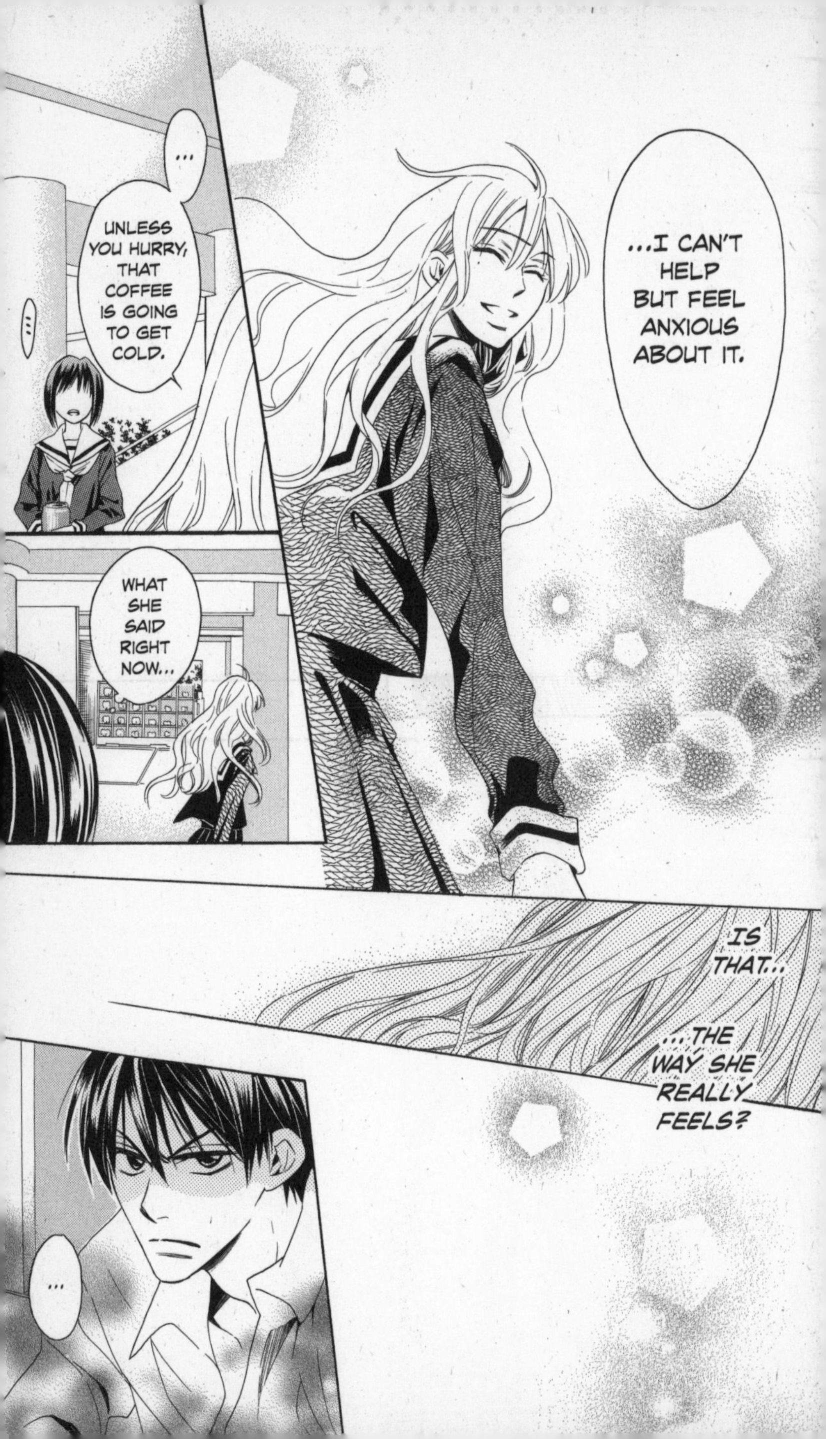
...I CAN'T HELP BUT FEEL ANXIOUS ABOUT IT.
...
UNLESS YOU HURRY, THAT COFFEE IS GOING TO GET COLD.
...
WHAT SHE SAID RIGHT NOW...
IS THAT...
...THE WAY SHE REALLY FEELS?
...

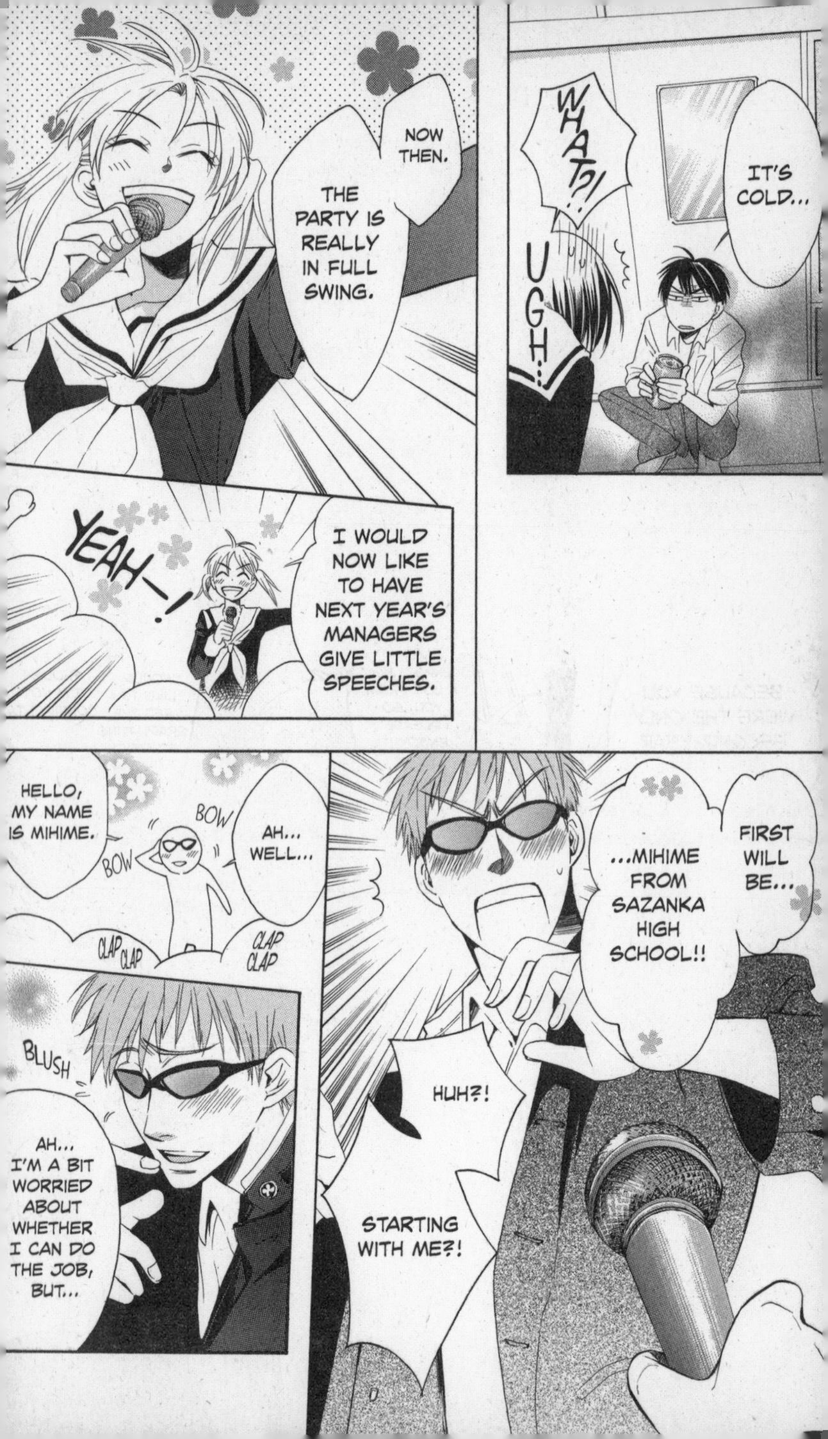
IT'S COLD...
WHAT?!
UGH...
NOW THEN.
THE PARTY IS REALLY IN FULL SWING.
I WOULD NOW LIKE TO HAVE NEXT YEAR'S MANAGERS GIVE LITTLE SPEECHES.
YEAH—!
FIRST WILL BE...
...MIHIME FROM SAZANKA HIGH SCHOOL!!
HUH?!
STARTING WITH ME?!
AH... WELL...
BOW
HELLO, MY NAME IS MIHIME.
BOW
CLAP CLAP
CLAP CLAP
BLUSH
AH... I'M A BIT WORRIED ABOUT WHETHER I CAN DO THE JOB, BUT...

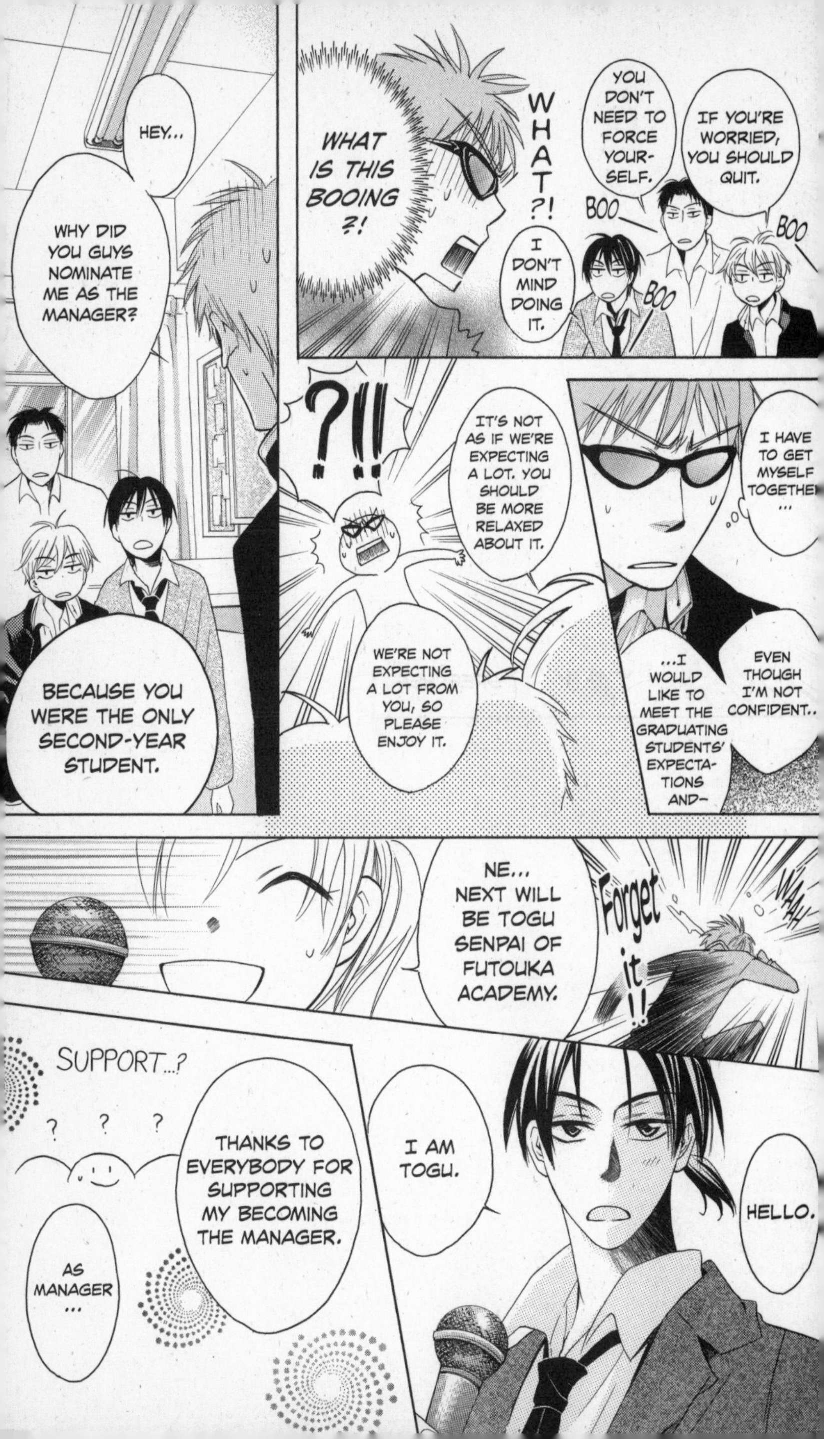

BOO
IF YOU'RE WORRIED, YOU SHOULD QUIT.
YOU DON'T NEED TO FORCE YOURSELF.
BOO
BOO
WHAT?!
I DON'T MIND DOING IT.
WHAT IS THIS BOOING?!
I HAVE TO GET MYSELF TOGETHER...
EVEN THOUGH I'M NOT CONFIDENT..
...I WOULD LIKE TO MEET THE GRADUATING STUDENTS' EXPECTATIONS AND—
IT'S NOT AS IF WE'RE EXPECTING A LOT. YOU SHOULD BE MORE RELAXED ABOUT IT.
?!!
WE'RE NOT EXPECTING A LOT FROM YOU, SO PLEASE ENJOY IT.
HEY...
WHY DID YOU GUYS NOMINATE ME AS THE MANAGER?
BECAUSE YOU WERE THE ONLY SECOND-YEAR STUDENT.
WAAH
Forget it!!
NE... NEXT WILL BE TOGU SENPAI OF FUTOUKA ACADEMY.
HELLO.
I AM TOGU.
THANKS TO EVERYBODY FOR SUPPORTING MY BECOMING THE MANAGER.
SUPPORT...?
? ? ?
AS MANAGER...

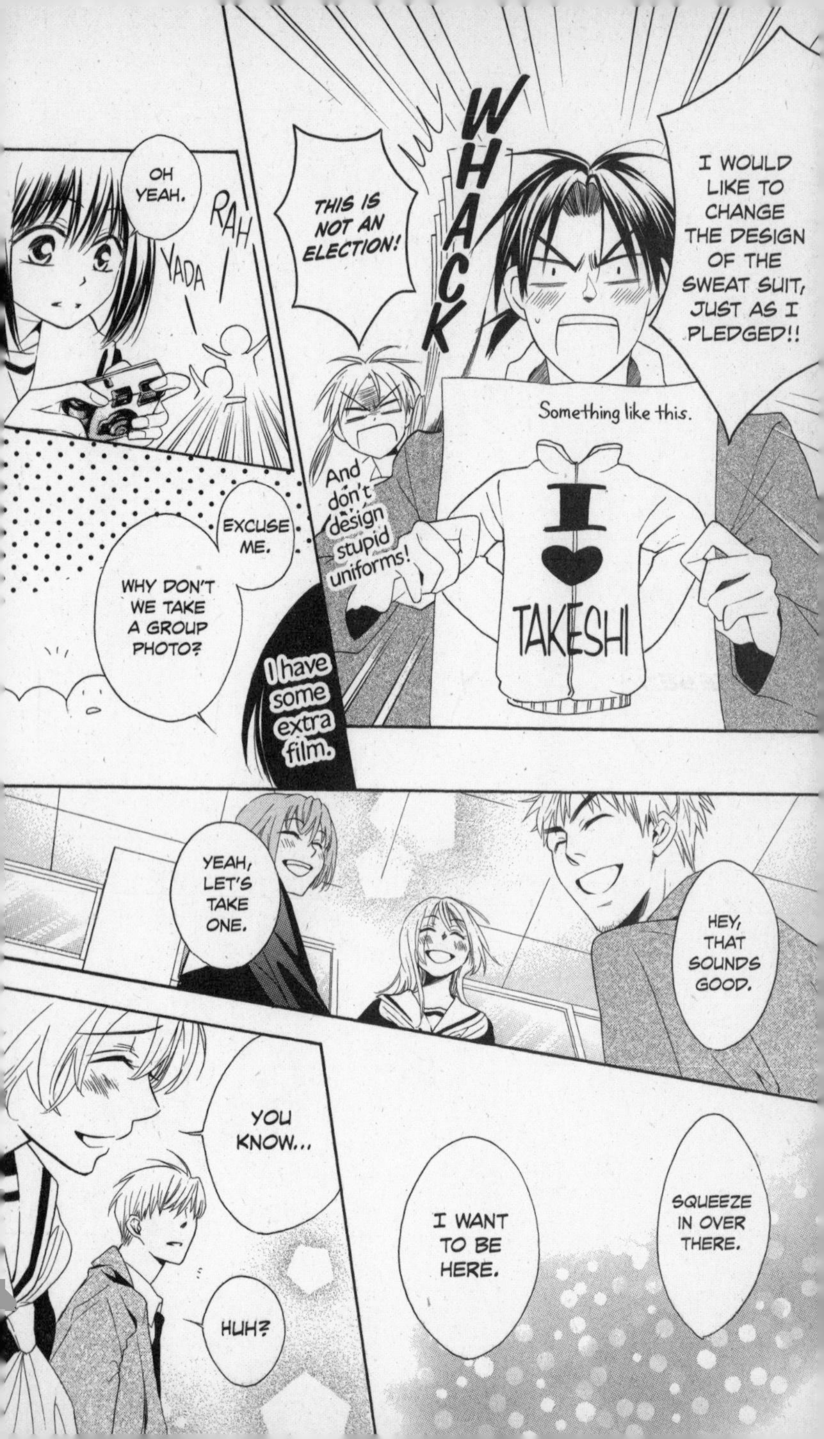
I WOULD LIKE TO CHANGE THE DESIGN OF THE SWEAT SUIT, JUST AS I PLEDGED!!
Something like this.
I ♥ TAKESHI
WHACK
THIS IS NOT AN ELECTION!
And don't design stupid uniforms!
OH YEAH.
RAH
YADA
EXCUSE ME.
WHY DON'T WE TAKE A GROUP PHOTO?
I have some extra film.
HEY, THAT SOUNDS GOOD.
YEAH, LET'S TAKE ONE.
SQUEEZE IN OVER THERE.
I WANT TO BE HERE.
YOU KNOW...
HUH?

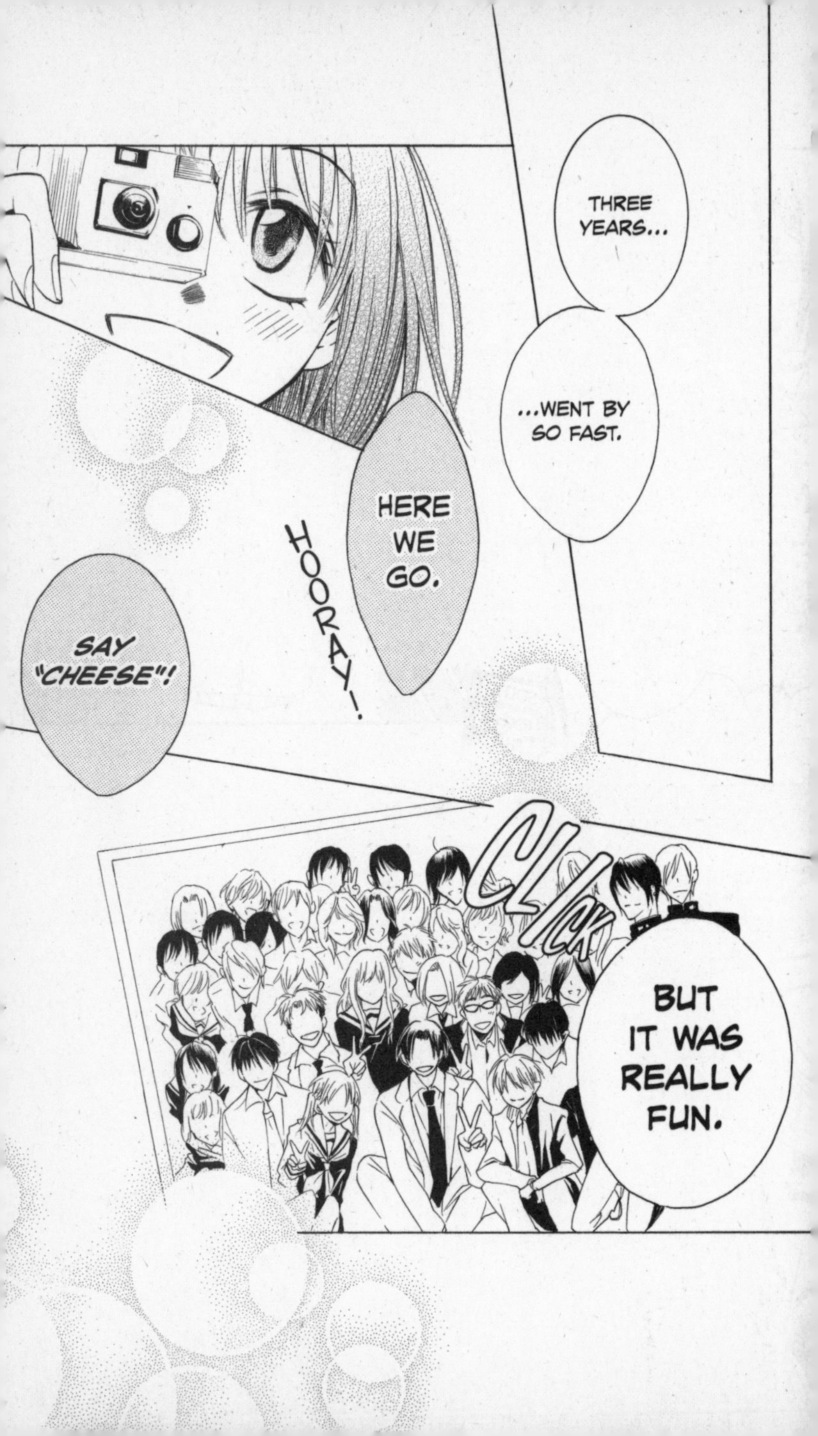
THREE YEARS...
...WENT BY SO FAST.
HERE WE GO.
HOORAY!
SAY "CHEESE"!
CLICK
BUT IT WAS REALLY FUN.

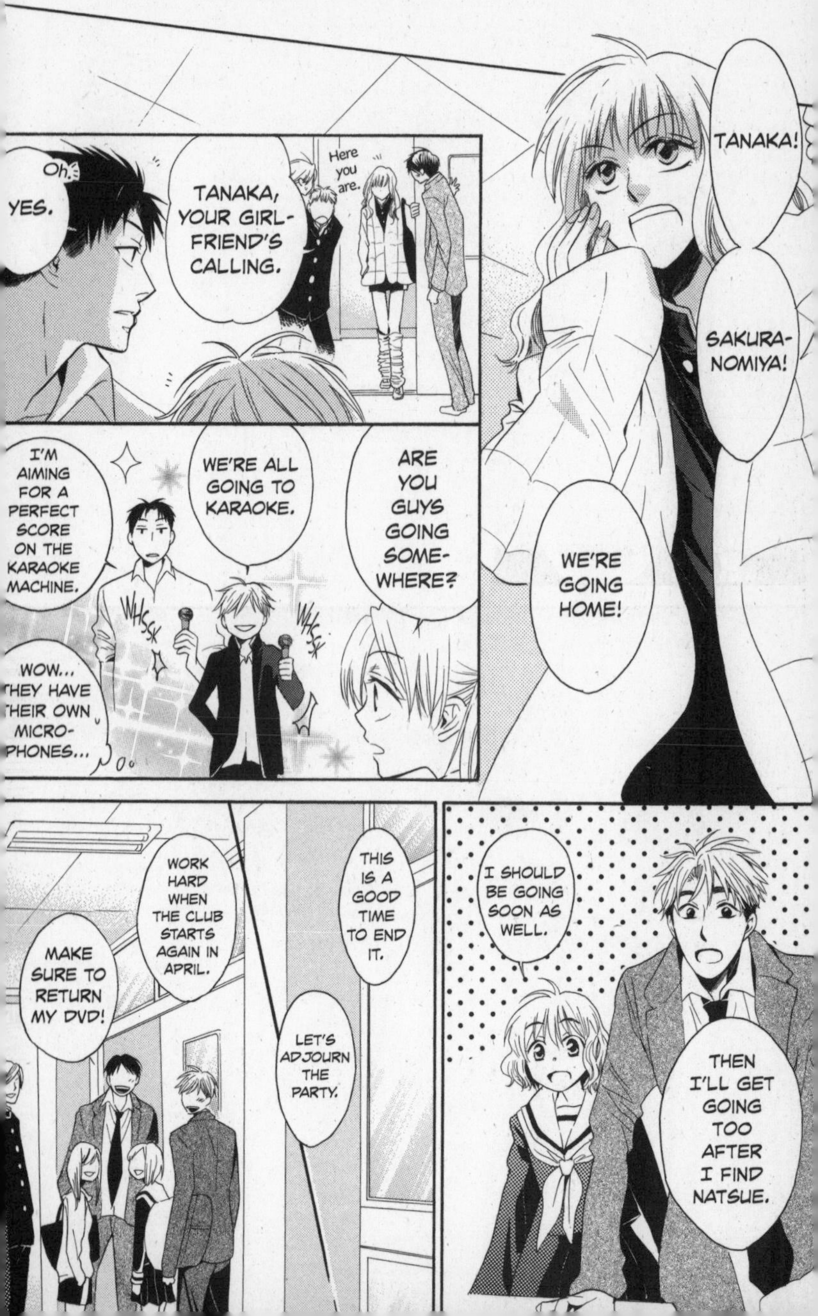
TANAKA!
SAKURA-NOMIYA!
WE'RE GOING HOME!
Here you are.
TANAKA, YOUR GIRL-FRIEND'S CALLING.
Oh.
YES.
ARE YOU GUYS GOING SOME-WHERE?
WE'RE ALL GOING TO KARAOKE.
I'M AIMING FOR A PERFECT SCORE ON THE KARAOKE MACHINE.
WHSSK
WHSSK
WOW... THEY HAVE THEIR OWN MICRO-PHONES...
I SHOULD BE GOING SOON AS WELL.
THEN I'LL GET GOING TOO AFTER I FIND NATSUE.
THIS IS A GOOD TIME TO END IT.
LET'S ADJOURN THE PARTY.
WORK HARD WHEN THE CLUB STARTS AGAIN IN APRIL.
MAKE SURE TO RETURN MY DVD!

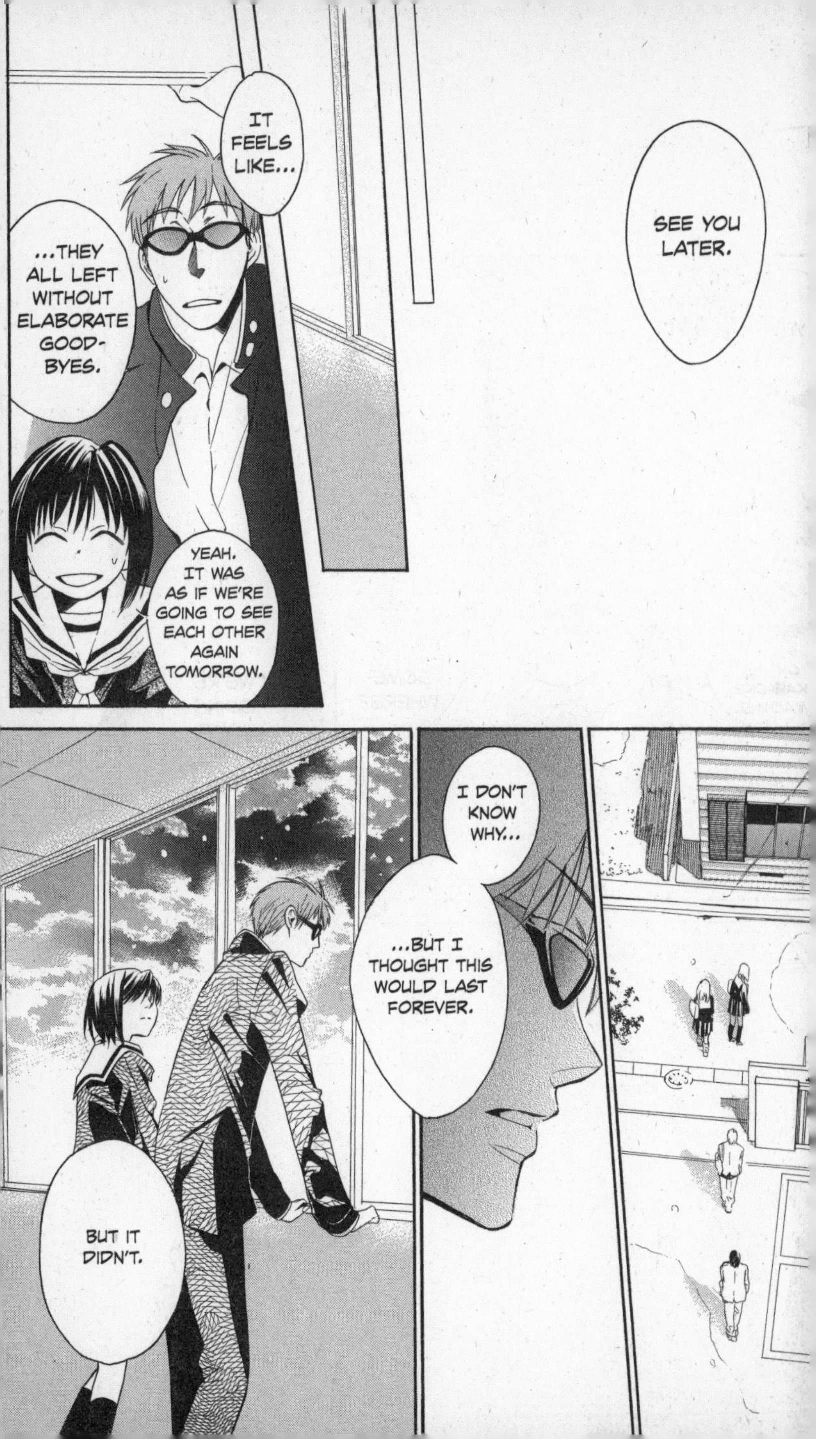
SEE YOU LATER.
IT FEELS LIKE...
...THEY ALL LEFT WITHOUT ELABORATE GOOD-BYES.
YEAH. IT WAS AS IF WE'RE GOING TO SEE EACH OTHER AGAIN TOMORROW.
I DON'T KNOW WHY...
...BUT I THOUGHT THIS WOULD LAST FOREVER.
BUT IT DIDN'T.

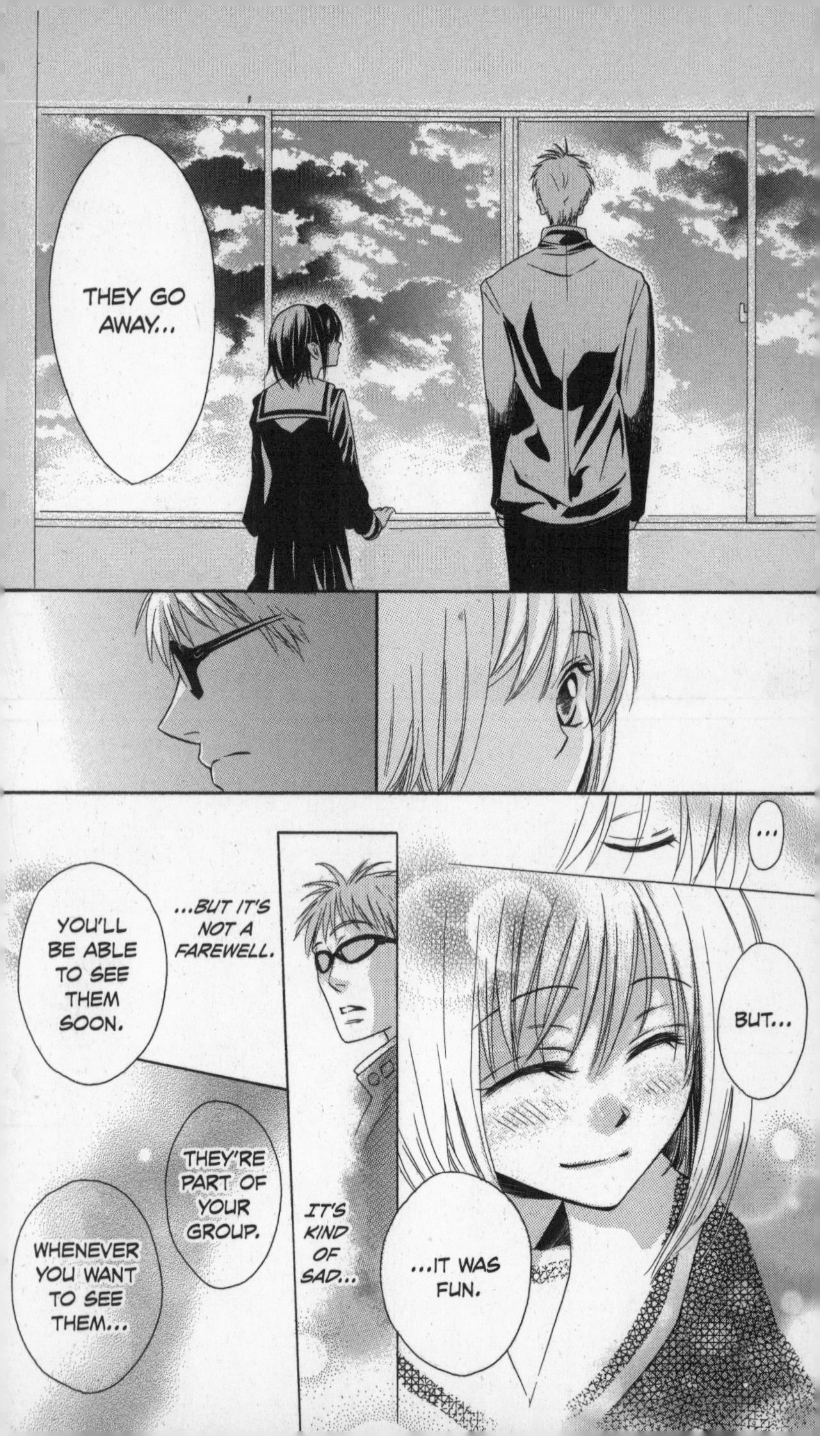
THEY GO AWAY...
...
BUT...
...IT WAS FUN.
IT'S KIND OF SAD...
...BUT IT'S NOT A FAREWELL.
YOU'LL BE ABLE TO SEE THEM SOON.
THEY'RE PART OF YOUR GROUP.
WHENEVER YOU WANT TO SEE THEM...

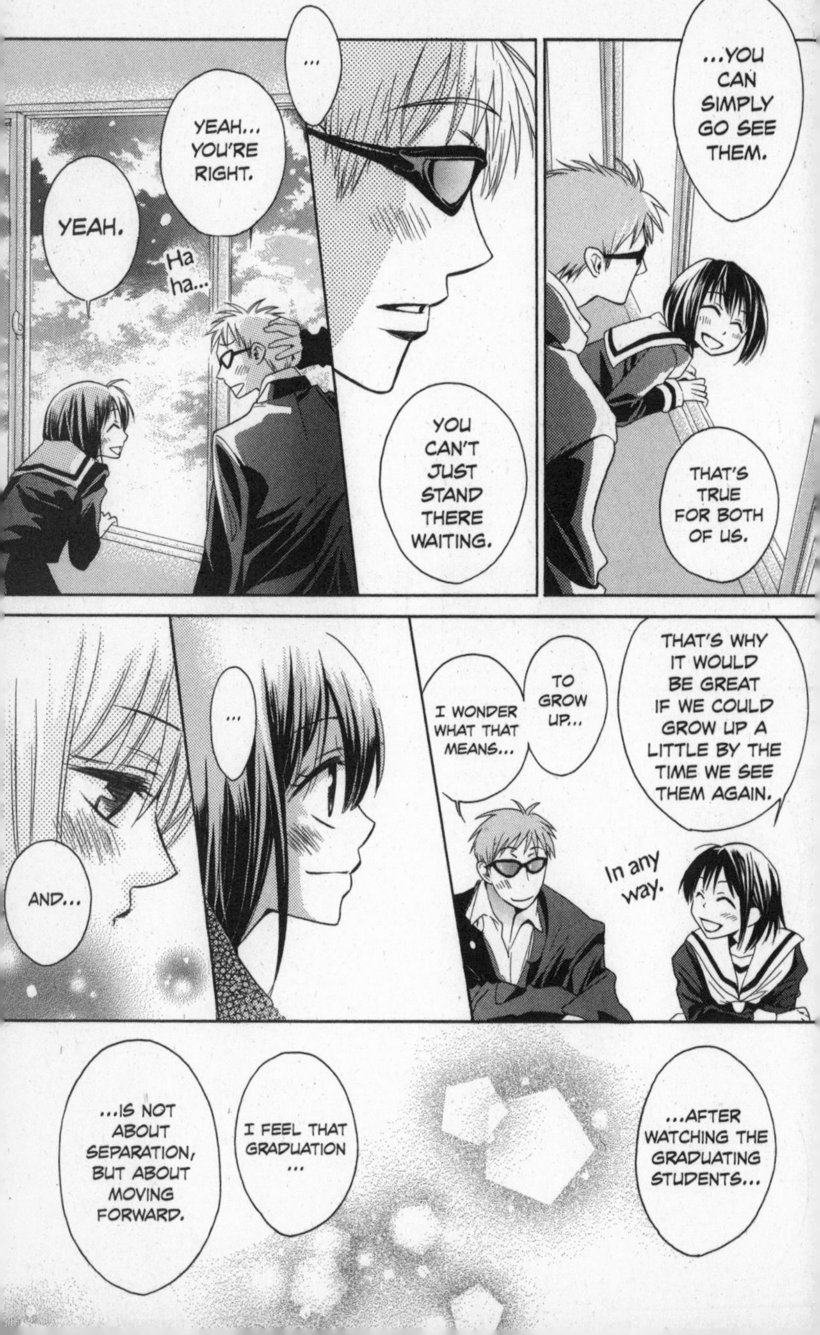
...YOU CAN SIMPLY GO SEE THEM.
THAT'S TRUE FOR BOTH OF US.
...
YOU CAN'T JUST STAND THERE WAITING.
YEAH... YOU'RE RIGHT.
YEAH.
Ha ha...
THAT'S WHY IT WOULD BE GREAT IF WE COULD GROW UP A LITTLE BY THE TIME WE SEE THEM AGAIN.
TO GROW UP...
I WONDER WHAT THAT MEANS...
In any way.
...
AND...
...AFTER WATCHING THE GRADUATING STUDENTS...
I FEEL THAT GRADUATION ...
...IS NOT ABOUT SEPARATION, BUT ABOUT MOVING FORWARD.

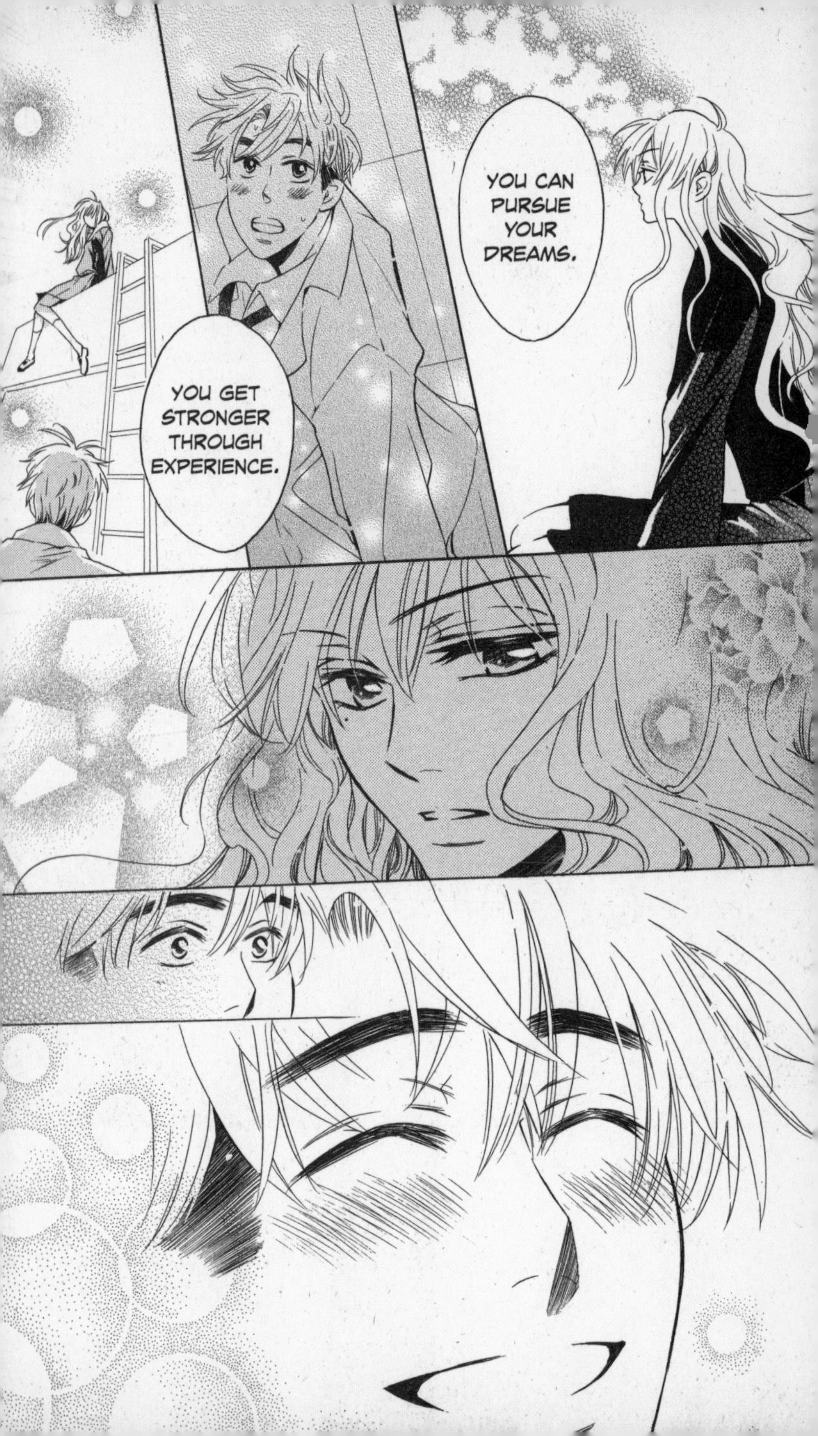
YOU CAN PURSUE YOUR DREAMS.
YOU GET STRONGER THROUGH EXPERIENCE.

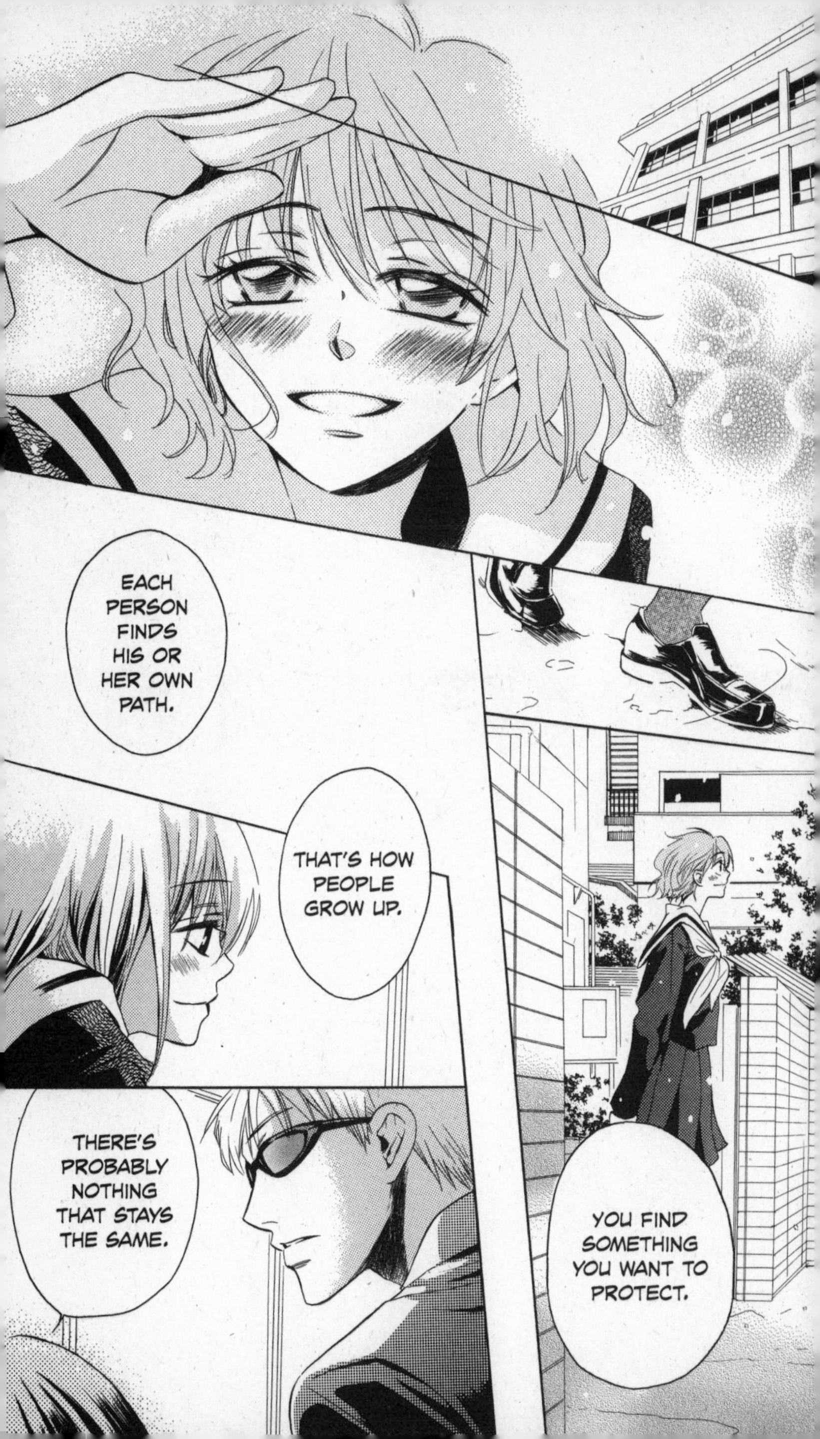
EACH PERSON FINDS HIS OR HER OWN PATH.
YOU FIND SOMETHING YOU WANT TO PROTECT.
THAT'S HOW PEOPLE GROW UP.
THERE'S PROBABLY NOTHING THAT STAYS THE SAME.

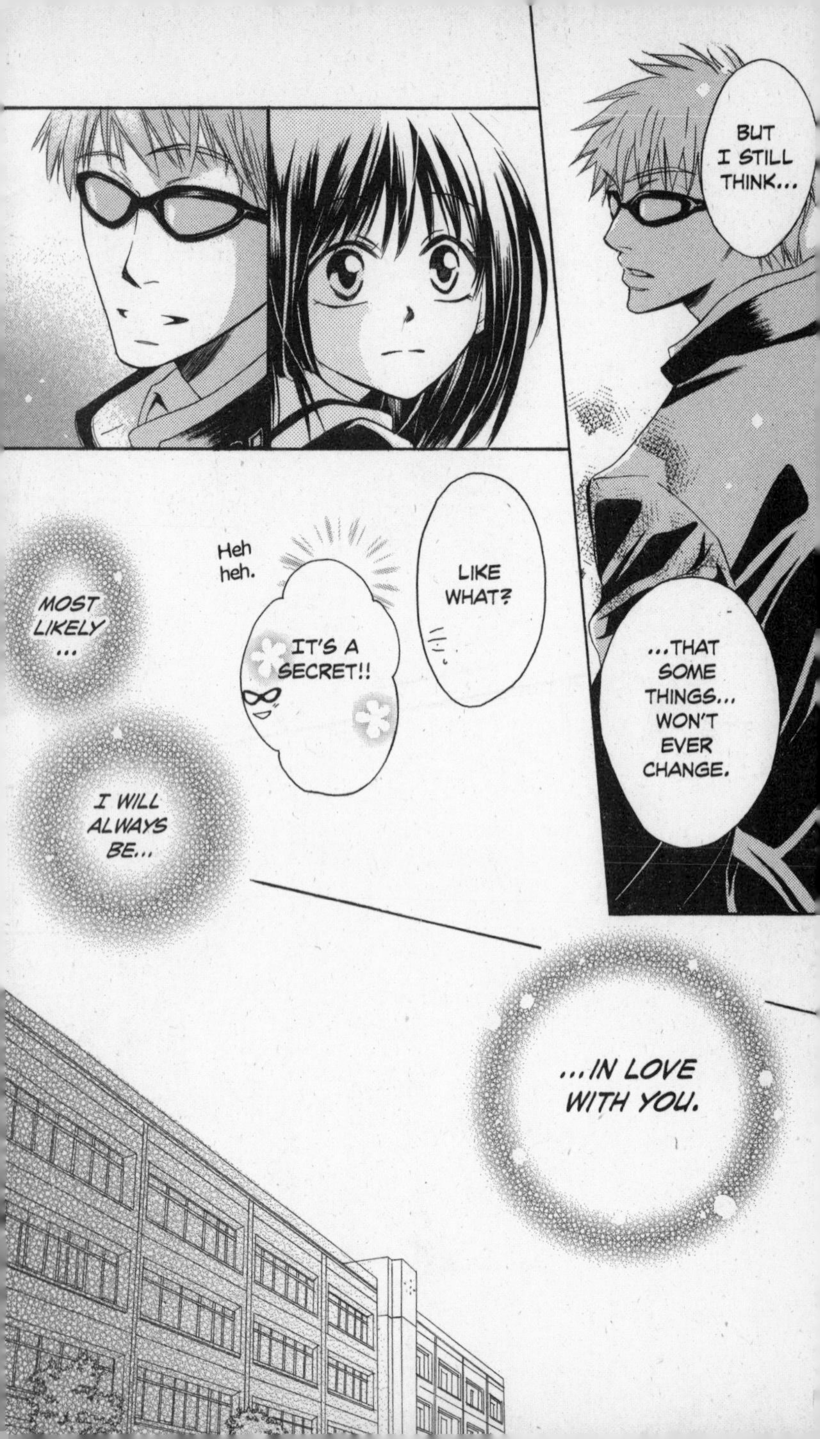
BUT I STILL THINK...
...THAT SOME THINGS... WON'T EVER CHANGE.
LIKE WHAT?
IT'S A SECRET!!
Heh heh.
MOST LIKELY...
I WILL ALWAYS BE...
...IN LOVE WITH YOU.

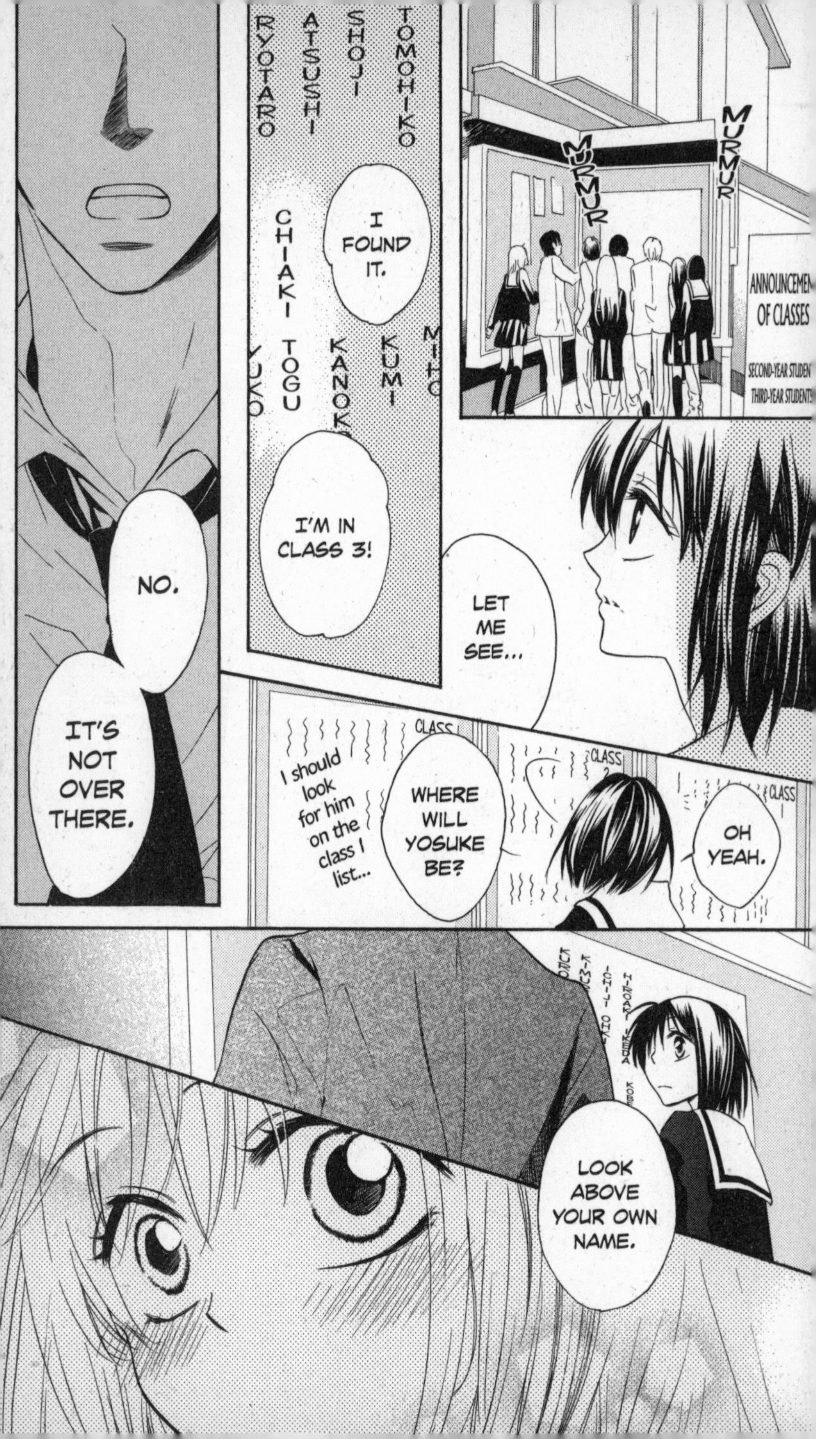
MURMUR
MURMUR
OF CLASSES
THIRD-YEAR STUDENTS
TOMOHIKO
SHOJI
ATSUSHI
RYOTARO
I FOUND IT.
KUMI
TOGU
CHIAKI
I'M IN CLASS 3!
LET ME SEE...
OH YEAH.
WHERE WILL YOSUKE BE?
I should look for him on the class 1 list...
NO.
IT'S NOT OVER THERE.
HIROAKI IKEDA
LOOK ABOVE YOUR OWN NAME.

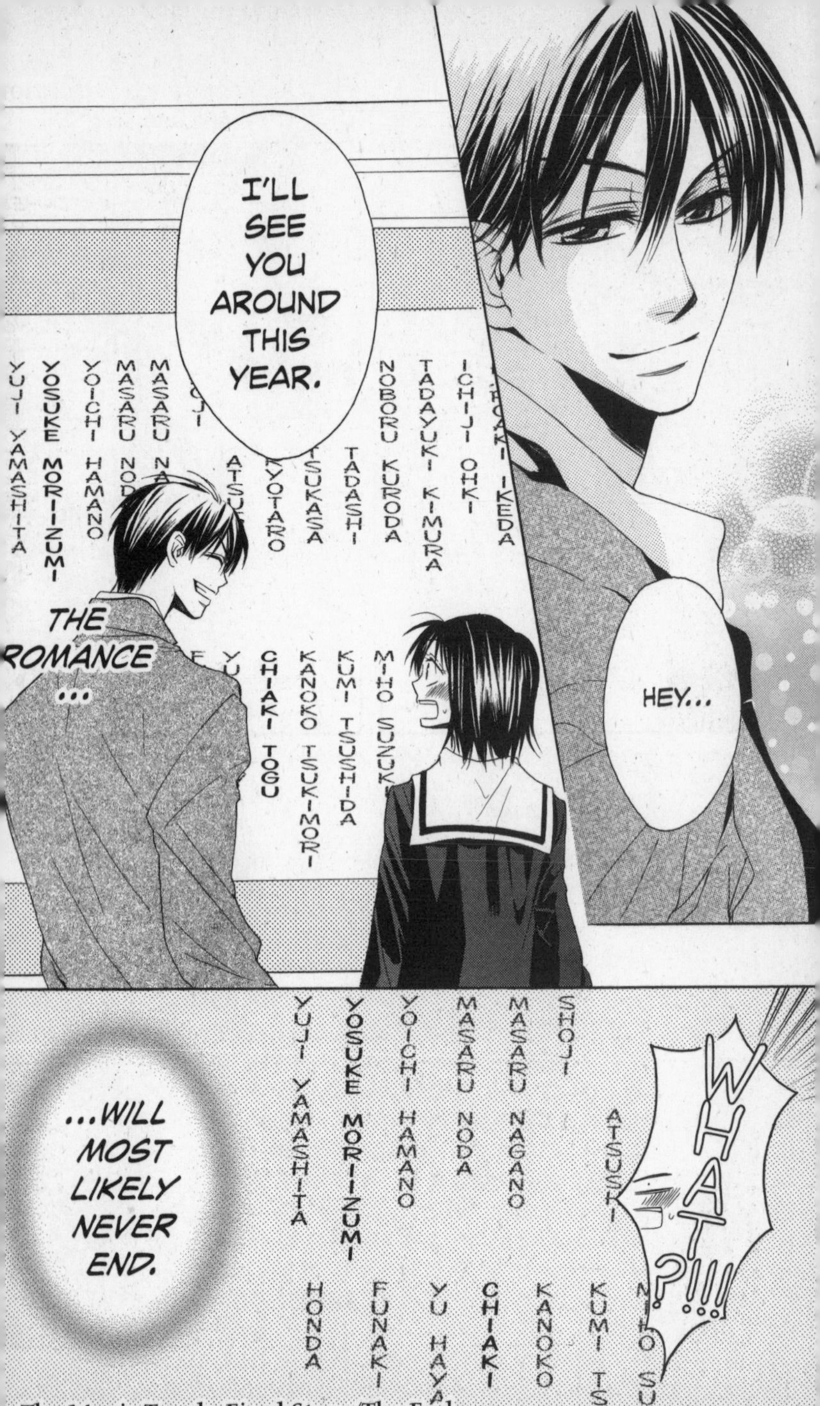
HEY...
I'LL SEE YOU AROUND THIS YEAR.
ICHIJI OHKI
TADAYUKI KIMURA
NOBORU KURODA
TADASHI
RYOTARO
YOICHI HAMANO
YOSUKE MORIIZUMI
YUJI YAMASHITA
THE ROMANCE...
KUMI TSUSHIDA
KANOKO TSUKIMORI
CHIAKI TOGU
WHAT?!!!
SHOJI
MASARU NAGANO
MASARU NODA
YOICHI HAMANO
YOSUKE MORIIZUMI
YUJI YAMASHITA
FUNAKI
HONDA
...WILL MOST LIKELY NEVER END.

The Magic Touch, Final Story/The End

POSTSCRIPT

Characters After Graduation
Keita and Ryo

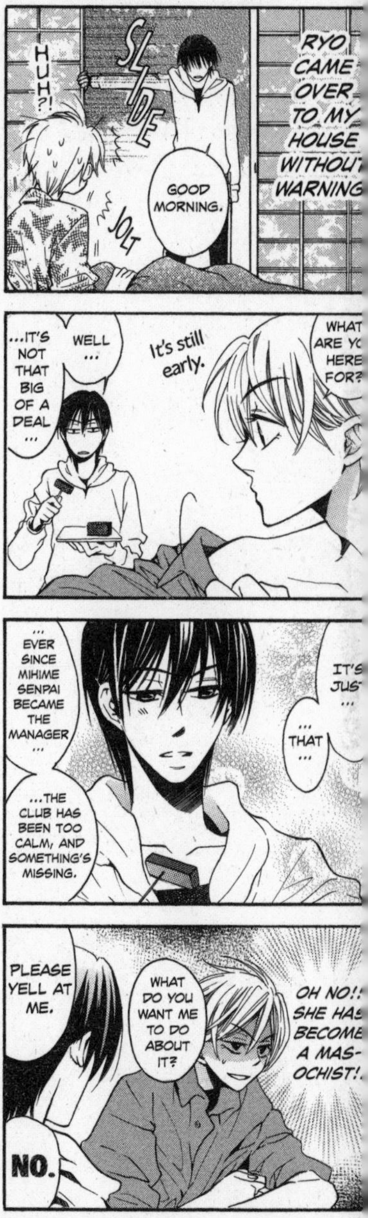
RYO CAME OVER TO MY HOUSE WITHOUT WARNING
SLIDE
HUH?!
GOOD MORNING.
JOLT
WHAT ARE YO HERE FOR?
It's still early.
WELL ...
...IT'S NOT THAT BIG OF A DEAL ...
IT'S JUST ...
... THAT ...
... EVER SINCE MIHIME SENPAI BECAME THE MANAGER ...
...THE CLUB HAS BEEN TOO CALM, AND SOMETHING'S MISSING.
OH NO!! SHE HAS BECOME A MAS-OCHIST!!
WHAT DO YOU WANT ME TO DO ABOUT IT?
PLEASE YELL AT ME.
NO.

Yuna

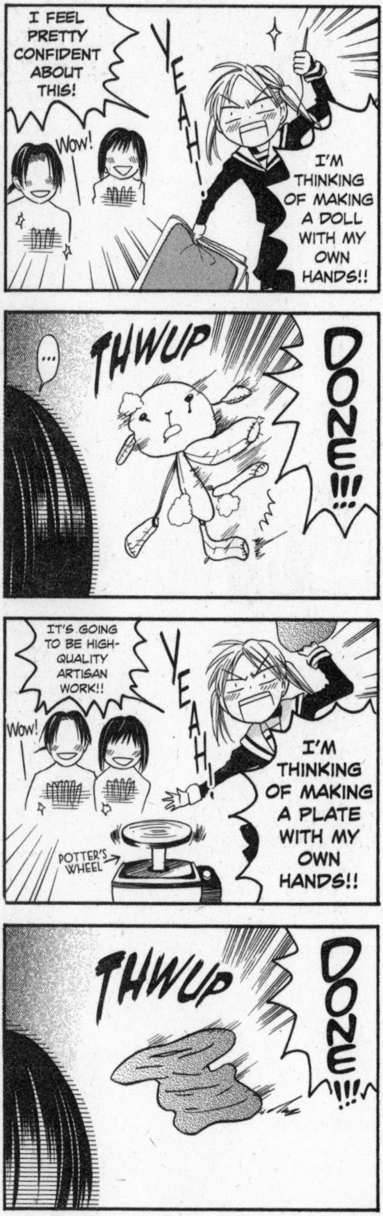
I FEEL PRETTY CONFIDENT ABOUT THIS!
YEAH!
I'M THINKING OF MAKING A DOLL WITH MY OWN HANDS!!
Wow!
DONE!!!
THWUP
...
IT'S GOING TO BE HIGH-QUALITY ARTISAN WORK!!
YEAH!
I'M THINKING OF MAKING A PLATE WITH MY OWN HANDS!!
Wow!
POTTER'S WHEEL
DONE!!!
THWUP

Liar...

Natsue and Manager 1: Before Graduation

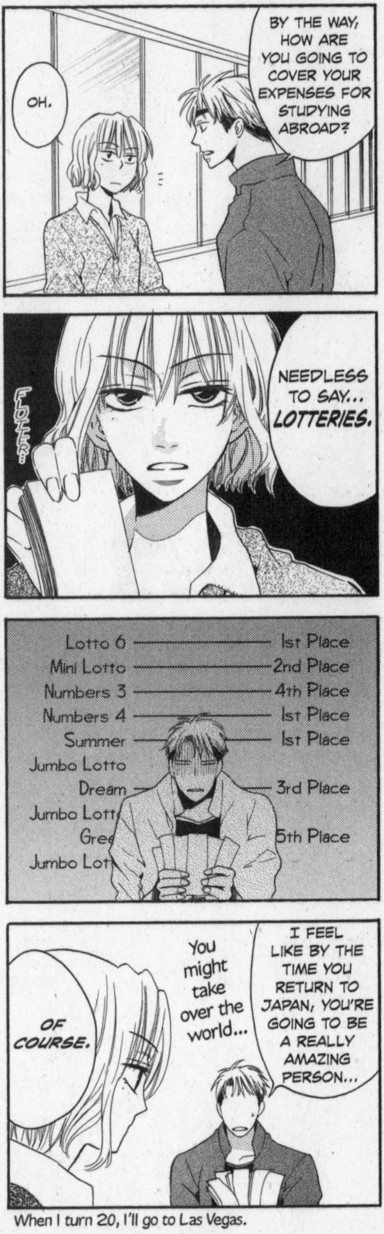
BY THE WAY, HOW ARE YOU GOING TO COVER YOUR EXPENSES FOR STUDYING ABROAD?
OH.
NEEDLESS TO SAY... LOTTERIES.
Lotto 6 — 1st Place
Mini Lotto — 2nd Place
Numbers 3 — 4th Place
Numbers 4 — 1st Place
Summer Jumbo Lotto — 1st Place
Dream Jumbo Lott — 3rd Place
Gree Jumbo Lot — 5th Place
I FEEL LIKE BY THE TIME YOU RETURN TO JAPAN, YOU'RE GOING TO BE A REALLY AMAZING PERSON...
You might take over the world...
OF COURSE.

When I turn 20, I'll go to Las Vegas.

atsue and Manager 2: Before Departure

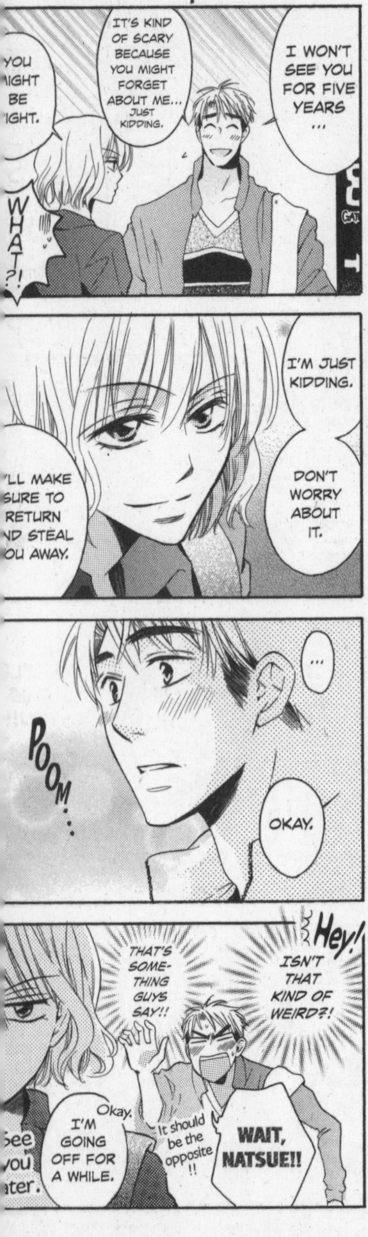
I WON'T SEE YOU FOR FIVE YEARS ...
IT'S KIND OF SCARY BECAUSE YOU MIGHT FORGET ABOUT ME... JUST KIDDING.
YOU IGHT BE IGHT.
WHAT?!
I'M JUST KIDDING.
DON'T WORRY ABOUT IT.
'LL MAKE SURE TO RETURN ND STEAL OU AWAY.
...
POOM...
OKAY.
Hey!
ISN'T THAT KIND OF WEIRD?!
THAT'S SOME-THING GUYS SAY!!
WAIT, NATSUE!!
It should be the opposite !!
Okay. I'M GOING OFF FOR A WHILE.
See ou ter.

Tanaka and Sanae

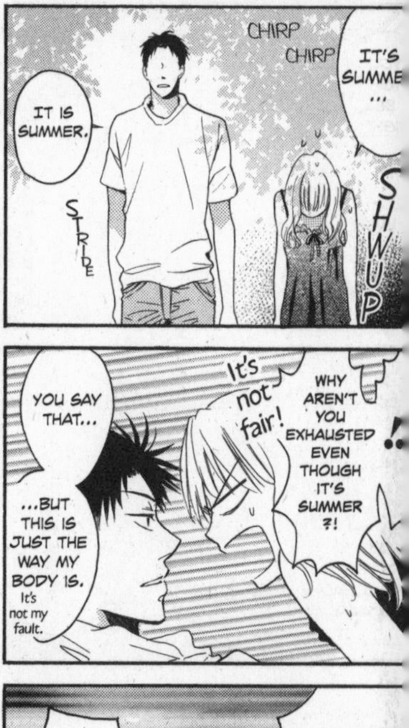

IT'S SUMME ...
CHIRP
CHIRP
SHWUP
IT IS SUMMER.
STRIDE
WHY AREN'T YOU EXHAUSTED EVEN THOUGH IT'S SUMMER?!
It's not fair!
YOU SAY THAT...
...BUT THIS IS JUST THE WAY MY BODY IS.
It's not my fault.
THEN I'LL DO THIS TO YOU!!
OH NO, PLEASE DON'T DO IT.
HEH HEH HEH! IT DOESN'T LOOK LIKE YOU HATE THIS!!
WUMP
...
You're really into it.
HOW'S THIS?! THE HEAT SHOULD BE TRANSFERRE OVER TO YOU NOW!!
SHE'S SO CUTE.
SQUEEZE

Tanaka is entranced by her.

Chiaki and Yosuke

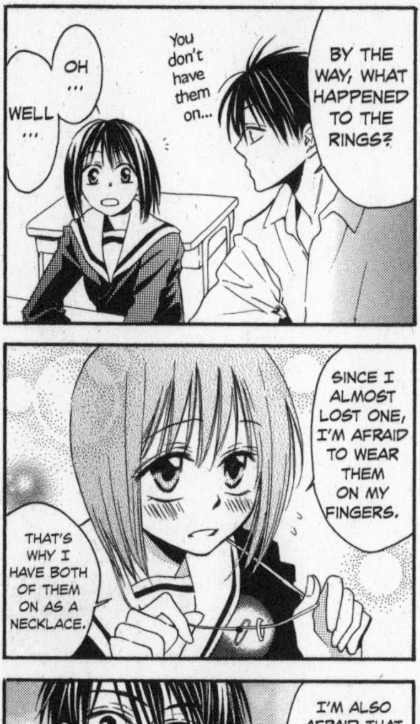

BY THE WAY, WHAT HAPPENED TO THE RINGS?
You don't have them on...
OH ...
WELL ...
SINCE I ALMOST LOST ONE, I'M AFRAID TO WEAR THEM ON MY FINGERS.
THAT'S WHY I HAVE BOTH OF THEM ON AS A NECKLACE.
I'M ALSO AFRAID THAT THE TEACHER WOULD CONFISCATE THEM IF THEY WERE ON MY FINGERS...
BABUMP
CHIAKI ...
HA HA HA HA
You're so cute.
TEE HEE HEE HEE
Hey... You guys...
THEY WILL BE CONFIS-CATED !!!

They'll probably be a silly couple forever.

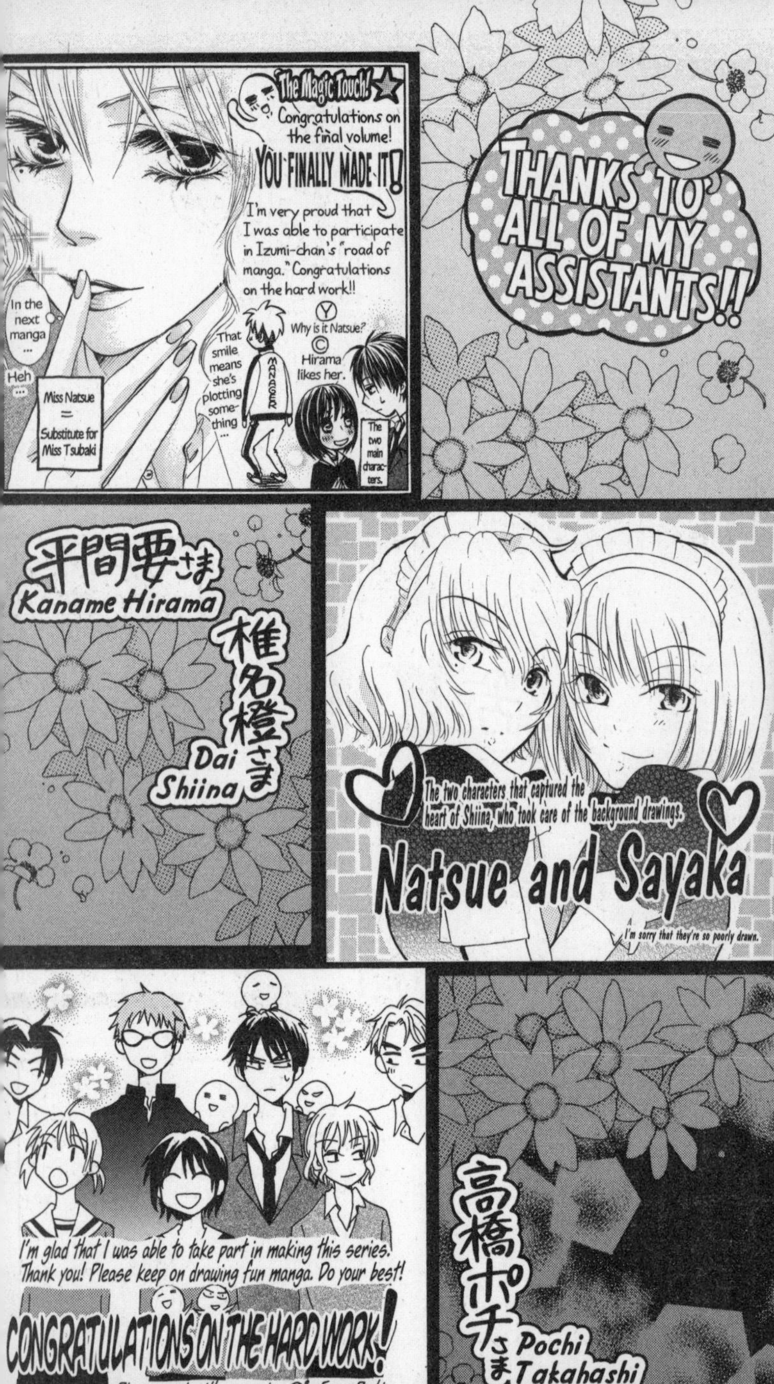
THANKS TO ALL OF MY ASSISTANTS!!
The Magic Touch!
Congratulations on the final volume!
YOU FINALLY MADE IT!!
I'm very proud that I was able to participate in Izumi-chan's "road of manga." Congratulations on the hard work!!
Y
Why is it Natsue?
C
Hirama likes her.
The two main characters.
That smile means she's plotting something...
MANAGER
In the next manga...
Heh...
Miss Natsue = Substitute for Miss Tsubaki
The two characters that captured the heart of Shiina, who took care of the background drawings.
Natsue and Sayaka
I'm sorry that they're so poorly drawn.
平間要さま
Kaname Hirama
椎名橙さま
Dai Shiina
高橋ポチさま
Pochi Takahashi
I'm glad that I was able to take part in making this series. Thank you! Please keep on drawing fun manga. Do your best!
CONGRATULATIONS ON THE HARD WORK!
Please work with me again. From Pochi.

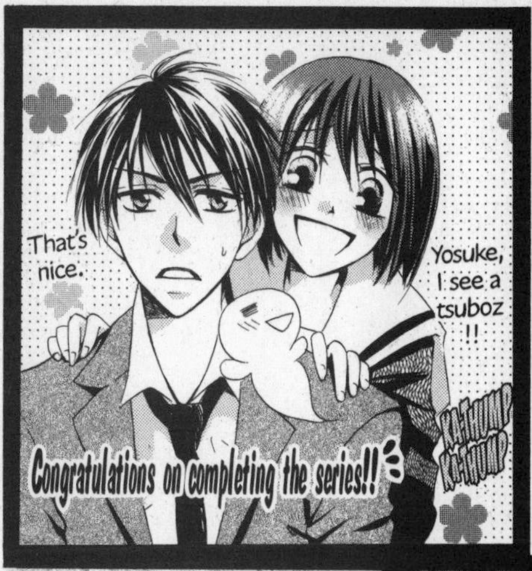
Yosuke, I see a tsuboz!!
That's nice.
KA-THUMP KA-THUMP
Congratulations on completing the series!!

Senri Toya
十夜千里さま

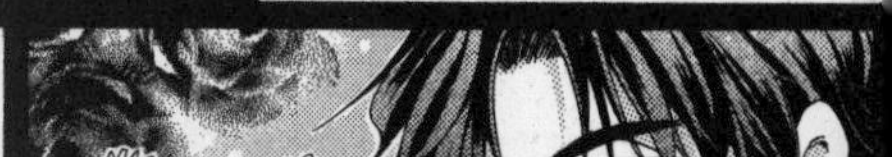
TRIO WITH TONED HAIR!
As the one responsible for the tones, working on Mihime's sunglasses gave me a really hard time. Take them off!

古賀よしき(妹)
Yoshiki Koga (younger sister)

Special Thanks!!

Editor S
Editor T
My Family
All of the Assistants
Friends

and you!!

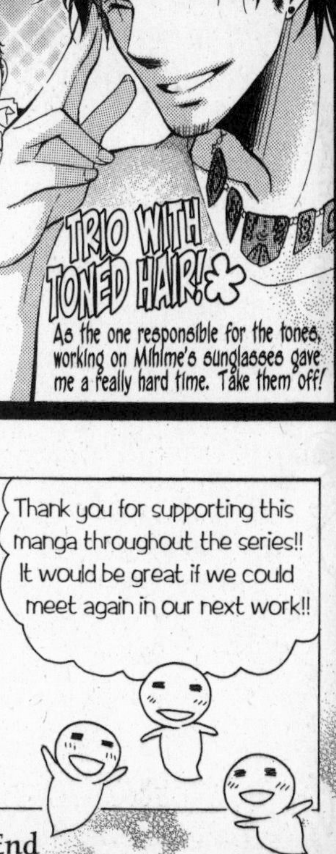
Thank you for supporting this manga throughout the series!! It would be great if we could meet again in our next work!!

Postscript/The End

Izumi Tsubaki began drawing manga in her first year of high school. She was soon selected to be in the top ten of *Hana to Yume*'s HMC (Hana to Yume Mangaka Course) and subsequently won *Hana to Yume*'s Big Challenge contest. Her debut title, *Chijimete Distance* (Shrink the Distance), ran in 2002 in *Hana to Yume* magazine, issue 17. In addition to *The Magic Touch* (originally published in Japan as *Oyayubi kara Romance*, or "Romance from the Thumbs"), she is currently working on the manga series *Oresama Teacher* (I'm the Teacher).

Tsubaki Sensei hails from Saitama Prefecture, her birthday is December 11 and she confesses that she enjoys receiving massages more than she enjoys giving them.

THE MAGIC TOUCH
Vol. 9
Shojo Beat Edition

STORY AND ART BY
IZUMI TSUBAKI

English Adaptation/Lorelei Laird
Translation/Nori Minami
Touch-up Art & Lettering/James Gaubatz
Design/Sean Lee
Editor/Eric Searleman

VP, Production/Alvin Lu
VP, Sales & Product Marketing/Gonzalo Ferreyra
VP, Creative/Linda Espinosa
Publisher/Hyoe Narita

Oyayubi kara Romance by Izumi Tsubaki © Izumi Tsubaki 2007
All rights reserved. First published in Japan in 2007 by HAKUSENSHA, Inc., Tokyo.
English language translation rights arranged with HAKUSENSHA, Inc., Tokyo.

Printed in Canada

Published by VIZ Media, LLC
P.O. Box 77010
San Francisco, CA 94107

10 9 8 7 6 5 4 3 2 1
First printing, August 2010

PARENTAL ADVISORY
THE MAGIC TOUCH is rated T+ for
Older Teen and is recommended
for ages 13 and up.
ratings.viz.com

VIZ
MEDIA
www.viz.com

Shojo
Beat
www.shojobeat.com

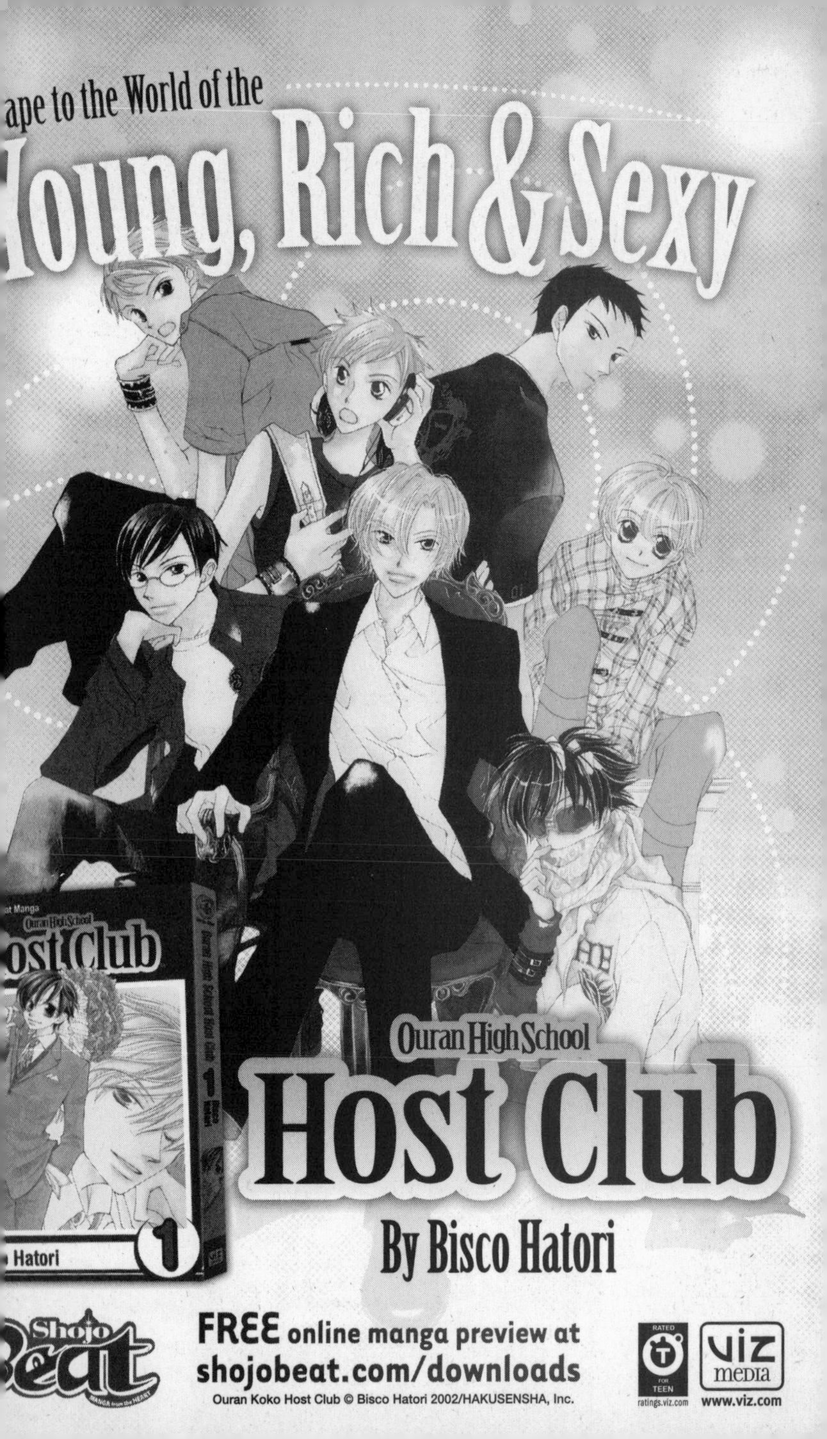
ape to the World of the
Young, Rich & Sexy
Ouran High School
Host Club
By Bisco Hatori
Ouran High School
Host Club
Hatori
1
FREE online manga preview at
shojobeat.com/downloads
Ouran Koko Host Club © Bisco Hatori 2002/HAKUSENSHA, Inc.
Shojo Beat
RATED T FOR TEEN
ratings.viz.com
VIZ media
www.viz.com

Don't Hide What's *Insic*

OTOMEN
by AYA KANNO

Despite his tough jock exterior, Asuka Masamune harbors a secret love for sewing, shojo manga, and all things girly. But when he finds himself drawn to his domestically inept classmate Ryo, his carefully crafted persona is put to the test. Can Asuka ever show his true self to anyone, much less to the girl he's falling for?

Find out in the *Otomen* manga—buy yours today!

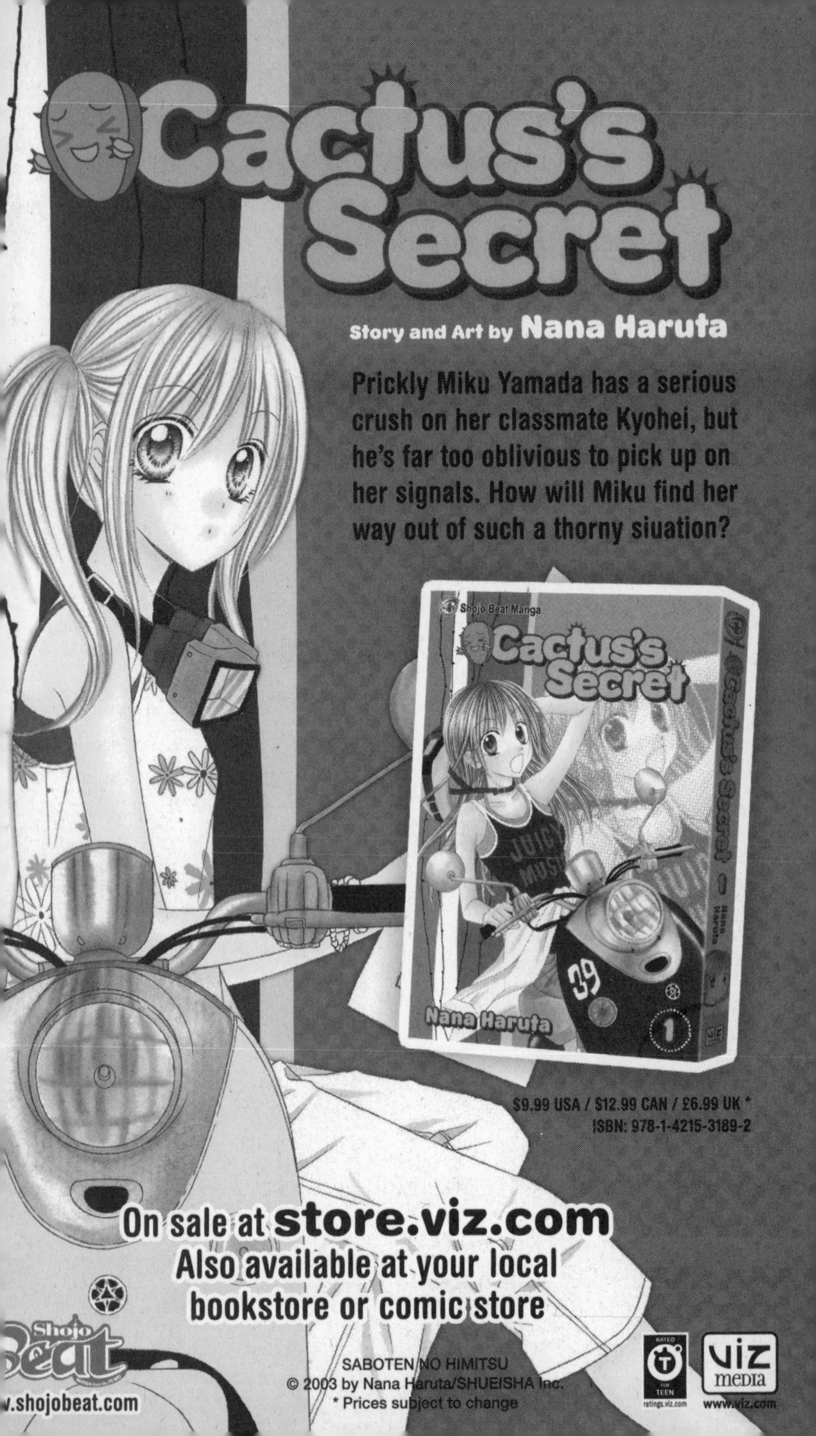
Cactus's Secret
Story and Art by Nana Haruta
Prickly Miku Yamada has a serious crush on her classmate Kyohei, but he's far too oblivious to pick up on her signals. How will Miku find her way out of such a thorny siuation?
Shojo Beat Manga
Cactus's Secret
Nana Haruta
1
$9.99 USA / $12.99 CAN / £6.99 UK *
ISBN: 978-1-4215-3189-2
On sale at store.viz.com
Also available at your local bookstore or comic store
Shojo Beat
v.shojobeat.com
SABOTEN NO HIMITSU
© 2003 by Nana Haruta/SHUEISHA Inc.
* Prices subject to change
RATED T FOR TEEN
ratings.viz.com
VIZ media
www.viz.com